ANNUAL EDITIONS

Homeland Security
Second Edition

EDITOR

Thomas J. Badey
Randolph-Macon College

Thomas J. Badey is an associate professor of Political Science and the director of the International Studies Program at Randolph-Macon College in Ashland, Virginia. He received a B.S. in Sociology from the University of Maryland (University College) in 1986 and an M.A. in political science from the University of South Florida in 1987. In 1993 he received a Ph.D. in political science from the *Institut für Politische Wissenschaft* of the *Ruprecht-Karls Universität* in Heidelberg, Germany. He served as a security policeman in the United States Air Force from 1979 to 1988 and was stationed in the United States, Asia, and the Middle East. Dr. Badey regularly teaches courses on international terrorism and homeland security and has written a number of articles on the subject. He is also the editor of McGraw-Hill /Contemporary Learning Series *Annual Editions: Violence and Terrorism.*

Contemporary Learning Series

2460 Kerper Blvd., Dubuque, IA 52001

Visit us on the Internet
http://www.mhcls.com

Credits

1. **The Concept of Homeland Security**
   Unit photo—U.S. Department of Homeland Security
2. **The Department of Homeland Security**
   Unit photo—CBP photo by Gerald Nino
3. **The Federal Government and Homeland Security**
   Unit photo—CBP photo by Gerald Nino
4. **State and Local Governments and Homeland Security**
   Unit photo—The McGraw-Hill Companies, Inc./Rick Brady, photographer
5. **First Responders**
   Unit photo—© 1997 IMS Communications Ltd./Capstone Design. All Rights Reserved
6. **New Technologies in Homeland Security**
   Unit photo—CBP photo by James R. Tourtellotte
7. **Vulnerabilities and Threats**
   Unit photo—PhotoLink/Getty Images
8. **Civil Liberties and Civil Rights**
   Unit photo—Copyright Thomas Hartwell/2003
9. **Intelligence and Homeland Security**
   Unit photo—Central Intelligence Agency
10. **The Future of Homeland Security**
    Unit photo—Jack Star/PhotoLink/Getty Images

Copyright

Cataloging in Publication Data

Main entry under title: Annual Editions: Homeland Security. 2nd Edition
1. Homeland Security—Periodicals. I. Thomas J. Badey. Title: Homeland Security.
ISBN-13: 978–0–07–339730–6   MHID-10: 0–07–339730–X

Second Edition

Cover image © Photos by Bill Kopiltz/FEMA and James Tourtellotte
Compositor: Laserwords Private Limited

Editors/Advisory Board

Members of the Advisory Board are instrumental in the final selection of articles for each edition of ANNUAL EDITIONS. Their review of articles for content, level, currentness, and appropriateness provides critical direction to the editor and staff. We think that you will find their careful consideration well reflected in this volume.

Preface

In publishing ANNUAL EDITIONS we recognize the enormous role played by the magazines, newspapers, and journals of the public press in providing current, first-rate educational information in a broad spectrum of interest areas. Many of these articles are appropriate for students, researchers, and professionals seeking accurate, current material to help bridge the gap between principles and theories and the real world. These articles, however, become more useful for study when those of lasting value are carefully collected, organized, indexed, and reproduced in a low-cost format, which provides easy and permanent access when the material is needed. That is the role played by ANNUAL EDITIONS.

On November 25th, 2002, 14 months after the attacks on September 11th, President Bush signed into law the Homeland Security Act of 2002. In what some have described as the most significant restructuring of the federal government since the National Security Act of 1947, a new Department of Homeland Security was created combining 22 federal agencies, over 170,000 employees, and a budget of over $40 billion. With the appointment of Tom Ridge, who championed its creation, as its first Secretary on January 24, 2003 the Department of Homeland Security began the monumental tasks of restructuring major elements of the federal government, while attempting to improve domestic security and prevent another 9/11. Much of this process has been completed. This massive transition however, has been not been without controversy. The swearing in of Michael Chertoff on February 15, 2005 as the second Secretary of the Department of Homeland Security marked an important step in the development of the DHS. Yet questions about the potential effectiveness of the organization remain. Natural disasters and terrorist threats have tested the capabilities of this new bureaucracy. The reviews have been mixed. Those critical of the lack of cooperation between government agencies prior to 9/11 are doubtful that adding another mammoth government bureaucracy has made America safer. Others remain convinced that only massive efforts by the federal government can prepare America for the inevitable biological, chemical, or radiological attacks from rogue states or international terrorist networks dedicated to our destruction. This anthology attempts to highlight the complex challenges and the potential pitfalls of contemporary homeland security policy.

The selections in this *Annual Editions: Homeland Security* were chosen to provide a broad overview and reflect a diversity of viewpoints and perspectives. This anthology is a complete revision of the previous edition. As homeland security continues to evolve the selection of current articles on the topic of homeland security continues to present a particular challenge. Articles in this introductory reader were chosen from a variety of sources and thus reflect different writing styles. Elements such as the timeliness and readability of the articles were important criteria used in their selection. It is our hope that this broad selection will provide easy access at various levels and will thus stimulate student interest and discussion.

This anthology is divided into 10 units. Unit 1 provides an overview of the myriad of challenges faced by the United States government in developing its plans for an effective homeland defense. Articles in this unit focus on the difficult task of identifying and setting priorities in homeland security. Unit 2 focuses on some of the organizational questions facing the Department of Homeland Security. It examines problems related to the merger of different functions and tackles important issues such as funding and oversight. Unit 3 examines the role of the federal government in homeland security. Issues such as immigration, port security, and disaster response are discussed. Unit 4 offers some insight into the problems faced by state and local governments in their efforts to develop and implement homeland security initiatives. Unit 5 focuses on the role of first responders while Unit 6 examines the role that new technologies may play in improving security. Existing vulnerabilities and potential future threats are the subject of Unit 7. Biological, chemical, and nuclear threats are discussed. Unit 8 examines the potential impact of homeland security legislation on civil liberties and civil rights. The Intelligence Community plays a vital role in protecting the United States from future threats. Unit 9 explores some of the problems associated with obtaining accurate and timely intelligence. Finally, Unit 10 examines the future of homeland security. Beginning with a speech by secretary Chertoff, it provides varying perspectives on the challenges that face the new Department of Homeland Security.

Annual Editions: Homeland Security provides a broad overview of the major issues associated with homeland security. It is our hope that this anthology will provide students with an introduction to the issues related to homeland security and serve as a stimulus for further in-depth exploration of this vital topic.

I would like to thank the individuals who have kindly agreed to serve as member of the advisory board for this anthology. I look forward to your comments and suggestions so that we can continue to improve the selections and materials in this anthology. I am also grateful to a group of undergraduate students who volunteered their time to help in the revision of this anthology. I would particularly like to thank Bobby Graves, Caitlynn Husz, Megan Kittle, Paul Patterson, as well as Jason Carmichael, Joseph Greenawalt, Jessica Kuehn, and Susan Landfried, for their help in sorting through and reviewing the numerous articles that were submitted for consideration. These students provided valuable insights and above all a critical students' perspective, which made my job much easier. I hope that you, will take the time to fill out the article rating form in the back of this anthology so we can continue to improve future editions.

Thomas J. Badey
Editor

Contents

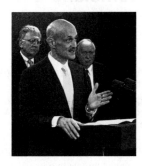

UNIT 1
The Concept of Homeland Security

UNIT 2
The Department of Homeland Security

The concepts in bold italics are developed in the article. For further expansion, please refer to the Topic Guide and the Index.

UNIT 3
The Federal Government and Homeland Security

UNIT 4
State and Local Governments and Homeland Security

The concepts in bold italics are developed in the article. For further expansion, please refer to the Topic Guide and the Index.

UNIT 5
First Responders

UNIT 6
New Technologies in Homeland Security

The concepts in bold italics are developed in the article. For further expansion, please refer to the Topic Guide and the Index.

UNIT 7
Vulnerabilities and Threats

UNIT 8
Civil Liberties and Civil Rights

The concepts in bold italics are developed in the article. For further expansion, please refer to the Topic Guide and the Index.

UNIT 9
Intelligence and Homeland Security

UNIT 10
The Future of Homeland Security

The concepts in bold italics are developed in the article. For further expansion, please refer to the Topic Guide and the Index.

The concepts in bold italics are developed in the article. For further expansion, please refer to the Topic Guide and the Index.

Topic Guide

This topic guide suggests how the selections in this book relate to the subjects covered in your course. You may want to use the topics listed on these pages to search the Web more easily.

On the following pages a number of Web sites have been gathered specifically for this book. They are arranged to reflect the units of this *Annual Edition*. You can link to these sites by going to the student online support site at *http://www.mhcls.com/online/*.

ALL THE ARTICLES THAT RELATE TO EACH TOPIC ARE LISTED BELOW THE BOLD-FACED TERM.

Internet References

The following Internet sites have been carefully researched and selected to support the articles found in this reader. The easiest way to access these selected sites is to go to our student online support site at *http://www.mhcls.com/online/*.

Annual Editions: Homeland Security, 2/e

The following sites were available at the time of publication. Visit our Web site—we update our student online support site regularly to reflect any changes.

UNIT 1: The Concept of Homeland Security

The Department of Homeland Security
http://www.dhs.gov/dhspublic/

The Department of Homeland Security (DHS) Web presence offers news and other vital information about emergencies and disasters, travel and transportation, immigration and borders, research and technology, and threats and protection.

International Information Programs: Response to Terrorism
http://usinfo.state.gov/is/international_security/terrorism.html

This Web site maintained by the U.S. Department of State's Bureau of International Information Programs contains information on international security.

National Homeland Security Knowledgebase
http://www.twotigersonline.com/resources.html

This important nongovernmental information source offers homeland security quick links and sections on nuclear, radiological, biological, and chemical emergencies, as well as facts on hazardous devices, bombs, and explosive ordnance emergencies and natural disasters. This page links to a great number of important related sites, including quick links to federal and state security agencies and organizations.

White House Homeland Security Policy
http://www.whitehouse.gov/infocus/homeland/

The White House's Web site dedicated to homeland security.

Global Security: Homeland Security
http://www.globalsecurity.org/security/index.html

Global Security's Web site provides news links U.S. and international security issues. Two very prominent issues, al Qaeda and pandemic influenza, have their own dedicated news link sections.

UNIT 2: The Department of Homeland Security

The Heritage Foundation: Homeland Defense Research
http://www.heritage.org/Research/HomelandDefense/

The Heritage Foundation maintains a "policy archive" relating to Homeland defense.

Federal Emergency Management Agency
http://www.fema.gov/

FEMA, whose presence was apparent at the site of the World Trade Center attack, reports on disasters of every sort and is part of the new homeland security organization. This home page of FEMA describes active disasters and emergencies, spotlights a guide for hurricane preparedness, the wildfire season, the federal response plan, and an "Are You Ready?" guide.

Mitretek Systems: Homeland Security and Counterterrorism
http://www.mitretek.org/
HomelandSecurityAndCounterterrorism.htm

This Web site discusses Mitretek Systems' focus on America's vulnerability to terrorist attacks, developing solutions that enable federal, state, and local officials to detect suspicious activities, respond to crises, and help with investigations. The site discusses Mitretek's present role in homeland security and counterterrorism.

Government Accountability Office: Homeland Security
http://www.gao.gov/docsearch/featured/homelandsecurity.html

The Government Accountability Office's Web site houses a number of documents that discuss homeland security issues.

UNIT 3: The Federal Government and Homeland Security

National Nuclear Safety Administration (NNSA)
http://www.nnsa.doe.gov/

This site maintains news on international nuclear programs, nonproliferation and defense programs. It features an article on the future of the nuclear weapons complex.

Federal Bureau of Investigation (FBI): National Security Branch

http://www.fbi.gov/hq/nsb/nsb.htm

The Federal Bureau of Investigation's National Security Branch Web site.

Transportation Security Administration

http://www.tsa.gov/

This is the site of the government agency responsible for creating new initiatives for port security. The TSA site features a news release on the subject by Secretary of Homeland Security Michael Chertoff.

U.S. Customs and Border Protection

http://www.customs.ustreas.gov/

News releases and fact sheets with regard to U.S. border security are provided on this Web site maintained by U.S. Customs and Border Protection.

UNIT 4: State and Local Governments and Homeland Security

New York State Office of Homeland Security

http://www.security.state.ny.us/

Information from New York states Office of Homeland Security.

NGA Center for Best Practices

http://www.nga.org/portal/site/nga/menuitem. 8274ad-9c70a7bd616adcbeeb501010a0 /?vgnextoid=e9a4d9b834420 010VgnVCM1000001a01010aRCRD

This site of the National Governors Association Center for Best Practices is devoted to homeland security issues that affect states. The site's weekly newsletter reports on federal policies affecting states, offers links to respected research, as well as quick analyses on hot topics.

UNIT 5: First Responders

U.S. Fire Administration (USFA)

http://www.usfa.dhs.gov/

As an entity of the Department of Homeland Security and the Federal Emergency Management Agency, the mission of the USFA is to reduce life and economic losses due to fire and related emergencies through leadership, advocacy, coordination, and support.

Responding First to Bioterrorism

http://www.nap.edu/firstresponders/

This page from the National Academies includes expert-selected resources for first responders on bioterrorism and public safety, with a search engine of more than 3,000 related Web pages. Browse by subject area, audience, source, or type of content.

Department of Health & Human Services: Emergency Preparedness & Response

http://www.bt.cdc.gov/

The Center for Disease Control has several dedicated pages providing information on Bioterrorism.

UNIT 6: New Technologies in Homeland Security

Government Technology

http://www.govtech.net/

The publication Government Technology maintains an archive of articles concerning Homeland security.

National Institute of Standards and Technology

http://www.nist.gov/public_affairs/factsheet/homeland.htm

The National Institute of Standards and Technology maintain online fact sheets on chemical and biological threats, infrastructure protection, and nuclear explosive materials.

UNIT 7: Vulnerabilities and Threats

National Homeland Security Knowledgebase

http://www.twotigersonline.com/resources.html

This site provides a large collection of links and resources devoted to Homeland security.

National Terror Alert Response Center

http://www.nationalterroralert.com/

This Web site provides fact sheets and preparedness guides as well as breaking news related to Homeland security. The site also indicates the current terror alert status.

U.S. Customs and Border Protection

http://www.cbp.gov/xp/cgov/border_security/antiterror_initia-tives/border_security_overview.xml

This site reviews the anti-terrorism initiatives being proposed by the U.S. Customs and Border Protection agency.

UNIT 8: Civil Liberties and Civil Rights

Homeland Security and Civil Liberties

http://www.strategicstudiesinstitute.army.mil/pubs/display. cfm?PubID5697

This site maintained by the Strategic Studies Institute of U.S. Army War College contains an archive of resources involving Homeland Security issues.

Center for Democracy and Technology: Security and Freedom

http://www.cdt.org/security/nsa/briefingbook.php

The NSA's Web site provides links to timely documents concerning domestic surveillance.

UNIT 9: Intelligence and Homeland Security

Office of the Director of National Intelligence

http://www.dni.gov/

This site provides information from the Office of the Director of National Intelligence, John Negroponte. It includes the Annual Threat Assessment which produced by Negroponte and provided to the White House and the Senate.

UNIT 10: The Future of Homeland Security

Securing Our Homeland: U.S. Department of Homeland Security Strategic Plan

http://www.dhs.gov/interweb/assetlibrary/DHS_StratPlan_FI-NAL_spread.pdf

This document produced by the U.S. Department of Homeland Security outlines its plan to secure the nation from terrorist threats.

We highly recommend that you review our Web site for expanded information and our other product lines. We are continually updating and adding links to our Web site in order to offer you the most usable and useful information that will support and expand the value of your Annual Editions. You can reach us at: *http://www.mhcls. com/annualeditions/.*

UNIT 1

The Concept of Homeland Security

Unit Selections

1. **Homeland Security,** Benjamin M. Friedman
2. **How Much Are We Willing to Take?,** Amanda Ripley
3. **Lethal Fantasies,** Sharon Ghamari-Tabrizi
4. **Why We Don't Prepare,** Amanda Ripley

Key Points to Consider

- Is the threat of terrorism over-emphasized?

- Has airport security improved? Is there such a thing as too much security?

- Should terrorism be the primary focus of the Department of Homeland Security?

Student Web Site

www.mhcls.com/online

Internet References

Further information regarding these Web sites may be found in this book's preface or online.

The Department of Homeland Security
   http://www.dhs.gov/dhspublic/
International Information Programs: Response to Terrorism
   http://usinfo.state.gov/is/international_security/terrorism.html
National Homeland Security Knowledgebase
   http://www.twotigersonline.com/resources.html
White House Homeland Security Policy
   http://www.whitehouse.gov/infocus/homeland/
Global Security: Homeland Security
   http://www.globalsecurity.org/security/index.html

The events of September 11th have left deep scars on the American psyche. It is almost inconceivable that the actions of so few could change the lives of so many. Fourteen months after 9/11, on November 25th, 2002, President George Bush signed into law the Homeland Security Act of 2002. In the most comprehensive reorganization of the nation's security apparatus since the passage of the National Security Act of 1947, a new Department of Homeland Security (DHS) was created. The change encompassed 22 existing federal agencies and impacted over 170,000 employees. In its efforts to consolidate the nation's response capabilities to disasters and emergencies, natural or man-made, the Bush Administration created a new super-bureaucracy eclipsed only by the existing Department of Defense.

As the primary legislative response to the attacks on September 11th, the new DHS is in the unenviable position of having to be everything to everyone. At first glance, the mission of the DHS appears simple—to make Americans safer. Accomplishing this mission, however, has been difficult. The department's slow response to hurricane Katrina, continuing gaps in airport security, the lack of effective border security, and the never-ending burden sharing battles with states and localities have led to public criticism. They have cast doubt on the ability of the DHS to complete its assigned mission.

The long-term success of the DHS, however, depends as much on its own ability to meet the complex challenges of the 21st century security environment as on the actions of others. The DHS is heavily dependent on the support of the President, Congress, the Intelligence Community, and local law enforcement agencies.

From the outset, President Bush championed the creation of the DHS. He has been and continues to be one of the strongest supporters of the new agency. Ongoing U.S. involvement in Iraq and Afghanistan however, has strained U.S. resources and tested the political will. Amidst shifting priorities, it remains to be seen how well the DHS will fare in inevitable interagency budget rivalries. As political leadership changes and as national priorities shift, continued executive support is critical for the long-term success of the DHS.

Congressional support is equally important. While the DHS was built on promises that it would cost no more than the operation of the already existing agencies, the reality is that even beyond so-called "transitional costs" the new department has required significant increases in funding. A record national debt, increasing deficits, escalating defense costs, and an uncertain economic future will continue to test congressional resolve in funding this new department.

Partly to calm the fears of the Intelligence Community that portions of its now $50 billion budget could be usurped by the creation of a new department, the DHS was left without its own intelligence collection capacity. Thus, the DHS remains heavily dependent on the analytical capabilities and the resources of an Intelligence Community known for its reluctance to share information with others. While directors of the CIA and FBI have pledged their support for the DHS, it remains to be seen how bureaucratic hurdles, interagency rivalries, and future turf wars may affect this commitment.

The DHS is also dependent on the cooperation of first responders and local law enforcement agencies. While many agree that local law enforcement agencies may be the key to the success of the DHS, beyond promises of additional federal funds and some joint disaster exercises, there has been only a limited effort to actively incorporate these agencies into the day-to-day activities of the DHS. Amidst rising criticism from state and local government officials of inadequate or inequitable distribution of federal counter-terrorism funds, the DHS continues to face an uphill battle as it tries to pacify the economic concerns of local law enforcement agencies and first responders, while eliciting their cooperation and support for national security priorities and policies.

As the Department of Homeland Security continues to negotiate its role in national security, the debate about what exactly that role will be continues. The articles in this unit focus on the broad context in which this role will be defined, and highlight the continued debate concerning its priorities. They explore the inherent tension between what, at times, appear to be contradictory missions. They question whether the DHS should focus its resources primarily on preparation for recurring natural disasters, or whether its resources are better spent in preparation for less likely, but potentially equally catastrophic, terrorist attacks.

Homeland Security

For the vast majority of Americans, the chances of dying in a terrorist attack are close to zero. There's a higher probability that you'll die by falling off a ladder than getting mixed up in some terrorist plot. So why is the U.S. Department of Homeland Security constantly telling every American to be afraid? That's a strategy that creates widespread fear without making America any safer. U.S. homeland security efforts should focus less on what is possible and more on what is probable.

BENJAMIN M. FRIEDMAN

"All Americans Should Fear Terrorism"

That's ridiculous. The odds of dying in a terrorist attack are minuscule. According to the U.S. Centers for Disease Control, the odds are about 1 in 88,000. The odds of dying from falling off a ladder are 1 in 10,010. Even in 2001, automobile crashes killed 15 times more Americans than terrorism. Heart disease, cancer, and strokes are the leading causes of death in the United States—not terrorism.

People overestimate risks they can picture and ignore those they cannot. Government warnings and 24-hour news networks make certain dangers, from shark attacks to terrorism, seem more prevalent than they really are. As a result, the United States squanders billions of dollars annually protecting states and locations that face no significant threat of terrorism. In 2003, Tulsa, Oklahoma, received $725,000 in port security funds. More than $4 million in 2005 federal antiterror funding will go to the Northern Mariana Islands. In 2003, Grand Forks County, North Dakota, received $1.5 million in federal funds to purchase trailers equipped to respond to nuclear attacks and more biochemical suits than it has police officers.

These small expenses add up. Federal spending on first responders grew from $616 million in 2001 to $3.4 billion in 2005, a 500 percent increase. Homeland security spending will approach $50 billion this year, not including missile defense—roughly equal to estimates of China's defense spending. Yet pundits call for more. A 2003 Council on Foreign Relations report hyperbolically titled, *Emergency Responders: Drastically Underfunded, Dangerously Unprepared*, recommmends increasing spending on emergency responders to $25 billion per year. To his credit, the new secretary of homeland security, Michael Chertoff, wants to trim the pork from the department's budget. But efforts in Congress to link funding with risk have failed largely because haphazard spending is consonant with the current U.S. strategy that tells all Americans to be afraid.

It's true that al Qaeda's attacks on Sept. 11, 2001, may be a harbinger of a more destructive future. But it is also true that parts of the war on terrorism are working. Tighter U.S. entry requirements, more aggressive European policing, the destruction of al Qaeda's Afghan sanctuary, and refined intelligence operations have crippled al Qaeda's ability to strike the United States. Most of al Qaeda's original leadership is dead or in prison. Few other Islamist terrorists—even the most wanted terrorist in Iraq, Abu Musab al-Zarqawi—are as capable or organized as al Qaeda once was.

"Terrorists Can Strike Any Place, Any Time, with Any Weapon"

Unlikely. This assertion is the guiding principle of our homeland security strategy, yet it ignores probability. When the U.S. Department of Homeland Security dispenses such silly advice as, "Ensure disaster supply kit is stocked and ready," or "During a nuclear incident, it is important to avoid radioactive material, if possible," it assumes all Americans face an equal threat and creates widespread fear without making America safer. The department should focus more on what is probable and less on what is possible.

Most Americans are safe from terrorist attack. And the most likely forms of attack remain conventional. The fact is, all terrorist attempts to use chemical and biological weapons have failed to cause mass casualties. True, a successful biological weapons attack could kill hundreds of thousands of people. But manufacturing, controlling, and successfully dispersing these agents is difficult—probably too difficult for today's terrorist groups. Synthesizing and handling chemical agents such as the deadly nerve agent VX, sarin, or mustard gas is complicated and extremely dangerous, often requiring access to sophisticated chemical laboratories. Most experts agree, for instance, that al Qaeda does not possess the technical capability necessary to produce VX. And even if terrorists procure and deploy chemical weapons, they are unlikely to kill many people. The 1995 sarin attack in Tokyo's subway system was limited to only 12 deaths. Official U.S. government reports, including that of the Gilmore Commission, which examines domestic responses to terrorism, show that it would take one ton of chemical agent, favorable weather, and considerable time to kill thousands of people with chemical weapons.

This is to say nothing of the fact that no terrorist organization is known to possess nuclear weapons. Even for nations with the requisite monetary resources and scientific infrastructure, building a nuclear weapon can take decades. Yes, terrorists might try to buy a stolen nuclear weapon or its parts on the black market. But the chances of terrorists heisting a working nuclear weapon or assembling one from stolen parts are low. Most nuclear weapons require delivery vehicles and activation codes. Stealing all of these elements is next to impossible. Smaller, more portable tactical nuclear weapons, especially those made by the former Soviet Union, are a greater danger. Yet, according to a 2002 report by the Center for Nonproliferation Studies, most of Russia's portable nuclear weapons are probably inoperable today. What about dirty bombs? They are relatively easy to construct, but much less destructive. Depending upon variables such as wind direction and the speed of evacuation, a dirty bomb might not be any more deadly than a conventional bomb.

A nuclear terrorist attack in the United States is possible. That possibility should be enough to produce a more active and well-funded nonproliferation policy than the United States has today, especially when it comes to vulnerable stocks of fissile materials around the world. But that policy should not include preparing all Americans for nuclear attack.

"Terrorists Will Attack Soft Targets as 'A-List' Targets Become More Secure"

Not necessarily. This claim is made repeatedly in the pages of the 2002 National Strategy for Homeland Security—without any supporting evidence. A look at past behavior shows that terrorists are likely to continue to attack well-defended, high-profile targets. Before hitting the World Trade Center in 2001, al Qaeda targeted the buildings in 1993. After bombing the U.S.S. Cole in a Yemeni port in 2000, al Qaeda struck a French oil tanker off the coast of Yemen in 2002. Al Qaeda targeted airlines in 1995, 1999, and 2001, and it has not stopped since. British would-be shoe bomber Richard Reid tried to blow up an airplane in December 2001. In 2002, al Qaeda terrorists fired missiles at planes in both Saudi Arabia and Kenya. In places such as Singapore and Uzbekistan, terrorist plots focused on U.S. embassies even after the 1998 embassy bombings in Kenya and Tanzania encouraged the United States to harden embassy defenses.

The idea that terrorists stealthily stalk America for weak spots implies levels of capability and cohesion that are more myth than reality. Different terrorist groups have different targets, not to mention discrepant information about where U.S. vulnerabilities lie. Some groups may be competent and organized; others are likely not. The assertion that terrorists continue to case American targets also stems from the idea that terrorists remain hidden in the United States. But FBI Director Robert Mueller told Congress in February that there is little evidence that so-called sleeper cells reside in the United States, even as he warned the U.S. Senate Select Committee on Intelligence that he remains "very concerned about what we are not seeing."

After years without a terrorist attack, perhaps Americans can take what they are not seeing seriously. The assumption that terrorists are flawless and ubiquitous results in unreasoned fear and overreaction. This ghost is worse than the reality.

"America Is Doing Far Too Little to Protect Its Ports"

Hardly. More than $600 billion in goods and nearly 50 percent of U.S. imports flow through American ports each year. U.S. ports are vulnerable to both weapons smuggled into the United States in containers and U.S.S. Cole-style attacks on ships. But there is little indication such attacks are likely. Since September 11, the United States has made significant investments in port security. Federal port security grant programs have distributed about $600 million in funding to hundreds of U.S. ports. The Coast Guard's budget has grown to $6.3 billion in the four years since Sept. 11, 2001. These efforts are enough.

The news media love to mention that U.S. Customs agents inspect only 2 to 5 percent of containers entering the United States. But the measure of success is which containers are searched, not how many. The key to protecting ports

3

without unduly burdening commerce is using intelligence to identify risky cargo. The Container Security Initiative, instituted by U.S. Customs and Border Protection in 2002, aims to identify and inspect suspicious cargo before it sails to the United States by stationing agents in foreign ports, requiring a manifest prior to a ship's arrival, determining the origin of containers, and developing electronic, tamper-proof container seals. This system is far from perfect. But it is superior to spending vast sums of taxpayer money to inspect every shipment. And, when one considers the cost to the U.S. economy of slowing commerce to a snail's pace, this is one solution that is worse than the present danger. Any additional port security spending should respond to known threats, not mere vulnerability.

"Corporations Should Spend More on Security"

False. The odds of any one business in the United States being attacked by terrorists are vanishingly small. Still, leading terrorism experts such as Stephen Flynn often tout the fact that 92 percent of America's CEOs believe terrorists will not attack their company. This, Flynn and others argue, is proof that businesses are underinvesting in security and that government regulation should force them to do more. In fact, these numbers show that businesses already spend too much.

Osama bin Laden has bragged of his ability to "bankrupt" the United States. The proper response to tactics such as these is to rationally evaluate risks while carrying on with business as usual, not to search frantically for holes to plug. Companies that deal with dangerous products, such as the chemical industry, or sports franchises that fill stadiums and create large public crowds, need to take security more seriously than others. Where the danger to society is high and companies have incentives to avoid spending more on security, the government may have to impose security standards or shift liability onto the company. But these types of situations are rare. Homeland security experts make much of the vulnerability inherent in modern economies. Manufacturing and food companies have international supply chains. Commerce relies on phone lines, power cables, and gas lines. These networks are ubiquitous and impossible to defend entirely. Because terrorists seek to frighten, attacks that produce much economic damage but little fear, such as electricity blackouts or the destruction of livestock, are unlikely. Companies whose vulnerabilities are exclusively economic have little to fear from terrorists and should not invest much in the defense against them.

"Terrorists Will Soon Mount a Crippling Cyberattack"

Nonsense. Cyberattacks are costly and annoying, but they are not a threat to U.S. national security.

Here, some historical perspective is useful. Alarmists warn that cyberterrorists could cripple American industry. Yet, even during World War II, the Allied bombing campaign against Germany failed to halt industrial production. Modern economies are much more resilient. A 2002 Center for Strategic and International Studies report, for instance, notes that just because the U.S. national infrastructure uses vulnerable communications networks does not mean that the infrastructure itself is vulnerable to attack. The U.S. power grid is run by some 3,000 providers that rely on diverse information technology systems. Terrorists would have to attack a large swath of these providers to have a significant effect. That's a difficult task. Hackers, unlike summer heat waves and thunderstorms, have never caused a blackout. The U.S. water system is similarly robust, as is the U.S. air traffic control system. Although dams and air traffic control rely on communications networks, hacking into these networks is not the same as flooding a valley or crashing a plane.

Viruses and denial-of-service attacks are everyday occurrences, but they are not deadly. Most attacks pass unnoticed. Because terrorists aim to kill and frighten, they are unlikely to find these sorts of attacks appealing. Even if they do, they will merely join a crowd of existing teenagers and malcontents who already make cyberattacks a major business expense. The annual costs of viruses alone reportedly exceed $10 billion in the United States. A 2003 Federal Trade Commission report put the annual cost of identity theft, much of which occurs online, at more than $50 billion. Cybersecurity gurus have far more to worry about from traditional hackers than from terrorists.

"Al Qaeda Remains the Largest Threat to U.S. Homeland Security"

Wrong. The organization bin Laden continues to run from Afghanistan or Pakistan is on the ropes. Today, the main threat to the United States comes in the form of extremist entrepreneurs with only tenuous links to bin Laden and from other Sunni terrorist groups. These groups include Ansar al Islam, Egypt's Jamaat al-Islamiyya and Egyptian Islamic Jihad, Southeast Asia's Jemaah Islamiah, the Islamic Movement of Uzbekistan, Algeria's Salifist Group for Preaching and War, the Moroccan Islamic Combatant Group, Zarqawi's Tawhid and Jihad, and a host of others.

The press often blithely refers to these groups as "al Qaeda linked." But the links refer to sympathy and personal contacts that date back years, not continuous communications, planning, or operational control. These groups can be referred to as a movement, but that does not mean that they are part of a unified organization. For instance, though communications between Zarqawi and bin Laden have reportedly been intercepted, their relationship is a loose alliance, not one that involves handing down orders or sharing finances.

Most of the large terrorist attacks carried out since September 11 have had little connection to al Qaeda's leadership. The recent attacks in Bali, Turkey, and Spain were independent operations conducted by local extremists. Consider Madrid. The press still commonly calls the commuter train bombing there on March 11, 2004, an "al Qaeda attack." But most recent evidence indicates that it was carried out by local Muslims, mostly Moroccans, who had some contacts with the Moroccan Islamic Combatant Group, but little or no connection to bin Laden or Zarqawi. The Madrid attackers planned and executed their attack without training, orders, or material assistance from other terrorist groups.

Some experts and policymakers call this collage of al Qaeda fellow travelers and wannabes a network—and treat it as some form of higher organization. But the fact that this collection of fundamentalists is the primary national security threat to the United States should be cause for celebration. These groups are dangerous, but, thankfully, they lack the geographic reach and organizational capacity that al Qaeda had in 2001.

BENJAMIN FRIEDMAN is a doctoral candidate in political science at the Massachusetts Institute of Technology.

From *Foreign Policy,* July/August 2005, pp. 22–24, 26, 28. Copyright © 2005 by the Carnegie Endowment for International Peace. Reprinted with permission. www.foreignpolicy.com

Terrorism. How Much Are We Willing to Take?

AMANDA RIPLEY

We should be feeling safer right now. British officials appear to have foiled a plot to blow up as many as 10 U.S.-bound passenger jets with liquid explosives hidden in carry-on luggage. Another batch of alleged operatives has been discovered and taken out of commission. Several thousand men, women and children did not die ghastly deaths over the Atlantic Ocean. "This," said Republican Congressman Christopher Shays when the arrests of 24 suspects was announced last week, "was a good day."

Then why did it feel so bad? Why did a bullet dodged feel like the beginning of something and not the end? Minutes after the news broke, counterterrorist experts popped up on TV screens like Pez dispensers to remind us that our homeland-security system is ill equipped to stop the kind of attack the suspected London bombers were said to be planning. President George W. Bush warned against false comfort, saying although he believes the U.S. is more secure than it was before 9/11, "we're still not completely safe." Worst of all, the Brits, who can normally be counted on to snuff out hysterics, warned that we had narrowly avoided "mass murder on an unimaginable scale."

The sense of dread can be attributed in equal parts to the identities of the suspects (24 men and women believed to have been born in Britain, one of whom has already been released without charge), to the supposed imminence of the attacks and to their purported targets: more planes falling out of the sky. But our collective shudder is by now practically instinctive. Since Sept. 11, 2001, we have conditioned ourselves to spike every triumph in the struggle against terrorism with a shot of anxiety. Try as we might to secure the perimeter, we walk in the shadow of risk. "This is the story of terrorist threats," says Bruce Hoffman, a counterterrorism analyst at the Rand Corp. "We close up one set of vulnerabilities, and they attempt to exploit another."

Our triumph last week was muted because it was also a test—a test of our understanding of terrorism. Do we continue to react reflexively to each new scheme, regardless of the probability of the threat and the feasibility of preventing it? Or do we have an honest discussion about risk and the costs of safety? After the discovery of the liquid-bomb plot, does it make sense to funnel billions more dollars into new machines that can detect liquid explosives, even though the past three sizable attacks pulled off by Islamic terrorists in major metropolises have been on trains in Madrid, London and Bombay? Banning cologne from planes and testing bottles of baby formula for explosives may make us feel proactive, but are we being smarter? "We can't just radically shift our strategy every time there's an event," Michael Chertoff, Secretary of the Department of Homeland Security (DHS), tells TIME. "The key is balance and constantly looking at the entire landscape."

Yet clear-eyed equanimity about how to best manage risk is exactly what gets lost every time a new, harrowing plot is uncovered. The U.S.'s response to the London arrests is already drifting toward overkill, as men with badges ask moms to taste the baby formula and women hide lipstick tubes in their bras. Two days after the arrests, British authorities, who have decades of experience dealing with terrorist bombings, were complaining to DHS about an excess of caution. More than one plane from London was turned back, and at least seven British Airways flights had to be canceled because U.S. officials took so long conducting background checks of passengers. "We understand the need for new security measures," says a British government representative. "But we are keen for the actions to impact as little as possible on passengers."

In a world where every successful antiterrorism operation serves only to highlight another vulnerability, trying to stop the next attack can seem like an exercise in futility. But that's exactly the point. Terrorists can't be deterred forever. Dealing effectively with the threat posed by al-Qaeda requires a more sober and rational approach than we have pursued over the past five years, one that involves figuring out how much we are truly willing to change our way of life to reduce the risk of another 9/11. Until that calculation is made, terrorists will continue to succeed even when they fail. "The secondary concern of all terror plots has always been the secondary impact of attacks—getting democracies and free societies so frenzied to prevent new attacks that we start eroding and violating the very freedoms and liberties that the authors of terrorism themselves want to destroy," says French terrorism expert Roland Jacquard. "There will always be holes. One-hundred-percent security doesn't exist. We can do everything possible or viable to increase our security, but cutting off your arm because your hand risks gangrene is going too far." The question is, How do you know when you have gone far enough?

What's lost in the hand wringing about the vulnerabilities and security holes exposed by the London plot is how much

Safer by Degrees

Terrorism has changed air travel dramatically. The Transportation Security Administration (TSA) has thousands of screeners and machines to detect weapons and explosives, but gaps remain:

Curbside

- **Improvement** National Guard troops now patrol airports
- **Problems** Curbside check-in, briefly suspended after 9/11, is again offered. The often hectic process at crowded airports can increase the potential for lethal suitcases to enter the system

Check-In

- **Improvement** Identifications are closely checked at counters
- **Problems** The growing use of electronic tickets means a passenger without bags no longer has to stop at the counter to get a boarding pass, eliminating one layer of scrutiny

Security

- **Improvement** Checked and carry-on bags are scanned and searched more often. The TSA has installed explosives-detection systems at most commercial airports to screen checked bags and is testing phone-booth-size machines that use puffs of air to detect explosives residue on passengers
- **Problems** Private security companies are increasingly being used, diluting the TSA's mandate and possibly creating greater vulnerability. Government reports have cited insufficient training and the need for better technology

Restaurants

- **Improvement** The TSA grants varying levels of clearance to the mostly minimum-wage employees of airport stores
- **Problems** Boarding-area concessions can pose a serious threat. A restaurant worker, for example, could pass a knife to a passenger

Boarding

- **Improvement** Only ticketed passengers and employees are allowed in boarding areas
- **Problems** Passengers connecting from smaller airports might have undergone less rigorous screening but still have full access to gates

On the Tarmac

- **Improvement** The process for obtaining worker credentials is tighter
- **Problems** Many people—including cleaners, caterers, mechanics, refuelers and baggage handlers—have access to planes, and the grounds of a large airport can be difficult to secure. In 2003, for example, three fishermen wandered onto a runway at New York City's John F. Kennedy International Airport and walked around for more than an hour until they sought police for an exit. At air-cargo facilities, neither cargo nor personnel undergo the same scrutiny as airline passengers and their luggage

---

the counterterrorism community got right. Over a year ago, Britain's MI5 launched an investigation that spanned at least three continents. Pakistani officials helped track the British suspects, and U.S. intelligence provided intercepts of the group's communications. "It was really a joint effort, the kind of cooperation you probably wouldn't have had before Sept. 11," says a U.S. official who is regularly briefed on terrorist threats.

On Thursday, after the suspects had been arrested, the FBI and DHS sent an internal memo to state and local law-enforcement agencies warning that peroxide-based explosives could be used in an attack. But the memo could offer only so much guidance. No one could tell airport searchers exactly what to look for. Even if they knew, they wouldn't have the tools to find it. So post-9/11 airport supplications reached a new low, as throngs of passengers handed over their deodorant, hair gel and bottled water. The airline industry, which had just reported its best quarterly profits in six years, faces a possible new cataclysm. London Heathrow Airport came to a standstill, and

one of aviation's most lucrative routes, between New York City and London, suddenly seems fraught with risk.

For many counterterrorism officials, the scale and depravity of the plot seem chilling enough to justify the drama. "Very seldom do things get to me," Chertoff told Congressman Peter King, chair of the House Homeland Security Committee, in a phone call late Wednesday night. "This one has really gotten to me." A British official says investigators believe the bombers planned waves of attacks. By blowing up planes over the Atlantic, they would make it nearly impossible to gather forensic evidence. Then after people returned to flying, the terrorists would strike again. That benign items—iPods and soda bottles, the stuff of teenagers' backpacks—could be turned into weapons of mass destruction seemed like a new, unsettling perversion. Or at least it felt new.

Despite the news-channel talk of a fresh threat, people have been trying for almost 20 years to blow up planes with liquid explosives packed in carry-on baggage. Terrorists, like movie

Spot the Bomb

None of the items newly banned by the TSA would explode if mixed. The fear is that those common containers could be refilled with bomb ingredients and carried openly onto aircraft, to be combined later

- **Good news** Liquid explosives tend to be quite volatile, and concocting a bomb on a plane in flight would be a difficult, noxious job
- **Bad news** Explosives can be made to look like almost anything—drinks, paper, even a child's toy. The use of machines that detect bombs and traces of explosives is spreading, but liquid-chemical sniffers aren't in airports—yet

"We can't just radically shift our strategy every time there's an event."

—DHS Secretary Michael Chertoff

studios and toddlers, don't like to try new things. In 1987 two North Korean agents posing as father and daughter put a radio packed with plastic explosives and a whisky bottle full of liquid explosives in a bag in the overhead bin of a South Korean airliner. Then they got off on a layover. The subsequent explosion sent the plane spinning into the jungle near the Thailand-Burma border, killing all 115 people onboard.

In 1994 al-Qaeda foreshadowed the London plot almost exactly when Pakistani terrorist Ramzi Yousef and Khalid Sheikh Mohammed, who went on to mastermind the 9/11 attacks, drew up a scheme to bomb 12 planes over the Pacific during a 48-hour period. They nicknamed the plan Bojinka. They intended to have five terrorists take liquid explosives in carry-on bags onto planes and then assemble the bombs onboard. All but one of the planes were to be U.S. bound. On Dec. 11, Yousef ran a dress rehearsal on a Philippine Airlines jet. He carried the explosives onboard in contact-lens-solution bottles. Like the North Koreans, he disembarked after positioning the bomb in the cabin. It successfully detonated, killing a Japanese passenger and injuring 10 others. But because of the very small quantity of explosives, it did not take down the plane. A month later, Yousef accidentally started a fire in his apartment while working with the explosives. The Bojinka plan was thwarted when police arrived to investigate and discovered a laptop containing details of the plot.

Since 1969, explosives have killed about 2,000 people on planes. "Explosive devices are—and will remain—the primary threat to aviation indefinitely," says Steve Luckey, a former security director of the Air Line Pilots Association. "Bomb components are easy to get, easy to hide, and the payoff is huge."

Liquid explosives are particularly diabolical. Like plastic explosives, a small amount of them can release a massive amount of force. And they can be easily disguised to look harmless. In 2002 the FBI issued a warning that al-Qaeda members had discussed sneaking onto planes liquid explosives disguised as coffee. The bombers who struck London's transit system in July 2005 used a variant of a peroxide-based explosive, triacetone triperoxide (TATP). "We didn't wake up and discover liquid explosives this week," says DHS Deputy Secretary Michael Jackson.

Then why does the system remain so vulnerable to that brand of attack? The explosives-detection machines in airports today are not able to sniff out liquid explosives in a sealed container. Airline-security experts interviewed by TIME were divided on the question of whether the technology even exists to effectively detect liquid explosives in airports. Private companies have been working on various devices for years, but it's not clear if any are sufficiently accurate, cheap and fast. The fix is elusive because explosives can literally appear in any form—from computer paper to Jell-O, solid to gas—and they can be detonated by an endless mosaic of everyday devices. "Unless you are prepared to conduct intimate body searches or scans of every single passenger on every single flight, you cannot guarantee security from smuggled explosives. It's as simple as that," says Charles Shoebridge, a British security analyst and former counterterrorism officer.

Still, some experts believe the U.S. should be doing more to defend against bombs in general. The White House's Homeland Security Advisory Council has a director for nuclear threats and one for biochemical threats but no one specifically tasked to handle explosives. As in other parts of DHS, some of the best minds in the explosives unit have left in frustration. "There has been a hemorrhaging of talent," says a former senior U.S. official.

DHS has spent $732 million this year on aviation R&D for explosives-detection programs. Jackson said he did not have figures on hand for how much went to detecting liquid explosives in particular. Far more is spent on homeland security now compared with before 9/11, but many security experts say it's still not nearly enough. "The Pentagon's budget is 10 times that of DHS," notes Clark Kent Erwin, a former inspector general for DHS.

But given the hard reality of limited resources, what is the rational thing to do next? "Some people say, Let's push all the money into something that happened last week," says Chertoff. "[But] we still have to think about all the other things that could happen." Shoulder-fired missiles, for example, could be just as dangerous to plane passengers as liquid explosives. Some politicians argue that we should develop Star Wars—style missile-defense technology to protect planes. But that would cost an estimated $10 billion to build and billions more to maintain.

It's worth considering the probability of an attack, not just the possibility. Once terrorists decide to bomb an airline with liquid explosives, how likely is it that they will succeed? Some 2,000 bombs are planted every year on U.S. soil, and almost none are liquid explosives. That's because they are extremely volatile. Some explode if dropped a couple of feet. Friction can set off TATP. It would be difficult, if not impossible, to check such a bomb in a suitcase. Even if the components are carried on separately—the safest strategy to avoid detection and premature detonation—mixing the materials produces a foul stench that would probably attract attention, according to a U.S. airline explosives expert.

Every time the government scrambles to defend against the newest threat, it runs the risk of shortchanging more pressing ones. Investing in body-scanning machines or prohibiting carry-on luggage might provide a degree of security against liquid explosives, but such steps would do nothing about the fact that most of the cargo shipped on passenger planes goes entirely uninspected—for bombs or anything else. DHS relies instead on a program it calls Known Shipper, which leaves it up to air carriers and freight forwarders to screen regular cargo customers so they can load boxes onto planes with only spot inspections. The Government Accountability Office warned last October that the industry isn't adequately investigating shippers. But the Bush Administration and the airlines, which make about $17 billion a year from cargo on passenger planes, have resisted introducing tougher rules.

The key, though, has less to do with the sheer number of searches than with trying to make sure we're conducting the right ones. Several security experts interviewed by TIME said they hope the London plot encourages Americans to do more sophisticated profiling of suspects. The U.S. already profiles all passengers, using computer software. But the methodology is outdated. The system searches for people who pay with cash or book their flight less than 24 hours in advance. The country has a legal, moral and political aversion to officially sanctioned discrimination. But there are ways to profile other than skin color. Software could search passengers' previous travel itineraries or their nationality, for example.

While the U.S. tries to improve its fragmented intelligence capabilities, the second best defense might be vigilance. Most terrorists make mistakes, just as other criminals do. Mohammed told CIA interrogators that he had inadvertently packed a copy of the Bojinka plan with all the targeted flights and explosion times in his bag on the Philippine Airlines test run. Nobody noticed. Today someone might—just as a flight attendant noticed Richard Reid trying to light his shoe in a failed attempt to blow up a transatlantic plane. "We're lucky the people we're up against are so incompetent," says Larry Johnson, a former State Department counterterrorism official.

The trick is to find that narrow space between vigilance and paranoia. After the Bojinka plot was uncovered in 1995, aviation officials banned carry-on aerosols and most liquids and gels heavier than an ounce on U.S. planes leaving Manila. Eventually, the ban faded away. And people kept flying.

Regular people are often more comfortable assessing risk than officialdom expects. They may not be perfect at it, but they do it every day. Nancy Bort of Arlington, Va., landed at Washington's Dulles International Airport on the first flight from London Heathrow after the arrests. The plane arrived nearly two hours late, and the passengers emerged clutching plastic bags for their passports and not much else. But Bort was unfazed. "I still think I have a greater chance of being hurt in a car accident than getting killed by a terrorist," she said.

Last year car crashes claimed the lives of an estimated 40,000 people in America. Terrorists? Zero.—*Reported by Jessica Carsen and J.F.O. McAllister/London, Simon Elegant/Beijing, Leo Cendrowicz/Brussels, Bruce Crumley/Paris, Mimi Murphy/Rome and Brian Bennett, Timothy J. Burger, Sally B. Donnelly, Tracy Samantha Schmidt, Douglas Waller and Michael Weisskopf/Washington.*

Lethal Fantasies

**With its eye on the "Universal Adversary," Homeland Security
is failing to prepare for more likely, foreseeable catastrophes.**

SHARON GHAMARI-TABRIZI

Several days after hurricane Katrina swept through the Gulf Coast in late August 2005, Sen. Susan Collins, a Maine Republican, furiously demanded to know how Department of Homeland Security officials could explain the pandemonium following the storm. After pouring billions of dollars into preparedness, if this was the nation's response to a disaster "where there was no enemy," she fumed, "then how would [government] . . . have coped with a terrorist attack that provided no advance warning and . . . was intent on causing as much death and destruction as possible?"

Hurricane Katrina was a damning demonstration of Homeland Security's inability to respond to a catastrophe with no enemy. What, then, has the government been preparing for? It might come as a surprise to learn that precisely because the government was preparing for a disaster touched off by no identifiable enemy, it was able to overlook the predictable dimensions of a tragedy that many saw coming.

The events of September 11, 2001 gave President George W. Bush the pretext to introduce a new strategic framework: the "global war on terror." This framework deflected the public's attention away from a world with observable contours and toward a ghostly enemy that encompasses all possible threats, including those not yet imagined. Homeland Security aligned itself with this larger mandate (what it called the "great calling of our generation") and began preparing to confront, in the words of Homeland Security Secretary Michael Chertoff, "a dangerous and merciless evil." Invoking the chaos at Ground Zero, in January 2005 Homeland Security introduced its National Response Plan, which called for "a new paradigm for incident management." Rather than sequestering responsibility for domestic terrorism from industrial accidents and the depredations of the weather, the plan reckoned it was better to think of them as belonging to "a broad spectrum of contingencies, from acts of terrorism, to natural disasters, to other man-made hazards (accidental or intentional)."

National preparedness would no longer be "event driven" but would subsume response and recovery under prevention. At first glance, it seems reasonable to lump together natural disasters with terrorist strikes. Both categories require first responders' attention and the tortuous coordination of local, state, and federal efforts. But there's a twist. After 9/11, preparedness came

to mean reducing U.S. vulnerabilities to terrorist attack. Or as Chertoff explained in April 2005: "As consequences increase, we respond according to the nature and credibility of the threat and any existing state of vulnerabilities." This attractively simple calculus became the logic for disbursing Homeland Security funds, including monies destined for the Federal Emergency Management Agency (FEMA) and other agencies within the department. "We'll be looking at everything through that prism," Chertoff promised. The result was that customary allocations for predictable natural disaster response were slashed.

Recognizing that it was "impossible to maintain the highest kind of preparedness for all possibilities, all of the time," Homeland Security sought to work out which incidents qualified as "catastrophic threats with the greatest risk of mass casualties, massive property loss, and immense social disruption." The centerpiece of Homeland Security's efforts was the National Planning Scenarios, which "illustrate a broad range of potential terrorist attacks, major disasters, and other emergencies." Rather than aiming for comprehensiveness, officials chose scenarios to dramatize response and recovery capabilities, selecting those "for which the nation is currently the least prepared."

Three scenarios involved natural disasters; twelve depicted terrorist arracks. Because the focus was on incident response, any old terrorist would do. The enemy was a cipher, identified simply as the "Universal Adversary." (In fact, the planning scenarios report declared, "The FBI is unaware of any credible intelligence that indicates that such an arrack is being planned." Rather, the scenarios "generally reflect suspected terrorist capabilities and known tradecraft.")

Think about it: Twelve of the fifteen scenarios used for determining Homeland Security's organizational and funding priorities were wholly untethered to evidence of the intentions and powers of actual people. More importantly, the scenarios justified the curtailment of federal support for disaster relief in annual weather events, such as hurricanes, floods, tornados, and wildfires—any one of which would surely, one day or another, develop into a disaster of catastrophic proportions. With Homeland Security's energies trained on the Universal Adversary, the humble necessities of levee construction could hardly be descried.

Why did responsible people accept the idea of a Universal Adversary? How did the featureless cunning of a phantom justify the diversion of public monies from actual needs to possible ones? How did we become spellbound by the fiend who threatened to skulk across our borders, infiltrate our ports, menace our power grid and communication hubs, and oppose us in our homes, workplaces, malls, sports arenas, and amusement parks?

Last February, in testimony before the Senate Select Committee on Intelligence, Deputy Secretary of Homeland Security Adm. James Loy obligingly allowed that a terrorist attack "could come in any form, at any place, on any timetable." This is the touchstone of the new paradigm. The Defense Department's 2001 Quadrennial Defense Review Report announced that uncertainty would henceforth frame national security analysis. Because no one can know "with confidence what nation, combination of nations, or nonstate actor will pose threats to viral U.S. interests," the report stated that it made better sense to guess what targets an enemy could plausibly attack.

This new "capabilities-based" model for threat assessment focuses more on "how an adversary might fight than who the adversary might be and where a war might occur," nudging national security analysis into the realm of the hypothetical, the generally suspected, the possible, and the conceivable. It swerves assessment away from actual political groupings with intelligible politics, means, and intentions to the self-referential conjectures of the American defender. One examines one's own capabilities and asks, as Defense Secretary Donald Rumsfeld put it in January 2002, "What design would I be forming if I were the enemy?" This is nor only solipsistic, it is ticklishly speculative. According to Rumsfeld, not only must one stand guard against "the unknown," "the uncertain," and "the unexpected," bur one must also prepare to defeat "adversaries that have nor yet emerged to challenge us." Capabilities-based threat assessment operates enigmatically, tolerates thin evidence, and generates an assumption train of trend analysis. It gives us the Universal Adversary.

The pity of it is that even Homeland Security thinks a terrorist strike against the American heartland is fairly unlikely. An internal document leaked to *Congressional Quarterly* last March concluded that America's enemies were few and unmotivated. The document, called Integrated Planning Guidance, Fiscal Years 2005–2011, identified Al Qaeda and other militant Islamist groups as the principal U.S. foes. Bur most astonishingly, it concluded, "We are not convinced that any of these organizations acting alone would pursue a major attack against the homeland." Nor did Homeland Security believe that terrorist groups would obtain state sponsorship. Of the six "countries of concern" that were cited, five were of "diminishing concern." Only Iran seemed to harbor "possible future motivation to use terrorist groups, in addition to its own state agents, to plot against the U.S. homeland." Stop and consider whether the Islamic Republic would truly dare to execute a catastrophic attack on U.S. soil.

For the past four years, U.S. officials have been engrossed in the contemplation of nightmares rather than identifiable social, political, and climatological realities. Advocates of the war on terror renounce the wisdom of engaging with the actual world—a world not entirely of our making, not entirely in our control, but a world we can know—in favor of their own best guesses. To the extent that we have succumbed to the Universal Adversary, we have smothered our good sense with a lethal fantasy.

Sharon Ghamari-Tabrizi is the author of *The Worlds of Herman Kahn: The Intuitive Science of Thermonuclear War* (2005) and a visiting professor in the Sociology Department and the Arms Control, Disarmament, and International Security program at the University of Illinois at Urbana-Champaign.

Floods, Tornadoes, Hurricanes, Wildfires, Earthquakes ...

Why We Don't Prepare

Katrina: one year later

AMANDA RIPLEY

Every July the country's leading disaster scientists and emergency planners gather in Boulder, Colo., for an invitation-only workshop. Picture 440 people obsessed with the tragic and the safe, people who get excited about earthquake "shake maps" and righteous about flood insurance. It's a spirited but wonky crowd that is growing more melancholy every year.

After 9/11, the people at the Boulder conference decried the nation's myopic focus on terrorism. They lamented the decline of the Federal Emergency Management Agency (FEMA). And they warned to the point of cliché that a major hurricane would destroy New Orleans. It was a convention of prophets without any disciples.

This year, perhaps to make the farce explicit, the event organizers, from the Natural Hazards Center at the University of Colorado, Boulder, introduced a parlor game. They placed a ballot box next to the water pitchers and asked everyone to vote: What will be the next mega-disaster? A tsunami, an earthquake, a pandemic flu? And where will it strike? It was an amusing diversion, although not a hard question for this lot.

Because the real challenge in the U.S. today is not predicting catastrophes. That we can do. The challenge that apparently lies beyond our grasp is to prepare for them. Dennis Mileti ran the Natural Hazards Center for 10 years, and is the country's leading expert on how to warn people so that they will pay attention. Today he is semi-retired, but he comes back to the workshop each year to preach his gospel. This July, standing before the crowd in a Hawaiian shirt, Mileti was direct: "How many citizens must die? How many people do you need to see pounding through their roofs?" Like most people there, Mileti was heartbroken by Katrina, and he knows he'll be heartbroken again. "We know exactly—exactly—where the major disasters will occur," he told me later. "But individuals underperceive risk."

Historically, humans get serious about avoiding disasters only after one has just smacked them across the face. Well, then, by that logic, 2006 should have been a breakthrough year for rational behavior. With the memory of 9/11, the worst terrorist attack

in U.S. history, still fresh in their minds, Americans watched Katrina, the most expensive disaster in U.S. history, on live TV. Anyone who didn't know it before should have learned that bad things can happen. And they are made much worse by our own lack of ambition—our willful blindness to risk as much as our reluctance to work together before everything goes to hell.

Granted, some amount of delusion is probably part of the human condition. In A.D. 63, Pompeii was seriously damaged by an earthquake, and the locals immediately went to work rebuilding, in the same spot—until they were buried altogether by a volcano 16 years later. But a review of the past year in disaster history suggests that modern Americans are particularly, mysteriously bad at protecting themselves from guaranteed threats. We know more than we ever did about the dangers we face. But it turns out that in times of crisis, our greatest enemy is rarely the storm, the quake or the surge itself. More often, it is ourselves.

A Tour of the American Hazardscape

So what has happened in the year that followed the carnival of negligence on the Gulf Coast? In New Orleans, the Army Corps of Engineers has worked day and night—like men bailing a sinking ship, literally—to rebuild the bulwarks. They have got the flood walls and levees to where they were before Katrina, more or less. That's, er, not enough, we can now say with confidence. But it may be all that can be expected from one year of hustle.

Meanwhile, New Orleans officials have, to their credit, crafted a plan to use buses and trains to evacuate the sick, the disabled and the carless before the next big hurricane. The city estimates that 15,000 people will need a ride out. However, state officials have not yet determined where the trains and buses will take everyone. The negotiations with neighboring communities are ongoing and difficult.

More encouraging is the fact that Louisiana Governor Kathleen Blanco and the state legislature managed to pass mandatory building codes this year. Most states already have such codes. Florida has had a strict one in place since 2001, and structures built under it tend to be the ones left standing after a 120 m.p.h. wind rips through. We know that for every dollar spent on that kind of basic mitigation, society saves an average of $4, according to a 2005 report by the nonprofit National Institute of Building Sciences. Then there's Mississippi, which, believe it or not, still has no statewide building code. Katrina destroyed 68,729 houses there. But this year a proposed mandatory code, opposed by many builders, real estate lobbyists and homeowners, ended up voluntary.

At the same time, Mississippi has helped coastal towns develop creative plans for rebuilding more intelligently. New Orleans, however, still has no central agency or person in charge of rebuilding. The city's planning office is down to nine people, from 24 before Katrina, and it really needs 65, according to the American Planning Association. And the imperative to rebuild the wetlands that protect against storms, much discussed in the weeks after Katrina and just as important as the levees, gets less attention every day. Worst of all, Mayor Ray Nagin and the city council are still not talking honestly about the fact that New Orleans will have to occupy a much smaller footprint in the future. It simply can't provide city services across its old boundaries, and its old boundaries cannot realistically be defended against a major storm anytime soon.

Here is the reality of New Orleans' risk profile, present and future: Donald Powell, the banker appointed by President George W. Bush to run the reconstruction effort, said last December, "The Federal Government is committed to building the best levee system known in the world." As of right now, the Corps plans to spend $6 billion to make sure that by 2010, the city will (probably) be flooded only once every 100 years. That's not close to the best in the world. The Netherlands has a system designed to protect populated areas against anything but a 1-in-10,000-years flood. Alternatively, the Corps could build 1-in-500-year protection for the city, but that would cost about $30 billion, says Ivor van Heerden, deputy director of Louisiana State University's Hurricane Center.

It may be unfair, but this is the reality New Orleans leaders should be talking about. In a TIME poll of 1,000 Americans taken this month, 56% said they did not think all of New Orleans should be rebuilt if it might flood again. But in New Orleans, a city cut through with racial distrust and anger over the Corps' faulty levees, the same conversation is laced with suspicion. There is enough high ground in New Orleans for the city to relocate the entire pre-Katrina population more safely. The mostly African-American Lower Ninth Ward could still exist; it would just need to be smaller. But for many locals, rebuilding in the same doomed locations has become a point of pride, of dignity—just the opposite of what it should be. When a planning panel brought in by Nagin's Bring Back New Orleans Commission—comprising 50 specialists in urban and post-disaster planning—late last year proposed holding off on redeveloping places that had flooded repeatedly until residents had more information, the traumatized population recoiled as one.

The city council quickly passed a defiant and suicidal resolution: "All neighborhoods [should] be included in the timely and simultaneous rebuilding of all New Orleans neighborhoods."

A National Culture of Unpreparedness

In the 12 months since Katrina, the rest of the U.S. has not proved to be a quicker study than the Gulf Coast. There is still no federal law requiring state and local officials to plan for the evacuation of the sick, elderly, disabled or poor. But in the past few months, both houses of Congress triumphantly passed bills that require locals to plan for the evacuation of pets.

In June the Department of Homeland Security (DHS) released an unprecedented analysis of state and urban emergency plans around the country, including assessments of evacuation plans and command structures. The report concluded that most "cannot be characterized as fully adequate, feasible, or acceptable." Among the worst performers: Dallas, New Orleans and Oklahoma City. (The best by far was the state of Florida.)

But it's not just bureaucrats who are unprepared for calamity. Regular people are even less likely to plan ahead. In this month's TIME poll, about half of those surveyed said they had personally experienced a natural disaster or public emergency. But only 16% said they were "very well prepared" for the next one. Of the rest, about half explained their lack of preparedness by saying they don't live in a high-risk area.

In fact, 91% of Americans live in places at a moderate-to-high risk of earthquakes, volcanoes, tornadoes, wildfires, hurricanes, flooding, high-wind damage or terrorism, according to an estimate calculated for TIME by the Hazards and Vulnerability Research Institute at the University of South Carolina. But Americans have a tendency to be die-hard optimists, literally. It is part of what makes the country great—and vincible. "There are four stages of denial," says Eric Holdeman, director of emergency management for Seattle's King County, which faces a significant earthquake threat. "One is, it won't happen. Two is, if it does happen, it won't happen to me. Three: if it does happen to me, it won't be that bad. And four: if it happens to me and it's bad, there's nothing I can do to stop it anyway."

Here's one thing we know: a serious hurricane is due to strike New York City, just as one did in 1821 and 1938. Experts predict that such a storm would swamp lower Manhattan, Brooklyn and Jersey City, N.J., force the evacuation of more than 3 million people and cost more than twice as much as Katrina. An insurance-industry risk assessment ranked New York City as No. 2 on a list of the worst places for a hurricane to strike; Miami came in first. But in a June survey measuring the readiness of 4,200 insured homeowners living in hurricane zones, New Yorkers came in second to last. They had taken only about a third of eight basic steps to protect themselves from a major storm (such as getting flood insurance or putting together a disaster evacuation plan or kit).

The conventional wisdom after Katrina was that most of the people who failed to evacuate were too poor to do so. But a recent survey of more than 2,000 respondents in eight hurricane-prone states showed that other forces may also be at play. The survey, led by Robert Blendon, professor of health policy and political analysis at the Harvard School of Public Health, attempted to determine what, if anything, would pry people from their homes in the face of another Katrina. Overall, 33% said they would not leave or were not sure whether they would leave if an evacuation order was given. But it was homeowners, at 39%, who were particularly stubborn. Lack of funds or transportation does play a role for stay-behinds, but according to the poll, a greater consideration is a vague belief that their home is built well enough to survive a storm—a justification offered by a whopping 68%.

People cherry-pick the lessons of Katrina to avoid taking action. Fifty-four percent of those who say they wouldn't evacuate are worried that the roads would be too crowded, and 67% believe shelters would be dangerous. That's understandable, unfortunately. One of the most damaging legacies of Katrina might be the TV images of looting and the graphic rumors of violence that crystallized our belief that we turn into savages in a disaster—a notion that is demonstrably untrue; after most disasters, including Katrina, the crime rate goes down. Ironically, 66% of those surveyed were also confident that if they stayed at home, they would eventually be rescued—a faith hardly justified by the Katrina experience. Ours is a strange culture of irrational distrust—buoyed by irrational optimism.

Heat waves bring out the same kind of self-delusion. Scott Sheridan, professor of geography at Kent State University, has studied heat-wave behavior—focusing particularly on seniors, who are at special risk in hot weather—in Philadelphia; Phoenix, Ariz.; Toronto; and Dayton, Ohio. He found that less than half of people 65 and older abide by heat-emergency recommendations like drinking lots of water. Reason: they don't consider themselves seniors. "Heat doesn't bother me much, but I worry about my neighbors," said an older respondent.

That optimism helps explain why construction along the Gulf Coast of Mexico and both coasts of Florida continues to boom, even though hurricane season is an annual affair. Keep in mind that dense coastal construction is the main reason storms are causing more and more damage every year in the U.S. More than 50% of Americans live in coastal areas, which means heavy weather increasingly runs into people and property. Also, the elimination of wetlands to make room for development means there's less and less of a buffer zone to absorb storm surges and mitigate damage. So our biggest problem is not the weather but our romantic urge to live near water.

Trickle-Down Apathy

When Americans cannot be trusted to save themselves, the government does it for them—at least that's the story of mandatory car insurance, seat-belt laws and smoking bans. But when it comes to preventing disasters, the rules are different. The message, says Paul Farmer, executive director of the American Planning Association, is consistent: "We will help you build where you shouldn't, we'll rescue you when things go wrong, and then we'll help you rebuild again in the same place."

In New Orleans, for example, many people in positions of power knew full well that the entire city should not be rebuilt after Katrina. They were quietly counting on the Federal Government to play the heavy. FEMA was expected to release new building rules for the first time since 1984. The rules would determine which areas and structures the Federal Government would insure against floods. Everything else would be lost, and the feds would be the perfect scapegoats. In April FEMA released its new guidelines. But instead of banning development in areas that are extremely likely to flood again, FEMA blinked. The major new requirement was that some houses be built 3 ft. off the ground—even though Katrina flooded up to 20 ft. in some neighborhoods.

Nationwide, only 20% of American homes at risk for floods are covered by flood insurance. Private insurers largely refuse to offer it because floods are such a sure thing. In certain flood-prone areas, the Federal Government requires people to buy policies from the government's National Flood Insurance Program to get a mortgage loan. But the program has never worked even remotely as insurance should. It has never priced people out of living in insanely risky areas. Instead, too few places are included in the must-insure category, and premiums are kept artificially low. This year, despite brave talk about finally fixing the program, Congress caved in to short-sighted constituents and real estate interests and failed to make major changes.

Despite Katrina, most Americans believe their homes will endure a storm

---

It may not be reassuring to hear that America's handicaps in this area are as old as the country itself. A federal system like ours is not built to plan for—or respond to—massive disasters, concedes George Foresman, the country's new Under Secretary for Preparedness. "Everything we're trying to do goes counter to how the Founding Fathers designed the system," he says, sitting in his office on the DHS campus in Washington, surrounded by pie charts documenting what needs fixing. Unlike other, more centralized governments, ours cannot easily force states or companies to act. And when the feds try to demand changes anyway, state and local officials bristle at the interference. Like teenagers, we resent paternalism—until we're in trouble. Then we expect to be taken care of.

Before he was appointed by President Bush to the new, post-Katrina preparedness job, Foresman spent more than 22 years in emergency-management in Virginia. His hiring in December was one of the few bright spots of the past 12 months, say veteran emergency planners who know him. He understands the importance of preparing for all kinds of disasters, not just terrorist attacks. But he does not soft-sell the challenge ahead. "Frankly, the American public doesn't do well with being told what not to do," he says. With reason: before James Lee Witt became FEMA director under President Bill Clinton, he was county judge in Yell County, Ark. In 1983 he made the mistake of trying to get the county to participate in the national flood-insurance program. "I almost got cremated by farmers. [They were] saying, 'Ain't no way in hell I'm going to let the Federal Government tell me where I can build a barn," he says.

If the feds want something to change, they have to suggest it—nicely. After the 1993 floods in the Midwest, the Federal Government, under Witt's direction, managed to do something rare: it offered to buy out flood-prone properties to prevent repeat disasters. Several communities accepted, and the government, in partnership with the state, bought back 25,000 properties. The thousands of acres left behind were converted into wetlands, which act like a sponge in storms. In 1995 the floods came again. "And guess what?" says Witt. "We never spent one dime on responding. Nobody lost everything they worked for."

Today relations between the different levels of government are at a low point. The natural tensions of a federal system have been exacerbated by an Administration that distrusts government even more than the average voter does. President Bush did not want to establish DHS to begin with. When he was pressured to do it anyway, he created a department weak in leadership, autonomy and funding.

So although DHS has received an unprecedented amount of money for emergency management, it's a fraction of what most security experts think is necessary. And most of the money has gone toward counterterrorism. While some counterterrorism equipment can be useful in other kinds of disasters, the money cannot be used to pay the salaries of state and local employees. That would violate an ideological position against making the Federal Government bigger (even though the Federal Government has grown under the Bush Administration through other outlays, like military and education spending). So $18 billion has gone out to states and cities, but most of it has been spent on shiny equipment like haz-mat suits and X-ray machines—even in cities that desperately need police and firefighters instead. Only 20% has gone to planning and training, which Foresman himself admits is not enough.

At the close of the Boulder workshop this year, Kathleen Tierney, head of the Natural Hazards Center, stood up to say, "We as human societies have yet to understand … that nature doesn't care. And for that reason, we must care." She was quoting herself intentionally. She had said the same thing the year before, seven weeks before Katrina. As she spoke, her voice rose: "Here we stand one year later. Where is the political will to protect lives and property?"

Then Tierney announced the hotly anticipated results of the Next Big One contest. There were some outliers. One person predicted that a gamma-ray flare would kill 90% of the earth's species. That is what is known in the disaster community as a hilarious joke. But the winner, with 32% of the votes, was once again a hurricane. After all, eight of the 10 costliest disasters in U.S. history have been hurricanes. This time, most of the hurricane voters predicted that the storm would devastate the East Coast, including New York City. History has left us all the clues we need. Now we wait for the heartbreak. —*With reporting by Jeffrey Kluger/New York*

UNIT 2

The Department of Homeland Security

Unit Selections

Key Points to Consider

- Is current homeland security spending making us more vulnerable?

- What changes can be made to the Department of Homeland Security to make it more effective?

- Should the size and population of a state be considered in the allocation of homeland security funds?

- Who should manage airport security? Why?

Student Web Site

www.mhcls.com/online

Internet References

Further information regarding these Web sites may be found in this book's preface or online.

The Heritage Foundation: Homeland Defense Research
   http://www.heritage.org/Research/HomelandDefense/
Federal Emergency Management Agency
   http://www.fema.gov/
Mitretek Systems: Homeland Security and Counterterrorism
   http://www.mitretek.org/HomelandSecurityAndCounterterrorism.htm
Government Accountability Office: Homeland Security
   http://www.gao.gov/docsearch/featured/homelandsecurity.html

One of the most difficult challenges facing the U.S. government is how to organize its domestic security efforts. As the military services, the Intelligence Community, federal law enforcement agencies, and state and local governments vie for funding and control of various aspects of the domestic security mission, the Department of Homeland Security continues to struggle with the problem of joining together formerly separate government bureaucracies into one cohesive, coordinated unit. Differing functions, management styles, corporate cultures, and internal rivalries notwithstanding, the DHS must continue its efforts to effectively integrate the activities of various agencies in order to be successful. While some have criticized the absence of a long-term strategic vision, the DHS has been organized by function into five broad areas of responsibility: Border Transportation and Security (BTS), Emergency Preparedness and Response (EPR), Science and Technology (S&T), Information Analysis and Infrastructure Protection (IAIP), and Management.

The largest of these five new divisions is the Directorate for Border and Transportation Security. Incorporating among others, the over 40,000 employees of the hastily created Transportation Security Administration, and the U.S. Customs Service—it includes some of the functions of the agency formerly known as the Immigration and Naturalization Service. While the U.S. Coast Guard maintains a separate identity, it works closely with the head of the BTS. The Directorate for Emergency Preparedness and Response houses the department's response capabilities to both natural and man-made disasters. Building on the work of the Federal Emergency Management Agency (FEMA), this directorate was tasked with planning and organizing the DHS's crisis response capabilities.

The research and development function of DHS is housed in the Directorate for Science and Technology. In addition to identifying and developing new technologies that may help in the war on terrorism, this directorate focuses on research related to biological, chemical, radiological, and nuclear threats. The Directorate of Information Analysis and Infrastructure Protection houses the limited intelligence function of the DHS. Focusing primarily on the analysis of data provided by others, the IAIP attempts to coordinate the assessment of intelligence regarding potential threats to homeland security. Finally, the Directorate of Management is charged with the management and budgeting function, as it continues to oversee the complicated merger of multiple agencies.

The articles in this unit look at the continued challenges that the Department of Homeland Security faces as it continues to establish its role in national security. Questions concerning homeland security funding and priorities weigh heavily on the DHS as congressional interference continues to undermine the efficiency and effectiveness of the DHS. Management issues resulting from the complicated merger of multiple federal bureaucracies remain a challenge for the DHS. Calls for organizational reforms and restructuring, particularly in the wake of hurricane Katrina, are gaining increased momentum. Due to its size and high visibility at U.S. airports, the Transportation Security Administration has also come under increased scrutiny. The confiscation of nail-clippers and tweezers, coupled with the enforcement of ever changing rules according to which a three ounce bottle of liquid is apparently safer if it is contained in a one quart plastic bag, have undermined public confidence and have highlighted bureaucratic ineptitude. Rather than making the public feel safer, the TSA has become a focal point for renewed criticism of homeland security policy.

Are We Ready for the Next 9/11?

The sorry state—and stunning waste—of homeland security spending.

VERONIQUE DE RUGY

What do gym memberships, the Fourteen Mile Bridge in Mobile, Alabama, and a promotional campaign for a child pornography tip-line have in common? Answer: They all were funded with your homeland security dollars.

Since September 11, Congress has appropriated nearly $180 billion to protect Americans from terrorism. Total spending on homeland security in 2006 will be at least $50 billion—roughly $450 per American household. But far from making us more secure, the money is being allocated like so much pork. States and cities are spending federal homeland security grants on pet projects that have nothing to do with homeland security; state and local officials fight over who will get the biggest share of the money, regardless of whether they have a legitimate claim to it. And when Congress isn't doling out cash indiscriminately, it's overreacting to yesterday's attacks instead of concentrating on cost-effective defenses against the most likely current threats. The result is an edifice that, far from preventing terrorist assaults, actually makes us more vulnerable by diverting resources from worthier projects.

How did this happen? There are four chief reasons.

1. The Oversight Problem

Homeland security spending occurs in an environment that is highly conducive to waste, fraud, and abuse, starting with the Department of Homeland Security (DHS) itself. When the department was created, proponents argued that we'd get an entity with sole fiscal responsibility for the government's efforts against terrorism, thus increasing transparency, enhancing efficiency, and facilitating information-sharing. Instead, the opposite happened.

Notwithstanding its name, DHS' activities are not strictly directed at protecting the homeland. Of a fiscal year 2006 budget of $41 billion, the department will spend only $27 billion on activities related to homeland security. The remaining $14 billion finances activities ranging from Coast Guard rescues to hurricane aid.

Conversely, much homeland security spending takes place outside of the department. The total amount directed to homeland security activities in fiscal year 2006 is roughly $50 billion. But $23 billion of that will be spent by departments other than DHS. Not surprisingly, a large portion—$9.5 billion—goes to the Department of Defense. But other funding decisions are more curious. Why, for instance, are the Environmental Protection Agency, the Commerce Department, and the National Aeronautics and Space Administration receiving homeland security funds?

With the money split between so many departments and programs, DHS and Congress cannot conduct effective oversight. The new department has authority over the agencies that were subsumed into it, whether or not it makes sense for them to be combined, but not over the many more security-related entities that remain outside its auspices. For example, the secret service, which is almost exclusively in charge of the president's security, was moved from the Department of Treasury to DHS, while the Federal Bureau of Investigation remains inside the Department of Justice with no DHS oversight.

Even more important, though, is Congress' failure to match the consolidation of DHS with the consolidation of its oversight of the DHS' constituent parts. Even after the combination of more than two dozen agencies, committee chairs have been unwilling to relinquish much of their jurisdiction over the 22 agencies and activities transferred to DHS. As a result, last year alone the leaders of DHS had to appear before 88 congressional committees and subcommittees.

Agencies are always aggressive advocates for expansion of their budgets and aggressive defenders of their statutory mandates. With so much of the spending so diffused, the current structure simply invites waste.

2. The Magic Word "Security"

Effective oversight is especially important in this area, given the political effect of the phrase *homeland security*, which tends to short-circuit skepticism. Even DHS activities unrelated to homeland security are apt to see their funding increase, on the assumption that they have something to do with the function indicated by the department's name. Programs that Congress might not approve if they were outside DHS now sail through because of their affiliation. In Christmas 2004, for instance, the department handed out $153 million to programs offering food and shelter for the poor, a significant increase from the previous year's budget. In September 2004, the Senate attached $2.9 billion to the fiscal year 2005 homeland security bill for disaster aid to farm states affected by droughts, floods, and freezes.

The surge in spending to strengthen homeland security has given lawmakers many opportunities to indulge in their common passions: bragging about protecting the country from terrorists and directing federal funds to their home districts. Federal coffers are wide open to fight terrorism, and lawmakers are predictably pushing projects allegedly aimed at protecting their constituents. 2002's infamous $190 billion farm bill, renamed the Farm Security and Rural Investment Act, is a good example of such congressional hornswoggling.

If power companies invested in infrastructure the way the Department of Homeland Security and Congress fight terrorism, a New Yorker wouldn't be able to run a hair-dryer but everyone in Bozeman, Montana, could light up a stadium.

Despite promises by appropriators to pass a pork-free homeland security bill and a presidential ban on earmarks forbidding lawmakers from slipping their pet projects into the bill at the last moment, Congress loaded the fiscal year 2006 homeland security bill with earmark projects having nothing to do with homeland security, and President Bush signed it. Among these projects: $7.9 million for investigations of missing and exploited children; $102,000 to promote public awareness of the child pornography tip line; $203,000 for Project Alert, a drug use prevention program for schools; $15.8 million to enforce laws against forced child labor; $500,00 to continue steel tariff training, a program "to ensure Customs and Border Protection (CBP) enforcement of U.S. trade laws benefits from the expertise of the steel industry in classifying steel goods"; and $15 billion for bridge alterations in Mobile, Alabama; LaCrosse, Wisconsin; Chelsea, Massachusetts; Galveston, Texas; Morris, Illinois; and Burlington, Iowa.

3. Failure to Prioritize

If power companies invested in infrastructure the way DHS and Congress fight terrorism, a New Yorker wouldn't be able to run a hairdryer but everyone in Bozeman, Montana, could light up a stadium. Efficient expenditures concentrate limited resources on the most cost-effective initiatives; not every need is worth funding, and the greatest priorities and risks must be addressed first. But because Congress is more interested in politics than security, it gives every threat, every state, and every interest group a share of the homeland security pie, regardless of risk.

It doesn't take a security expert to realize that some anti-terror expenditures are more cost-effective than others. Simple

cockpit barricades, which the airline industry has now installed at relatively low cost, can prevent all 9/11-style attacks. In contrast, the burgeoning U.S. system for screening the bags of every airline passenger has already cost $18 billion during the last four years but will do little to prevent 9/11-style hijacking. Nor does the screening system prevent the destruction of airplanes, since it doesn't systematically check carry-on bags or air freight for explosives.

Another example: Congress insists that DHS hand out ever greater portions of its budget to "first responder" programs—essentially federal funds for state and local police and fire departments. But as James Carafano has shown in a 2005 study for the conservative Heritage Foundation, a dollar spent on preventing the next terror attack is vastly more cost-effective than a dollar spent recovering from it.

That's not to say it isn't prudent to prepare for an attack. But federalizing first-responder programs accentuates the incentive problems that already plague the political process. When such programs are a state responsibility, legislators have a strong incentive to accurately assess the risk and potential damages to their states. They have to decide whether to spend more on homeland security or on other accounts. When these programs are funded at the federal level, by contrast, a congressman from Wyoming has no incentive to admit that his state is not a likely target or that if it ever were a target, the damages would be limited. He has no incentive to turn down federal money and even less incentive to volunteer taxpayers' dollars for other states.

To make matters worse, Congress provides every state with a guaranteed minimum amount of grant money regardless of risk. As a result, rural, less-populated areas receive a disproportionate amount of money. Of the top 10 grant recipients, only the District of Columbia also appears on a list of the 10 places most at risk of attack.

The theory underlying the grant distribution formula is that terrorists could strike anywhere. That's true. But not every target is equally likely or equally important. By trying to protect us everywhere, Congress ensures that we're adequately protected almost nowhere.

The lack of risk-based funding, combined with the absence of federal terrorism preparedness standards or a goal to guide the expenditure of funds, has resulted in some ridiculous uses of terrorism preparedness grants. We've seen $63,000 spent on a decontamination unit that is stored in a warehouse in rural Washington because the state does not have a hazardous materials team to use it; $350,000 spent by a small volunteer fire department in Virginia on a custom-made fireboat; $1.5 million spent by Grand Forks County, North Dakota (population 70,000), to buy decontamination tents, a semi-armored van, two trailers equipped with gear for responding to weapons of mass destruction, and more biochemical suits than there are police officers to wear them; $500,000 spent by Outagamie County, Wisconsin (population 165,000), to buy chemical suits, generators, rescue saws, disaster response trailers, emergency lighting, and a bomb disposal vehicle; and $557,400 spent by North Pole, Alaska (population 1,570), on homeland security rescue and communications equipment.

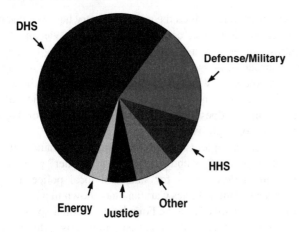

Source: U.S. Budget, FY 2006

Figure 1 Recipients of Homeland Security Funding.

The waste of homeland security funds does not occur exclusively in low-risk cities. Washington, D.C., incontestably one of the most at-risk areas in the country, used the region's first wave of homeland security aid as "seed money" for a computerized car-towing system Mayor Anthony Williams had promised for three years to help combat fraud by private towing companies. The city also used $100,000 in homeland security money to fund the mayor's popular summer jobs program.

The department's spending has been the subject of many audits, none of which found systemic fraud or abuse. Indeed, many of the questionable purchases made with DHS funds were allowed by department guidelines. To end the discussion there, however, ignores the larger point that the system for disbursing homeland security funds is based on warped priorities. While the audits did not find systemic problems, some of their specific recommendations reinforce the impression that the system is a joke. The DHS inspector general's audit of first-responder grants declares that "efforts to monitor and measure the impact of first responder grants needs to be improved" The inspector general's report on the Port Security Grant Program notes that many grants were given to projects that "appeared to be for a purpose other than security against an act of terrorism."

Spending $58,000 on a rescue vehicle capable of boring through concrete to search for victims in collapsed buildings in Colchester, Vermont (population 18,000), may be permitted by DHS guidelines, but are those guidelines appropriate? And while there may be ways to justify spending homeland security funds in this location, does anyone really believe that Vermont, North Dakota, and Wisconsin are the front lines of the war on terror?

Instead of stopping the flow of money to low-risk areas, Congress created another pot of grant money called the Urban Area Security Initiative. The program's backers said it would allocate money based on an objective evaluation of risks and that political considerations would not be allowed to intrude.

So what happened? In early 2003, Congress announced that it would pay $100 million in Urban Area Security Initiative money to seven high-risk cities—New York, Washington, Los Angeles, Seattle, Chicago, San Francisco, and Houston. Immediately, members of Congress started receiving calls from urban officials who felt they had been unfairly left out. The list

Selected Examples of Wasteful Homeland Security Spending

- $200,000 for Project Alert, a school-based drug prevention program
- $7,100,000 for forensic support and grants to the National Center for Missing and Exploited Children
- $100,000 for the Child Pornography Tipline
- $10,000,000 to Intercity Bus Security to improve security for operators and passengers by providing bus security enhancements and training to bus companies and others
- $22,000,000 to the trucking industry security program to promote security awareness among all segments of the commercial motor carriers and transportation community
- $2.5 billion for "highway security," which consists of building and improving roads
- $50,000,000 to provide an exercise program that meets the intent of the Oil Pollution Act of 1990
- $38 million to fully cover all remaining fire claims from the Cerro Grande Fire in New Mexico
- $20,000,000 to renovate the Nebraska Avenue Headquarters of the Department of Homeland Security
- $500,000 for a homeland security program at the Morehead State University Institute for Regional Analysis and Public Policy
- $22,800 for Mason County, Washington, to buy six radios that are incompatible with county radios
- $30,000 for a Tennessee high school to have a defibrillator on hand for a basketball tournament
- $98,000 for training courses by the Tecumseh, Michigan, fire department—that no one attended
- $557,400 to North Pole, an Alaska town of 1,570 people, for homeland security rescue and communications equipment

Sources: DHS Inspector General reports, press accounts

of qualifying cities started to expand. By May 2003, the number of most-at-risk cities had grown from seven to 30. That was followed by an increase in funding from $100 million to $700 million. Today more than 80 cities and mass transit agencies, including Indianapolis, Louisville, and Columbus, are getting extra homeland security cash out of an $830 million budget.

4. Preventing Yesterday's Attack

Inappropriate security spending is often a knee-jerk reaction to the news of the day. The surest way for a mode of transportation to get a boost in federal funding is to be attacked by terrorists.

Within days of 9/11, Congress ordered a federal takeover of airport passenger screening and created a 45,000-employee bureaucracy. Protecting the country against hijackings became *the* priority, and the Transportation Security Administration (TSA) became the key player.

The TSA's budget reflects Congress' overreaction. Its $5.9 billion represents more than 10 percent of homeland security spending and more than 15 percent of DHS' budget. Its funds exceed those of the FBI or the Secret Service. And although Congress originally charged the TSA with protecting all modes of transportation, it has done little beyond aviation. More than 90 percent of the TSA's budget request for fiscal year 2006 is devoted to air transport. The TSA has established itself as a multibillion-dollar centralized bureaucracy whose main function is to guarantee that security screeners, many of whom barely speak English, spend endless hours harassing pilots, confiscating dangerous mustache scissors, and pawing grandmothers and children.

Programs that Congress might not approve if they were outside DHS now sail through because of their affiliation. In Christmas 2004, for instance, the department handed out $153 million to programs offering food and shelter for the poor.

At first mass transit received its security funding through the broad State Homeland Security Grant Programs. Transit officials complained that little of the money would make its way to them because they had to compete with first responders and many other competitors. But when coordinated bombings on the Madrid train system killed 191 people in March 2004, Congress immediately created a separate $150 million grant program for transit and rail security.

In the aftermath of the two attacks on the London subway system last July, lawmakers proposed still more money for public transit systems. Sen. Judd Gregg (R-N.H.) suggested an increase of $100 million. Sen. Charles Schumer (D-N.Y.) talked of $200 million. Sen. Richard Shelby (R-Ala.) called for a $1.2 billion increase, and Sen. Hillary Clinton (D-N.Y.) upped it to $1.3 billion. That was nothing compared to the $6 billion requested by William Millar, president of the American Public Transport Association.

Yet if the London bombings teach us anything, it's that throwing money at transit security is unlikely to have any impact. After decades of combating Irish Republican Army terrorists, the London subway system is known to be one of the best protected in the world, but the large public investment in surveillance did not prevent the two terrorist attacks. The second incident occurred even while the system was in maximum alert mode. Experts agree that options are limited, if not nonexistent, for preventing such strikes. So why spend money on it?

Fortunately, lawmakers never got around to increasing transit security funding. Only a few weeks before they passed their homeland security spending bill, the Gulf Coast was devastated by Hurricane Katrina. Because they have the attention spans of 2-year-olds, members of Congress immediately turned all their attention to firefighters and natural disaster preparedness. During the debate on the spending bill, dozens of amendments were introduced to increase funding for everything from natural disaster relief efforts to firefighters. Among other things, lawmakers included an amendment (ultimately defeated) that would have provided $1.7 billion more for first responders and for disaster planning and mitigation.

The Alternative

It's hard to see how we are safer from terrorist attack now that the Princeton, New Jersey, Fire Department owns Nautilus exercise equipment, free weights, and a Bowflex machine, all paid for with homeland security grants.

If Congress were serious about homeland security, it would scrap the requirement that every state be guaranteed a part of the homeland security budget, abolish all grants to state and local governments, ban all earmarks from homeland security bills, and create better oversight for its homeland security spending. These steps would help root out wasteful spending and ensure that funds were allocated based on risk rather than politics.

The Transportation Security Administration's $5.9 billion represents more than 10 percent of all homeland security spending and more than 15 percent of DHS' budget. Its funds exceed those of the FBI or the Secret Service.

In 2004 the members of the independent, bipartisan 9/11 commission stated that the current system is in danger of turning homeland security funding into "pork-barrel" spending and making security subsidies just another state entitlement program. They suggested that homeland security funding be based strictly on an assessment of risks. While mainly ignored by

Table 1 Risk vs. Reward

Cities Facing the Highest Risk of a Terrorist Attack	Entities Receiving the Most Homeland Security Funding Per Capita	
1 New York, NY	Virgin Islands	$104.35
2 Chicago, IL	Guam	90.36
3 Washington, DC	Northern Marina Islands	54.00
4 San Francisco, CA	Wyoming	37.74
5 Los Angeles, CA	American Samoa	37.54
6 Boston, MA	District of Columbia	34.16
7 Philadelphia, PA	Vermont	31.43
8 Houston, TX	North Dakota	30.82
9 Newark, NJ	Alaska	30.18
10 Seattle, WA	South Dakota	26.32

Source: Author's calculation based on Office of Domestic Preparedness, "Fiscal Year 2004 Homeland Security Grant Program" and Rand's 2005 Study "Estimating Terrorist Risk."

lawmakers, their conclusions did trigger public debate. Greater public outrage about the deeply flawed spending process may have encouraged DHS to become a stronger advocate for reform ideas unpopular in the pork hungry Congress.

Indeed, the greatest potential for reform today is coming from DHS. Following the 9/11 recommendations, it has started pushing for a complete overhaul of the grant formula and a more risk-based approach to homeland security in general. A possible sign of that new attitude is the Transportation Security Administration's recent decision to allow passengers to carry some knives onto airplanes. It certainly isn't enough, but it's a step in the right direction. Meanwhile, the department's inspector general has produced several extensive reports exposing bad practices and suggesting ways to curb wasteful spending. If Congress is waiting for guidance before it acts, it need wait no longer.

But that might be wishful thinking. Congress, by nature, is an inefficient institution driven by self-interested politicians. Wasteful spending is par for the course. And if it is sad that lawmakers treat homeland security the same way they treat everything else, it certainly isn't surprising.

VERONIQUE DE RUGY (vderugy@aei.org) is a research scholar at the American Enterprise Institute.

Revisiting Homeland Security

Lawmakers with second thoughts about their creation have moved from criticizing the troubled department to chipping away at it.

TIM STARKS

The Homeland Security Department's announcement last month that it was cutting counterterrorism aid to New York and Washington and giving more to small cities such as Ft. Lauderdale and Memphis set lawmakers' teeth on edge. Like the color-coded threat levels and ordering old ladies to take their shoes off at the airport, it seemed to the politicians like just another bureaucracy-driven decision that had little regard for common sense and even less for political realities.

And in a way, it was an insult added to injury: It came just at a time when Congress was trying to figure out how to funnel more money—not less—to the metropolitan areas that are considered the most threatened, especially after Sept. 11, 2001.

"As far as I'm concerned, the Department of Homeland Security and the administration have declared war on New York," railed Rep. Peter T. King, the New York Republican who oversees the department as chairman of the Homeland Security Committee.

"It's a knife in the back to New York," said King, who lost friends, neighbors and constituents in the 2001 attacks, "and I'm going to do everything I can to make them very sorry they made this decision."

Members of Congress have spoken harshly before about the Homeland Security Department, complaining about its response to Hurricane Katrina, for instance, and its inability to control illegal immigration. But for the first time, lawmakers are going beyond talk to action, actively promoting legislation to remove pieces of the department.

This could lead, in time, to a wholesale dismantling of the department that was created with such urgency more than three years ago. No one is going that far yet, but members of Congress are increasingly asking themselves whether they and the Bush administration made a mistake in agglomerating 22 government agencies, bureaus and offices into one department to handle domestic security.

"What we're now seeing is the kind of rethinking of the organization that should have taken place before it was created," said Norm Ornstein, a resident scholar at the American Enterprise Institute, a conservative think tank. "First of all, there should have been a recognition that pulling together any kind of disparate agencies is an enormously difficult task that can take years to do, sometimes decades."

The forced merger of these various agencies is one of the main reasons that Homeland Security is not working as Congress intended. Each agency brought with it a distinct culture and, in some cases, its own problems. FEMA had been a government backwater, and sometimes a dumping ground for unwanted political appointees, long before Sept. 11. The Coast Guard had for decades struggled to find the resources to handle its various missions.

Once created, the department was put in the hands of a former state governor—Pennsylvania Republican Tom Ridge—who some critics said was a better politician than he was a manager. His successor, Michael Chertoff, is a former judge with no experience running a major agency.

Finally, some critics say that the Bush administration and Congress were not prepared to give the new department the level of resources it needed to fulfill such an ambitious mandate.

The result has been more a confederation of agencies than a cohesive department, leaving little wonder that members of Congress have proposed removing some of those agencies and letting them operate on their own.

In May, two House committees approved legislation to pull FEMA out of the Homeland Security Department and let it operate on its own. Committee members thought an independent FEMA could devote more effort to disaster recovery.

That is much the same reason other lawmakers think the Coast Guard should be removed, too. Its civilian responsibilities, such as search and rescue, they say, are not inherently related to homeland security. And a House committee in May approved a bill to take away some of the department's responsibilities for medical response to disasters.

Such views are not widely held in Congress; the consensus seems to be that it is too soon or would be unwise to make such changes. The administration opposes removing any agencies. For one thing, it might threaten the entire structure.

"Once you start tearing this thing apart, it's all open for consideration," said Paul C. Light, a New York University professor who specializes in the federal bureaucracy. "Congress should be very careful about taking things out. It could be a house of cards."

It is also not clear that those who want to remove certain agencies are driven by policy alone. Creation of the department scrambled congressional committee jurisdictions and left some chairmen with less power than they previously had. A reorganization could give some of it back. (*Turf wars, p. 1776*)

But never before have the congressional complaints about the department been so insistent. Even the chairman of the House Appropriations subcommittee that funds the department, Kentucky Republican Harold Rogers, indicated recently that there may come a day when he would favor dismantling it.

"I'm not quite there yet," Rogers said, though his subcommittee's fiscal 2007 bill withholds $1.3 billion until the department produces strategies, planning documents and other material Rogers has asked for.

Early Warnings

Once, and not that long ago, a Homeland Security Department was a shiny new idea about good government. In February of 2001, the U.S. Commission on National Security/21st Century predicted that a terror attack on U.S. soil was likely within the next 25 years. If that happened, the commission warned, it would decimate lives and wreak destruction that would damage U.S. pre-eminence in the world. And the government would not be ready.

"In the face of this threat, our nation has no coherent or integrated governmental structures," said the members of the panel, nicknamed the Hart-Rudman Commission, in their final report. "We therefore recommend the creation of an independent National Homeland Security Agency (NHSA) with responsibility for planning, coordinating and integrating various U.S. government activities involved in homeland security."

The expected attack came months, not years, later. Sept. 11 drove President Bush to appoint a homeland security czar to oversee the agencies, bureaus and operations spread out across the federal government that had any responsibility for defending the country against such attacks. This adviser would operate from the White House in the Office of Homeland Security.

Tom Ridge was not in the job long before reports began to surface of agencies that did not want to take his direction. Congress became angry when Ridge, citing executive privilege, refused to testify at committee hearings. Rep. Jane Harman, a California Democrat, brandished a chart demonstrating how complicated, dissolute and uncoordinated federal homeland security was. Lawmakers began discussing in earnest the work of Hart-Rudman.

Bush resisted the idea, pushed mostly by Democrats, of a Homeland Security Department. But when revelations of intelligence failures made headlines in the spring of 2002, he proposed his own plan for a department. Republicans got on board. Very few members of Congress voted against the final bill, approved late the same year.

Department supporters point to accomplishments since. "Their track record, outside of Katrina, is pretty good," said Adam H. Putnam of Florida, chairman of the House Republican Policy Committee. "There have been no terrorist attacks inside the U.S. since 9/11."

In the early days of the department, the focus was on vision and strategy. Retired Coast Guard Adm. James Loy, who served

Homeland Uncertainty

If Congress changes the structure of the Homeland Security Department, the most likely targets will be the Federal Emergency Management Agency (FEMA), which has been plagued by mistakes, and the Coast Guard, an agency Congress dotes on and had misgivings about adding to Homeland Security in the first place. So far, lawmakers have done little more than talk about altering the department, but action is likely if the problems persist. Here's a rundown on some of the proposals:

- **FEMA** Lawmakers were so upset by FEMA's fumbled response to Hurricane Katrina and with Homeland Security's management of the agency that 11 bills to do something about it have been introduced. Eight would yank FEMA out of the department altogether. Alaska Republican Don Young's bill to make FEMA its own agency with Cabinet status has been approved by his Transportation and Infrastructure Committee and by Government Reform. The administration opposes the idea and GOP congressional leaders have not gotten involved. The House Homeland Security Committee has approved a competing bill to give FEMA more responsibility and clout but leave it where it is.
- **Coast Guard** When Congress created the department some members, such as Young, worried that the Coast Guard's traditional maritime roles, such as search and rescue, would get short shrift in a department primarily dedicated to counterterrorism and border security. Their concerns have only increased as the Coast Guard tries to handle multiple roles with limited resources. Lawmakers probably won't try to move the Coast Guard anytime soon, but Alaska Republican Ted Stevens, chairman of the Senate Commerce, Science and Transportation Committee, is considering legislation on the subject.
- **National Disaster Medical System** When Congress created the department it incorporated teams that coordinate the medical response to disasters. These teams, which had been under the Department of Health and Human Services (HHS), were attached to FEMA. Last month, the House Energy and Commerce Committee approved legislation to move them back, saying they could operate better as part of HHS. "Unless we want these agencies to suffer the fate of FEMA, we will need to remain vigilant," said John D. Dingell of Michigan, the committee's ranking Democrat. Both the administration and the Homeland Security Committee oppose the move.

as deputy secretary and in other capacities, said one of Ridge's great accomplishments was setting forth the key operational principles of the department: awareness, prevention, preparedness, response and recovery. A similar iteration of those principles still guides the department.

The department, said current deputy secretary Michael Jackson, has increasingly focused on "systemic discipline." An anthrax scare at the Pentagon led the department to develop specific lists of actions for each kind of attack, listed in a book that Jackson can flip through to find recommended responses and tasks for, say, a "chlorine tank explosion."

Each secretary can claim responsibility for reducing a variety of vulnerabilities. Both Loy and Jackson praised the department's progress on the difficult task of guarding critical infrastructure—the chemical plants, computer networks and other structures that pose tempting terror targets. The overdue National Infrastructure Protection Plan is ready for release this week, Jackson said.

Under Ridge, the department went from executive order to interim plan, Loy said. Under Chertoff, it has begun to expand on that work, not only finalizing the plan but completing an inventory of all critical infrastructure, prioritizing it and recommending action for some of the higher-risk chemical plants in the nation.

In several ways, the department also has consolidated its operations—under Ridge, it cut the number of bill-paying centers from 19 to six—and benefited from synergy among its agencies that its creators envisioned. The department's grants and training division, which distributes aid to states and first-responders, has called upon the expertise of the Transportation Security Administration, FEMA and other agencies for information about vulnerabilities and needs in such areas as mass transit and disaster preparedness.

However fragmentary those achievements are, they are close to the way government agencies in general grow and evolve. Experts warned when the department was created, and still caution today, that building an effective structure could take years, even decades.

As such, Jackson said, Congress' impatience is healthy and expected; the country cannot afford to wait 10 years to have a fully functioning department when the threat of terrorism still looms. But it is not a reason to do something drastic. The department must be given time to mature.

"We had the right vision," he said. "We ought to have the courage of our convictions to stand by what we created."

In Light's view, "Congress just has to be patient and avoid the temptation to undo the merger with continued bad news from the department."

Bag and Baggage

And yet, there is general agreement that the department is a mess—more so than members of Congress expected it would be at this point.

At least part of that is because of the merging of agencies with vastly different cultures and missions. Some of the agencies had only a small connection to security. The Coast Guard was primarily focused on search and rescue and fisheries, and devoted just 25 percent of its efforts to homeland security. Likewise, FEMA was not a protective agency like the Secret Service—it had always focused on natural disasters.

After three and a half years, Homeland still has a split personality. According to the administration's fiscal 2007 budget request, 40 percent of the department's spending would be for activities not related to homeland security.

And plenty of the government's homeland security spending is in agencies outside the department, such as the FBI. Another Bush budget document places the total federal homeland security budget at $58.3 billion, of which nearly half is for the Homeland Security Department.

Some agencies also brought baggage as well. At the time, the Immigration and Naturalization Service was referred to as the most dysfunctional agency in the federal government. The Coast Guard was a good agency but historically starved of needed funding, said Elaine Kamarck, a Harvard University Kennedy School of Government Professor who managed Clinton's "reinventing government" initiative.

Combine that with the stress of any reorganization, and ineffectualness was bound to reign. "The simple act of moving something is extremely disruptive and distracting to the core mission," said Michael O'Hanlon of the Brookings Institution.

Kamarck said some of the decisions made during the merger compounded the woes of the department. Customs was combined with the INS, then split into three units—Customs and Border Protection, Immigration and Customs Enforcement, and Citizenship and Immigration Services.

That led to problems for all three agencies, according to the department's inspector general, such as the detention and removal of aliens and a lack of coordination in intelligence-gathering and investigations.

Furthermore, the initial merger of the 22 agencies was not the last shakeup. Last summer, after months of review, Chertoff ordered a department-wide reorganization that merged several divisions and created new ones. "They've been reorganizing internally at a relatively rapid pace," Light said. "The department has been in turmoil since the beginning."

Jackson, though, said Chertoff's reorganization was designed at least in part to chop away at internal dysfunction, some of it inherent to the foundation of the department. For instance, Congress mandated the creation of an Information Analysis and Infrastructure Protection Directorate. For a while, it was considered the most dysfunctional portion of the department, and the different divisions of the directorate, with different kinds of expertise and goals, did not always see eye to eye. Chertoff separated them, creating a special intelligence office and putting infrastructure protection into a

Preparedness Directorate—a better fit for the respective tasks, Jackson said.

"There was a profound operational dysfunction in the way that was glommed together," he said. "Now they're aligned and doing a good job."

Managing Change

The Hart-Rudman Commission assumed that a department devoted to homeland security was not the only answer to protecting the country. "There is no perfect organizational design, no flawless managerial fix," the members wrote. "The reason is that organizations are made up of people, and people invariably devise informal means of dealing with one another in accord with the accidents of personality and temperament. Even excellent organizational structure cannot make impetuous or mistaken leaders patient or wise, but poor organizational design can make good leaders less effective."

Ridge and Chertoff, the two secretaries of the department, have each received mixed reviews on their management. Ridge, a capable politician, proved most adept in front of the camera, communicating to the public. Internally, he engendered loyalty among aides.

Chertoff, an admired intellectual, brought the regimented thinking of an attorney from his time as a judge and top official in the Department of Justice.

But their strengths have also sometimes been a detriment. And in the views of their critics, each also brought a similar flaw.

"They are not operations guys. You need a heavy-duty operations guy in there," Kamarck said. Chertoff, she said, is a "brilliant lawyer and brilliant judge, and he's never run a major operation involving thousands of people. Frankly, Tom Ridge wasn't much better, either. He was a politician. They've had two inadequate directors."

Ridge, insiders said, had a tendency to let internal disputes drag on too long, a result of his politician's instinct not to displease anyone. He also gained a reputation for letting other departments tread on his turf, such as in 2003 when he signed a memorandum with the Department of Justice that granted them lead authority for terrorism finance investigations, much to the dismay of investigators in his own department.

Chertoff has a tendency toward frankness, for instance saying repeatedly that not everyone and everything in the country can be protected, a message that often offends lawmakers.

And more than a few insiders quietly wished Chertoff had half of Ridge's political savvy when Hurricane Katrina hit. His unwillingness to take control of the situation when FEMA Director Michael D. Brown was floundering was a setback for his department, said Kamarck.

Democrats began calling on him to resign as early as last summer. But during the fury over the fiscal 2006 state grants, for the first time a Republican, Rep. John E. Sweeney of New York, joined the chorus. Some of Chertoff's early supporters have begun to abandon him.

"I've lost a lot of confidence in Secretary Chertoff," said King. "It's getting more and more difficult to defend him."

Neither Ridge nor Chertoff granted interview requests last week, but their deputies, Loy and Jackson, defended them in a similar fashion: The secretaries may not have been former chief operating officers, but they brought their own skills to bear in the job and surrounded themselves with people who possessed the skills they lacked.

The department's management problems extend far below the secretary's office. The department has had trouble finding candidates for management jobs who are both capable and willing. Only three of the more than 20 top managers in the department today served under Ridge for more than a day.

"Sometimes you'll find people who just don't want the grief," said Jackson. Testifying before Congress "is not always a lovefest, and there's a risk to your career if you leave after getting beat up on things."

A survey last year ranked the Department of Homeland Security the second-worst place to work among large agencies. The worst was the Small Business Administration.

When Homeland Security sought a replacement for Brown, several candidates rejected the offer flat out. Critics say the department has not often enough taken responsibility for finding top managers. The result is that those who are brave enough to stay sometimes end up taking on added responsibilities, serving as "acting" director of an agency while maintaining their old jobs as well.

"The joke on our side is that we could really start a local at DHS for the Screen Actors' Guild, there are so many people 'acting,'" said Rep. Bennie Thompson of Mississippi, ranking Democrat on the Homeland Security Committee.

The appointment process also stalled last year during Chertoff's reorganization review, when it was not clear what the department's deck chairs would look like, and the administration declined to appoint leaders to agencies that might not exist once the review was through.

Some of those who have been willing to come work at the agency have had their qualifications questioned. Most prominent is Julie L. Myers, head of Immigration and Customs Enforcement, who had limited experience with most of the agency's work, but was the wife of John F. Wood, Chertoff's chief of staff, and is the niece of Air Force Gen. Richard B. Myers, the departing chairman of the Joint Chiefs of Staff.

"Maybe we should fix the appointment process and make changes in how we select top officers at homeland security," Light said, citing the Myers appointment.

Jackson said the department has had success finding capable job candidates with its pitch to prospective employees: "There's no more exciting place to be in government than the Department of Homeland Security. And nothing exceeds the importance of what we're doing."

Three Years On, Turf Wars Persist

CONGRESS MAY HAVE CREATED the Department of Homeland Security, but it has done no better than the department itself in coming to grips with the disparate and interwoven missions of the various agencies it oversees.

Legislation on the protection of seaports and railroads and the security of airline cargo has been left hanging because lawmakers cannot agree on solutions, cannot find the money to pay for solutions or refuse to compromise on committee jurisdictions. Lawmakers have not even been able to reauthorize the department they built.

After it created the department, the House created a Homeland Security Committee to oversee these issues. The Senate more recently gave its Senate Governmental Affairs Committee jurisdiction over domestic security issues. But given the department's vast and disparate responsibilities, congressional oversight of its operations remains diffuse—spread across no fewer than 65 committees and subcommittees.

That has left the new committees feeling a little like the new kid on the block, with veteran chairmen from other panels balking at attempts to consolidate oversight of the Homeland Security Department.

For example, Don Young, the Alaska Republican who chairs the Transportation and Infrastructure Committee, has refused to share much jurisdiction over the Coast Guard even though it is part of the Homeland Security Department. Wisconsin Republican F. James Sensenbrenner Jr., chairman of the Judiciary Committee, has been unwilling to give up much oversight of immigration, which also is under the control of Homeland Security. The House Energy and Commerce Committee, meanwhile, has tried to maintain control of technology issues such as the emergency radio spectrum.

John Gannon, a former staff director for the House Homeland Security Committee, says that while he was there he spent much of his time battling over jurisdiction. "We got clobbered by the other committee chairmen," he says. "There was a dismissive attitude."

Turf also has been an issue on port security, which Congress has been arguing about for years. Last year, Senate Commerce, Science and Transportation Committee Chairman Ted Stevens, an Alaska Republican, guided a bill through the panel to authorize $729 million over three years for port security. This spring, Maine Republican Susan Collins persuaded her Homeland Security and Governmental Affairs Committee to approve a similar port security bill that calls for spending $835 million a year.

There has been no progress in merging the two. "That's just a jurisdictional fight," Stevens said after the Collins bill was approved. Just because Collins has homeland security as part of her panel's jurisdiction, Stevens said, "that doesn't mean they have control over ports."

Controlling the Spending

The usual struggles between appropriators and the authorizing committees also plague homeland security oversight. The tough task of investigations has been overshadowed by the lure of Homeland Security appropriations, which allow members of Congress to send anti-terrorism money back to their home districts.

Kentucky Republican Harold Rogers, chairman of the House Homeland Security Appropriations Subcommittee, has come under fire for steering homeland security business to companies in his district, including language that helped a business in Corbin, Ky., win federal work making identification cards for transportation workers.

Bringing appropriations home is nothing new, but critics say the power that appropriators have over homeland security far outweighs that of the authorizing committees, making it hard to have an impact on spending levels or formulas for anti-terrorism grants. For instance, appropriators, especially those from rural or small-town districts, have opposed homeland security grant formulas that would benefit high-threat areas such as New York, Washington or Los Angeles.

House Homeland Security Committee Chairman Peter T. King, R-N.Y., says a department authorization bill modeled after the annual defense authorization—in which authorizers set a Pentagon spending blueprint, but the appropriators make specific funding decisions—would give Congress a firmer hold over programs, funding levels and priorities for the far-flung department. "In the ideal world it would send a message to the department and would set a structural base for the department," King says. "And it's important to establish credibility for the committee." But he isn't holding out hope.

King is hoping to have his committee take a stab at an authorization bill again this summer. The House last year passed a fiscal 2006 reauthorization, but the Senate did not take it up, and this year again it has no plans to mark up a Homeland Security authorization.

'Taking a While to Shake Out'

Collins says that with a department as large as Homeland Security, "it's no surprise this [jurisdiction] is taking a while to shake out." Her committee has marked up bills dealing with chemical plant security, grant formulas and port security.

The House panel has been more active since King took over. In the past year it has held a dozen markups on bills ranging from the handling of ammonium nitrate to port security. "We are working in a pretty bipartisan way, and we are the prime committee of jurisdiction," the chairman says. But none of this legislation has passed Congress. "Legislatively, there's not a lot of successes to look at," says James Jay Carafano, a homeland security and defense analyst at the Heritage Foundation, a conservative think tank. "Jurisdiction is a problem ... and it just isn't getting any better."

It is not that Homeland Security officials have avoided Capitol Hill. Since its inception in 2003, the department has participated in 601 congressional hearings and provided nearly 6,000 congressional briefings. The department's two secretaries, Tom Ridge and Michael Chertoff, have testified 38 times.

But while all of these hearings show that House and Senate committees are interested in homeland security issues such as port security and the federal response to Hurricane Katrina, the diffuse mission of the committees means that one panel is not there to hold the new department accountable. And the turf wars further complicate the problem, experts say. "Congress has tragically failed in its oversight," says Timothy J. Roemer, a member of the Sept. 11 commission and a former Democratic House member from Indiana. "Congress needs to do less finger-pointing at the agency and look in the mirror."

Rep. Bennie Thompson of Mississippi, the ranking Democrat on House Homeland Security, scoffs when asked about congressional oversight of the biggest government reorganization since World War II. "You mean the lack of congressional oversight," he says.

Gannon, a former CIA deputy director who is now an executive at the aerospace firm BAE Systems, says that if the department fails, it is ultimately a reflection on Congress. "The department," he said, "needs focused, strong congressional oversight."

—Martin Kady II

An Evolving Bureaucracy

The Bush administration's original plan was to build the Homeland Security Department by reorganizing 22 existing agencies and offices into four divisions—dedicated to border and transportation security, emergency preparedness, defense against weapons of mass destruction, and information analysis—and adding the Secret Service (formerly in the Treasury). Some components, such as FEMA, stayed much as they had been when the department was created in a 2002 law (PL 107-296). Others, such as the FBI's domestic preparedness office, disappeared. A few became hybrids—the Animal and Plant Health Inspection Service is run jointly by the Homeland Security and Agriculture departments. Congress, meanwhile, specified that the Coast Guard and Secret Service would be part of DHS while retaining their own identities. A reorganization last summer changed the original lineup. How the agencies drawn into Homeland Security are arranged now:

THE 22 AGENCIES BEFORE SEPT. 11

	Bush's fiscal 2003 budget
Border & Transportation Security	
INS/Border Patrol (*part of the Justice Department*)	$6.4 billion
Customs Service (*Treasury*)	$3.8 billion
Animal and Plant Healthy Inspection Service (*Agriculture*)	$1.1 billion
Transportation Security Administration (*Transportation*)	$4.8 billion
Coast Guard (*Transportation*)	$7.3 billion
Federal Protective Service (*General Services Administration*)	$418 million
Federal Law Enforcement Training Center (*Treasury*)	not available
Office for Domestic Preparedness (*Justice*)	not available
Emergency Preparedness & Response	
Federal Emergency Management Agency (*Independent agency*)	$6.2 billion
Strategic National Stockpile of Vaccines and the National Disaster Medical System (*Health and Human Services*)	$2.1 billion
Nuclear Incident Response Team (*Energy*)	not available
National Domestic Preparedness Office (*FBI*)	$2 million
Chemical, Biological, Radiological & Nuclear Countermeasures	
Civilian Bio-Defense Research Programs (*HHS*)	$2 billion
Lawrence Livermore Lab (*Energy*)	$1.2 billion
National Biological Warfare Defense Analysis Center (*Defense*)	$420 million
Plum Island Animal Disease Center (*Agriculture*)	$25 million
Information Analysis & Infrastructure Protection	
Critical Infrastructure Assurance Office (*Commerce*)	$27 million
Federal Computer Incident Response Center (*GSA*)	$11 million
National Communications System (*Defense*)	$155 million
National Infrastructure Protection Center (*FBI*)	$151 million
Energy Security and Assurance Program (*Energy*)	$20 million
Secret Service	$1.2 billion

THE DEPARTMENT TODAY

Preparedness Directorate: Primarily makes grants to state and local agencies, and helps them identify risks and train workers. (*Fiscal 2006 appropriation: $4 billion*)

Science & Technology Directorate: Research and development on counter-terrorism. (*$1.5 billion*)

Management Directorate: Includes an intelligence analysis office that was downgraded after the department lost turf battles with the CIA and the Pentagon. (*$946 million*)

FEMA: Prepares for and coordinates federal response to natural disasters and terrorist attacks. (*$2.6 billion*)

TSA: Largely unchanged since it was created by Congress in 2001 to protect airports and planes. (*$3.9 billion*)

Customs & Border Protection: A marriage of the Customs Service's inspection system and the Border Patrol. (*$5.9 billion*)

Immigration and Customs Enforcement: The combined investigative functions of the former Immigration and Naturalization Service and the Customs Service. (*$3.2 billion*)

Citizenship and Immigration Services: The part of the old INS that deals with naturalization, visas and policy. (*$114 million*)

Federal Law Enforcement Training Center: The Georgia training base for law enforcement personnel. (*$280 million*)

Coast Guard: Combines border security with maritime services such as search and rescue. (*$7.7 billion*)

Secret Service: Protects the president and other officials and investigates financial crimes. (*$1.2 billion*)

SHARE OF FY2006 BUDGET
TOTAL: $31.6 billion

- Coast Guard: 24.4%
- Customs and Border Protection: 18.7%
- Preparedness Directorate: 12.7%
- TSA: 12.3%
- Immigration and Customs Enforcement: 10.1%
- FEMA: 8.2%
- Science and Technology: 4.8%
- Secret Service: 3.8%
- Management Directorate: 3.0%
- Less than 1% each: Federal Law Enforcement Training Center; Citizenship and Immigration Services; Other

Finding the Money

The importance of that mission has led President Bush to declare that only two department budgets should be protected from cuts: Defense and Homeland Security. Given that the president originally opposed creating Homeland Security, that would be something of a turnaround.

But the funding numbers are somewhat deceptive. While the fiscal 2007 budget request for Homeland Security did recommend an increase, some of it was predicated on Congress enacting fees that the administration knew lawmakers would almost certainly reject. Not counting fees, the department's budget would increase by just 1 percent.

That budget has hovered just above $30 billion since the department's inception. Democrats say that's not enough to shore up an infinite list of vulnerabilities and get the department's management in order.

"Money would fix some obvious things, like if you had more people on the border," said Thompson. "Money would fix some of the interoperability problems" for incompatible first-responder radio equipment, he said.

That unwillingness to spend the significant amounts of money that would have helped first-responders from different jurisdictions communicate with one another during Katrina "is scandalous," said Ornstein.

On the other hand, Homeland Security has often spent its money wastefully. A contract with Boeing to install bomb-detection machines in airports, worth a little more than $500 million originally, mushroomed to $1.2 billion over the span of 18 months. According to former inspector general Clark Kent Ervin, the contract structure allowed the company to profit from its costs and its subcontractors' costs, for a total of $82 million. Ervin documented $500,000 spent on artwork and silk plants for an operations center at the Transportation Security Administration.

Problems keeping track of money persist. Immigration and Customs Enforcement has been so beset by money woes that it once instituted a hiring freeze and cut back on expenses such as cell phone calls and gasoline. This month, the Government Accountability Office concluded an investigation at the direction of the House Homeland Security Committee that found about $1 billion worth of waste, fraud and abuse in Katrina disaster aid, with some of the money being spent on items such as a sex-change operation and some being spent by people in jail.

Congress has itself to blame for some of the department's resource problems, because it often cuts money from management accounts to pay for other priorities. Last year, negotiators on the annual Homeland Security spending bill agreed to give the administration a little more than half of what it wanted for a new personnel system.

Some aspects of that personnel system are unpopular in Congress because government employee unions allege that it would strip them of basic rights. But in a department trying to unify its pay system, thereby better integrating the department as a whole, the funding reduction hurt.

Boiling Over

Nothing is likely to change in fiscal 2007. During House debate of the latest Homeland Security spending bill, more than $100 million was pulled from the $255 million for the Management Directorate, the secretary's office and related programs, which was already $51 million less than the president sought.

"Why not help them get the resources they need to succeed?" Light asked of Congress. "They still don't want to spend any money. They still don't want to fix the personnel system."

Among the lawmakers starting to reconsider the Homeland Security Department's structure, no two better illustrate that movement than Sen. Trent Lott of Mississippi and Rep. Thomas M. Davis III of Virginia, both Republicans.

Each played a role in creating the department in 2002: Lott was Senate Republican leader and Davis was a subcommittee chairman of House Government Reform, which reviewed the legislation. Last summer, though, the department's response to Katrina gave them second thoughts about the wisdom of putting FEMA into Homeland Security.

"Preliminarily, my opinion is absolutely that was a mistake," Lott said after the storm. "You can't blame that on anybody but us."

Both Lott and Davis have now cosponsored bills to make FEMA an independent agency, and the House version might come to the floor this week.

FEMA would lose one of its own agencies under a bill approved in May by the House Energy and Commerce Committee. It would return the National Disaster Medical System to the Health and Human Services Department. Under the bill, HHS would become the primary agency in charge of coordinating federal assistance to state, local and tribal governments in preparing for or responding to bioterrorist attacks or public health or medical emergencies.

"Unless we want these agencies to suffer the fate of FEMA, we will need to remain vigilant," warned ranking Democrat John D. Dingell of Michigan.

Even though the Coast Guard performed heroically during Katrina as part of Homeland Security, there are some who still believe it, too, does not belong in the department.

Senate Commerce, Science and Transportation Chairman Ted Stevens, R-Alaska, said he was preparing legislation to remove the Coast Guard from the Homeland Department. "That's a very burdensome overlay of supervision it doesn't need, and we're devoting some of the money that could be used to modernize the Coast Guard to provide it with more supervision that it doesn't need," Stevens said.

Others simply argue that the department is a hopeless affair, what Massachusetts Democrat Jim McGovern called "a bureaucratic nightmare." For them, it is up to Congress to reconsider a number of aspects of the 2002 legislation.

At a Rules Committee hearing in May, Putnam asked Rogers, the Appropriations subcommittee chairman, whether he thought the department should be broken up, eliciting Rogers' comment that he was "not quite there."

"The point of my questioning that particular day was not to lob grenades at the DHS," Putnam said, "but to ask the question of myself and my colleagues, because we are the ones who created this.

"Isn't it time for us to take a long hard look at what we have done and determine whether we accomplished what we have set out to? Aren't we the best ones to ask that question, since we're the ones that created it? The longer it exists, the less likely we'll be able to make the big decisions, the tough decisions to reform it."—*Patrick Yoest, Victoria McGrane and Martin Kady II contributed to this story.*

Shifting Priorities: Congressional Incentives and the Homeland Security Granting Process

Small states receive more homeland security grant money per capita than large states because of the structure of representation and decision making in Congress. Beyond per capita allocations, the homeland security granting process affects the structure of state and local emergency management agencies, shifting priorities away from natural and technological disasters toward counterterrorism. I suggest using competitive grants, increasing the salience of the granting process, and changing the institutional setting in order to rationalize the granting process.

PATRICK S. ROBERTS
Virginia Tech

In the wake of the terrorist attacks of September 2001, the federal government has demonstrated an unprecedented commitment to homeland security through a massive reorganization and the creation of a new cabinet-level department as well as through exponentially greater spending on counterterrorist security. The Department of Homeland Security (DHS) has spent $11 billion on emergency preparedness and response from 2001 to 2004. According to the textbook picture of government, federal agencies use budget and personnel increases to take on new tasks in addition to old ones, in this case defending the nation against terrorism while preserving the capacity to respond to natural and technological disasters.[1]

But rather than textbook efficiency, the federal government's response to the threat of terrorism is an example of the triumph of symbolic and distributive policies over more straightforward attempts to address the real problems of homeland security. I show how Congress has funded counterterrorism initiatives without serious risk analysis while reducing its commitment to emergency preparedness and response to natural and technological disasters. Small isolated states receive far more money per capita for homeland security than do large high-risk states, and furthermore within each state money and attention appear to be diverted from more frequent natural disasters toward the terrorist threat. The essential reason for this imbalance is that the incentives for public agencies are different than they are for private firms. Scholars such as Mayhew (1974) and Fiorina (1977) have shown how Congress structures policies to further the reelection ambitions of individual members, resulting in outcomes that may be optimal for an individual member's district but suboptimal for the country as a whole. In practice, Congress often uses spending as wealth transfers—in other words, "pork"—rather than as coherent solutions to policy problems. Faced with these structural limitations, the best strategy for policymakers interested in a coherent approach to emergency management is to make the issue of risk analysis salient to the public in order to bypass the usual veto points while employing risk analysis during funding decisions as much as possible through the use of competitive grants.

The differences between government and private firms provide reasons to suspect that emergency management agencies will not be able to respond to the new mission of homeland security in an "efficient" manner. One meaning of efficiency in government is the lowest cost way for a legislator to achieve desired outcomes, which is usually a maximum of goods for a particular legislator's district (Weingast & Marshall, 1998). Most people, however, think of governmental efficiency as the lowest cost way in which institutions can achieve a general good or resolve a shared problem. In the case of hazard response, the problem is clear: the United States must incorporate the heightened threat of terrorism into its strategy for preparation and response to disasters in general.

Unless agencies develop autonomy, the first step in problem solving will depend upon Congress.[2] It is in federal agencies' relationships with Congress, rather than with consumers in a private market, where the notion of efficiency becomes cloudy. In the words of Wallace Sayre, a student of public administration, "public and private management are fundamentally alike in all unimportant respects" (Allison, 1990, p. 16). Government agencies cannot distribute the benefits of greater earnings to employees in the way that private firms can. Federal bureaucracies are also constrained because they cannot allocate the factors of production in accord with the preferences of agency leaders and they generally lack control over the missions they pursue. Authority over federal agencies rests to a great degree in entities outside the agency—the president, Congress, courts, interest groups, states and localities, and public opinion (Wilson, 1989, pp. 114–136).

These entities have far different motives than the consumers who shape the functions of the private market. While customers of private firms may want the highest quality product available at a low price, agencies cannot easily make efficiency a goal since it is not always clear what their products are. In emergency management policy, the federal government is charged with helping victims of disaster recover while also developing an effective mitigation strategy so that people take actions that reduce their potential losses before disaster occurs.

Like many of the goals agencies pursue, these two are potentially in conflict since people who are given assistance with recovery may calculate that it is worth the risk not to change their behavior because they can count on the federal government to cover their losses (Platt & Rubin, 1999). In public management, efficiency is a slippery concept both because of confusion over missions at the agency level and because members of Congress may face conflict between serving their districts and serving the nation as a whole.

In an environment of multiple and contradictory goals, policymakers often fall back on vague rhetoric to unify the public such as "securing the homeland," which obscures the relative costs and benefits involved in such a task. In truth, the United States will never be impervious to attack, but it can be more or less vulnerable. One way in which Congress addressed the terrorist threat was by funding emergency preparedness and response entities at the state and local levels, first through a formula in the Patriot Act and then through subsequent legislation. The result was a distortion in the allocation of funds, both away from high-risk states such as New York and toward low-risk but well represented small states, as well as away from high-probability natural disasters toward the terrorist threat. These shifts in attention and funding demonstrate shortcomings in the decision-making process in government.

The most frequent incentives for congressional spending are the relative costs and benefits of a particular policy as perceived by a legislator's constituents. General costs and benefits are those that fall on citizens equally, such as a feeling of threat or safety from a terrorist attack (Arnold, 1990, pp. 26–27). Geographic and group costs and benefits fall on some segments of society more than others. In public administration, these costs and benefits fall on a unique set of consumers: the public, which acts through legislators who represent particular districts. The public feels the threat of a general cost of terrorism, which leads politicians to compete with each other to provide even greater levels of funding. The financial costs of terrorism funding are general too, since they flow from general revenue. The actual costs of a terrorist attack, however, will fall on particular communities and regions that suffer damage. The challenge is to send enough money to those regions at greatest risk while not sacrificing attention to previous missions such as emergency management.

The mismatch between the public's perceived costs and benefits and the system of legislative representation produces two problems for homeland security performance. The first is an incentive structure that does not send federal homeland security funds to regions with the highest risk but rather apportions them according to congressional power. The second is an incentive system that funds the high-profile threat, terrorism, at the expense of the more frequent, but lower profile, dangers of natural and technological disasters.

Shifting Resources from Natural Hazards to Terrorism

Congress has long funded grants for the fields of law enforcement and disaster preparedness but after the terrorist attacks of 2001 it debated how to grant money to a new field which combined both: homeland security (Ransdell, 2004). Grant money was distributed to states and localities through the DHS Office for Domestic Preparedness, the Department of Justice, the Department of Health and Human Services, and the DHS Emergency Preparedness and Response Directorate, which includes the Federal Emergency Management Agency (FEMA). Congress faced a challenge in allocating money based on the analysis of the risk of a particular threat compared to the cost, rather than based on short-term political incentives that favored allocating massive resources quickly to a salient threat.

While the United States should devote resources to the growing threat of terrorism, there are many reasons to continue to devote resources to other kinds of disasters. Natural and technological disasters occur with greater frequency and cause more damage on average each year than terrorist attacks. Natural and technological disasters are also more predictable than terrorism because we possess historical data on floods, earthquakes, hurricanes, and even oil spills, while data on domestic attacks are sparse.

Congress, however, reduced funding for natural and technological disaster grants and increased funding for counterterrorism grants after 2001, as Figure 1 shows. DHS funding for state homeland security grants in 2004 was more than 10 times the amount it was in 2001, reaching $1.7 billion that year. Meanwhile, the primary emergency preparedness programs lost funding, reaching $170 million in 2004 in money used to help state and local agencies maintain and improve their emergency management capabilities.[3] Emergency management grants help states and communities prepare for hurricanes, fires, floods, oil spills, and other disasters. Figure 2 shows how the locus of granting activity shifted from the Emergency Preparedness and Response directorate to the Office for Domestic Preparedness, signaling a new focus for disaster money.

Natural and technological disasters are more frequent and historically more costly than terrorism. In addition, agencies at all levels of government have experience with responding to fires, floods, hurricanes, and tornadoes and have developed procedures for addressing disaster preparation and response that have become more efficient over time. FEMA is a government agency that works fairly well in responding to hurricanes. Agencies responsible for counterterrorism, however, do not yet have the same kind of institutional apparatus and knowledge to support them. As a result, much of the new homeland security grant money went to either preexisting state and local government "wish-lists" or to fashionable counterterrorism gear. Some of the most egregious examples include: $1.5 million spent by the County of Grand Forks, North Dakota (population 70,000) to purchase more biochemical suits than the county had police officers, as well as to decontamination tents and trailers; and in 2004 alone $962,000 to Juneau, Alaska, for a robot to deactivate bombs, decontamination equipment, pharmaceuticals, and night vision goggles. Juneau's emergency programs manager, Michael R. Patterson, put it succinctly, saying "I don't have to go looking for grants, they are coming to me" (Lipowicz, 2002; see also Murphy, 2004). When Congress directs granting programs to emphasize terrorism, states and localities follow because they have an almost insatiable appetite for new money: in a survey of emergency management agencies, most said that they needed new crisis management software gear and 5% said that they needed "spline reticulation," a nonexistent fictional feature included in the survey to test which agencies would request money for *anything*.[4]

Changes in federal funding priorities lead to changes in organization of emergency management agencies at the state and local levels.[5] In the 1990s, state and local emergency preparedness agencies shifted from being primarily concerned with civil defense against nuclear attack and riots to concern for natural and technological disaster preparation. Professional emergency managers replaced many of the law enforcement officials in preparedness leadership, and the offices gradually added programs aimed at mitigation and prevention of natural disasters rather than mere recovery. After September 11, however, the state and local agencies underwent a second major change to become homeland security offices. In some cases the change was in name only, but in others the agencies were given new missions and new funds to prepare for terrorist attacks.

By 2004, most state agencies have reoriented their organizational structures to address the threat of terrorism. In the state emergency management context, the term homeland security refers to prevention

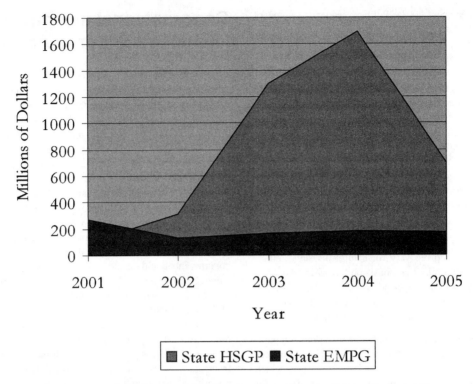

Figure 1 Differences in Federal Funding for State Homeland Security Grant Program versus State Emergency Management Performance Grants, 2001–2005 (Estimated)
Source: Select Committee on Homeland Security, 2004.

and response to terrorist attacks that use either conventional weapons or chemical, biological, or radiological agents.[6] The vision set forth in the National Strategy for Homeland Security stresses the need to strengthen the entire emergency management system to be able to deal with any emergency—natural or manmade. States vary in the degree to which they have integrated homeland security into their responsibilities for natural and technological disasters, but all have taken on counterterrorism to some degree. For example, by 2003 almost all states had designated a homeland security office or officer. Some states responded to

the vision of all hazards presented in the National Strategy by integrating existing emergency response organizations with the new homeland security tasks so that they function in lockstep. Emergency managers in these states have been successful in convincing their leaders that homeland security is simply an extension of current emergency management responsibilities, similar to FEMA's approach to all hazards management.[7]

In other states, the reorganization was more thorough; at least 13 states underwent reorganizations to create new homeland security

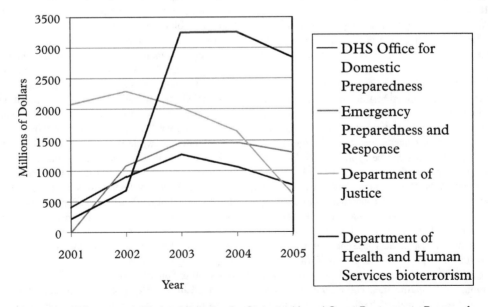

Figure 2 Differences in Federal Funding for State and Local Grant Programs to Prepare for and Respond to Terrorism, Natural Hazards, and Other Disasters, 2001–2005 (Estimated)
Source: Select Committee on Homeland Security, 2004.

agencies (Hembree & Hughes, 2003). Political leaders in some of these states concluded that homeland security is the broadest category in emergency preparedness and moved natural disaster organizations under homeland security agencies. Other states created new organizations solely responsible for homeland security. Almost all made some organizational changes; by 2003, 47 states had created a terrorism committee or task force (Hembree & Hughes, 2003).

Even in cases where homeland security is integrated into an all hazards approach—in which managers are trained to deal with disasters of all kinds—concerns about terrorism can still dominate. For instance, Indiana's designated homeland security advisor is the terrorism council director, but the state emergency management agency has also shifted its workload to prepare for terrorism. Phil Roberts (personal communication, October 6, 2003), the deputy director of the Indiana State Emergency Management Agency, explains that:

> Our priorities used to be placed primarily on mitigation, preparedness, response and recovery for natural disasters and haz-mat incidents, with a minor emphasis on terrorism issues. Now, I would have to say that we spend probably 75 percent to 80 percent of our time strictly on homeland security/terrorism issues. September 11th changed our lives, I believe, forever.

Shifts in organizational structure and time spent on hazards preparation are two indicators of how homeland security has affected offices of emergency management. A third indicator is the degree to which homeland security programs have become a budget priority. Funds for emergency management programs overall have not kept pace with new missions of counterterrorism and biological/chemical disaster preparation. Federal funds for disaster agencies have been mostly stagnant over the last ten years, with the exception of homeland security grants in the past four years (shown in Figures 1 and 2), most of which have been directed toward purchasing new "first responder" technology (Hembree, 2002; Hembree & Hughes, 2003).[8] In fiscal year 2003, a tight budget year in which states cut services across the board, 14 states appropriated funds in addition to federal grants to support specific homeland security-related programs, including increased building security, local government planning, training, equipment for first responders, and increased state public health lab capacity.[9] The net effect is a stagnant or decreasing emergency services budget combined with increased monies for homeland security.[10]

State and local emergency management agencies reorganized to meet the terrorism threat to a much greater degree than has FEMA. While FEMA expanded its programs for terrorism preparation and recovery, it did not alter its basic organizational structure in the way that many state and local agencies did.[11] Many state preparedness agencies, however, did undergo organizational restructuring to emphasize homeland security and terrorism. Two explanations for the change in mission and organizational structure stand out. First, the all hazards approach—the idea that emergency management should emphasize disaster procedures and spending that can be applied to all disasters rather than those tailored for specific threats—did not take hold uniformly at the state and local levels. This led to minor confusion about agencies' missions and core tasks, which prevented them from building a reputation.[12] Second, many state emergency management agencies may have simply been too small and weak to withstand the funding and attention shift toward the terrorist threat. These agencies depend on federal and state grants for their operational budgets, and when grant criteria emphasized the terrorist threat, state and local agencies shifted their priorities. In addition, the law enforcement culture, which is more concerned about terrorism than is the natural hazards culture, is stronger in some state and local agencies than at FEMA.

Congressional Incentives to Fund Homeland Security Across States

The increase in grant funds for counterterrorism has had a greater effect than simply increasing resources at the state and local levels; it has shifted priorities away from other hazards. Congress behaved like the proverbial bull in the china shop: its funding decisions had consequences for organization and procedures at all levels of government. Congress lacks the "adaptive flexibility" of the private market because even though it has 435 decision makers, its policy solutions are often hierarchical and monolithic and therefore not well suited to respond to changing circumstances. True adaptive flexibility would require decentralized decision making and mechanisms for eliminating ineffective grant programs while rewarding effective ones (North, 1990, pp. 80–81). In theory, homeland security block grants to states and localities would be a paradigm of decentralization. Subnational governments could develop solutions tailored to local needs and states would be the proverbial "laboratories of democracy." In reality, emergency management agencies were not well prepared to balance the use of the new grant funds with preexisting missions. State and local agencies had few resources to tap for guidance on how to apportion new money toward the potential mix of terrorist, natural, and technological disasters. Congress provided plenty of money but little guidance aside from the message that counterterrorism was a priority: it moved the majority of granting programs away from FEMA's direct oversight to supervision by Department of Homeland Security officials primarily concerned with terrorism.

Congress not only failed to calculate the probability and potential costs of various hazards in apportioning money between terrorism and other disasters, it also failed to grant money based on which states faced a greater terrorist threat. First responder grants, like most grants, follow a formula that provides a minimum amount of money to each state. The law behind the first responder grants, passed as part of the Patriot Act, guarantees each state 0.75 percent of the total that DHS apportions for terrorism preparedness grants. Though other granting programs typically have 0.25% or 0.5% guarantees, small-state legislators demanded more for homeland security. Since the Senate has equal representation for each state, the body has a "bias" toward small states that build coalitions to ensure that they receive a high level of allocations per capita (Lee, 1998).

For each of the homeland security grant packages, small, low-risk states received more money per capita than large or high-risk states, as Tables 1 and 2 show. For FY 2003 New York state received 4.68% of the total federal grant money for state homeland security programs, even though its population is 6.55% of the nation's total. Wyoming, however, has 0.17% of the nation's population but received 0.85% of the grant money. That means that New York received $5.10 in grant money per capita while Wyoming received $35.30.

Publicly, small states argued that the terrorist threat is unpredictable and so the United States should prepare for attack everywhere; citizens of Wyoming deserve to be protected just as much as citizens of California. Former Washington Senator Slade Gorton suggested that small states are legitimately concerned about being left vulnerable if the bulk of counterterrorism money goes to dense population centers, saying that "If you harden some targets, you soften others" (Murphy, 2004; see also Daunt & Fox, 2003; Gorman, 2003; Hernandez, 2003; Russakoff & Sanchez, 2003).

Terrorism is not entirely unpredictable, however. Insurance companies develop prices for terrorism insurance based on a calculation of risk. In 2003 an insurance underwriter analysis firm, the Insurance

Table 1 Per Capita Homeland Security Grant Spending, FY 2003

Wyoming	35.3	South Carolina	8.0
District of Columbia	31.5	Louisiana	7.7
Vermont	29.4	Alabama	7.7
North Dakota	28.7	Colorado	7.7
Alaska	28.4	Minnesota	7.3
South Dakota	24.6	**US Average**	**7.2**
Delaware	23.5	Wisconsin	7.1
Montana	21.3	Maryland	7.1
Rhode Island	18.7	Arizona	7.1
Hawaii	16.7	Missouri	7.1
New Hampshire	16.4	Tennessee	6.9
Maine	16.2	Washington	6.8
Idaho	15.8	Indiana	6.8
Nebraska	13.2	Massachusetts	6.7
West Virginia	12.8	Virginia	6.4
New Mexico	12.6	North Carolina	6.1
Nevada	11.4	New Jersey	6.1
Utah	10.9	Georgia	6.1
Kansas	10.0	Michigan	5.8
Arkansas	10.0	Ohio	5.6
Mississippi	9.7	Pennsylvania	5.5
Iowa	9.5	Illinois	5.5
Connecticut	8.7	Florida	5.2
Oklahoma	8.7	New York	5.1
Oregon	8.6	Texas	5.0
Kentucky	8.0	California	4.7

Source: DHS Office for Domestic Preparedness and the United States Census.

Services Office, surveyed intelligence experts and applied their risk ratings to a database of potential targets in order to price terrorism insurance rates. The federal government first attempted to apply risk analysis to homeland security funding decisions through the Urban Area Security Initiative grant program. In 2003, a formula that combined measures of population density with a measure of critical infrastructures and credible threat was used to allocate $100 million to seven cities determined to be at a high threat level. After the list was announced, cities that were left out complained to Congress and to the department that they needed money for security. By May 2003, there were 30 cities on the threat list and by FY2004 the list included 50 cities and a budget of $625 million (Ripley, 2004).[13] Electoral incentives to reward cities that felt threatened were more powerful than expert risk analysis in determining funding levels. The homeland security granting process is a story of political incentives that lead legislators to use their influence to distribute as much money to their districts as possible—and to claim credit for addressing the salient threat of terrorism—without substantial room for reasoned risk analysis and careful adaptation to the terrorist threat.

Remedies

The point of this paper is not to say that Congress is hopelessly ineffective. Electoral incentives provide many useful benefits; chief among them is tying the political class to actual communities. The structure of congressional decision making, however, presents several obstacles for policymakers concerned with how the federal government should respond to the terrorist threat alongside other hazards. Experience with other facets of homeland security and with the grant process provides a few options for improving Congress' deliberations.

Use Competitive Grants Rather Than Block Grants

Block or formula grants are popular with legislators because they provide a way for Congress to claim that it is addressing a problem, essentially by providing money to states and localities, while also rewarding their districts. The problem with homeland security block grants is that they are not apportioned based on risk analysis and once they reach the states they are not always used wisely. One remedy is for Congress to issue competitive grants instead. Competitive grants require states to submit proposals for how to use the money to expert panels that rank proposals and decide how to award funds. Even under most competitive grant programs, states are allocated minimum amounts so that no state is left out. Even so, competitive grants would place some distance between granting decisions and political incentives and they would force states to invest in developing creative and well-reasoned uses for the money.[14]

Table 2 Per Capita Homeland Security Grant Spending, FY 2004

Wyoming	37.74	South Carolina	8.52
District of Columbia	34.16	Louisiana	8.24
Vermont	31.43	Alabama	8.24
North Dakota	30.82	Colorado	8.17
Alaska	30.18	Minnesota	7.81
South Dakota	26.32	**US Average**	**7.63**
Delaware	24.86	Wisconsin	7.57
Montana	22.66	Maryland	7.53
Rhode Island	20.00	Missouri	7.45
Hawaii	17.75	Arizona	7.43
New Hampshire	17.44	Tennessee	7.37
Maine	17.26	Washington	7.22
Idaho	16.65	Indiana	7.21
Nebraska	14.10	Massachusetts	7.14
West Virginia	13.73	Virginia	6.75
New Mexico	13.39	North Carolina	6.49
Nevada	11.84	New Jersey	6.45
Utah	11.56	Georgia	6.40
Kansas	10.65	Michigan	6.19
Arkansas	10.63	Ohio	6.00
Mississippi	10.32	Pennsylvania	5.89
Iowa	10.20	Illinois	5.85
Connecticut	9.30	Florida	5.45
Oklahoma	9.27	New York	5.41
Oregon	9.18	Texas	5.24
Kentucky	8.57	California	4.97

Source: DHS Office for Domestic Preparedness and the United States Census.

Change the Institutional Setting for Decision Making

To rationalize the process—and effectively generate policies in the public interest—politicians must manipulate the institutional setting so that policymakers do not feel like their first priority must be to satisfy narrow geographic or group interests. One way to stack the deck in favor of the public interest is to bypass the typical congressional approval structure, with its many opportunities for logrolling and veto points. When congressional leaders wanted to create the DHS with minimal revisions to the original proposal, House Speaker Dennis Hastert decided to appoint a nine-person select committee to vet the proposal rather than employing the usual multicommittee process, which could have stalled or diluted the bill (Brill, 2003, pp. 504–505). Chairmen from regular committees were able to file comments with the select committee but they were not able to formally alter the bill. If Congress had given a single homeland security committee oversight for the granting process as well as other homeland security activities, there might have been a greater opportunity for creating a budget that reflects a consensus about how to balance funding for counterterrorism with other disasters and about how to distribute money among states. In other words, decreasing committee involvement may strengthen Congress' capacity to coordinate on a comprehensive set of emergency management grants. Changing the institutional setting is difficult since there are large disincentives for smaller states to cooperate in efforts that result in less money for them. The last time Congress bypassed the usual guarantees for small states in a major grant program was in 1956 when it spent $31.5 billion over 13 years to build interstate highways.

Raise the Salience of the Issue

Reforms in the public interest stand a chance of passing when they are particularly salient. Airline and trucking deregulation succeeded after an expert consensus brought the issue to the attention of politicians (Derthick & Quirk, 1985; Patashnik, 2003). Increased salience could help build support for more risk analysis in the homeland security granting process since the current arrangement seems suboptimal to most people. The challenge is to lower citizens' information costs so that they can easily recognize and reward good policy. Think tanks and journalists can—and are—distributing information about funding disparities.[15]

Putting an issue on the agenda need not be a long process during a crisis. In normal times, institutions can become sclerotic as interests organize and lobby to serve narrow goals, but during a crisis these interests lose their efficacy and policymakers jettison normal procedures (Baumgartner & Jones, 1993; Olson, 1982). Legislators bypassed normal procedure during the creation of the DHS because of the terrorist crisis, and political entrepreneurs might be able to persuade them to do the same under either the threat of continued terrorism or the threat of a budget collapse.

Notes

1. For an argument that political markets are as efficient as economic markets, see Wittman (1995). A central assumption of a classic text on policy analysis and public administration, David Weimer and Aidan Vining's *Policy Analysis,* is that public policy is a way to make Pareto improvements in the general welfare in instances where there is market failure (See especially pp. 116–146.)

2. Sometimes congressional sclerosis can be overcome by an agency that develops a measure of autonomy and can substantially structure policies on its own.

3. Working within the standard federal government grant administration process, EMPG provides the support that state and local governments need to achieve measurable results in key functional areas of emergency management: (1) Laws and Authorities; (2) Hazard Identification and Risk Assessment; (3) Hazard Management; (4) Resource Management; (5) Planning; (6) Direction, Control, and Coordination; (7) Communications and Warning; (8) Operations and Procedures; (9) Logistics and Facilities; (10) Training; (11) Exercises; (12) Public Education and Information; and (13) Finance and Administration.

4. Data from a 2003 survey by a major consulting firm of 94 state and local emergency management agencies.

5. As Martha Derthick (1970) demonstrated in her study of a federal assistance grants in Massachusetts, power tends to flow toward the center; money from the federal government can rearrange the organization and culture of even the most recalcitrant state and local agencies.

6. The National Strategy for Homeland Security defines homeland security as a "concerted national effort to prevent terrorist attacks within the United States, reduce America's vulnerability to terrorism, and minimize the damage and recover from attacks that do occur." The overall vision set forth in the document outlines the need to strengthen the nation's emergency response system to be adaptable to deal with any emergency—natural or manmade. See http://www.whitehouse.gov/homeland/book/index.html.

7. Most states have maintained the all hazards language in their emergency response plan: at least 23 have integrated terrorism into the plan using all hazards language. Others have developed a terrorism "annex" or special section to the plan, while still others have developed terrorism-specific plans.

8. The national average for state emergency management agency budgets was $50.6 million in fiscal year 2002, up from an average of $49 million in 2000.

9. To take one example, the King County (Seattle), Washington, Office of Emergency Management (OEM) takes an explicitly "all hazards" approach according to its website, meaning that it prepares for all kinds of disasters using similar procedures, but even King County has had to reduce the time emergency managers spend preparing for flood and fires in order to plan for homeland security. The number of hours King County emergency management employees spent on non-homeland security natural and technological disaster programs went from 75% of the total work hours in 2001 to 32% in 2003, largely because of time spent on counterterrorism and WMD (weapons of mass destruction) preparation. In 2001, 19% of the OEM time was spent on leave and administrative duties, while 6% was spent on recovery and mitigation programs. In 2003, 18% was spent on leave and administration, 13% on recovery and hazard mitigation, and 37% on homeland security. The 2003 data is from January to June only. Data is from Eric Holdeman, Manager, King County Office of Emergency Management, personal communication, Boulder, Colorado, July 14, 2003.

10. Phil Roberts notes that the Indiana State Emergency Management Agency has not seen a change in state funding, but it nevertheless has over "10 times the amount of [federal] funding that [it] used to administer prior to September 11th" in the form of homeland security grants for equipment, training, and planning (personal communication, October 6, 2003).

11. States are required by the Department of Homeland Security to develop a homeland security strategy before they are eligible to use the grant funds provided by DHS, so there is a baseline approval process that defines what homeland security activities can be funded with federal dollars (e.g., planning, exercises, first responder equipment, bioterrorism preparedness, regional collaboration and coordination, and mutual aid planning). If the state identifies an activity that it thinks is integral to its security but does not fit in these new streams of funding, most likely it would generate the funds for itself (e.g., extra capitol/government building security).

12. Recent works argue that a strong reputation is the source of bureaucratic autonomy and, in many cases, success (see Carpenter, 2001, for example). FEMA was able to go from being threatened with extinction to becoming one of the most popular agencies in government by building a reputation for effective disaster response.

13. A description of the granting program is in Office of Domestic Preparedness, "Fiscal year 2004 Urban Areas Security Initiative Grant Programs," http://www.ojp.usdoj.gov/docs/fy04uasi.pdf.

14. Eli Lehrer (2004) makes the case for competitive grants.

15. One example is de Rugy (2004).

References

Allison, G. T. (1990). Public and private management: Are they fundamentally alike in all unimportant respects? In F. S. Lane (Ed.), *Current issues in public administration* (4th ed., pp. 16–33). New York: St. Martin's Press.

Arnold, R. D. (1990). *The logic of congressional action.* New Haven, CT: Yale University Press.

Baumgartner, F. R., & Jones, B. D. (1993). *Agendas and instability in American politics.* Chicago: University of Chicago Press.

Brill, S. (2003). *After: How America confronted the September 12 era.* New York: Simon & Schuster.

Carpenter, D. P. (2001). *The forging of bureaucratic autonomy: Reputations, networks, and policy innovation in executive agencies, 1862–1928.* Princeton, NJ: Princeton University Press.

Daunt, T., & Fox, S. (2003, February 23). Anti-terror readiness still lacking. *The Los Angeles Times,* p. B1.

Derthick, M. (1970). *The influence of federal grants: Public assistance in Massachusetts.* Cambridge, MA: Harvard University Press.

Derthick, M., & Quirk, P. J. (1985). *The politics of deregulation.* Washington, DC: Brookings Institution.

Fiorina, M. P. (1977). *Congress, keystone of the Washington establishment.* New Haven, CT: Yale University Press.

Gorman, S. (2003, August 9). Homeland Security's intractable problem. *National Journal,* p. 2548.

Hembree, T. (2002). Future challenges of state emergency management. In *The book of the states* (pp. 427–429). Lexington, KY: The Council of State Governments.

Hembree, T., & Hughes, A. (2003). Strategies for national emergency preparedness and response: Integrating Homeland Security. In *The book of the states* (pp. 493–497). Lexington, KY: The Council of State Governments.

Hernandez, R. (2003, March 26). Pataki feels shorted by president's security budget. *The New York Times* p. D1.

House Select Committee on Homeland Security. (2004). *An analysis of first responder grant funding.* Retrieved May 16, 2005, from http://homelandsecurity.house.gov/files/FirstResponderReport.pdf.

House Select Committee on Homeland Security. (2004). *Federal funding to prevent, prepare for, and respond to acts of terrorism and other emergencies.* Retrieved May 16, 2005, from http://homelandsecurity.house.gov/files/HomelandSecurityFundingChart.pdf.

Lee, F. E. (1998). Representation and public policy: The consequences of Senate apportionment for the geographic distribution of federal funds. *Journal of Politics, 60*(1), 34–62.

Lehrer, E. (2004). Money can't buy you safety. *Weekly Standard, 9*(37). Retrieved November 10, 2004, from https:///www.weeklystandard.com/Check.asp?idArticle=4162&r=jadfa.

Lipowicz, A. (2003, October 22). North Pole receives homeland security funds. *CQ Homeland Security.*

Mayhew, D. (1974). *Congress: The electoral connection.* New Haven, CT: Yale University Press.

Murphy, D. E. (2004, October 12). Security grants still streaming to rural states. *The New York Times* p. A1.

North, D. C. (1990). *Institutions, institutional change and economic performance.* Cambridge: Cambridge University Press.

Olson, M. (1982). *The rise and decline of nations.* New Haven, CT: Yale University Press.

Patashnik, E. (2003). After the public interest prevails: The political sustainability of policy reform. *Governance, 16*(2), 203–234.

Platt, R. H., & Rubin, C. B. (1999). Stemming the losses: The quest for hazard mitigation. In R. H. Platt (Ed.), *Disasters and democracy* (pp. 69–107). Washington, DC: Island Press.

Ransdell, T. (2004). *Federal Formula Grants and California: Homeland Security.* San Francisco, CA: Public Policy Institute of California.

Ripley, A. (2004). How we got Homeland Security wrong. *Time.* Retrieved October 11, 2004, from http://www.time.com/time/archive/preview/O,10987,1101040329-603192,00.html/.

Rugy, V. d. (2004). *What does Homeland Security spending buy?* (Working Paper). Washington, DC: American Enterprise Institute.

Russakoff, D., & Sanchez, R. (2003, April 1). Begging, borrowing for security. *The Washington Post,* p. A1.

US Census and the Department of Homeland Security Office for Domestic Preparedness. (2003). *Fiscal year 2003 Homeland Security Grant Programs.* Retrieved May 16, 2005, from http://www.ojp.usdoj.gov/odp/grants_programs.htm.

US Census and the Department of Homeland Security Office for Domestic Preparedness. (2004). *Fiscal year 2004 Homeland Security Grant Programs.* Retrieved May 16, 2005, from http://www.ojp.usdoj.gov/odp/grants_programs.htm.

Weimer, D. L., & Vining, A. R. (1999). *Policy analysis* (3rd ed.). Upper Saddle River, NJ: Prentice Hall.

Weingast, B. R., & Marshall, W. (1988). The industrial organization of congress; or why legislatures, like firms, are not organized as markets. *Journal of Political Economy, 96*(1), 132–163.

Wilson, J. Q. (1989). *Bureaucracy.* New York: Basic Books.

Wittman, D. A. (1995). *The myth of democratic failure.* Chicago: University of Chicago Press.

PATRICK S. ROBERTS is Assistant Professor in the Center for Public Administration and Policy in the School of Public and International Affairs at Virginia Tech.

From *Review of Policy Research,* Vol. 22, No. 4, July 2005, pp. 437–449. Copyright © 2005 by American Political Science Association. Reprinted by permission of Blackwell Publishing, Ltd.

Airport Security Screening: Privatize or Federalize?

The 9/11-inspired airport security screening system has been the center of controversy ever since it was created in 2001. Although the federalized system is held in high esteem by the traveling public, two tests of the system by the Department of Homeland Security (DHS) in 2003 and 2004 to 2005 found significant shortcomings, despite large changes made to the security screening process as a result of the first test. The article identifies other criticisms of the Transportation Security Administration (TSA) from both an operational and philosophical perspective, and from functions the TSA does do right. Finally, the article identifies why airport security privatization has not progressed and how potential changes to the TSA structure could make it a better functioning entity, including the author's proposal to transfer TSA oversight responsibility to the U.S. Coast Guard.

KEITH MEW

Background

Between 1973 and 2001, airport security screening in accordance with FAR 108, was conducted by private contractors hired and paid for by the airlines located at the airport at which they operated. The security screening system had many problems driven by strong competition, intense pressure from airlines to lower costs, and contractors' hiring poorly educated, poorly trained, and poorly paid workers. Morale was low, the annual employee turnover in some firms exceeded 90%, and the security-screening system proved difficult to regulate. Attempts by the Federal Aviation Administration to improve contractor performance often proved ineffective (Moss & Eaton, 2001) and contracting-out security services discouraged data sharing with law enforcement agencies. The industry appeared to be unable to assure security and even after September 11, 2001, reports of security breaches at major airports were frequent, even infamously shown by network news exclusives (NBC Dateline, 2001).

In contrast to the above scenario, a recent Transportation Security Administration (TSA) commissioned survey of 17,000 passengers conducted by BearingPoint Inc. (Airport Security Report, 2005a) at 25 airports indicated that the traveling public is largely satisfied with the federalized security screening system in place today (see Table 1).

The decision to federalize airline security in 2001 might appear to represent a change in public management policy. The apparent increase in safety and the satisfaction with the system by the traveling public, would lead one to think that a federalized airport system might remain in place for a long period of time. Although the majority of U.S. airports appear to want the current system to remain in place, an operational and philosophical rationale argues that the system should be privatized, albeit with a different form of privatization than what existed prior to 9/11.

The Present System of Airport Security Screening

The present system of airport security screening stems from the Aviation and Transportation Security Act (ATSA) of 2001, passed in the wake of the 9/11 attacks. When creating the TSA, Congress sought to correct a structural and regulatory failure in airport security. The regulatory failure was the lack of oversight provided by the FAA. The structural failure was the previous practice of lodging responsibility for screening with individual competing air carriers. Because of their competitive position, the costs of airport security became yet another cost the airlines sought to minimize. In seeking to fix these two problems, Congress eliminated the airlines' role in passenger screening, deciding instead that a single provider at each airport should carry out this function, rather than individual firms selected by the various airlines.

The TSA employed tough new standards and the strong regulatory oversight that was lacking in the FAA's approach to this task. Congress authorized the TSA to become that single provider of passenger screening. The TSA hired thousands of passenger and baggage screeners to accomplish this task using a variety of machines to identify bomb making materials and other threats. According to the 9/11 Commission Report (2005), airport security takes more than 90% of the TSA budget, despite

Table 1 Passengers Rating of Transportation Security Administration (TSA) Screener

How confident are you in TSA's ability to keep air travel secure?	82%
How satisfied are you with your experience at the passenger security checkpoint?	91%
How satisfied are you with the courtesy of the passenger screeners?	92%
How would you rate the thoroughness of passenger screening you received?	94%
How satisfied are you with the time it took to screen you and your carry-on items?	89%
Was the length of time you waited in line at the passenger security checkpoint—	
Much shorter or shorter than you expected?	54%
About what you expected?	33%
Longer or much longer than you expected?	24%

Source: Airport Security Report, March 9, 2005.

the fact that the commission considered maritime or surface threats equal to or greater than that from the air. However, it would appear that airports are deemed to be a greater threat by the TSA. Using the guided missile theory, the TSA believes terrorism on an airplane or using an airplane to attack a facility would have the most significant impact. The cost of providing security screening services is increasing and expected to cost $3.9 billion in financial year 2006 (see Table 2).

The current organization of airport screening proved to be a political compromise; the Senate bill had called for a 100% federal takeover, the House had called for federal standards and oversight of screening provided by each airport, using either its own staff, or contractors. The compromise called for creating a federal screening workforce under the TSA, but allowed five airports to privatize security operations during an initial 2-year period, obtaining their screeners from TSA-certified private contractors. After the 2 years, in November 2004, all U.S. airports had the option of continuing with the TSA, or opting-out and using certified private contractors.

The five-airport pilot program (San Francisco, Kansas City, Rochester, Tupelo, and Jackson Hole) was evaluated by three separate entities whose reports all appeared early in 2004: the

Inspector General's Office of the Department of Homeland Security, the consulting firm BearingPoint Inc., and the Government Accountability Office. All three reached broadly similar conclusions. The screening services at the airports were about the same as those of other airports of comparable size that employed TSA screeners.

Criticisms of the Current System

All three above reports criticized the TSA for over-centralizing operations. For example, all screener hiring and training is controlled from TSA's Washington headquarters, which makes it impossible, even for potentially quicker and more flexible screening contractors, to respond to changes in airline service that increase or decrease the numbers of passengers and bags to be screened.

An overarching criticism of the TSA by airport executives is the lack of hiring and staffing flexibility. Flight activity levels at airports often change rapidly, yet the passenger screening staffing system appears unable to respond to changes in these levels, resulting in unacceptable delays in passenger screening (Segal,

Table 2 Cost of Passenger Screening Aviation Security: Screener Workforce and Equipment

Program	FY 2004	FY 2005	FY 2006	Change
Screener workforce	$2.33B	$2.42B	$2.67B	$245M
Screener training & other	408M	494M	468M	(26M)
Checkpoint support	37M	124M	157M	34M
Secure flight	45M	35M	0	(35M)
Crew vetting	18M	10M	0	(10M)
Registered traveler	6M	15M	0	(15M)
EDS/ETD systems	840M	400M	367M	(33M)
Mandatory authority (ASCF)		250M	250M	0
Total	$3.70B	$3.50B	$3.66B	$160M
Total (with mandatory authority)		$3.75B	$3.91B	$160M

Source: FY 2006 Transportation Security Administration Budget Request (http://tsa.gov).
Note: FY = fiscal year.

2003). Only recently, nearly 4 years after 9–11, has the TSA been allowed to hire part-time screeners. These part-time staff positions can be scheduled to more efficiently staff the airports' changing passenger flows throughout the day. In the case of some small non-hub airports, screeners are actually transported to and from these airports with a round-trip travel time of 3 to 4 hours to work perhaps one or two commercial flights that in some instances utilize small commuter aircraft with very few passengers. The ability for the TSA to staff these small airports with local part-time screeners and to staff the larger airports to more efficiently meet peak-period passenger demand is long overdue.

The same over-centralization and lack of flexibility is manifested in equipment maintenance. An example from a Midwest airport involves the breakdown of an Explosive Detection System (EDS) machine in an airport terminal. Its repair unleashed a decision chain from TSA headquarters in Washington to Boeing, the manufacturer, to a return to the local area in the form of a vendor who completed the work. Several other criticisms can be made at an operational level.

Airport executives are concerned about the organizational problems associated with the management of a 45,000-person workforce. A common note of criticism by many airport executives is that the multiple layers of TSA management create a burdensome challenge for airports and constitute a waste of financial resources. Most airports are assigned a federal security director (FSD), a deputy federal security director (DFSD), numerous assistant federal security directors (AFSD) with additional management support personnel. The larger airports many times are also assigned an attorney (sometimes more than one) and even logistics engineers. At most medium- and large-hub airports, AFSDs are assigned to be the liaison to the stakeholders (airports and airlines), another liaison is assigned to local law enforcement, another liaison to the community, and yet another AFSD may be assigned to oversee regulatory responsibilities associated with the airport. Using these positions as examples of TSA management layers, the AFSD assigned to regulatory responsibilities would be similar to the pre-TSA period when the FAA had these responsibilities. This position is deemed appropriate by most airport executives. However, airport executives many times seriously question the need for the other various liaison positions. These responsibilities could easily be carried out by the FSD or the AFSD, perhaps assisted by a lower level management-support position. It should be noted that the AFSD assigned to law enforcement was initially put in place when the TSA was planning to hire law enforcement positions assigned to airports. Airport executives around the country opposed the need for TSA law enforcement professionals that would be layered with local airport police. The TSA administration eventually backed off from their plans to hire these individuals, but even without TSA law enforcement personnel being hired, the law enforcement AFSDs were still put in place around the country and asked simply to serve as a liaison to the airports police department. Once again, these various liaison responsibilities could easily be carried out by the FSD or the DFSD. These positions mentioned above are only examples of the layers of bureaucracy within the TSA for which

airport executives seriously question the need and the benefit of the associated fiscal expense.

These identified layers of inefficient management have enormous financial repercussions, yet are just examples of general wasteful spending by the TSA. Lavish spending by the authority has been well documented (Office of the Inspector General [OIG], 2005a), and several commentators (e.g., de Rugy, 2005; Frank, 2005; Strohm, 2005) have itemized specific examples. Applebaum (2005) asserts that that the total TSA budget ($5.6 billion) is as large as that for the FBI and far less productive, while the detection equipment bought for screeners is outdated. Seidenstat (2004) is concerned with the cost of running the current security screening system ($3.66 billion, 2006—see Table 2) and argues for comparing the financial costs of the current system to a public-private approach.

At a more philosophical level, the Reason Foundation points out an inherent conflict of interest in the TSA: on one hand by running the system, and on the other hand being responsible for its maintenance (Poole, 2005a). They also argue that airport security is compromised by the fragmentation of security organization between the TSA, responsible for screening, and the airport authority, responsible for most nonterminal security (Poole, 2005b).

All the above criticisms are minor compared to the findings of several tests of the security screening system itself—the TSA is not successfully screening weapons and explosives. In 2003, the Department of Homeland Security (DHS) (OIG, 2005b) conducted a test of aviation security screening at 15 domestic airports to evaluate the TSA's ability to detect explosives and weapons. They tested both passenger screening and checked baggage by covertly sending agents through the system with fake explosives in checked baggage and sending threat objects through security checkpoints. Although the exact results of the tests have not been published, it is safe to assume that the security screeners did not do a very good job because seven recommendations were made to improve the system covering four broad areas—training, equipment and technology, policy and procedures, and management and supervision. The TSA accepted and apparently implemented these recommendations.

The DHS undertook a follow-up test of the system between November 2004 and February 2005. Hundreds of screening checkpoint and checked baggage tests were completed at different sized airports. In their report of the test, the DHS (OIG, 2005b) revealed no improvement from the previous audit despite the diligence of the majority of screeners in the performance of their duties.

What the TSA Is Doing Right

From the above discussion, one might conclude that the TSA screeners are not doing a very good job. However, the DHS (OIG, 2005b) report also stated that the demonstrated TSA diligence in the performance of their duties might make it difficult for them to improve their performance without better equipment. Congressman DeFazio writing in the *Washington Post* (2005), agreed, stating that screeners are working with "outmoded machines that fail to detect plastic explosives and other threats" (online).

Without question, airport security is being performed by a better-trained and more highly qualified work force than existed before 9/11. The screeners perform their job in a more professional manner, supervision has improved, background checks are more rigorously applied, the turnover rate has decreased, and screeners receive better salaries and benefits. The TSA has also updated its basic screener training course, established a recurrent training requirement, and created an online learning center.

It is this air of professional diligence that apparently makes the public confident of the veracity of their performance. Table 1 makes clear that passengers have a high regard for airport screener performance and their ability to keep air travel secure. A survey of 265 passengers at Long Beach Airport (LGB) conducted by California State University, Los Angeles, aviation administration students in March 2005 also revealed that 71% of passengers rejected the notion of privatizing airport screeners. The results are based on a 95% confidence level with a 6% margin of error.

Privatization of the System

Nevertheless, given federal auditors' dissatisfaction with TSA's operation of airport security, and airport managers' of management inefficiencies, one might expect the possibility of opting out of the federalized screening process, 2 years after the ATSA was enacted, to be embraced by airports.

In June 2004, the TSA issued preliminary guidance on how an opt-out or "Security Partnership Program" process would work. Although still planning to keep control of contractor selection and maintain its management system at airports, TSA indicated it would give airport executives input into the selection process, be willing to let airports act as security contractors, and permit a unified approach to airport security under a single management. The TSA, although acknowledging the problems with the centralized approach to hiring and training, has yet to make a decision regarding airport involvement.

This uncertainty has affected airport executives' decision-making process and to date only Elko Regional Airport (EKO) has decided to privatize its airport screening system under this scheme. Interestingly, their reasons for embarking on this policy are largely financial. The EKO airport security director, Art Moses, stated, "With about 80 private security companies in the United States figuring they could make a profit providing airport security services, we figure we can do it too" (Airport Security Report, 2005b, p. 3).

Between the restrictions contained in the legislation, and the TSA interpretation of them, most airports felt they would not gain much from shifting to a private contractor. Overall, as many airport officials evaluated their participation in the TSA opt out program, they were very concerned about liability and potential lawsuits. If an airport were to opt out, they would most likely be subject to any liability incurred due to the failure of airport-employed screeners. The 2002 Fostering Effective Technologies Act, (known as the SAFETY Act) does provide a system of limited liability in the event of acts of terrorism when utilizing a qualified service (such as airport screeners) certified by the DHS; despite the law, many airports are still not sure that they would have enough protection. Initially, some airport executives felt that if they were to opt out of the TSA screening process, some of the layers of management bureaucracy of the TSA might be eliminated or at least reduced. However, as the opt-out program was unveiled, TSA officials made it very clear to the industry that the various bureaucratic layers of management would still exist at those airports that opt out. Therefore, as earlier noted, one small airport chose to participate in the opt-out program. Airport executives decided the advantages simply did not outweigh the liabilities, given the requirements and guidelines of the opt-out program.

Conclusion

The differences between public satisfaction and federal and airport dissatisfaction with TSA security are interesting and beg the question: Why is there such a difference? That no commercial aircraft acts of terrorism occurred in the United States since 9/11 is a factor. Also, airport screeners are better trained and look far more professional than their counterparts before 9/11. However, given the ease with which covert break-ins have occurred, one must conclude that their professionalism is more perception than reality.

Given the above considerations, one has to ask if the privatization of airport security screening would be justified considering the actual costs and the efforts the aviation industry would have to endure. What real benefits would privatization bring to the aviation industry and to the flying public? The current TSA screeners are experienced, pass a standardized training and certification examination, the agency has an established infrastructure, and operation has improved. Many airports feel that they would not gain much from shifting to a contractor. However, here are several agencies and commentators who do feel that a better system should be in place.

One system purports that airport security screening should follow the to-date successful European model and allow airports to directly contract-out security screening services. In Europe and Israel, nearly all large airports have shifted from civil-service workers for passenger and baggage screening to private security firms in the past decade. Their governments set training and performance standards and provide strong oversight of private contractors (Segal, 2003).

The Reason Foundation (Poole, 2005a) argues that the U.S. system should be privatized, and that federal government should only provide regulatory oversight. Using this model, TSA would focus only on standard-setting and high-level supervisory functions, and airports would be responsible for hiring and managing privatized security.

A proposal by the Heritage Foundation reorganizes the TSA to make a solely operational agency with no oversight or infrastructure protection policy functions. Restructuring TSA's mission and renaming it the Aviation Security Administration would create a more focused agency that could concentrate on trying to do one thing well rather than many things poorly (Carafino, 2005).

The author of this article believes another concept would function better than others proposed: privatize screeners, completely dismantle the TSA, and replace their oversight function by another federal agency that has successfully managed security from overseas threats—the United States Coast Guard. This federal agency also operates under the DHS and has a successful history of managing and providing regulatory oversight and the overall protection of our coast lines. This concept would replace the TSA bureaucracy at local airports with Coast Guard officers (perhaps renamed the "Air Guard"), enlisted personnel, and required support staff. These individuals would provide regulatory oversight of the security requirements at the commercial service airports and would be responsible for the contract administration of a private-security contractor providing the passenger-screening function. These private-security companies would be selected and retained by the Coast Guard and would be required to adhere to strict training and performance-related standards.

One would expect the U.S. Coast Guard management of aviation security to be less bureaucratic than that of the TSA. Coast Guard officers are professionally trained to strict military standards and historically have earned the respect of the nation. The Coast Guard's historical record proves its relative efficiency and fiscal responsibility, especially when compared to the TSA. Further advantages are the various components of the Coast Guard operating structure already in place. By comparison, the TSA structure is still new, is very inefficient, and continues to evolve into even more of a bureaucratic-layered entity.

References

Airport Security Report. (2005a, March 9). *Passengers rate TSA screeners* (p. 2). Potomac: Access Intelligence, LLC.

Airport Security Report. (2005b, April 6). *Airports remain in "holding pattern" on returning to private screening* (p. 3). Potomac: Access Intelligence, LLC.

Applebaum, A. (2005, June 15). Airport security's grand illusion. *Washington Post*. Retrieved June 22, 2005, from http://www.washingtonpost.com

Carafino, J. (2005, May 6). Safer skies: Air security priorities for the next four years. *The Heritage Foundation*. Retrieved on June 18, 2005, from http://www.heritage.org/Research/HomelandDefense/em969.cfm

DeFazio, P. A. (2005, May 25). Airport screeners: A federal workforce works. *Washington Post*. Retrieved June 18, 2005, from http://www.washingtonpost.com

de Rugy, V. (2005, May 5). TSA Disaster. *National Review Online*. Retrieved June 24, 2005, from http://www.nationalreview.com.

Frank, T. (2005, April 19). Government audit of TSA finds money wasted. *USA Today*. Retrieved June 24, 2005, from http://www.usatoday.com/news/washington/2005-04-19-tsa-waste_x.htm

Moss, M., & Eaton, L. (2001, November 15). Security firms ever mindful to cut costs. *New York Times*, p. B1.

NBC Dateline. (2001, December). *Fear of flying: Are airports safe?* Retrieved June 18, 2005, from http://130.182.123 .66/loaddoc. asp?doctype=U&docformat=Link&cid=153&docid=4114&crid=0&ctrlid=Ch%5F6%5F%2D% 5FPrivatization%2Eppt&clinkid=153&dlinkid=

Office of the Inspector General. (2005a, March). *Follow-up audit of passenger and baggage screening procedures at domestic airports* (Unclassified Summary). Office of the Inspector General, Department of Homeland Security. Retrieved May 5, 2005, from http://www.dhs.gov/interweb/assetlibrary/OIG_05–16_Mar05.pdf

Office of the Inspector General. (2005b, March). *Irregularities in the development of the Transportation Security Operations Center*. Office of the Inspector General, Department of Homeland Security. Retrieved June 24, 2005, from http://www.dhs.gov/interweb/assetlibrary/OIG_05-18_Mar05.pdf

Poole, R. W. (2005a, January/February). Security: A time to pause. *Airport Business*, pp. 32/34.

Poole, R. W. (2005b, March).Transportation security aggravation; Debating the balance between privacy and safety in a post 9/11 aviation industry. *Reasononline*. Retrieved June 18, 2005, from http://www.reason.com

Seidenstat, P. (2004, May). Terrorism, airport security, and the private sector. *Review of Policy Research*, 21 (3), 275.

Segal, G. F. (2003). *Cato handbook for Congress. Recommendations for the 108th Congress*. Cato Institute. Retrieved April 18, 2005, from http://www.cato.org/pubs/hb108/hb108-32.pdf

Strohm, C. (2005, April 24). Senators seek assurances that TSA will stanch wasteful spending. *GovExec.com*. Retrieved June 24 from http://www.govexec.com/dailyfed/0405/042605c1.htm

The 9-11 Commission Report. (2005). *Final Report of the National Commission on terrorist attacks upon the United States*. Washington DC: U.S. Government Printing Office.

Transportation Security Administration. (2005). *Screening Partnership Program*. Transportation Security Administration official Website. Retrieved April 18, 2005, from http://tsa.gov

KEITH MEW has worked in the aviation industry for more than 20 years, as an airport project and systems manager in both the public and private sectors, and as an educator. For more than 10 years he has taught at public universities in Indiana and California. He is currently a professor of aviation administration at California State University, Los Angeles, and has written several articles on airport privatization.

From *Public Works Management & Policy,* Vol. 10, No. 1, July 2005, pp. 3–9. Copyright © 2005 by Sage Publications. Reprinted by permission.

UNIT 3

The Federal Government and Homeland Security

Unit Selections

Key Points to Consider

- Has spending on new technology and military equipment made America safer?

- Is it possible to stop illegal immigration?

- Should FEMA become independent of the Department of Homeland Security?

- How can U.S. port security be improved?

Student Web Site

www.mhcls.com/online

Internet References

Further information regarding these Web sites may be found in this book's preface or online.

National Nuclear Safety Administration (NNSA)
http://www.nnsa.doe.gov/

Federal Bureau of Investigation (FBI): National Security Branch
http://www.fbi.gov/hq/nsb/nsb.htm

Transportation Security Administration
http://www.tsa.gov/

U.S. Customs and Border Protection
http://www.customs.ustreas.gov/

Despite efforts to merge homeland security functions within the Department of Homeland Security, individual agencies continue to play a critical role in our domestic security. The criticisms of the agencies involved in various aspects of homeland security mirror those of other parts of the federal government. Supporters of a federalist approach to problem solving would argue that only the federal government has sufficient economic, bureaucratic, and legislative resources to effectively address threats to our security. Thus, the federal government must be the primary organizer of homeland security functions. Skeptics warn of unbridled growth, massive bureaucracies, and inefficient spending. They argue that state and local governments should be the focal point of homeland security activities. Students of American history and politics will quickly recognize that this debate is not a new one. It is an integral part of American political culture to question government—particularly the federal government.

The long-term success of homeland security policy is heavily dependent on the ability of individual federal agencies to contribute to the homeland security mission. Border security and illegal immigration, port security, and disaster response have been among the areas most often criticized in the press.

The articles in this unit focus on key agencies with seemingly impossible tasks. Despite massive government spending and the resulting economic boom spurred by the emergence of a seemingly endless array of new security, defense, and technology contactors, key questions remain unsolved. And despite the passage of recent legislation to construct a 700 mile fence on the southern border of the United States, the issue of border security and illegal immigration has yet to be resolved. Immigration reform has once again been delayed amidst continuing partisan discord. While some warn of the potential threat of infiltration by Middle Eastern terrorist via our southern border, there appears to be little evidence to support such assertions. Middle Eastern terrorists are more likely to arrive in the U.S. by means of a first class ticket than by a two-day trek through the Mexican desert, but the lack of effective border control continues to undermine the federal government's credibility on homeland security.

The Federal Emergency Management Agency also continues to be a subject of criticism. Overwhelmed by the magnitude of the destruction of hurricane Katrina, an agency that had earned high regards as an independent agency, failed miserably under the management of the DHS. How to fix FEMA remains a subject of much controversy and debate.

Lastly, the issue of port security has garnered much public attention. Wrestling between the security imperative and economic necessity, U.S. Customs and Coast Guard officers struggle with limited resources to devise and implement security systems that balance the desirable with the possible. So far—despite on-going efforts—this balance appears elusive.

The Doom Boom

Washington's economy hums to the tune of the war on terrorism

DAVID VON DREHLE

Late one winter afternoon, not long before he stepped down as chief of the U.S. Capitol Police, Terrance Gainer was discussing security in the age of catastrophic terrorism. Behind him, his office windows displayed a spectacular view: nearly 180 degrees of Washington skyline, anchored by a huge, incandescently white dome. To some people, the Capitol dome stands for power. To others, freedom. To the Americans who watched as the dome was built during the desperate years of the Civil War, its alabaster gleam represented the idea of the nation itself.

Gainer would see the dome and think: "Quite a target."

And the Mall, with its monuments, memorials, artifacts and treasures? "It's like a runway," Gainer observed. Macabre? Perhaps, but Gainer, like many others in Washington, was paid to think unpleasant thoughts, including one in which a terrorist steers a jet down the wide landing path of the Mall, descending over the Reflecting Pool, accelerating above the Washington Monument, the Smithsonian Castle on his right, the National Gallery on his left, to slam spectacularly into the dome.

The White House, with its low profile and wooded surroundings, is a much trickier objective, Gainer noted.

This was all said matter-of-factly. It's just the world we live in today. See plane, think missile; see landmark, think fireball; feel breeze, think anthrax. And so I found myself nodding agreeably as Gainer continued in this apocalyptic vein, comparing the relative threats posed by deadly germs in the air vents, a dirty bomb, a suicide bomber in a room full of VIPs. He spoke smilingly about the inevitable panic, the gridlocked roads, the trapped humans frantic to escape. Is evacuation even a good idea in most cases? Gainer asked rhetorically. After all, a basement makes a sturdy bunker against even a violent blast. On the other hand, if the basement fills with highly flammable jet fuel . . .

"And what if a bomb the size of the Hiroshima bomb was set off around here?" Gainer asked finally, then answered his own question. "Well, we'd all be dead, so we wouldn't have to worry about a mass evacuation."

For a brief moment, I imagined a blinding flash outside Gainer's windows, and a rush of superheated wind, and the windows bursting as the walls imploded. But just as quickly, the vision retreated to the grim corner of the brain where most Washingtonians endeavor to keep it. In place of the horror there was, once more, a fine view of the coppery winter dusk. The dome. A construction crane. Lights winking on. Another construction crane. The Washington Monument. Another construction crane.

And another construction crane.

And another.

Construction cranes occupied nearly every point of the compass, in the foreground and in the background, looming nearby, tiny on the horizon. Bombs and missiles aren't the only things that go boom. Economies do, too.

Thus, the yin and yang of life in Washington were balanced there amid the homey confines of Chief Gainer's office. Visions of disaster alongside hard evidence of good times. The fact is, since the al-Qaeda attacks of September 11, 2001, life has been fat in the cross hairs (apart from the occasional night sweat). The Washington area has enjoyed the best economy in the nation during the past four years—by a mile. What doesn't kill us makes us richer.

Those who live in Washington may have found themselves wondering whether they should stay. Maybe the thought crossed someone's mind the day the folks from Human Resources distributed plastic escape hoods, mini-flashlights and whistles to blow should you find yourself pinned under rubble. Or maybe it was the day your spouse came home with an armload of duct tape and plastic sheeting for your "safe room." Maybe it was when the guys in the mailroom started walking around in surgical masks, or when you attended that dinner party where your neighbors explained their strategy for evacuating via bicycle or canoe. But you stayed, and seemingly everyone else did, too. And many thousands more poured into the region, filling the subdivisions and condo blocks and office towers rising from Dulles to downtown, Leesburg to Largo, Dale City to Hyattsville, Md.

Meanwhile, this thriving metropolis has been forested with strange, man-made flora: the hardened posts, known as bollards, cemented into the ground at strategic points to thwart car bombs; the slender poles blossoming with surveillance cameras; the stumpy boxes that give no outward sign of the radiation detectors inside. Above it all, like a forest canopy, rise the busy booms (that word again!) of the construction cranes. The stubby bollard and the towering crane, one representing fear, the other prosperity—incongruous, yes, but also ubiquitous. They are the symbols of our time.

The first reactions to 9/11 included panic, disbelief, outrage, shock, sorrow, fury and a righteous patriotism. There was a lot of speculation about crowds at the military recruiting stations and a general wave of bear-any-burden determination. It was a blood, sweat, toil and tears sort of moment. President Bush, congressional leaders and Pentagon brass gathered at the National Cathedral a few days after the attacks to pray for God's assistance in the smiting of our enemies. As they stood to leave, the pipe organ roared out "The Battle Hymn of the Republic"—which, you may remember, is not exactly a pastoral. Some fateful lightning was about to be loosed from our terrible, swift sword.

And indeed there has been lightning in distant places around the world. Closer to home, however, the response has been less martial than monetary. Military recruitment is down, not up. Rather than meet any hardship, we have loosed the fateful charge cards of America's fat wallet.

Which makes a certain brand of sense: A basic doctrine of war says to mass your strength against your enemy's weakness, and the United States has no more tangible, flexible strength than its economy. It's no coincidence that, among the five living former secretaries of defense since 1977, four have become financiers (the other is vice president). Our money and our muscle are strategically meshed. Experts can argue about the long-term vitality of America's money muscle, given our outsourced jobs, sagging industrial base, looming old-age crisis and national debt. But for the time being, U.S. cash flow remains awesome. The federal government is the world's largest consumer of goods and services. The United States produces more buying power each year than the 25 European Union nations combined, though Europe has 160 million more people. With less than 5 percent of the world's population, we produce more than 20 percent of the world's dough. Faced with a crisis, our leaders did what they know best. They started shoveling money.

It's impossible to say precisely how much the U.S. government has spent in response to 9/11. The National Commission on Terrorist Attacks Upon the United States—better known as the 9/11 Commission—noted in 2004 that the country's defense and security spending was escalating more steeply than at any time in the past 50 years. This money is contained in thousands of budget items, some of which are misleading, others of which are classified. We can see the tips of some icebergs, though. According to the Congressional Budget Office, funding specifically for homeland security, one small part of the overall security spending spree, more than doubled in the first two years after the attacks, from $20 billion to more than $40 billion.

Some federal spending is an obvious response to Osama bin Laden, such as the billions to fortify federal office buildings and update government computer networks. Some comes under less obvious headings, such as the billions in new spending at military hospitals to treat and rehabilitate the wounded soldiers of the Iraq war. Some money remains inside government agencies, such as the billions in new spending at the National Institutes of Health in Bethesda, funding research into anthrax, smallpox and other germ terrorism. Some of it pours into private companies, especially private companies with big Washington area offices. All told, it's safe to say that hundreds of billions have gushed forth in a torrent of money that has washed across the globe, puddling in pockets from Kandahar to Kansas City. And the great lakes of cash have collected right here in the government's back yard.

"What you see in all the new construction, all the new jobs and so forth, is the benefit the Washington area receives from having a very rich uncle—you know, Uncle Sam," says Stephen Fuller, director of the Center for Regional Analysis at George Mason University. "Every quarter, and especially on April 15, we receive an enormous transfer of wealth from the rest of the country."

Fuller is a slim, graying fellow who has built a small empire on his diligent collection and smooth explication of Washington area economic data. He has numbers for everything, usually right at his fingertips, from the size of the federal workforce under Lyndon Johnson to the current growth rate of the dry-cleaning sector. Merchants, developers, politicians and journalists look to Fuller and his PowerPoint slides for illumination of the world outside their windows. Suppose you want to know why the unemployment rate in Northern Virginia has been the lowest in the country for much of the past four years. Fuller has a slide to explain it.

"Government procurement," he summarizes.

Fuller continues. "In Fairfax County, federal procurement amounted to $16 billion last year alone." That is the richest windfall in America, by far—roughly 10 times as much, per capita, as the government doled out for goods and services in Los Angeles, for example. "Procurement" does not describe all government spending, just the goods the government buys and the outside work it commissions. So that $16 billion, while huge, doesn't include the salaries of government workers, who are legion in Fairfax and throughout the Washington region. Nor does it include the rent the government pays for office space, even though the feds and their contractors are this area's biggest tenants, by far. Since 9/11, the Washington region has boasted the strongest commercial real estate market in America, with low vacancy rates producing rents second only to New York City.

All these spending streams flow into the region, but procurement spending "is something far more potent," Fuller says. "We've found that procurement dollars have twice as much impact in the economy as government payroll dollars. The money churns more through the economy. There's a bigger bang for the buck."

That bang is reflected in the huge new houses with the two-story foyers, in the fancy late-model cars, in the oversubscribed private schools, and, most of all, in the chain of construction cranes sited in the past few years from the Pentagon to past Dulles International Airport. In terms perfectly chosen for the prosperous citizens of Northern Virginia, Fuller compares this stretch to a high-class galleria, with the Defense Department and the airport as the anchor stores. "The Pentagon is like Neiman Marcus," he says, "and Dulles is like Nordstrom." Between them lies a long line of upscale boutiques doing record business—weapons contractors, management consultants, data processing giants, communications providers, information technology firms. Big names, such as Accenture, BearingPoint, Computer Sciences Corp., General Dynamics, Titan, Oracle, Raytheon and SAIC. Countless smaller contractors as well. These companies are selling everything from missiles to disaster-modeling software to computer integration at the Department of Homeland Security.

Northern Virginia has prospered the most, but don't cry for Maryland or the District. According to another of Fuller's slides, federal procurement spending has been frenzied there, too. From 2003 to 2004, to focus on a single year, federal contracting increased 16 percent in the District and 19 percent in the Maryland suburbs.

If you spend it, they will come: Since al-Qaeda hit the Pentagon, more people have moved to greater Washington than to any other non-Sunbelt region. Call it denial, call it playing the odds; having weighed the certainty of good jobs versus the threat of future catastrophe, people have voted with their moving vans. The threat is real. Last year, Rand Corp., the granddaddy of national security think tanks, proposed a complex formula for estimating the risk of major terrorist attacks in U.S. cities. The cities with the most dense urban cores, New York and Chicago, ranked first and second because of the prospect of many deaths in a relatively small area. Washington, despite much lower density, was third, because of its obvious strategic importance.

That's enough risk to inspire the bollards and cameras and radiation detectors, but not enough to persuade people to leave. If you want perfect safety, you could buy a government-surplus missile silo in sparsely populated Kansas or Wyoming. They come on the market from time to time. Once you seal the hatch on an Atlas E silo, encased in 18 inches of steel-reinforced concrete beneath at least six feet of prairie sod, you can ride out a nuke more than 50 times the size of the Hiroshima bomb. But the silo market is slumping, while two-bedroom condos in Kalorama, within walking distance of prime al-Qaeda targets, are going for $750,000 and up.

Government procurement was rising even before the attacks, because presidents going back to Ronald Reagan have shared a belief that contracting with private companies for services is better than hiring more government employees to do the work. Everything about the United States has grown significantly since the 1980s—the population, the economy, the federal budget—except for the size of the federal workforce. Still, Fuller has a pretty good handle on how much the war on terror has supercharged the spending.

"We've calculated that, without 9/11, procurement spending in the region would have grown $5.5 billion over the last four years," he explains. "But 9/11 happened, and the actual growth was $18.5 billion." The difference between those two numbers—$13 billion—is another way of glimpsing the prosperity that has followed after the fireballs. "Each billion in additional procurement spending generates approximately 7,000 new jobs," Fuller adds.

What kinds of jobs? Fuller has still more PowerPoint slides. Washington leads the nation in total job production over the past five years, thanks to the post-9/11 rush, with other thriving cities far, far behind. This region has created some 200,000 new jobs in that period.

And yet, the Washington area actually trails the rest of the country in the growth of most job categories. Even with all the construction cranes and federal office renovations, we're a bit behind the average in construction jobs. We're way behind in retail, in financial services, in education and health-care jobs. Our new jobs are concentrated in just two categories, Fuller says. First, "professional services"—meaning highly paid technical, scientific, managerial, consulting and computer-design jobs. And the second category, more mysterious: "other services."

"Those are the people who baby-sit, cut lawns, do dry cleaning and clean the homes of the professional services people," Fuller explains.

The war on terror has given Washington an E-Z Pass for the turnpike to the future. These are precisely the sort of jobs that experts believe will hold the key to tomorrow's economy. The region has roughly 2 percent of the total American workforce, but more than 10 percent of the computer systems designers, 8 percent of the consultants and the scientific researchers, 6 percent of the professors and the technologists and the Internet operators. "This is the new economy," Fuller sums up. So we should be very well positioned to prosper indefinitely, provided we don't get incinerated.

Money is how government says, "I Care." Frowny politicians can hug disaster victims amid scenes of devastation, and that's fine for a day or two. Then people want the bottom line: What's the appropriation? When President Bush went to flooded New Orleans in September to talk about Hurricane Katrina, the key quote was, "I have asked for, and the Congress has provided, more than $60 billion."

The collapse of the twin towers on live television, and the direct hit on the Pentagon, focused governmental concern—meaning spending—to an intensity not seen in generations, going back to Pearl Harbor. But something had changed in the intervening decades. After Pearl Harbor, it was easy to see exactly where the money was going. Millions of young men and women joined the government as soldiers, seamen, airmen and clerks. Tanks, airplanes, destroyers and aircraft carriers rolled out of factories and shipyards on round-the-clock shifts. The work never stopped. Bombs, bullets, guns, uniforms, packs, tents, Jeeps, mess kits—all highly tangible and easily understood. Even the most highly classified supersecret expenditure went searingly public less than four years after Pearl Harbor, when Hiroshima was destroyed by a single bomb.

Today, the output is more elusive. Where is the money going? You can read about a spending bill. You can visit one of the publications or Web sites devoted to tracking the parade of new, rich, inscrutable-sounding government contracts awarded each day. A sampling from a January issue of Washington Technology magazine:

ManTech International Corp., Fairfax, Va., won a $300 million, two-year subcontract from VSE Corp., Alexandria, Va., to provide the Army with support services in Afghanistan and Iraq . . .

Multimax Inc., Largo, Md., won two five-year contracts worth a total of $75.7 million from the Air Force for communications support, testing and IT security services to Air Force organizations at Manas Air Base in Kyrgyzstan for $32.8 million; and Maxwell Air Force Base, Ala., for $42.9 million. . . .

Science Applications International Corp. . . . won two contracts worth a total of $68.4 million over three years from the Centers for Disease Control and Prevention to help implement and support the agency's BioSense national syndromic surveillance program . . .

Or you can tour the bollards and cranes.

But it's all amorphous, compared with the sheds full of government workers thrown up on the Mall in the 1940s.

Hoping for a peek at the new wartime economy, I visited last year's Government Security Expo & Conference, or GOVSEC, at the Washington Convention Center. Launched in 2002, GOVSEC is an annual event "for those responsible for protecting government's physical, information and cyber security at the federal, state and local levels." The 2005 conference attracted 6,000 people, many of whom obviously had influence over government spending, because more than 500 companies—from small inventors to charter members of the military-industrial complex—waited eagerly to meet them in the exhibition hall.

Booths covering acres of floor space displayed products ranging from flashlights to speedboats. Some of the merchandise was brutally prosaic: jacks for lifting rubble, protective suits for cleaning up toxic debris, civil defense sirens, gas masks, stretchers, shatter-resistant windows. Some of the gear was old technology repackaged for new sales: traffic cones as evacuation markers; police vans souped up into mobile crisis command centers.

Other offerings were snazzy and high-tech; for example, a computer software package called VIS2TA. It was sold by Northrop Grumman, a Los Angeles company that happens to have four offices in Northern Virginia and yet another in Maryland. During World War II, the companies that now make up Northrop Grumman built airplanes and ships. Now they're raking in money writing software. VIS2TA was designed to reduce reams of emergency information into a single database. Suppose a bomb exploded in a VIS2TA town. The computer would quickly produce a city map showing every building in the vicinity of the blast. Click on a building, and up would pop a detailed floor plan and evacuation route. Every hospital, firehouse and police station would feed information into the map, updated as the crisis unfolded. Another layer of data would reveal the weather conditions and project the fallout based on prevailing winds.

But no one would buy just the software package. The same officials who would want VIS2TA would want a powerful new computer network to run it. They would want to house the network in a custom-built command center, like the one Gainer showed me last year inside Capitol Police headquarters. There, inside a secure room, I counted at least 10 big flat-panel displays and dozens of smaller screens showing views from surveillance cameras planted throughout Capitol Hill. There were also scores of phones and computer consoles. One display tracked the direction of the wind, and another reported the locations of key members of Congress. Yet another displayed the paths of nearby aircraft.

What chief would not like to have a space-age setup like this, whether or not he has Gainer's obvious reasons for needing it? And, of course, the command post must be connected to a mobile headquarters, which must be linked to rescue unit crews wearing new hazmat suits and carrying pricey hand-held radios. Multiply all those chiefs times all that gear, connect them through lobbyists and members of Congress to the pipeline of federal money, and you can begin to picture one tributary of the great Doom Boom. One of many.

Strolling up one aisle of GOVSEC and down the next, I was chilled at first by the horrible assumptions underpinning the bazaar. Portable anthrax tests. Bomb-defusing tents. Personal climate systems, for hunting terrorists in extreme heat or cold. Holographic weapons sights. Everything trailed a stink of death and dismemberment. But soon enough an almost giddy feeling of gee whiz replaced the horror: Wow, can they really do that? Have they actually perfected a voice-analyzing "truth verification system"? Is it true that sensors can identify people based on their unique pattern of blood vessels beneath the skin? Can a lightweight barrier really be strong enough to stop a speeding truck? And look at all this James Bond stuff: a cellphone that performs video surveillance; another cellphone that eavesdrops on the conversations of callers nearby.

Not every company hawking a product was based locally, of course. One of the most intriguing devices on display was produced by American Science and Engineering (AS&E), of Billerica, Mass. The company's ZBVs—"Z Backscatter Vans"—appeared to be ordinary white delivery trucks, but inside they were packed with supersensitive scanning machines. According to the company sales pitch, one driver in a ZBV can thoroughly search more than 100 cars, trucks, shipping containers, Dumpsters, boxcars—you name it— every hour, just by driving slowly past. From the sidewalk, it looks like Mr. Repairman needs a parking space, but, in fact, the van is emitting "backscatter X-rays," whatever those are, in a search for bombs, hidden passengers, illegal drug stashes and so on. Another machine, at the same time, is probing the air for radioactive telltales of nukes and dirty bombs. A ZBV can look through the walls of some buildings and the clothes of passersby. It can park at the curb and scan traffic, or it can race along at highway speeds, scanning the cars alongside. And if you paint FTD on the side, everyone will think it's roses.

AS&E makes these vans in Billerica, but Washington is the place to turn sneaky vans into profits. This is where America keeps its checkbook. This is where the grants are bestowed for purchasing bomb-finders and nuke-sniffers. This is where the money comes from for research and development on the next generation of scanning technologies. This is where a company's executives can have lunch with their lobbyists, should they wish to seek counsel on the best way to dip their corporate pail into the government's cataract of cash.

And so the convention center was a hive of government employees and the smiling salespeople waiting to meet them. Above the bustle, banners announced the presence of mega-companies such as Philips, Raytheon, Glock, Mitsubishi, CompuDyne and many more. Everyone had converged on Washington to think about explosions, fires, piles of rubble, chaos, deadly germs, radiation. And then to translate those thoughts into the more soothing contemplation of moneymaking. And, of course, to enjoy the shops and restaurants.

Is it bad to prosper in a crisis, to thrive on adversity? The moral factors are not clear. Doctors do well in an epidemic, and everyone says thank you. On the other hand, a lawyer who passes out cards in the emergency room after a school bus crash is slime. So what about Washington? Are we more like the healers or the ambulance-chasers?

However you answer that one, the link between bad news and good times is central to this city's history. The Civil War worked wonders for the development of Washington. In 1860, on the eve of the catastrophe, Washington had just two paved streets, no standing police force and an open sewer behind the White House. A Union private, arriving from New York shortly after the first shots were fired at Fort Sumter, was disappointed to find the capital "little better than a country town." Within a few months, however, 100,000 soldiers had followed him to Washington, and the transformation had begun.

That boom surely felt a bit like our own, at least in the beginning: tense, anxious, rife with intrigue and rumors of an impending attack. And yet, the hotels were packed, the saloons bustling, the theaters sold out. Inventors streamed to the capital carrying prototypes for repeating rifles, machine guns, artillery and bombs. The big hotel run by the Willard brothers at 14th Street and Pennsylvania Avenue became "a 'seething cauldron' of commercial intrigues," in the words of writer Ernest B. Furgurson, "jammed with cigar-smoking salesmen and lobbyists touting materials of war." In his history of Civil War Washington, "Freedom Rising," Furgurson described a frenzied scramble for the barrels of money that Lincoln poured into saving the Union—fantastic sums for the time, more than $1 million a day.

James "Big Jim" Fisk, for instance, was a failing salesman for the Boston retailer Jordan, Marsh. He heard Lincoln's call for volunteers and, rather than joining a regiment, "remembered the thousands of unsold blankets he had once seen moldering in the store's attic," Furgurson recounted. "Confident that the army would be needing blankets, he came to Washington and set up at Willard's. Stocking the best suite in the house with food, liquor and lighthearted ladies, he became a generous, cork-popping host" to squads of freshly minted government purchasing clerks. Fisk "soon disposed of the moldy blankets for such an absurd profit that the firm was delighted for him to stay on."

"You can sell anything to the government at almost any price you've got the guts to ask," Fisk confided. He wasn't the only person who noticed. One-third of all military contract spending went to overcharges in the early months of the Civil War, a congressional investigation later concluded.

As the war continued, Washington grew into the nerve center for the largest armies the continent had ever seen. Thousands of clerks collected hundreds of millions in new taxes, and spent the money on countless tons of weaponry, food and supplies. True, these Washingtonians weren't dying at places like Antietam and Chickamauga, and not every dollar they spent was spent wisely, honestly or well. But money was the tide that bore the North to its victory, so their frenzy was not in vain.

Some of those clerks stayed in Washington after the crisis was over—the population of the city grew by 80 percent from 1860 to 1870. Thus, a pattern was begun: What Washington gains in bad times, it never gives up. We see the pattern repeat 70 years later, during the back-to-back disasters of the Great Depression and World War II. Again, Uncle Sam opened wide the money tap. As before, clerks and contractors flocked to the capital for jobs or a piece of the action. The population rose by nearly two-thirds from 1930 to 1950, to more than 800,000 people in the District, with more in the newly sprouting suburbs. The size of the federal workforce in Washington nearly doubled in the five years from 1940 to 1945, from 139,000 to 265,000.

David Brinkley noted in his book about World War II, "Washington Goes to War," that many economists predicted a gloomy future for the Washington region once peace returned and the bureaucrats went home. But "they did not understand the basic nature of government," Brinkley explained. "They did not see that with the wartime innovation of the withholding tax, previously unimaginable amounts of money were being extracted from the American people with relatively few complaints. Federal tax collections in 1940 had totaled $5 billion. In 1945, $49 billion. And it was all spent."

It is almost always all spent. The great lesson of Washington, according to veteran lobbyist Ed Rogers, who has watched budgets be made by both Democrats and Republicans, is that "whoever wants to spend the most, wins."

Instead of a postwar recession, the boom continued in peacetime—a fact, Brinkley noted, that stamped many government leaders as disciples of the British economist John Maynard Keynes. In simplest terms, Keynes advised governments to increase spending during economic downturns as a way to stimulate growth. Sure enough, Washington's unbridled spending on the war had cured the national depression. A generation would go by before Washington saw the rise of a competing school of thought. Economist Robert Mundell's "supply-side" economics contended that, instead of borrowing and spending to spur the economy, government should cut taxes and let the private sector allocate the cash.

Today's Doom Boom might be seen as an experiment in combining the two—substantial tax cuts and massive spending. The supply-siders in the Bush administration and the Republican Congress have dramatically cut taxes while simultaneously saturating the capital with new spending. Two stimulants instead of one. Like sugar-coated chocolate, like diet pills washed down with coffee, this combination has been so economically potent that the whole region is practically vibrating. Most economists are forecasting yet another year of brisk growth in the Washington area, with tens of thousands of new jobs added, new office buildings filling with new tenants, and home prices stabilizing at or near record highs.

The Wall Street Journal recently reported record revenue for the lobbying industry. There's a $68 steak on the menu at Charlie Palmer's on the Hill. And, as I write this sentence, there is a construction crane going up outside my downtown Washington window.

Can this be what bin Laden had in mind?

Anyone who hopes to defeat the United States must have a strategy for neutralizing our money. In 1941, Adm. Isoroku Yamamoto, commander of the Japanese Combined Fleet, prepared the surprise attack on the American Navy at Pearl Harbor. Having completed two tours at the Japanese Embassy in Washington as naval attache, Yamamoto had no illusions about American money muscle. Therefore his strategy was to cripple the U.S. fleet just long enough for Japan to seize control of Southeast Asia, which was rich in the natural resources, such as oil and rubber, that Japan needed for its dreams of empire. The best Japan could hope for, Yamamoto told his superiors, was to set the United States back 18 months—and then seek a treaty. Beyond that, American industry was too strong to be defeated.

As it turned out, the United States needed just six months, not 18, to snap the spine of Yamamoto's navy, but the admiral was correct on the larger point. By 1943, a year and a half after Pearl Harbor, American factories had increased their production of tanks a hundredfold, and were turning out more tanks in a year than Germany produced during the entire war. Construction of warships was up more than tenfold: In 1943, the United States built 15 aircraft carriers—nearly as many as Japan produced in its entire history. America built nearly 86,000 airplanes in 1943, roughly equal to Japan's output for the whole war. As military historian Alan Gropman of the National Defense University has documented, all this happened despite bureaucratic bungles and nagging inefficiencies from the top of the production chain to the bottom. Still, 18 months after Pearl Harbor—as the U.S. economy approached its peak wartime effort—this country was "manufacturing munitions almost equal to the combined total of both its friends and adversaries," Gropman wrote.

And the U.S. economy has only grown mightier since then.

However, bin Laden and company have a very different strategy than Japan did, a "policy in bleeding America to the point of bankruptcy," as bin Laden put it in a videotaped address to the American people just before the 2004 presidential election. It is a sort of judo, a leveraging of weakness into strength, known as asymmetric warfare, in which small investments by al-Qaeda defeat huge investments by the United States. Asymmetrically speaking, the cost of destroying the tallest buildings in Manhattan, in 2001, was little more than a plane ticket and a box cutter, given ideologues willing to do it. So it didn't matter that, according to intelligence estimates, the U.S. military was outspending al-Qaeda by more than 10,000 to 1.

Since then, the United States has increased spending on security by more than two-thirds, but our foes are still working that same judo, blowing up commuter trains and military convoys with surplus explosives and junk from around the house: backpacks, trash bags, cellphones, toy cars. The United States has hundreds of billions of dollars' worth of surveillance equipment on the ground, in the air and orbiting in space, but none of those gadgets can find bin Laden or his deputy, Ayman al-Zawahiri. The only time we see or hear from them is when they smuggle another cheap audio or videotape to al-Jazeera television. As Secretary of Defense Donald Rumsfeld summed up in a 2003 memo to his staff: "The cost-benefit ratio is against us! Our cost is billions against the terrorists' cost of millions."

Exactly, bin Laden said in the videotape. It worked during the 1980s in Afghanistan. Using "guerrilla warfare and the war of attrition" jihadists "bled Russia for 10 years until it went bankrupt and was forced to withdraw in defeat," the al-Qaeda leader said.

Can they do the same to the United States?

You may not be surprised to learn that experts disagree about how much damage our budget deficits are doing to the country. Over time, large deficits soak up capital that could go to more useful investments, and America potentially becomes vulnerable to the demands of overseas lenders. But that doesn't mean that, as bin Laden seemed to suggest, the United States is as fragile as the old Soviet Union was. As the Bush administration points out, the U.S. economy has survived more intense spending binges than this one. "Spending as a percentage of the economy is lower than it was under four of the last five presidents," White House strategist Peter Wehner argued in a recent memo, "and the high-water mark for the budget deficit as a percentage of the [economy] . . . is significantly less than was the case in the 1980s."

So the immediate problem may not be bankruptcy. It might be frustration, if Americans conclude that the massive expenditures since 9/11 aren't buying results. While the federal government has been flexing the money muscle of the United States—hyperstimulating the Washington economy—the enemy has drawn strength from the economic and political weakness of the Arab world. There's that judo, again. Our strong economy is cranking out software and sensors, bollards and cranes, but weak Muslim economies are cranking out extremists just as fast or faster. "The combined gross domestic product of the 22 countries in the Arab League is less than the GDP of Spain," the 9/11 Commission noted in its 2004 report. "Forty percent of adult Arabs are illiterate, two-thirds of them women. One-third of the broader Middle East lives on less than two dollars a day. Less than 2 percent of the population has access to the Internet."

The Joint Chiefs of Staff recently completed a broad review of American strategy in the war on terror. In the fifth year of Washington's Doom Boom, the generals concluded that we need to be building up Muslim countries with at least as much enthusiasm as we have shown for building up the corridor between Dulles and the Pentagon. If the United States could figure out how to transplant a bit of the energy and prosperity of the Doom Boom to the failing countries of the Middle East, it would do us more good in the long run than bollards in every driveway and scanners on every roof.

This will take a long time, the Joint Chiefs acknowledged, but America will not win this war until ordinary Muslims can safely bet on a moderate future. "The conditions that extremist networks exploit to operate and survive have developed over long periods," the new strategy declared. And so "the effort to alter those conditions will require a long-term, sustained approach," as well.

Leaders from across the political spectrum talk about a Marshall Plan for the Middle East, but, as scholars Derek Chollet and James M. Goldgeier explained in a recent essay, the task may be even more complicated than the successful rebuilding of war-ravaged Europe, if only because building a modern country is more complicated than rebuilding it. They quoted former German chancellor Helmut Schmidt explaining the difference. "Europe possessed a long-standing entrepreneurial heritage, a base of business acumen, a high level of general education and technological knowledge as well as engineering capabilities," Schmidt said. "No Marshall Plan can succeed where such prerequisites do not exist."

Let's hope the government is spending a lot of money on smart people to solve this problem.

If so, maybe someday these smart, prosperous people can live in posh apartments and walk to work in new offices and shop in upscale stores—all built on the site of the old Washington Convention Center, demolished in 2004. Not long ago, I visited the site at 10th and Eye streets NW. Thanks to the Doom Boom, it is one of the most valuable undeveloped pieces of real estate in America, prime downtown acreage in a thriving city, close to subways and hotels and theaters. My purpose in wandering over was to picture the latent possibilities of such emptiness in this time of extraordinary growth. I tried to think of the space as seeded with future wealth and luxury, requiring nothing but the current government money rain to bring it bloom.

Instead, I found myself thinking: Here's what it looks like after a Washington landmark is destroyed. A huge, fenced scar. An aid to the imagination, should you need one. A glimpse of how failure might look in the battle with bin Ladenism.

David Von Drehle is a Washington Post Magazine staff writer.

Immigration and National Security

The greatest threat to U.S. homeland security comes from illegals who enter the country through its porous borders in order to attack. The tide of illegal immigration must be stemmed in order to secure the United States against terrorism. It is all too easy for illegal immigrants to slip in beneath the radar, eschewing the legalization process and never being detected and deported. And as long as the benefits of illegally immigrating outweigh the costs, the influx will continue. Legal immigration itself needs reform, too; particularly the visa-waiver program and the rules governing dual citizenship, which pose further security challenges. Federal government officials must overcome their fear of alienating ethnic voters and American business, enhance border security, and reform the nation's immigration policies.

JAN C. TING

The July 7, 2005, terror bombings in London and additional terrorist attempts there since then have brought new attention to the Islamist threat. They also highlighted the striking difference between U.S. and European concerns over the Islamist threat. In Europe, the greatest concern is the threat from its own resident immigrant population—particularly the young second and third generations, born in Europe. In the United States, the greatest concern is not its own population, but the threat of those sent from abroad to attack America.

Europe is now paying the price for open borders, past and present non-enforcement of immigration laws, and overly generous asylum policies. Despite government efforts to integrate Muslims, Europe's high-tax, high unemployment, and high welfare-benefits economic model has led to alienation among Europe's growing Muslim minority and a lack of economic and cultural integration.[1] With acts of violence from Muslim citizens in Europe increasing in number and scale, many Europeans feel that the Islamist threat needs to be addressed at home, not in Iraq.

But four years after 9/11, America's national borders remain open and uncontrolled. Our government seems unconcerned about this, even as it spends billions of dollars and thousands of lives in Iraq and Afghanistan fighting terrorism, and even as it worries about protecting the nation's ports, power supply, mass transit, and every other possible target against terrorist threats. The border with Mexico poses particular problems, but so too do our visa-waiver program and our rules governing dual citizenship.

Illegal Immigration

The Pew Hispanic Center reported in September 2005 that illegal immigrants now outnumber legal immigrants to the United States.[2] Every night, thousands of foreigners covertly enter the United States, and we have little idea who they are. Those we do intercept provide us with an idea of how many are illegally crossing the borders to enter the United States. The official estimate is that the U.S. Border Patrol apprehends 1 out of every 4 illegal border crossers.[3] But current and former Border Patrol officers say that the ratio of those intercepted is much lower—probably more like 1:8 or 1:10. The number getting in is always many times higher than the number of those who are apprehended. And because of the immigrants' remittances of U.S. dollars back to their home country, Mexico in particular has been supportive of its citizens who choose to enter the U.S. illegally.[4]

Table 1 shows Border Patrol apprehensions for fiscal years (ending September 30) 2000–05. The total number of apprehensions was highest in 2000 and then declined over the next three years, following 9/11. It then rose again in 2004 and 2005, after President Bush announced his proposal for guest-worker amnesty in January 2004. Apprehensions along the southern border make up about 97–98 percent of total apprehensions. Most of those apprehended near the United States' southern border are Mexicans, but there are also numerous "Other than Mexicans," or OTMs.

As Mexicans have known for years, the border is wide open, and anyone who wants to can easily enter the United States covertly. According to research by Wayne Cornelius of the Center for Comparative Immigration Studies at the University of California–San Diego, 92 percent of Mexicans seeking to enter the United States illegally eventually succeed.[6] Even children can easily enter. The New York Times Magazine reported in 2003 that the Border Patrol has also apprehended unaccompanied Mexican children as they were brought into the United States by smugglers to join parents who were already in the country illegally.[7] The children were processed and returned to Mexico, but by the time the article was published, all the children it had followed had successfully entered the United States and been reunited with their illegal alien parents.

Importantly, the number of OTMs apprehended near the southern border has been clearly and dramatically increasing since 2000, from 28,598 that year to 65,814 in 2004 and 100,142 in the first eight months of fiscal year 2005 alone. What happens upon apprehension is very different for OTMs

Table 1 U. S. Border Patrol Apprehensions, Fiscal Years 2000–05[5] (*in Thousands*)

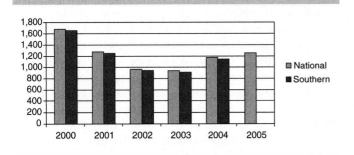

than for Mexicans, who can be immediately returned to Mexico in what is described as "voluntary departure." In the case of adult Mexicans, U.S. authorities simply take them back to the border (fully expecting to see them again). But the Mexican government does not allow the United States to send OTMs back into Mexico. This is perhaps understandable. No country would want other countries sending it their unwanted third-country nationals. But since these OTMs clearly entered the United States through Mexico, Washington might usefully and legitimately put some diplomatic pressure on Mexico City either to take the OTMs back or to prevent their entry into Mexico in the first place.

An OTM has to be scheduled for a hearing with an immigration judge, who can issue a removal order. A scheduled immigration hearing may be days, or more likely weeks, later, and even if a removal order is issued, the alien has statutory rights to appeal administratively to the Board of Immigration Appeals, and if that fails, to the federal courts. The U.S. government therefore has a dilemma. It can either detain the alien until the hearing (and, if a removal order is issued, until all appeal rights are exhausted, to ensure the alien's removal), or it can release the alien on his "own recognizance," and hope that the alien will voluntarily appear for the scheduled hearing and, if ordered removed and after exhausting all appeals, voluntarily appear for deportation.

Because the government has only authorized and funded a small number of detention spaces (a total of 19,444 in 2004, with another 1,950 added in May 2005),[8] increasing numbers of OTMs are released on their own recognizance. While fewer than 6,000 OTMs were released on their own recognizance in each of 2001 and 2002, that number increased to 7,972 in 2003, jumped to 34,161 in 2004, and already numbered 70,624 for the first eight months of fiscal 2005. The failure-to-appear rate at one immigration court near the southern border, in Harlingen, Texas, is 98 percent.[9] A removal order is typically issued in absentia for those who fail to appear. When the statutory appeal rights all expire, the names are added to the list of alien "absconders" who have actually been caught by the government, ordered removed by an immigration judge, and exhausted all their appeal rights, but are still in the country anyway. The list of such absconders is now 465,000 and growing, out of a total illegal alien population of 8 to 12

million, per a December 2003 estimate by Tom Ridge, then Secretary of Homeland Security. Lou Dobbs of CNN, among others, uses 20 million as a more realistic number.[10]

The release rate for apprehended OTMs is now so high, Border Patrol agents report that instead of hiding from the authorities, illegally entering OTMs actually seek them out in order to obtain the document charging them with illegal entry. They call this "Notice to Appear," which informs them of the date and place of their scheduled hearing before an immigration judge, a permiso; some agents call it a "Notice to Disappear," since that is what it permits them to do. If illegal immigrants are challenged while moving deeper into the United States from the border, they can produce the document to show that they have already been apprehended and charged and have scheduled appointments before immigration judges.[11]

The overwhelming majority of the millions of illegals, and even of the absconders, are not terrorists. But the sea of incoming illegal aliens provides a cover and a culture in which terrorists can hide, and a reliable means of entry. We need only recall that the Madrid train bombers resided easily in Spain (some came from Morocco, where Spanish is widely spoken) to appreciate that many Islamist terrorists are fluent in Spanish. Border Patrol apprehension figures show that among the OTMs apprehended in 2004 and 2005 were hundreds of persons from 35 "special interest" countries, almost all of which are Muslim. They include Afghanistan, Egypt, Iran, Iraq, Lebanon, Saudi Arabia, Somalia, Sudan, Syria, and Yemen; the number-one country in the group, with the largest number of aliens apprehended, is Pakistan. Again, these are just the apprehensions: for every alien apprehended entering the United States illegally, an estimated 3 to 9 others succeed.

Another threat to national security is presented by the significant number of violent criminals who are able to enter the U.S. illegally. In Los Angeles, two-thirds of all outstanding fugitive felony warrants, and 95 percent of outstanding fugitive homicide warrants, are for illegal aliens.[12] The Mexican government refuses to extradite its criminals to the United States, where they would face the death penalty, because the Mexican constitution does not permit capital punishment. In October 2001, the Mexican Supreme Court ruled that life imprisonment also violates the Mexican constitution.[13] So illegal aliens committing serious crimes in the United States, including the murder of police officers (for example, Los Angeles County deputy sheriff David March, who was shot to death in 2002 during a routine traffic stop) can and do seek refuge in Mexico, from which extradition is impossible unless U.S. prosecutors agree to seek only a determinate sentence. California prosecutors estimate that as many as 360 individuals who have committed murder or other serious crimes in the state have not been extradited. An estimated 60 fugitives charged with or wanted for murder in Los Angeles County are believed to be at large in Mexico.[14]

Political Gap

The main barrier to tightening the border is the absence of political will to take any effective action to stem the tide of illegal immigration. On no other issue is the gap wider between the views of ordinary Americans, who overwhelmingly want to see the uncontrolled influx of illegal aliens halted, and those of the national political elite of both parties, who overwhelmingly feel that nothing can or should be done about our porous borders.[15]

Politicians are pressured on two fronts when it comes to addressing the illegal alien population. First, American business, which is an important source of campaign funds, counts on plentiful, cheap labor. Illegal immigration serves its need, and also helps keep the wages of competing American and legal resident workers in check. And illegal immigrants offer revenue opportunities to many other businesses. Some U.S. banks are even granting mortgages to illegal immigrants.[16] The other major influence on politicians is electoral: the fear that any action to restrict illegal immigration will create a backlash among the growing number of ethnic voters. However, this fear may be misplaced. It is precisely those who have recently immigrated legally to the United States who feel most keenly the competition from illegal alien labor and the impact of that competition on their own wages. But the two considerations, business and political, act together to maintain a political majority in favor of doing nothing to effectively curb illegal immigration.

This pro-illegal alien coalition works in interesting ways. In 2004, following some worksite raids in Los Angeles by the Immigration and Customs Enforcement bureau of the Department of Homeland Security, rumors spread that more raids were coming. Businesses complained that their workers were afraid to come to work, and political activists attacked any immigration enforcement actions as inherently racist. In response, Asa Hutchison, then DHS's undersecretary for border security, announced that there would be no more worksite raids and stated that ending racial profiling was a DHS priority.[17]

President Bush's plan for immigration reform is a guest-worker program that would allow illegal aliens in the U.S. to obtain legal status if they can find a job. Business interests thought this was a fine idea when it was announced in 2004, and for pro-illegal alien activists it was better than nothing. But it amounts to amnesty for illegal aliens, as would any proposal that rewards illegal aliens who have violated our statutes, disadvantaging foreign nationals who have respected our immigration laws by waiting their turn to immigrate legally to the United States. Millions of fully qualified would-be legal immigrants have remained in their home countries pending approval to legally live and work in the United States. Some have been on a waiting list for legal immigrants for twenty years or more. Rewarding illegality makes those who respected and complied with our immigration laws appear foolish.

Congress did the same thing with the last large-scale amnesty of illegal aliens, in 1986, when it thought the adoption of employer sanctions—punishment for those who employ illegal aliens—would put an end to illegal immigration. In order to qualify for the amnesty, aliens had to prove they were in the United States in violation of our immigration laws. Those who had kept their student and work visas current were out of luck. Because they had respected U.S. laws, they were ineligible for the amnesty. Only those who had flaunted the laws were given legal status and the right to become American citizens. Nor did employer sanctions work, because the law was written so as to

protect employers, requiring only the most superficial efforts at compliance, and also because there was no enforcement.

A month after President Bush's announcement of his guest-worker amnesty proposal, more than half of the aliens being apprehended in the San Ysidro sector of the border near San Diego, and 90 percent in South Texas, were reporting to the Border Patrol that they were coming in order to get amnesty. Washington thereafter ordered Border Patrol to stop collecting this information.[18] Indeed, Washington seems determined to prove that nothing can be done to tighten our borders. According to Border Patrol sources, the Border Patrol was ordered in May to stop arrests of illegal aliens along the Arizona border. The Minuteman Project, an anti-illegal immigration group of volunteers, had conducted a one-month patrolling campaign in April, and Washington did not want the number of arrests to show an increase after it ceased.[19]

While it will be difficult to secure our entire 2,000-mile long southern border, there is plenty that we could do if only we had the political will to do so. We can put more people on the border, either using volunteers like the Minutemen, or using the U.S. Army Reserve and the border states' National Guards. We can resume worksite raids to arrest illegal aliens. And we can make employer sanctions work. A few years ago a pilot project was carried out to see whether employers would comply with a requirement to verify that a prospective employee's social security or other work authorization number presented by the alien was in fact a legally issued number. The project had good results but was never made mandatory. Today it might be done through the Internet, to be even faster and less burdensome for employers.[20]

But the most effective thing that could be done is to change the cost/benefit calculation of aliens considering illegal entry to the United States. The poor are as capable as anyone of determining what is in their best interests. If we allow the situation to continue where the benefits of illegal entry into the U.S. are large, with plentiful job opportunities available to illegal aliens, while the risks of apprehension and deportation are low, potential border-crossers will make the same decision that anyone would make in their position. We cannot blame them for coming to the United States illegally in all the circumstances: they are making rational decisions which we might also make if we were in their shoes.[21] The blame for illegal immigration properly belongs on U.S. political leaders, who enable and protect the flow of illegal aliens into the United States.

Defenders of the status quo try to blur the distinction between legal and illegal immigration, calling opponents of illegal immigration "anti-immigrant." This misleads some people, who are mindful that we are in fact a nation founded upon immigration. Every American is either an immigrant or the descendent of ancestors who came here, or were brought here, from somewhere else. That includes Native Americans. Our legal immigration system is appropriately the most generous in the world, admitting each year 1 million legal permanent resident immigrants with a clear path to full citizenship, more than all the rest of the nations of the world combined.[22] It is more than possible to champion legal immigration while advocating restrictions on illegal immigration, and even those seeking changes to our legal immigration system can see that addressing the problem of illegal immigration must come first in order to give legal immigration meaning.

The Visa-Waiver Program

Prior to 1986, the United States required visas of nearly all foreigners traveling to the United States, the exceptions being Canadians and Mexicans with border-crossing cards. To obtain a U.S. visa, a foreigner was required to apply for one at a U.S. consulate abroad, submitting his or her foreign passport, which allowed inspection of the passport to determine whether it was counterfeit or stolen, and an opportunity to ask questions before issuing a visa, or withholding a visa in appropriate cases. To board an airplane headed to the United States, a foreign national had to show a U.S. visa in his or her passport.

But in 1986, the U.S. Congress enacted a reciprocal visa-waiver program to allow the citizens of certain favored countries, mostly in Europe and now numbering 27, to enter the U.S. for up to 90 days without a visa, and vice versa.[23] (In order for a country to be eligible for the program, the refusal rate for nonimmigrant visas for its citizens cannot exceed 3 percent.) Visa waiver entrants may board an airplane to the United States merely by showing their passport. Visa waiver had long been sought by the U.S. tourism industry and by the airlines, and was also supported by the U.S. State Department, the staff of which was freed from having to process visa applications. (Visa-waiver entrants have lately numbered around 13 million per year.)

Who else was able to enter the United States without a U.S. visa using visa waiver? Zacarias Moussaoui, sometimes referred to as the 20th hijacker, entered the U.S. before 9/11 by showing his French passport. Moussaoui, who was arrested while taking lessons in Minnesota on flying a commercial airplane, admits to being an Al Qaeda agent. Richard Reid, the "shoe bomber," was able to board an airplane headed for the United States without a U.S. visa by showing his British passport. And one of the 1993 World Trade Center bombers, Ramsi Yusuf, was able to enter the U.S. through visa waiver after presenting a counterfeit European passport.

One might think that after 9/11, the visa-waiver program would have been eliminated. But its supporters swung into action to defend the program. At House Judiciary Committee hearings held in February 2002, witnesses testified that 9/11 changed nothing and that the case for visa waiver was as sound as ever. The number of entrants intent on mass murder who had entered the United States under visa waiver was declared to be statistically insignificant, and persons deemed unacceptable upon inspection on arrival could always be turned away. But how would this latter mechanism help against someone such as Reid, who boarded with the intent of blowing up the airplane?[24]

Congress tried to demonstrate concern by requiring better passports of visa-waiver applicants. The USA Patriot Act required that by October 2003, visa waiver applicants present machine-readable passports, but implementation was delayed until June 26, 2005. Deadlines for additional requirements under the Enhanced Border Security and Visa Reform Act of 2002 have been extended to October 26, 2005, for inclusion of a digital photo, and to October 26, 2006, for new passports issued by visa-waiver countries to be e-passports equipped with integrated computer chips capable of storing other biometric information.[25] It is not clear, however, how these passport requirements mitigate the national security threat presented by visa waiver.

Especially since the London bombings and with our growing awareness of the large Islamic populations in Europe qualifying for visa waiver, commentators have begun to note the danger visa-waiver presents, since it permits entrants from nations known to have populations of Islamist terrorists, such as Spain, Germany, France, and the UK. But observers often conclude that nothing can be done because ending visa waiver and reverting to pre-1986 visa requirements would adversely impact the airline and tourist industries and burden our State Department with visa applications.[26] Washington's consensus on visa waiver is the same as it is on our porous border: nothing can be done.

Indefinite Permanent Residence and Dual Citizenship

When a legal immigrant is admitted to the United States, he or she becomes a legal permanent resident (LPR) and receives what is commonly referred to as a green card. Typically, after five years of residence, LPRs become eligible for U.S. citizenship, and it has always been U.S. policy to encourage them to apply for citizenship and to naturalize. Doing so is not required, however, and perhaps it should be. The current policy allows millions of noncitizens who owe no loyalty to the United States to reside and work here permanently. A limitation on the duration of LPR status, perhaps to five years or as long as a citizenship application is pending, would encourage and facilitate the assimilation of immigrants.

Current U.S. policy actually encourages dual citizenship and the divided loyalty that comes with it. Unless U.S. citizens explicitly give up their citizenship, they may vote in foreign elections, serve in a foreign army hostile to the United States, or take an oath of allegiance to a foreign power—even if that oath includes a renunciation of all other loyalty—without relinquishing their U.S citizenship. Under current law, many benefits flow from dual nationality. These include the ability to carry and travel on two different passports, to work freely in each country without specific authorization, and to transmit dual citizenship to one's children. Although the Supreme Court has ruled that U.S. citizenship may not be involuntarily removed if a citizen intends to retain it,[27] Congress could legislate and State Department give appropriate notifications that certain specified actions inherently express a citizen's intent to relinquish U.S. citizenship.

Conclusion

The illegal immigrant himself or herself is not primarily to blame for the tide of illegal immigration which conceals and facilitates the presence of those hostile to our national security and interests. The problem continues to be the lack of political will among our leaders in Washington to recognize and respond to the flaws in our immigration system. Concerned citizens who have already written multiple letters to their elected representatives should consider running for elected office themselves on an anti-illegal immigration platform. They don't have to win, but only use the occasion to get politicians to see that their inaction on immigration reform could affect the results on election day.

Notes

1. See Robert S. Leiken, "Europe's Angry Muslims," *Foreign Affairs*, July/Aug. 2005; Zachary Shore, "Can the West Win Muslim Hearts and Minds?" *Orbis*, Summer 2005.

2. Stephen Ohlemacher, "Report: Illegal Immigration has Increased," AP, Sept. 27, 2005.

3. Sen. John McCain (R-Ariz.) stated that the Border Patrol apprehends only one out of four or five illegal entrants on CNN's *Lou Dobbs Tonight*, June 17, 2004. Video clip available at www.americanpatrol.com.

4. "Mexicans Send Records 20B South of the Border," *NewsMax.comWires*, Apr. 19, 2005.

5. 2005 annualized from data for first eight months of the year. Source for OTM and 2005 statistics: Associated Press, " 'Other Than Mexican' Migrants Routinely Released," *Tucson Citizen*, July 5, 2005. Source for 2004: Gentry Braswell, "Agency's Illegal Immigrant Apprehensions Continue to Rise," *Sierra Vista Herald*, July 1, 2005. Source for 2000–2003: U.S. Border Patrol fax, July 28, 2004, available at www.theamericanresistance.com. It is remarkably difficult to gather official data on border apprehensions. Many searches on Department of Homeland Security websites lead to a Freedom of Information Act request form, which suggests that the government has the data but is unwilling to provide it without an FOIA request. To observe the absence of recent enforcement statistics on government websites, see http://uscis.gov/graphics/shared/statistics/index.htm.

6. Quoted by John M. Broder, "With Congress's Blessing, a Border Fence May Finally Push Through to the Sea," *New York Times*, July 4, 2005.

7. Ginger Thompson, "Crossing with Strangers," *New York Times*, Nov. 3, 2003.

8. AP, " 'Other Than Mexican' Migrants."

9. Cited in Jerry Kammer, "Loophole to America," *San Diego Union-Tribune*, June 4, 2005.

10. AP, " 'Other Than Mexican' Migrants"; U.S. Border Control website, www.usbc.org; "Ridge's Immigration Remarks Draw Fire," *NewsMax.com Wires*, Dec. 11, 2003, at www.newsmax.com; transcript of "Lou Dobbs Tonight," Mar. 2, 2005, at http://transcripts.cnn.com. Roben Farzan, "Urban Migrant," *New York Times*, July 20, 2005, notes that the PewHispanic Center estimates 10.3 million immigrant workers in the United States. See also U.S. Border Patrol Local 2544 website, www.local2544.org.

11. Kammer, "Loophole to America."

12. "In Los Angeles, 95 percent of all outstanding warrants for homicide (which total 1,200 to 1,500) target illegal aliens. Up to two-thirds of all fugitive felony warrants (17,000) are for illegal

13. aliens." Heather MacDonald, "The Illegal Alien Crime Wave," *City Journal*, Winter 2004, www.city-journal.org.

13. Kate O'Beirne, "Like a Good Neighbor? Mexico and Its Refusal to Extradite," *National Review*, Feb. 9, 2004.

14. Ibid.

15. See Roy Beck and Steven A. Camorata, "Elite vs. Public Opinion: An Examination of Divergent Views on Immigration," *Center for Immigration Studies* Backgrounder, December 2002, at www.cis.org. "The results of [a Chicago Council on Foreign Relations] survey indicate that the gap between the opinions of the American people on immigration and those of their leaders is enormous. The poll found that 60 percent of the public regards the present level of immigration to be a 'critical threat to the vital interests of the United States,' compared to only 14 percent of the nation's leadership—a 46 percentage point gap."

16. See "Chicago: Banks Allow Mortgages to Illegal Immigrants," *Realtor Magazine,* Dec. 10, 2003, www.realtor.org.

17. Heather MacDonald, "Homeland Security? Not Yet," *City Journal*, Autumn 2004, www.manhattan-institute.org.

18. Matt Hayes, "Bush Amnesty Sparks Surge in Border Crossings," Fox News, Feb. 19, 2004. See also William Branigan, "Bush Proposal Prompted Surge in Illegal Immigrants," *Washington Post*, June 28, 2005, and the Judicial Watch Special Report, "U.S. Border Patrol Survey Analysis," June 28, 2005, at www.judicialwatch.org.

19. Jerry Seper, "Border Patrol told to stand down in Arizona," *Washington Times*, May 13, 2005.

20. For a discussion of these pilot programs, which Congress mandated in 1996 and which were evaluated by a Congressional committee as "far superior to the current program," see Thomas Alexander Aleinikoff, David Martin, and Hiroshi Motomura, *Immigration and Citizenship: Process and Policy*, 5th ed. (Thomson-West, 2003), pp. 1150–51.

21. See Miriam Jordan, "Convoy to Tennessee brings Immigrants to Shelter After Storm," *Wall Street Journal,* Sept. 19, 2005, for an account of how illegal immigrants displaced from New Orleans by Hurricane Katrina quickly found work in other states, so that they could continue the remittances home on which their families rely.

22. In recent years, about one-third of immigrants have come from Asia, one-third from Central and North America, and one-third from other regions of the world, including Europe, Africa, South America, and Oceania. See Nancy F. Rytina, "U.S. Legal Permanent Residents: 2004," June 2005, Homeland Security Office of Immigration Statistics, at http://uscis.gov/.

23. The 27 countries are: Andorra, Australia, Austria, Belgium, Brunei, Denmark, Finland, France, Germany, Iceland, Ireland, Italy, Japan, Liechtenstein, Luxembourg, Monaco, the Netherlands, New Zealand, Norway, Portugal, San Marino, Singapore, Slovenia, Spain, Sweden, Switzerland, and the United Kingdom.

24. See Jan C. Ting, "Close the Visa Loophole," *National Law Journal*, Jan. 28, 2002; Jan Ting, "Immigration Law Reform After 9/11: What Has Been and What Still Needs to Be Done," *Temple International & Comparative Law Journal,* Fall 2003, p. 503.

25. "DHS Releases Guide to Passport Rules for Visa Waiver Program," PR Newswire, July 19, 2005.

26. Visa Program Could Open U.S. Door to Terrorists," Gannett News Service, *Tucson Citizen*, July 22, 2005; James Jay Carafano

and Richard Weitz, "Building the Alliance for Freedom: An Agenda for Improving and Expanding the Visa Waiver Program," Heritage Foundation Backgrounder #1850, May 6, 2005, www.heritage.org; and Robert S. Leiken, "Europe's Mujahideen: Where Mass Immigration Meets Global Terrorism," Center for Immigration Studies, Apr. 2005, www.cis.org.

27. *Afroyim v. Rusk,* 387 U.S. 253 (1967). For the excessively lenient State Department interpretation of this ruling, see the Department's 1990 statement of evidentiary standards quoted in Aleinikoff, Martin, and Motomura, *Immigration and Citizenship,* pp. 142–3.

JAN C. TING (jan.ting@temple.edu) is professor of law at Temple University's Beasley School of Law and an FPRI senior fellow. This article is based on a lecture he gave on July 12, 2005, as part of FPRI's Summer School Lecture Series.

From *Orbis,* Winter 2006, pp. 41–52. Copyright © 2006 by Foreign Policy Research Institute. Reprinted by permission of Elsevier Science Ltd.

Senators Say Scrap FEMA and Start Over

But lawmakers split over removing agency from Homeland

Tim Starks

A recommendation from Senate investigators to abolish and replace the Federal Emergency Management Agency (FEMA) promises a fight that will begin as early as this month to determine the agency's future.

A seven-month review of the government response to Hurricane Katrina by investigators for the Senate Homeland Security and Governmental Affairs Committee culminated in a list of 86 recommendations. At the top of that list is a suggestion to create a National Preparedness and Response Authority to take the place of FEMA.

"Sometimes an organization becomes so dysfunctional and disreputable it is beyond repair," Sen. Joseph I. Lieberman of Connecticut, the ranking Democrat on the panel, said April 27 at a news conference where the recommendations were released. "FEMA is sick."

Committee Chairwoman Susan Collins, R-Maine, and Lieberman plan to press their panel's recommendations in legislation, although they set no fixed timetable for a markup. But lawmakers in both parties are sharply divided on whether FEMA or any successor agency should be independent or part of the Homeland Security Department.

The proposed new structure would reunite emergency preparedness and response functions, an issue upon which both Homeland Security committees agree. Homeland Security Secretary Michael Chertoff last year split the two functions in a departmental reorganization. But the committee did not recommend taking FEMA out of the department, which Collins and Lieberman were instrumental in creating.

Some lawmakers argue that the only cure for FEMA's problems is its removal from Homeland Security.

The department has indicated it does not like either idea. Spokesman Russ Knocke criticized the Senate investigators' recommendation on abolishing FEMA.

"At this point in time, it really doesn't make sense to be playing around with the organizational charts," he said.

Those competing views about FEMA's fate should collide in May. In the House, the Transportation and Infrastructure Committee will consider legislation that would restore FEMA's independence. *(House bills, CQ Weekly, p. 1034; House's FEMA report, CQ Weekly, p. 488)*

"FEMA was neglected and deteriorated so quickly because its disaster mission cannot compete with DHS's terrorism prevention mission," said Rep. Bill Shuster, R-Pa., who chairs a Transportation subcommittee that will consider the bill. "Putting FEMA back together, strengthening it and changing its name under the same roof will not address the root cause of DHS's failure."

An aide to the House Homeland Security Committee said Chairman Peter T. King, R-N.Y., would move a bill in May similar to the Senate investigators' proposal: FEMA would not be abolished but would have control over disaster preparedness as well as response.

"Whether we call the agency charged with emergency preparedness and response FEMA or something else, the Senate's report echoes our urgent call to strengthen disaster preparedness and response within the department," said Bennie Thompson of Mississippi, the ranking Democrat on the Homeland Security panel.

On the Senate side, members of the Homeland Security and Governmental Affairs Committee will consider the report—"Hurricane Katrina: A Nation Still Unprepared"—at a May 2 meeting. Some members, such as Sen. Daniel K. Akaka, D-Hawaii, have said FEMA should be restored to independence.

Several members, including Norm Coleman, R-Minn., and Mark Pryor, D-Ark., said April 27 that they were still reviewing the report's recommendations but were open to the proposal to replace FEMA.

Collins and Lieberman said they thought an independent FEMA would create overlapping and redundant response agencies, since most proposals for removing FEMA would limit its authority to natural disasters and leave terrorism incidents to the Homeland Department.

By Any Other Name

Outside experts were divided.

"The call for creating a new organization within DHS is simply renaming FEMA, and despite Shakespeare's belief that 'a rose by any other name would smell as sweet,' renaming FEMA won't make it smell any better, and it will create an even greater deal of confusion than there already is," said former FEMA director James Lee Witt. "The most important step in fixing FEMA is to return it to its independent status."

On the other side of the issue was Herman B. "Dutch" Leonard, professor of public management at the John F. Kennedy School of Government at Harvard University.

"This represents a clean break from history both in terms of the reputation and baggage that FEMA has," Leonard said.

Panel Addresses Preparedness

Concluding that "our leadership and systems must be prepared for catastrophes we know will be unlike Katrina, whether due to natural causes or terrorism," the Senate Homeland Security panel made the following recommendations to meet that goal:

- **FEMA:** Abolish FEMA and create a National Preparedness and Response Authority within the Department of Homeland Security (DHS), giving it a full range of responsibilities.
- **Regional operations:** Enhance regional operations to provide better coordination between federal agencies and the states. Establish regional strike teams.
- **Coordination:** Create a National Operations Center to communicate with and coordinate various government agencies before, during and in the wake of a disaster.
- **Resources:** Provide enough resources and funding to ensure that the new response agency, and other federal agencies with disaster-related responsibilities, can be effective.
- **Planning:** Develop clear operational plans and training programs and require DHS to work with federal and regional agencies and states to ensure that they are aware of the plans and well-trained in their details and execution.

UNIT 4

State and Local Governments and Homeland Security

Unit Selections

Key Points to Consider

- How have state law enforcement agencies changed since 9/11?

- Can the Oklahoma model be applied to other states?

- Should urban areas, like New York, receive more homeland security funding? Why?

- Who is responsible for response failures during hurricane Katrina?

Student Web Site

www.mhcls.com/online

Internet References

Further information regarding these Web sites may be found in this book's preface or online.

New York State Office of Homeland Security
   http://www.security.state.ny.us/

NGA Center for Best Practices
   http://www.nga.org/portal/site/nga/menuitem.8274ad9c70a7bd616adcbeeb501010a0/
   ?vgnextoid=e9a4d9b834420010VgnVCM1000001a01010aRCRD

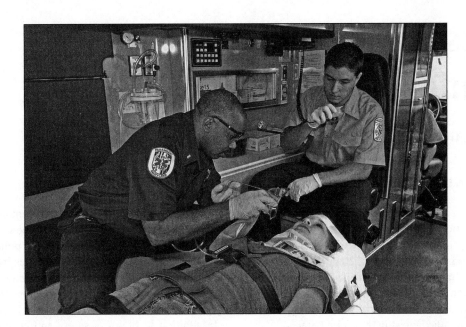

Major disasters, by definition, tend to quickly overwhelm the resources and capabilities of local governments. When challenged beyond their means, cities and localities have come to rely on state governments for assistance. The involvement of state governments in disaster response is nothing new. Most states have had significant experience in disaster response and emergency management. Through years of trial and error—exposure to natural disasters such as earthquakes, floods, wild-fires, tornadoes, hurricanes; and snowstorms and man-made disasters such as plane crashes, train crashes, and chemical spills—states have managed to build up effective emergency management and disaster response capabilities.

States have developed significant infrastructures to assist in such responses. Command and control facilities, specialized equipment, and designated emergency personnel—to include, when needed, National Guard units—are important components of most states' disaster response plans. While existing infrastructure may vary from state to state, based on threat perception and the availability of resources, it is an illusion to think that the federal government is more capable at planning for and organizing local disaster response than those who know the area and have been doing it for years.

The federal government can, nevertheless, play an important role. To effectively expand their response repertoire to include potential threats to homeland security, the two most important things that states need from the federal government are information and funding.

Information is the most important thing the federal government can contribute to state and local efforts. While a number of federal agencies are working on more effective ways to exploit data collected by local and state police departments, little has been done to eliminate the barriers that prevent the distribution of intelligence to these departments. The lack of information and lack of feedback from the federal government continue to be a source of frustration for state and local authorities. State and local police forces can not become effective "eyes and ears" for federal homeland security efforts if they aren't told specifically who and what to look for. In addition to timely intelligence and accurate threat assessments, states need improved access to specialized knowledge and training that will allow them to prepare themselves for new types of threats.

One of the biggest sources of contention between state and local governments and the Bush Administration is homeland security funding. While most states and municipalities support the desire for improved security, few have sufficient economic resources to sustain this effort. In a time of deficits and budget cuts preparing for future threats while responding to heightened terrorist "alert-levels" has become a near impossible task. Federal money to acquire new specialized equipment, conduct training, and field additional security forces is needed. As the Bush Administration has increasingly shifted its attention to problems overseas, federal spending on state and local efforts has slowed. As a result, states and municipalities have become increasingly critical of federal support.

The articles in this unit focus on the challenges that state and local governments faced in their homeland security efforts. The first article in this unit highlights how the homeland security focus has changed the role of state law enforcement agencies. It argues that with economic support from the federal government, states must take the lead in improving and insuring public safety. In the second article, Kerry Pettingill, Director of the Oklahoma Office of Homeland Security, discusses a new regional disaster response system. He identifies factors that must be considered in developing an agile, multi-tier response system. Article three focuses on the continuing dissatisfaction among states and localities with distribution of federal funds for homeland security. It raises the concern that large cities like New York are being ignored in favor of smaller cities like Louisville and Omaha. Finally, the fourth article examines the response to Hurricane Katrina. It argues that since the U.S. disaster relief system is set up primarily on the state and local level, Louisiana Governor Kathleen Blanco and New Orleans Mayor Ray Nagin are primarily responsible for its failure.

Terrorism's Impact on State Law Enforcement

CSG work group examines new roles and changing conditions

CHAD FOSTER AND DR. GARY CORDNER

In recent years, Arizona established the Arizona Counter Terrorism Information Center, a combined facility/information system that supports the analysis and sharing of law enforcement information. New York hired 120 new state troopers to guard critical infrastructure along the northern border. The state of Washington implemented an explosive detection canine program to provide additional security screening at terminals to its ferry system, the largest in the United States.

These developments all suggest heightened roles for state law enforcement agencies since the September 11, 2001 terrorist attacks. Not only are state police organizations taking on these new terrorism-related responsibilities, they and their local counterparts are shouldering many new burdens because of shifting federal priorities.

In 2004, The Council of State Governments and Eastern Kentucky University conducted a 50-state survey of law enforcement agencies and convened an expert work group to examine how these changing conditions are affecting police and their traditional duties and to form recommendations for states. As state policy-makers and legislators seek policy improvements, results from this terrorism-prevention study and recently drafted guidance may help them understand current conditions and strategic directions for the future.

State Law Enforcement— Yesterday and Today

General purpose state law enforcement agencies exist in all states but Hawaii. These agencies or departments typically fall under the rubric of state police, state patrol or highway patrol departments. One of the oldest and most well-known state police organizations is the Texas Rangers, established in 1835. Most state agencies, however, are relatively new. The proliferation of the interstate highway system during the mid-20th century and the need for traffic safety and enforcement forced most states to establish or expand their state law enforcement agency.

Although the structure and function of these agencies varies among states, they share similar characteristics. A common component of most state law enforcement agencies is a criminal investigation division. Roughly 50 percent of all states use a unified model or one that combines police/highway patrol function and investigation responsibilities into a single department. The other half of states have a separate bureau of criminal investigation that works independently or within the state attorney general's office.

In addition to highway safety and criminal investigations, general purpose agencies play many other lead and supporting roles in the states. For example, these agencies often provide states with special weapons and tactics teams; search and rescue units; marine and aviation assets; crime labs; criminal history repositories; uniform crime reporting; statewide information systems; training for local law enforcement; and statewide communication, intelligence and analysis.

According to the Bureau of Justice Statistics, there were roughly 700,000 full time, sworn state and local law enforcement personnel in 2000. Within this total, state law enforcement agencies account for roughly 56,000 officers. The Federal Bureau of Investigation, on the other hand, employed just 11,523 special agents in 2000. Law enforcement numbers substantially increase at all levels of government, especially at the state und federal levels, once special jurisdictions with arrest and firearm authorities are considered (e.g.. alcoholic beverage control, fish and wildlife, state park services).

Local police departments and sheriffs' offices provide the bulk of law enforcement services to rural communities. As with many other services, however, rural areas are severely constrained by the lack of law enforcement resources. In 1999, for example, 52.4 percent of all local law enforcement agencies employed less than 10 sworn officers while 5.7 percent employed just one sworn officer. For this reason, state police departments often play enhanced roles in rural areas by providing critical support services to smaller local agencies.

Generally speaking, state law enforcement agencies existed in a fairly stable environment before Sept. 11 fulfilling traditional roles. And then the attacks occurred, creating and shifting responsibilities and paradigms among all layers of law enforcement.

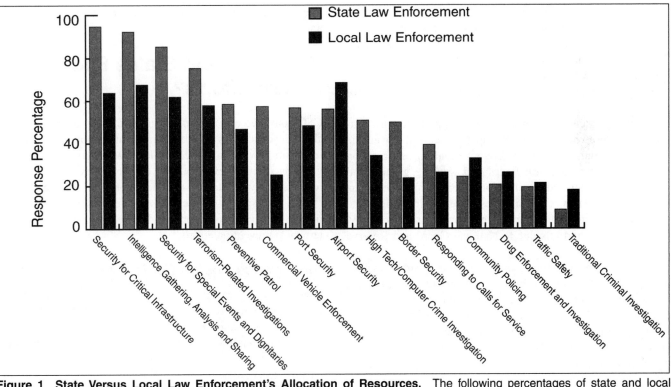

Figure 1   State Versus Local Law Enforcement's Allocation of Resources. The following percentages of state and local law enforcement agencies say they have allocated more or many more resources toward certain operational responsibilities since Sept. 11.

Source: CSG and EKU National Survey of State and Local Law Enforcement Agencies, 2004.

Key Research Finding

Traditionally, state-level law enforcement has represented about 10 percent of total police employment in the United States. In keeping with this employment level, state law enforcement has historically played an important but relatively small role in the overall picture of policing in America. The information collected for this project, however indicates an expanding role for state law enforcement since 2001, partly because of new roles and responsibilities associated with homeland security, and partly because state police are filling gaps and vacuums created by shifts in federal law enforcement priorities, Thus, while it is true that all types of police agencies have been significantly affected post-Sept 11, it seems that state law enforcement agencies have been affected the most.

According to the 50-state survey carried out by CSG and EKU in the spring of 2004. state law enforcement agencies are very involved in their state's homeland security initiatives, and they are being stretched thin today because of these new roles and changing federal priorities.

Roughly 75 percent of state agencies say they either have a great amount of involvement or serve as their state's leader in terrorism-related intelligence gathering, analysis and dissemination. In addition, more than 50 percent of state agencies report

similar involvement in homeland security planning and coordination at the state level, conducting vulnerability assessments of critical infrastructure, providing protection for this infrastructure and dignitaries, and emergency response to terrorism-related incidents.

How are these responsibilities affecting state police in terms of resource allocation? In comparison to the period before Sept. 11, more than 70 percent of state agencies report allocating more or many more resources for security of critical infrastructure, special events and dignatories: intelligence gathering, analysis and sharing: and terrorism-related investigations. Furthermore, at least 50 percent of state police organizations say more or many more resources have been allocated for airport, border and port security; commercial vehicle enforcement; high-tech/computer crime investigation; operational assistance to local agencies; and preventive patrols.

These resources are likely generated from a number of possible sources; the survey results and interviews suggest three. First, more than 10 percent of state agencies report allocating fewer resources for traditional criminal investigation and drug enforcement following Sept. 11. Therefore, it is likely that some resources have been shifted internally among competing public safety problems and priorities. Interviews with state officials in 2004 support the conclusion that other crime-fighting efforts have suffered as a result of new terrorism related demands. This may be especially troublesome for states experiencing problems with other types of crime, such as synthetic drugs (e.g., methamphetamines and prescription drug abuse), new violent gang activities, identity theft and cybercrimes.

Second, state police organizations are receiving funds and resources through a number of federal grant programs such as the State Homeland Security Program and Law Enforcement Terrorism Prevention Program. Although state law enforcement agencies will likely see a small portion of these funds, roughly $1.5 billion was allocated to states for these two programs in 2005.

Third, interviews with state officials suggest they are simply doing more with less. For example, much of the overtime pay incurred during heightened levels of alert, participation on multi-jurisdictional task forces and working groups, and exhaustive planning and coordination have been absorbed internally. And, these new responsibilities come at a time when state police organizations, like local agencies across the country, face personnel shortfalls due to National Guard and Reserve activations.

How do state law enforcement agencies measure against local agencies? In general, law enforcement relationships and responsibilities continue to be assessed and redefined at all levels, and they will continue to evolve because of the changing nature of terrorist threats, prevention needs and transforming operations and tactics. The survey results do suggest, however, that certain responsibilities are more state or local in nature. State agencies were more likely to report allocating more or many more resources to the following operational responsibilities: intelligence gathering, analysis and sharing; security for critical infrastructure, special events and dignitaries; and commercial vehicle enforcement. Conversely, local agencies were more likely to indicate allocating more or many more resources to community policing, drug enforcement and traditional criminal investigation.

Shifting Federal Priorities

According to the *9/11 Commission Report* in 2004, "the concern with the FBI is that it has long favored its criminal justice mission over its national security mission." In 2002, the FBI announced a reshaping of priorities to guide future activities, with the new number one priority being "protecting the United States from terrorist attacks."

Shifting federal law enforcement priorities since Sept. 11 have forced state and local agencies to assume greater roles for those previously held federal responsibilities (e.g., financial crimes, bank robberies, organized crime and drug trafficking). These public safety and crime issues have not disappeared since Sept. 11, and state and local law enforcement agencies are obligated to address these deficiencies by assigning new personnel and shifting resources. Although the FBI may still be involved in these cases, they are much more selective today than before 2001.

In addition to the strain on state resources., state officials are concerned that the shift by the FBI away from traditional crimes will cascade to the state and local levels, thus hindering efforts to screen and analyze possible precursor crimes for linkages to larger-scale terrorist activities. There is a strong indication that a nexus exists among types of criminal activity, including illegal drug operations, money laundering, fraud, identity theft and terrorism.

Where Should States Focus Future Efforts?

CSG convened an expert work group in 2004 to explore these changing conditions and a broad range of alternatives to improve terrorism prevention at the state level. As states develop strategies concerning prevention and, to a lesser extent, emergency response, they should consider the following recommendations. (Visit *www.csg.org, keyword: protect,* for a comprehensive listing and description of recommendations for states on improving terrorism prevention efforts.)

Intelligence Fusion Centers and Analysts

"Fusion centers are an integral part of a state's strategy regarding the prevention of terrorism," said Colonel Bart Johnson of the New York State Police. The centralization of intelligence sharing and analysis at the state level, through one physical center or network of facilities, provides a means to gather and analyze disparate networks of information more effectively and efficiently.

Arizona was one of a handful of states to establish an information fusion center after Sept. 11. The Arizona Counter Terrorism Information Center is nationally recognized for providing tactical and strategic intelligence support to law enforcement officials across the state and for being uniquely located with the FBI's Joint Terrorism Task Force.

According to the National Criminal Intelligence Sharing Plan released in 2004, "Analysis is the portion of the intelligence process that transforms the raw data into products that are useful . . . without this portion of the process, we are left with disjointed pieces of information to which no meaning has been attached." Today, terrorism and crime prevention missions require a much more proactive approach to identify terrorists before they act and interdict attacks that are occurring. To meet this new need, states should pursue specialized intelligence analysts and improved analytical tools. The Florida Legislature, for example, authorized more than 30 new intelligence analyst positions following Sept. 11 to address this need.

Collaboration Among Law Enforcement Partners

"Terrorism prevention and response requires law enforcement agencies at all levels to work together, exchange information, train and coordinate efforts to a much greater extent than has ever occurred," said Sheriff Al Cannon of Charleston County, South Carolina.

The 9/11 Commission also recognized the importance of integrating law enforcement assets at all levels of government. The commissioners cite the nation's 66 Joint Terrorism Task Forces as a model intergovernmental approach. According to the commission, state and local law enforcement agencies "need more training and work with federal agencies so that they can cooperate more effectively with those federal authorities in identifying terrorist suspects."

To foster intergovernmental cooperation, the work group recommends that states do the following: draft and implement a statewide counterterrorism program for the law enforcement community; develop standardized training programs and tools; build partnerships with key residential, commercial property owners and security personnel and provide them with resources and tools to identify and report suspicious activities; and develop and implement a public education and outreach plan that establishes and formalizes public information policies and procedures that relate to terrorism prevention and response.

Integration with the Criminal Justice System

Not only must state agencies work closely with their local and federal counterparts, they must integrate terrorism prevention responsibilities into the criminal justice system at large. "It's now more important than ever to incorporate terrorism prevention into law enforcement's toolbox of crime fighting programs," said Rep. John Millner of Illinois.

Law enforcement officials generally agree that an association exists among types of criminal activity and terrorism. "Some terrorist operations do not rely on outside sources of money and may now be self-funding, either through legitimate employment or low-level criminal activity," said the 9/11 Commission. "Counterterrorism investigations often overlap or are cued by other criminal investigations, such as money laundering or the smuggling of contraband. In the field, the close connection to criminal work has many benefits."

Therefore, states should embrace an "all crimes" approach to terrorism prevention. This strategy ensures that possible precursor crimes are screened and analyzed for linkages to larger-scale terrorist activities. Also, states should develop and implement protocols to leverage all criminal justice and regulatory personnel, resources and systems, including local law enforcement; probation and parole officers; court documents such as pre-sentence investigations; and other state and local regulatory agencies.

Governance and Legal Issues

The work group addressed a number of state-level governance, planning and legal issues affecting state law enforcement and general terrorism prevention duties. First, states should consider regional approaches for homeland security planning and operational purposes. Creating or realigning existing regions or zones helps to remove or reduce local jurisdictional barriers for operational purposes and may enhance the distribution of federal grants.

States should also assign a principal point of oversight and review for homeland security through a legislative committee or multibranch commission. In many states, disparate oversight is provided through individual disciplines and policy areas such as agriculture, military affairs, public health and public safety. Similarly, certain aspects of the homeland security mission should be codified into law, such as key terms and definitions, general duties and responsibilities for the primary state-level stakeholders, and strategic planning processes.

Finally, as a condition of accepting federal funds, states should ensure that state and local agencies have plans in place to sustain newly acquired equipment and capabilities for the long term. Future homeland security grant proposals and initiatives, therefore, should sufficiently demonstrate these long-term obligations, strategies and plans.

States' Critical Role

Today, state police organizations are taking many lead and supporting roles in terrorism prevention. They provide a critical information sharing and analysis capability at the state level and a link between local and federal authorities. Their role is especially important in rural areas where resources are scarce. Thus, they provide a critical link among large and small local agencies.

In addition, state troopers patrol the interstate and state highways and serve as "eyes and ears" for suspicious activities, and would play a critical role in managing mass evacuations and

---

State Police in the United States—2000

- Every state except Hawaii has a state police or highway patrol agency.
- State police agencies range in size from 126 sworn officers (North Dakota) to 6,678 sworn officers (California).
- The average size of state police agencies is more than 1,000 sworn officers, compared to roughly 40 sworn officers for local police and sheriffs' agencies.
- State police agencies represent about 7 percent of all the non-military sworn law enforcement personnel in the United States. After factoring in other special-jurisdiction agencies at the state level (e.g., Bureaus of Investigation, Alcoholic Beverage Control Agencies), the states likely account for about 10 percent of all the sworn police in the United States.
- The states with the most sworn state police officers per population are Delaware (74 officers per 10,000 residents), Vermont (50) and West Virginia (38). These states also have the largest percentage of state police when compared to the entire law enforcement presence in the state. State police account for 33 percent of all sworn officers in Delaware and 29 percent in Vermont.
- The states with the fewest sworn state police officers per population are Wisconsin (9 officers per 10,000 residents), Georgia (10), Florida (10) and Minnesota (11) . Georgia has the smallest percentage of state police when compared to the entire law enforcement presence statewide—4 percent of all sworn officers.

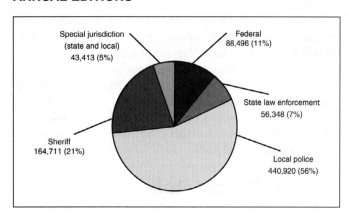

Figure 2 State, Local and Federal Law Enforcement Personnel, 2000 Full-Time Sworn Personnel.
Source: Bureau of Justice Statistics

aid for disaster areas. State police continue to play important roles guarding border crossings, seaports, airports and critical infrastructure. Furthermore, their specialized services (e.g., SWAT, canine units, air and marine assets) are often requested at the local levels, and are important assets to deter, interdict and respond to acts of terrorism.

State policy-makers should be informed about these changing conditions, as well as the risks that accompany them. For example, should drug enforcement resources be sacrificed at the expense of terrorism prevention? What new structures, capabilities and resources benefit both responsibilities? Police organizations are becoming more proactive through new information-led policing initiatives and tools such as crime mapping. Can state-level fusion centers support these new general crime fighting initiatives?

"The fact remains that the Sept. 11 terrorists lived and shopped in small towns across the country, frequented bars and other establishments in these small towns, rented cars and drove across states, and took flying lessons at small regional airports," stressed Sheriff Cannon. "If not the state, then who should take the lead in establishing and maintaining the unprecedented cooperation required to prevent a future attack?"

Today, a tremendous opportunity exists for states to leverage their law enforcement resources to prevent future acts of terrorism and to improve overall public safety.

This project was supported by Grant No. 2003-DT-CX-0004 awarded by the National Institute of Justice, Office of Justice Programs, U.S. Department of Justice. Points of view in this document are those of the authors and do not necessary represent the official policies of the U.S. Department of Justice.

CHAD FOSTER is chief public safety and justice policy analyst with The Council of State Governments. **GARY CORDNER, PH.D.,** is a professor with the College of Justice and Safety at Eastern Kentucky University.

From *State News*, March 2005, pp. 28–33. Published by the Council of State Governments. Reprinted with permission of the publisher and the authors.

State of Readiness

Oklahoma takes a collaborative approach to building a state-of-the-art regional emergency response system.

Doug Brandes

The people of Oklahoma know about disasters. In April 1995, domestic terrorism struck the Alfred P. Murrah Federal Building in Oklahoma City. In May 1999, a massive F-5 tornado with the highest wind speed ever recorded ripped through Oklahoma City and its suburbs. Since Nov. 1, wide-sweeping wildfires have ravaged more than half a million acres of the state. Oklahoma takes emergency response very, very seriously.

In more than two decades with the Oklahoma Highway Patrol, Major Kerry Pettingill served in specialized positions that include certified bomb technician, commander of the tactical teams and bomb squad, and liaison to the FBI's joint terrorism task force. He is also an IFSAC-certified hazmat technician and a graduate of the FBI's National Academy. In January 2004, Oklahoma Gov. Brad Henry appointed Pettingill as the director of the Oklahoma Office of Homeland Security.

Pettingill says the state is better prepared than ever for a natural disaster or a terrorist attack, and he would know. As one of the first responders on-scene at the Murrah Building bombing, be has witnessed the need first hand and has since led the way in building Oklahoma's state-of-the-art regional response system by collaborating with fire departments across the state.

"I don't want to say we've seen more disasters than other parts of the country," Pettingill says, "but we've had our share. The Murrah Federal Building attack instantly made everyone more aware. And because of that we focused on our statewide emergency response solutions before perhaps a lot of other states did."

How Is Oklahoma's Regional Response System Set Up?

Our regional response system includes 53 units representing multiple levels of response. It's funded through a U.S. Department of Homeland Security grant program. We just received delivery of five bedrock vehicles that form the core of the program—five large regional hazmat units. The next tiers are comprised of 20 intermediate units and 24 small decontamination units. Two urban search and rescue units and two mass-decontamination units round out the system.

The large hazmat/CBRNE units are manufactured by Pierce. Each requires a 20-membcr team consisting of personnel from several disciplines to operate, The intermediate units in the second level of the system have the same capabilities as the larger units, but need only nine people per team—that allows even the far corners of the state, much of which is rural, to have a response capability similar to the large units, with a smaller number of personnel. The small units require just six people to operate.

What Process Did You Go Through to Determine the Types of Vehicles and Equipment?

I was actually part of a team that started strategizing this in 2000, even before the World Trade Center attack. As a member of the Oklahoma Highway Patrol, I had been tasked with organizing a working group to deal with some Department of Justice finding that was coming into the state, and we were hoping to use it to enhance existing hazmat teams and bomb squads.

Then 9/11 happened. More federal funding became available, and we were designated by the governor as the state administrative agency to deal with these new DHS funds and to formulate a plan for a statewide emergency response program that would address a CBRNE attack. We knew the funding would be limited and instead of giving everyone a little, we determined a better use of the funds would be to build a statewide system.

Initially, we thought we'd position three large trailers across the state. But then one of the working group members suggested dividing the response into three groups—large, intermediate and small—with each type of vehicle able to do something a little bit different. That was an idea that I thought had merit, and we decided to go in that direction.

Eventually, the group defined the role of each unit. Small units for decontamination, then a significant step up for intermediate units to handle chemical, biological, radiological, nuclear and explosive response. We strategically placed the different units across the state in an effort to provide some level of response—quickly—to every Oklahoman. Originally, the group suggested that the large units be a larger truck and trailer. But then it was proposed that the large truck and trailer be changed to a single unit, because it would be more maneuverable and would better serve the large metropolitan areas. I, however, resisted that idea.

Why Were You Against It?

Well, DHS wouldn't allow single, integrated vehicles because they were afraid people would try to buy fire trucks with the grant money, and that wasn't acceptable for this program. But I decided to listen to the fire department chiefs on our committee who really thought this was a better way to go. We knew another state was in the process of disputing the rule with DHS, and we petitioned as well. As a result, DHS granted us a waiver to purchase the single units. Once the vehicles were delivered, I was really glad the chiefs had convinced me to change my mind.

It Sounds as Though You've Had a Good Relationship with the Fire Chiefs.

Most definitely. In fact, the chiefs influenced another significant change in our plans. They came back from responding to Hurricane Katrina damage with lessons learned and suggested we change our vehicle specs for the intermediate units right before we placed the order. From their experience in the Gulf Coast, they felt we needed more technical-rescue units that could support urban search and rescue.

I called together those chiefs who would be receiving an intermediate unit for a presentation from those proposing the change. It was after that meeting we switched eight of the intermediate hazmat units to technical-rescue team vehicles.

How Did You Decide Where the Response Units Would Be Housed to Provide Coverage Throughout the State?

Even before it was required by DHS, we divided the state into eight response regions—and that is not an easy thing to do. . . . Everyone from the legislators to the health-care officials had very strong opinions about how the boundaries should be determined. Ultimately, we decided to build the backbone of our program along the 1-44 corridor that runs across the state northeast to southwest—that's where nearly 75% of the population resides.

The five large hazmat units are placed in Lawton, Oklahoma City, Tulsa, Claremore and Moore/Norman, cities that are either on 1-44 or within close proximity. The intermediate units and decontamination units are scattered throughout the state. Most units are housed in fire departments; one is at a police department; one is at an emergency management agency; one is with a tribal group.

What Is the Nature of the Relationship Among Fire Departments and Other First-Response Groups in This System?

To take advantage of important support personnel, and to share costs, we are collaborating with a variety of organizations—mostly fire departments, but also police, emergency management and tribal groups. They assume primary responsibility for vehicle storage, maintenance, replenishment of supplies and personnel training at the levels that are required. In exchange, they are able to use the vehicle to respond to emergencies in their area. Most important, they're also on call as part of our statewide effort to provide blanket coverage to all of our citizens.

How Is Training Being Coordinated?

Our responders in Oklahoma are already trained at a high level. Thousands of them have received specialized training, and now

Now That's a Rapid Response

Lawton (Okla.) Fire Chief Bart Hadley

The day after its arrival, one of five hazmat vehicles was called into action at a 3,000-gallon jet-fuel spill that spread across 1-44 in Lawton, Okla.

Even with fire department pumpers and foam systems responding to clean up the scene, it was a day-long incident. And it was the perfect opportunity for Lawton's new hazmat response vehicle to show what it can do.

"Even though it wasn't yet fully equipped, we were able to deploy it as a command vehicle," says Lawton Fire Chief Bart Hadley. "It's not uncommon for an incident commander to operate out of the back of an suv for a short duration. But when you have a situation like this was, that can last hours, if not days, to have a piece of equipment like this response unit is just invaluable. It's just a huge benefit to be able to stand up inside it, to get away from the crowd and think straight while assessing the situation."

Hadley is certain the vehicle will improve the department's response in major tornadoes, too. "We'll be able to light up an area with some pretty amazing stadium lighting that can go up 25 or 30 feet. There's a weather station for wind speed and direction, And we'll have the ability to detect and determine what chemicals we're dealing with if something is unknown in a situation. I think it's going to greatly enhance the safety we can provide to citizens in our part of the state," he says.

everyone who will operate the regional response units in their community will receive additional training. With efficiency and ease of use in mind, each of the 53 units is interoperable, and training will be standardized. We think that's vital, so all responders have the confidence that their peers have received the same training. Last summer, [we] surveyed all the agencies that would be receiving one of the response units to determine exactly who has already received the hazmat and rescue training and who needs instruction. We've developed the appropriate courses, and they will be provided at no cost.

Communications Are a Huge Part of Emergency Response. Are You Addressing Those Issues?

Absolutely. One of the key things we learned from the Murrah Building bombing was how crucial it is—and how very difficult it can be—for various emergency responders to be able to communicate with each other at a disaster scene. We secured funding for the initial phase of an interoperable communications system that will expand the state's 800MHz radio system, so we can synchronize public safety radio frequencies during statewide emergencies.

Each of our intermediate and large units will have an interoperable switch that allows them to connect to disparate radio systems so they can all talk freely, using whatever radio systems the individual departments have. They'll be able to talk with the command center or set up other groups within the systems. . . .

This will be an ongoing program, and it will take several years to put it into operation throughout the state. Just recently, we've seen communications problems with other fire departments coming in from other states to help us with the wildfires. We've been trying to improve the communications systems for a long time, but this is the first time money has been available to actually fund a project of this magnitude.

Speaking of the Oklahoma Wildfires, What Other Types of Emergencies Do You Anticipate These Response Vehicles Addressing at the Local Level?

As you know, tornadoes are a major concern across Oklahoma. What many people don't realize is that nearly every time a tornado touches down, the destruction caused also involves some sort of hazmat situation, with turned-over tanks and broken lines. These vehicles will definitely be put into service then. There are certainly occasions when we have chemical spills and a variety of other types of situations, like train derailments.

The five large units, along with the other units in the system, give us capabilities that are state of the art. They're outfitted with the higher-end equipment that departments always want. . . .

The Heart of the Regional Response System

The Oklahoma Office of Homeland Security was one of the first to successfully petition DHS to allow the use of large single-unit vehicles instead of a truck/trailer configuration, citing the need for maximum versatility and maneuverability.

The five large regional hazmat response units that form the heart of the system are Pierce Command Response Vehicles, built on Pierce Lance chassis. Features include:

- Seating for six.
- Three-door cab.
- 22-inch raised roof.
- TAK-4 independent front suspension.
- Command Zone advanced electronics.
- 450hp Cummins engine and 400-amp alternator.
- Roll-up compartment doors and full-length awning on both sides.
- Adjustable tool boards and slide out trays.
- 30kw Onan PTO generator.
- Recessed walkway and tower.
  A partial list of other equipment includes:
- Fully interoperable communications system.
- Six-station computer network.
- Command and office supplies.
- Weatherpak-400 weather station.
- Global positioning system.
- Thermal-imaging camera.
- Satellite phone.
- Chemical detector.
- Radiation dosimeters.
- Hazmat suits and personal protective gear.
- Decontamination and cleaning equipment.
- Foam and agents.
- Absorbents, booms and containment equipment
- Plugging and patching supplies.
- Large tools and small hand tools.
- Lighting equipment.
- Safety supplies.

Now they'll have satellite capabilities for Internet connections. They'll be able to access information from Internet libraries on-scene. They can monitor air quality in hazmat situations. Overall, it's a very practical system.

With All of This in Place, How Close Is the Oklahoma Office of Homeland Security to Meeting Its Goals for the State?

We're well on our way. The goals of our program are three-fold: To prevent terrorist attacks, to reduce the state's vulnerability to attacks, and to respond and recover if a terrorist attack should occur. We want to provide every Oklahoman a level of security and peace of mind that if a response to a natural disaster or weapon of mass destruction is needed, we have the capability to respond within about a two-hour timeframe. With the system we're implementing, we believe we'll be able to do that.

We have a good start with our regional response system, but the project continues to evolve. As we see a need we are open to incorporating additional units. I don't think you can ever be satisfied. Our duty is to use what grants we receive so that the greatest number of Oklahomans benefit. I think we're doing just that.

DOUG BRANDES is a freelance writer.

New York State of Mind

Is the Department of Homeland Security really shortchanging New York?

JAMIE DEAL

New York officials, along with the New York Times and other media, recently blasted Homeland Security secretary Michael Chertoff for announcing cuts in anti-terror funding to New York City. Instead of the $208 million given last year, the city will receive $124 million.

In response, an irritated Mayor Michael Bloomberg declared his city the most at risk. "When you stop a terrorist," he explained, "they have a map of New York City in their pocket. They don't have a map of any of the other 46 or 45 places." Representative Peter King labeled the reduction "indefensible and disgraceful," and went so far as to threaten the Department of Homeland Security: "It's a knife in the back of New York, and I'm going to do everything I can to make them very sorry they made this decision." Senator Hillary Clinton followed suit by calling the cuts "outrageous" and stating that they "demonstrate this administration's continued failure to grasp the unique security threats that face New York." Senator Chuck Schumer scoffed at the announcement with a hint of big-city condescension: "Georgia got a 40 percent increase. Somehow this administration thinks that Georgia peanut farmers are more at risk than the Empire State Building."

On cue, the New York Times published an editorial, "Pork 1, Antiterrorism 0," in which it accused the DHS of "dangerously [shortchanging]" New York and Washington while "[showering] money on Omaha and Louisville." As the Times sees it, this slash in spending just goes to show how little President Bush and the Republicans have prepared the nation for another attack.

But these criticisms ignore some key facts. The Urban Areas Security Initiative—the grant program through which DHS funds are distributed—was allotted $757.3 million this year ($119 million less than last year) and 46 metropolitan areas received money. Even after its 40 percent decrease to $124.4 million, New York got over 16 percent of the total funding this year. Instead of being "dangerously shortchanged," New York is getting more than its fair share—especially considering Chertoff's explanation for the funding readjustments:

"First of all . . . I don't think it's fair to describe them as cuts," the Homeland Security chief told a group at the Brookings Institution on June 1. "Last year, New York got $200 million. This year, we're going to give them $124 million under this particular program. But last year was an artificially elevated number to make up from the very low grant the year before. If you average out the prior three-year grants, you're going to see this year is directly in line with what we've done over the past four years."

This year's grant is not punishment for New York; it is a return to normalcy. Furthermore, this readjustment has not only expanded the Urban Areas Security Initiative to other large and vulnerable cities, but also reduced the program's overall budget.

Because of the reduction in New York and other cities' grants, the Los Angeles/Long Beach area got an $11.4 million increase, and previously neglected cities such as Jacksonville and Sacramento also benefited. In addition, Georgia's 40 percent increase—the one lamented by Senator Schumer—will help not only that state's peanut farmers; it will provide greater security for Atlanta, the state capital and home to the largest skyscraper in the South.

Mayor Anthony Williams of Washington, D.C.—a city that saw a $31 million reduction to $46.5 million in grants—claims the nation's capital has been mistreated, too. But by April last year, Washington had left $120 million unused. At the time, former Rep. Christopher Cox, who chaired the Homeland Security Committee, cited this as a prime example of government waste. Washington accepted the grants but lacked the organization required to effectively use those funds. It makes sense that the city would get less money this year.

Philadelphia and Phoenix, two of the nation's largest cities, were truly shortchanged. Philadelphia received $19.5 million, while Phoenix got $3.9 million—a little over three percent of New York's grant. Phillip Gordon, the mayor of Phoenix, called this year's grant "incomprehensible," as his city's dams and nuclear power plant make it highly vulnerable.

As with any such grant program, there are certainly flaws in the Urban Areas Security Initiative. Perhaps Homeland Security should reevaluate cities like Omaha and Louisville, and give more funding to places like Philadelphia and Phoenix. But this does not excuse the clumsy rhetoric of those who have unfairly maligned the department and ignored facts.

JAMIE DEAL is an intern at The Weekly Standard.

Blame Amid the Tragedy

Gov. Blanco and Mayor Nagin failed their constituents.

BOB WILLIAMS

As the devastation of Hurricane Katrina continues to shock and sadden the nation, the question on many lips is, Who is to blame for the inadequate response? As a former state legislator who represented the legislative district most impacted by the eruption of Mount St. Helens in 1980, I can fully understand and empathize with the people and public officials over the loss of life and property.

Many in the media are turning their eyes toward the federal government, rather than considering the culpability of city and state officials. I am fully aware of the challenges of having a quick and responsive emergency response to a major disaster. And there is definitely a time for accountability; but what isn't fair is to dump on the federal officials and avoid those most responsible—local and state officials who failed to do their job as the first responders. The plain fact is, lives were needlessly lost in New Orleans due to the failure of Louisiana's governor, Kathleen Blanco, and the city's mayor, Ray Nagin.

The primary responsibility for dealing with emergencies does not belong to the federal government. It belongs to local and state officials who are charged by law with the management of the crucial first response to disasters. First response should be carried out by local and state emergency personnel under the supervision of the state governor and his emergency operations center.

The actions and inactions of Gov. Blanco and Mayor Nagin are a national disgrace due to their failure to implement the previously established evacuation plans of the state and city. Gov. Blanco and Mayor Nagin cannot claim that they were surprised by the extent of the damage and the need to evacuate so many people. Detailed written plans were already in place to evacuate more than a million people. The plans projected that 300,000 people would need transportation in the event of a hurricane like Katrina. If the plans had been implemented, thousands of lives would likely have been saved.

In addition to the plans, local, state and federal officials held a simulated hurricane drill 13 months ago, in which widespread flooding supposedly trapped 300,000 people inside New Orleans. The exercise simulated the evacuation of more than a million residents. The problems identified in the simulation apparently were not solved.

A year ago, as Hurricane Ivan approached, New Orleans ordered an evacuation but did not use city or school buses to help people evacuate. As a result many of the poorest citizens were unable to evacuate. Fortunately, the hurricane changed course and did not hit New Orleans, but both Gov. Blanco and Mayor Nagin acknowledged the need for a better evacuation plan. Again, they did not take corrective actions. In 1998, during a threat by Hurricane George, 14,000 people were sent to the Superdome and theft and vandalism were rampant due to inadequate security. Again, these problems were not corrected.

The New Orleans contingency plan is still, as of this writing, on the city's Web site, and states: "The safe evacuation of threatened populations is one of the principle [sic] reasons for developing a Comprehensive Emergency Management Plan." But the plan was apparently ignored.

Mayor Nagin was responsible for giving the order for mandatory evacuation and supervising the actual evacuation: His Office of Emergency Preparedness (not the federal government) must coordinate with the state on elements of evacuation and assist in directing the transportation of evacuees to staging areas. Mayor Nagin had to be encouraged by the governor to contact the National Hurricane Center before he finally, belatedly, issued the order for mandatory evacuation. And sadly, it apparently took a personal call from the president to urge the governor to order the mandatory evacuation.

The city's evacuation plan states: "The city of New Orleans will utilize all available resources to quickly and safely evacuate threatened areas." But even though the city has enough school and transit buses to evacuate 12,000 citizens per fleet run, the mayor did not use them. To compound the problem, the buses were not moved to high ground and were flooded. The plan also states that "special arrangements will be made to evacuate persons unable to transport themselves or who require specific lifesaving assistance. Additional personnel will be recruited to assist in evacuation procedures as needed." This was not done.

The evacuation plan warned that "if an evacuation order is issued without the mechanisms needed to disseminate the information to the affected persons, then we face the possibility of having large numbers of people either stranded and left to the mercy of a storm, or left in an area impacted by toxic materials." That is precisely what happened because of the mayor's failure.

Instead of evacuating the people, the mayor ordered the refugees to the Superdome and Convention Center without adequate security and no provisions for food, water and sanitary conditions. As a result people died, and there was even rape committed, in these facilities. Mayor Nagin failed in his responsibility to provide public safety and to manage the orderly evacuation of the citizens of New Orleans. Now he wants to blame Gov. Blanco and the Federal Emergency Management Agency. In an emergency the first requirement is for the city's emergency center to be linked to the state emergency operations center. This was not done.

The federal government does not have the authority to intervene in a state emergency without the request of a governor. President Bush declared an emergency prior to Katrina hitting New Orleans, so the only action needed for federal assistance was for Gov. Blanco to request the specific type of assistance she needed. She failed to send a timely request for specific aid.

In addition, unlike the governors of New York, Oklahoma and California in past disasters, Gov. Blanco failed to take charge of the situation and ensure that the state emergency operation facility was in constant contact with Mayor Nagin and FEMA. It is likely that thousands of people died because of the failure of Gov. Blanco to implement the state plan, which mentions the possible need to evacuate up to one million people. The plan clearly gives the governor the authority for declaring an emergency, sending in state resources to the disaster area and requesting necessary federal assistance.

State legislators and governors nationwide need to update their contingency plans and the operation procedures for state emergency centers. Hurricane Katrina had been forecast for days, but that will not always be the case with a disaster (think of terrorist attacks). It must be made clear that the governor and locally elected officials are in charge of the "first response."

I am not attempting to excuse some of the delays in FEMA's response. Congress and the president need to take corrective action there, also. However, if citizens expect FEMA to be a first responder to terrorist attacks or other local emergencies (earthquakes, forest fires, volcanoes), they will be disappointed. The federal government's role is to offer aid upon request.

The Louisiana Legislature should conduct an immediate investigation into the failures of state and local officials to implement the written emergency plans. The tragedy is not over, and real leadership in the state and local government are essential in the months to come. More importantly, the hurricane season is still upon us, and local and state officials must stay focused on the jobs for which they were elected—and not on the deadly game of passing the emergency buck.

MR. WILLIAMS is president of the Evergreen Freedom Foundation, a free market public policy research organization in Olympia, Wash.

UNIT 5
First Responders

Unit Selections

Key Points to Consider

- How can the two competing paradigms in antiterrorist policing be reconciled?

- Why is communication between first responders critical?

- What role does the community college system play in first response?

Student Web Site
www.mhcls.com/online

Internet References
Further information regarding these Web sites may be found in this book's preface or online.

U.S. Fire Administration (USFA)
   http://www.usfa.dhs.gov

Responding First to Bioterrorism
   http://www.nap.edu/firstresponders

First responders play a critical role in any disaster response. The heroic efforts of firefighters, police officers, and emergency medical personnel in New York City and Washington D.C. on September 11th and the sacrifices that they made are eternalized in the many lives that they helped save. As the United States prepares for future attacks, the role of first responders clearly merits closer examination. The term first responder, however, does not only apply to local emergency personnel. It includes people at various levels that may be directly involved in homeland security efforts.

While the battles over increased federal funding and training for police and fire departments continue, most have come to realize the importance of individuals in homeland security. As the actions of the passengers on United Airlines flight 93—which crashed outside of Pittsburgh, Pennsylvania on September 11th—indicate, once people understand the nature of the threat, they are willing to become involved, and when necessary, even give their lives to save others. Realizing the plans of the terrorists, the passengers of flight 93 decided that they would rather take their chances fighting the hijackers than be used in a terrorist plot to harm others. The selfless action of these passengers may have done more to prevent another terrorist attack than billions of dollars spent on airport security.

Beyond response to major disasters, local law enforcement, fire prevention, and medical personnel play an important role in homeland security. They provide a first point of contact for citizens and are in a unique position to detect, report, and help prevent terrorist activity. Respect for people and good policing builds trust and support for police officers in local communities. Information from these communities may help in the early detection of potential threats. Fire departments play a critical role in the early identification of possible vulnerabilities and the planning of emergency responses and evacuations. Their contacts with local businesses and industry put them in a position to conduct emergency response training and help in emergency planning. Local medical personnel are the first point of contact for threats to public health. Specialized training and access to appropriate equipment and resources can help in the early detection and containment of public health threats.

Managing the interactions among the first responders from various levels of government continues to be a challenge. Lack of planning and coordination can lead to conflicts, confusion, and duplication of efforts. As federal emergency management exercises provide opportunities to practice these interactions, the lack of interoperability, communication problems, and jurisdictional disputes continue to impede effective cooperation.

The articles in this unit examine how first responders have adapted to continuing changes in the homeland security environment.

Antiterrorist Policing in New York City after 9/11: Comparing Perspectives on a Complex Process

After the attacks on September 11, When the World Trade Center was attacked on the morning of September 11, 2001, there was a significant redeployment of law enforcement in the United States, especially in New York City, which included: greater public displays of weapons; increased suspicion, surveillance, registration, detention and deportation of Arab and Muslim immigrants; the prevention of bias crimes against those same people; training for first response to future disasters; and greater investigation co-operation between municipal and federal agencies. This article explores aspects of these changes through the security-civil liberties debate, but goes beyond this dichotomy to include less explicit aspects of antiterrorist policing like dealing with trauma and popular myths of the hero. The process is described from three perspectives, each situated in a different paradigm of social analysis and practice: the rational-Enlightenment paradigm, the power paradigm, and the psycho-cultural paradigm. Some behaviors can be accurately described from a one of these points of view, but no single perspective exhaustively explains all behaviors, especially complex changes in large institutional settings. This article explores simultaneous dimensions of a multilevel process allowing for a causal pluralism, rather than mere relativism.

Avram Bornstein

When the World Trade Center was attacked on the morning of September 11, 2001, the familiar order of activity quickly unraveled across New York City. Thousands of police were immediately pulled from their usual assignments and put on the streets. Officers who normally taught at the academy, drove the bus to the jail, verified the backgrounds of new recruits, or investigated property crimes, found themselves guarding the United Nations, the Empire State Building, bridges and tunnels, Grand Central Station, and dozens of other locations that supervisors decided were possible targets. Even police academy cadets were sent into the streets to direct traffic.

The police went on twelve hour shifts to increase the number of uniformed bodies on the streets. Many officers explained that, with the commute, twelve hour shifts often meant fourteen to sixteen hour days. Sleep deprivation became a frequent topic of conversation. In addition to guarding and directing traffic, they were digging in the destruction at Ground Zero, sifting through the debris, and helping identify bodies. The New York Police Department (NYPD) started spending about $2.2 million per day on overtime—over $200 million in the first three months (see Gardiner 2001). In all of 2000, with a budget swollen by aggressive street enforcement funding, the Department only spent a total of $237 million for overtime. By comparison, the Fire Department spent $49 million in related overtime, the Sanitation Department spent $23 million in overtime for cleanup, and the Department of Design and Construction spent $199 million to hire private companies to clear over a million tons of debris.

Besides the overtime and sleeplessness, the emotional experience of the job changed after the attack. Most obviously, the death of police, firefighters and emergency service workers made all of them heroes in the eyes of New Yorkers and beyond. Baseball caps and tee-shirts with NYPD and FDNY letters or insignia became ubiquitous. Professionally printed posters and handmade signs honoring their service were plastered on walls. New Yorkers brought flowers to police and fire stations and applauded officers in the streets. One officer said he received thanks and praise from a man he was arresting for a petty larceny. Police-community relations, formerly tainted with high profile shameful events like the torture of Abner Louima and the shooting deaths of Amadou Diallo and Patrick Dorismond, shifted to adoration.

These changes were only the beginning. While the increasing presence and power of armed forces in public life was a trend before 9/11 (see Kraska 2001; Parenti 1999), a surge in militarism occurred immediately after the 9/11 attack. Not only did armed forces enter Afghanistan and eventually Iraq, but armed personnel inside the United States were redeployed with new and greater force. Across the country, airports, bridges, tunnels, train and bus stations and American landmarks had permanent guards. In New York City, special NYPD operations with names like Hercules and Atlas deployed a massive uniformed, and sometimes heavily armed force to the streets.

Explaining the Organization of State Arms

There has been disagreement to the point of controversy about the motivation for the armed and policing responses domestically (not to mention internationally) in the wake of 9/11. For some, the expansion of policing in the United States has been welcomed. Hardly an inconvenience at all, it has made them feel safer and more secure from the danger of political violence. For others, the new policing is political opportunism and tyranny at the expense of democracy. Many journalistic debates, panels and lectures have been framed around the problem of balancing the needs of security and civil liberties. One side criticizes the use of state force, and the other side defends it as necessary. Aware of these arguments, politicians regularly pay lip-service to both, and both seem to influence institutional change.

The security argument is the operative public logic of policing in most secular democracies (e.g. Bratton 1998). This perspective exists within a rational-Enlightenment paradigm that sees society as a thing to be measured in statistical forms and managed with policy for the common good. The security argument says that violence and suffering can be minimized in a society by empowering specialized state agents, police and soldiers, to defend against the threats of other states or domestic criminals. State organized force is a tool to be used efficiently and judiciously to establish order, safety, and security. Among social scientists, Silverman (1999) provides a valuable example from this perspective in his study of the reorganization of the NYPD administration in the 1990s. According to Silverman, rationally planned methods of preemption, like aggressive summonsing for "quality of life" violations, and of greater managerial accountability, such as increasing statistical scrutiny and decentralizing command, succeeded in lowering crime for everyone's benefit.

The civil liberties argument, often critical of security theory and practice, usually stems from a power paradigm. This paradigm is often suspicious of the "common good" inherent in the rational-Enlightenment vision of society and sees state agents as political participants in a contest between oppressed people and ruling groups, or between different factions of ruling groups. From this perspective, policing is not about defending the community, but fighting the community, or a segment of it, for a ruling group. For example, Parenti (1999) argues that the "war for all seasons"—the drug war—was introduced for "managing and containing the new surplus populations created by neoliberal policies" (45). As Reaganomics exacerbated existing inequalities of wealth, he argues, more police, mandatory sentencing, and prisons repressed the disadvantaged. The power paradigm contends that the rational-Enlightenment focus on security is only an ideological cover for what is *really* happening, which is a calculated political contest of power and domination.

The security-civil liberties debate, while ubiquitous in public discourse, is too narrowly conceived. Neither the security nor civil liberties orientations can exhaustively account for developments of antiterrorist policing in New York City. While relevant and useful, they are both too strategic. There are aspects of behavior that may be contrary to any clearly stated, or even knowingly concealed interest. Behavior cannot always be reduced to such instrumental logic or self-serving goals. Action may be more expressive of meaning or myth than organized around achieving clear ends, and humans sometimes do things contrary to self-preserving interests.

Psychologists and anthropologists often specialize in the interpretation of different kinds of behavior and meaning. When it comes to violence, psychological theories emphasize individual development and the role of frustration in the creation of aggression projected either toward the source of frustration or a substitute object. Desires to hurt or destroy often come from experiences of injury or loss that produce reactive aggression. From the cultural angle, anthropologists describe how aggression and violence are constructed through local meanings, shared languages, or other symbolic systems. Stories, myths, and social life become the emotional and practical framework through and in which individual and collective acts of violence are organized. With somewhat fluid disciplinary boundaries, both anthropology and psychology can explain violence with reference to issues of emotion, identity or recognition.

Among such studies of police in the United States, Mastrofski, Reisig and McCluskey (2002) examine how disrespect, a very subjective experience communicated in locally specific ways, is a key to factor leading to arrest. Jerome Skolnick and James Fyfe (1993) describe how bad policing is often the result of a police department "culture" that tolerates or promotes "the siege mentality," the "Dirty Harry" personality, or the "code of silence" (see also Kappeler, Sluder and Alpert 1994). The choice to name one pattern of behavior after the famous movie character played by Clint Eastwood indicates the authors' awareness of the symbolic power of Hollywood. Despite the common rhetoric of technocratic efficiency, from this paradigm state violence is as much a performance of self as a pragmatic, instrumental plan.

This article provides an overview of the growth of antiterrorist policing in New York City post 9/11 from these three paradigms. The goal is not to decide which perspective is privileged over the others, nor to explore the debates within each paradigm, but to see how multiple motives simultaneously operate in multilevel institutional change. This is intended to allow for a causal pluralism, rather than mere relativism. After describing this plurality in the case at hand, the conclusion considers how these anthropological insights complement either of the other operating logics.

In addition to collecting articles from local newspapers, the data here were gleaned from conversations and observations in New York City, particularly among two of the populations most affected by the changes: Arab New Yorkers and police. As a resident of the City and following years of research with Palestinians in the West Bank (see Bornstein 2001, 2002), I have been in contact with New York Arabic communities in some way for over a decade. Formally, I began documentary video work on Arab life in New York City in 1997, producing two 50 minute documentaries based on over sixty hours of video taped interviews and observations. 1 have participated in dozens of conferences, panels and public conversations mainly on Israel-Palestine, but also on the tragedy of 9/11 and the new wars in the Muslim world. Informally, I have been in close conversation with a handful of Arabic speaking friends, neighbors, and students. Indeed, on the morning of 9/11 I witnessed the disaster in the company of two recent Syrian immigrants who had spent the night in my downtown Manhattan apartment.

Since June 2001, I have also been leading a discussion-based course exclusively for NYPD officers on racial and ethnic discrimination in policing in New York City. I was teaching the course in September 2001 when the disaster occurred, and have taught continuously since. I and a co-professor sit in a circle with about 20–25 police officers, approximately 150 over seven semesters, for 3 credit-hours a week, asking questions to elicit discussion on racism and anti-racist strategies in their jobs. The classes are voluntary, so officers are self-selected and not representative of the NYPD in terms of race and gender: there are always a number of women and significantly more than half are people of color, both unlike the Department, which is disproportionately comprised of white men in comparison to the City's population.

There are clearly limitations to generalizations based on anecdotal data collected while participating in these roles. However, the tremendous sense of vulnerability among many Arab Americans, as well as the aversion of police, like other workers and managers, from public investigation, make such participant-observation critical to describing patterns of behavior and experience that may be hidden from other methods of inquiry.

Security and the Rational-Enlightenment Paradigm

In the United States, policing agents are organized into hierarchical bureaucratic agencies, with their own internal divisions, sanctioned to use force to maintain public order and uphold state laws. Like other large bureaucracies, efficient management in police organizations is a central orienting ideal. The NYPD has been celebrated as a model department for its adaptation during the 1990s of modern management principles such as clarifying mission statements, evaluating performance with timely data, enforcing accountability, and supporting innovative responses to emerging problems. Specifically, the NYPD implemented a system of evaluation and accountability called CompStat, for Computer Statistics, in which precinct commanders are regularly called to police headquarters, where "top brass" publically review the numerical counts of complaints, summonses, and arrests from their command area (see Silverman 1999; Weisburd et. al. 2003). Decision making based on timely numerical data has made the NYPD a leading example of the rational-Enlightenment paradigm in policing. In the wake of 9/11, the rational-Enlightenment paradigm dominated the public face of police decision making in the expanded investigation and protection of New Yorkers.

Management Decisions

What happened in New York City occurred in the context of administrative changes in law enforcement at the federal level. The Transportation security Administration, a federal agency, took airport security away from private contractors and increased the number of marshals riding on planes. By March 2003, the newly created Department of Homeland security (DHS) headed by Tom Ridge took responsibility for 21 government agencies. This centralization of authority was meant to overcome the glaring failure, noted by the Joint Inquiry of the House and Senate intelligence committees into the 9/11 attacks, of the Central Intelligence Agency (CIA) to share the names of two suspected assailants with the Federal Bureau of Investigation (FBI) and immigration authorities. The DHS' Operation Liberty Shield centralized policing and called on a number of Federal, state and local agencies to provide greater security at borders, transportation systems, power plants, farm and food facilities, chemical plants and other critical locations (Ridge 2003). Among other significant changes, the DHS took immigration and customs away from the Justice Department's Immigration and Naturalization Service (INS) and gave it to two new agencies, the Bureau of Immigration and Customs Enforcement and the Bureau of Customs and Border Enforcement, both of which are under the leadership of Under Secretary for Border and Transportation Security Asa Hutchinson.

In the NYPD, major changes were initiated less than three and a half months after 9/11 when Michael Bloomberg replaced Rudolph Giuliani as mayor, and invited a previous commissioner, Raymond Kelly, back to New York to serve a second time. Kelly made appointments that brought significant international experience and high-level connections to the NYPD including Deputy Commissioner of Counterterrorism Frank Libutti, a retired US Marine Corps lieutenant General (who left a year later), and Deputy Commissioner of Intelligence David Cohen, a former CIA operations chief.

The NYPD began to strengthen investigation capacity. They initiated an antiterrorist telephone hot-line campaign on busses and subways, which urged people to report suspicious people or objects. A new high-tech counter-terrorism center was built. The number of antiterrorist detectives quickly rose from 20 to 120 to investigate public tips and vendors of supplies useful to terrorists such as chemical distributors or scuba equipment retailers. The Department conducted a language survey that revealed only 27 Arabic speakers on the force (Gardiner and Parascandola 2002). Besides community affairs, several Arabic speaking officers were transferred to intelligence and more were sought in recruiting.

NYPD investigators have been sent across the country and overseas to train with police in cities including London, Hamburg, Toronto, Lyon, and Tel Aviv (Weiss 2002). Many officers have received an assortment of tactical training from the Federal government and other outside experts, from terrorist profiling to first response protocols for future attacks. Terrorism drills, some involving over a thousand first responders, have tested how agencies like the NYPD, the FDNY, and the city's Department of Environmental Protection, respond and interact in a mock emergency (El-Ghobashy 2004). Assignment to the Joint

Terrorist Task Force put officers in contact with the DHS, the FBI, the U.S. Marshals Service, the U.S. Department of State's Diplomatic security Service, the Bureau of Alcohol, Tobacco and Firearms, the New York State Police, the New York/New Jersey Port Authority Police Department and the U.S. Secret Service. One of the main difficulties these agencies face in coordination is deciding who has jurisdiction over complex cases and who is best able to execute investigations.

There has also been a heavily militarized aspect of the response. The NYPD rotates six helicopters to surveil the city from above. New Yorkers also witnessed Operation Hercules on the ground in which heavily armed special interdiction forces show up at different locations with no obvious pattern (Horowitz 2003). According to Police Commissioner Raymond Kelly, the random nature of this show of force is meant to throw off possible terrorists. Kelly said:

> "We have done a fairly comprehensive examination of al-Qaida doctrine, al-Qaida handbooks. We know that they make a major commitment to reconnaissance, they make a major commitment to planning. So if you change the pattern of normal security or normal enforcement, we believe that can be disconcerting and disruptive" (Interview on 60 Minutes, March 23, 2003).

While such special tactics police are only a small group, almost any police officer can participate in Operation Atlas, which involves about 1000 officers and costs about $5 million a week in overtime. Since 9/11, this program has paid for 24-hour police patrol at priority locations in New York City like bridges, tunnels, transportation hubs, important landmarks and other potential targets.

Bias Backlash

Arab and South Asian Muslim communities in the New York metropolitan area were traumatized by the 9/11 attack like most New York communities, but they suffered an additional fear: the fear of being considered the enemy and of retribution. The Arab American Anti-Discrimination Committee reported that in the United States in the first nine weeks after 9/11 there were over 700 violent incidents, including several murders, targeting Arab Americans, or those mistaken for Arabs or Muslims like Sikhs and other South Asians (Ibish 2003; see also Human Rights Watch 2002). New York City was no exception to this trend. Before 9/11, there were 301 hate crimes recorded for the year, an average of 33 a month. In the month after 9/11, there were 142, with about 100 involving people of Middle Eastern descent (Hamil 2001). Common objects of such hate crimes were neighborhood mosques, deli-supermarkets owned by immigrants, and taxi drivers.

Potential victims responded in a variety of ways to their new situation. Some taxi drivers hid their Muslim names and plastered the car with American flags. Some men shaved their beards, stopped wearing traditional dress and tried to be discreet in their expressions of tradition, although two female students chose to wear hijab to support their "sisters." Abdo Zindani of the Yemeni American Association, advised fellow Arabs in the United States

to "keep a low profile" by avoiding going outdoors, especially as groups of young men or in traditional dress (Upadhyay 2003). Community activists organized escorts for women dressed in hijab head-coverings and Sikhs who wear turbans.

Most police departments were caught unprepared for bias attacks despite previous problems such as those during the first Gulf War or following the bombing in Oklahoma when people mistakenly assumed the perpetrators were Muslim. There were few plans to prevent hate crimes. In New York City, police were not systematically deployed to sensitive locations. Some members of the community said that patrol officers even dissuaded victims from pressing charges by expressing sympathy for, or naturalizing the rage of the assailants. Complainants were told to stay off the street, which some resented.

However, as the phone calls began to come in, precinct commanders with significant Arab or Muslim populations, or noticeable mosques or Muslim schools, like the 68th Precinct in Bay Ridge Brooklyn, organized meetings with identifiable groups and leaders to open communication. Supervisors developed protocols to prevent hate crimes when world events, like the invasion of Iraq, make them more likely to occur. According to a survey by the Arab-American Anti-Discrimination Committee, once the problems were reported, the police department responded well to the needs of local communities for protection from hate or bias crimes. By the summer 2003, the Department had also spent tens of thousands of dollars adding a new segment to their "Streetwise" sensitivity training for rookies and cadets to educate them about the Arab and Muslim residents in the City.

The NYPD, faced with a problem from outside the City of potentially apocalyptic proportion, made fighting terrorism a priority in many ways. They focused the rank and file on guarding high-profile targets, trained for future disasters, increased the numbers of dedicated investigators who work locally, nationally and internationally, deployed highly visible armed forces, and addressed security for communities threatened by backlash bias crimes. For those from a security or rational-Enlightenment paradigm, these Department decisions address the explicit goals to protect and serve the community in the context of an international conflict.

Civil Liberties and the Power Paradigm

In contrast to the rational-Enlightenment paradigm on the reorganization of state security, the power paradigm, often heard in the media and in government opposition, is suspicious of the ruling administration and the police. Common in the community of activists who came together to support those Arabs, Muslims and Sikhs who suffered post-9/11, this paradigm sees government officials exploiting the fears of 9/11 to increase policing powers to consolidate political control for their patrons. Like the Federal exclusion of Chinese immigrants, President Wilson's deportation of thousands of immigrants during the Palmer Raids, President Roosevelt's internment of 120,000 Japanese Americans, McCarthy's blacklisting and Hoover's

COINTELPRO, to mention just a few famous examples, these new panicked measures are considered unnecessary to preserve national security. On the contrary, they violate civil liberties raising the danger that these new powers will be used to repress political opponents. Groups such as Operation Rescue, People for the Ethical Treatment of Animals, the Environmental Liberation Front, Greenpeace, fair trade advocates, or any other form of vocal political dissent can be investigated under the banner of fighting terrorism. Those protesting the wars in Iraq and Afghanistan have also felt what they consider political opposition in the name of security. Two particular recent changes are highlighted by this paradigm: the expansion of surveillance permitted in the Patriot Act and the selective enforcement of immigration laws.

Targeting Immigrants

The main brunt of the Federal government's antiterrorist efforts have fallen on immigrants from Arab and Muslim countries. In the days following 9/11 there was a roundup of over 1,000 men, most of them Arabs and Muslims. The number is unclear because, despite lawsuits for disclosure, the Justice Department stopped releasing figures after the number reached 1,200. Chief Immigration Judge Michael Creppy issued a memo to all immigration judges on September 21, 2001, that all deportation proceedings directed by the Justice Department were to be closed to the public and the press (ACLU 2002a). More than 600 Arab and Muslim immigrants were soon deported on immigration violations. According to the Office of Inspector General of the Department of Justice, there was misconduct by federal officials including indiscriminate arrests, severe confinement at the federal detention facility in Brooklyn, denial of access to lawyers and family, physical and verbal abuse by guards and hundreds held longer than their alleged immigration violations, many minor, warranted (NYCLU 2003a).

In June 2002 the Department of Justice issued notices of the new National Security Entry-Exit Registration System requiring all non-citizen men over the age of 16 from a list of 25 countries, mostly but not exclusively Muslim, deemed to be of "highest terrorism risk" to register in person at Federal offices by certain deadlines to be fingerprinted, photographed, and questioned.

The NYPD was enlisted by the FBI to carry out about 80 investigations (New York Law Journal 2001). Although previously forbidden from contacting the INS, the NYPD may have been asked to help the Federal government track and deport absconders. An ACLU lawsuit, *National Council of La Raza et al. v. Ashcroft*, filed in December 2003 in a U.S. District Court on behalf of a coalition of seven civil rights and immigrant rights groups, seeks disclosure of a new Department of Justice policy that reverses Federal policy by giving local police powers to arrest and detain immigrants believed to be in violation of non-criminal provisions of Federal immigration laws (ACLU 2003). NYPD officers have said that making contact with immigration was not allowed in the past, and that the present is somewhat unclear. Several understood the old logic that such actions may harm their relationships with immigrant communities and divert local law enforcement resources. If undocumented people were hesitant before 9/11 to report to the police serious criminal activity, knowledge of police cooperation with immigration officials will make them avoid it completely. For example, even when assaulted and stabbed by five men while walking home in Midwood in January 2003 because of his "Middle Eastern" looks, a Muslim immigrant told the hospital the wound was self-inflicted and did not file a crime report because his visa had expired (Ruiz 2003). "According to one estimate, 80 percent of hate crimes go unreported in the United States due to a variety of factors, such as fear of police, lack of knowledge about civil rights and the failure to classify incidents as bias-motivated" (Upadhyay 2003).

Community-based Organizations

Undocumented immigrant men in the United States for years, married to legal residents, who have citizen children and applications pending with immigration authorities, thought the registration would be easy. Unfortunately, reports of problems were widespread. Hundreds of men and teenage boys were again being arrested and detained on immigration violation charges, and 13,000 Arab and Muslim men who registered faced deportation (Casimir 2003a, 2003b; Hall 2003). As a consequence, "the fabric of neighborhoods is thinning. Families are packing up; some are splitting up. Rather than come forward and risk deportation, an unknowable number of immigrants have burrowed deeper underground. Others have simply left—for Canada or for their homeland" (Swarns 2003). Some young men already working illegally on non-immigrant or out-of-status visas quickly arranged to marry American citizens for a payment.

In the summer 2002, Emira Habiby Browne, the executive director of the Arab-American Family Support Center in Brooklyn, said 500 people came to her organization looking for legal help (Casimir 2003a). The Family Support Center, and other organizations like the Council for American Islamic Relations (CAIR), the Council of Pakistan Organization, the Salam Arabic Lutheran Church of Brooklyn, the Saint Mary and Saint Antonius Coptic Orthodox Church of Queens and Brooklyn's Islamic Society of Bay Ridge helped members find legal counsel with the Migration Policy Institute, the Immigrants' Rights Project of the American Civil Liberties Union (ACLU), Washington Square Legal Services at New York University School of Law and private pro bono lawyers (Adcock 2003). The Arab-American Anti-Discrimination Committee, Alliance of Iranian-Americans, CAIR, and the National Council of Pakistani-Americans also filed an injunction to prevent the INS from further detention of individuals who were in the process of applying for residency.

There were also efforts by community groups outside the courtroom. The Muslim Public Affairs Council (MPAC) stationed human rights monitors at INS registration stations in ten cities around the country. Demonstrations in the streets in front of detention centers in New Jersey and New York were organized by a broad coalition of groups including the Blue Triangle Network, Brooklyn Heights Peace Action, Brooklyn Parents for Peace, Center for Immigrant Families, Desis Rising Up and Moving, the Green Party, the International Action Center, the International Socialist Organization, Jews For Racial and Economic Justice, the Malcolm X Grass Roots Movement, New Yorkers Say No To War and South Asians Against Police Brutality & Racism. Organizations active for many years in a social movement against multiple issues such as police brutality, mandatory minimum sentencing, and the death penalty, provided a broad base for mobilization against the detentions. Linked to the ongoing conflict in Israel-Palestine, there was also a flowering of "dialogue projects" that organized discussion groups of Muslim and non-Muslim neighbors. This loose acephalous network of social movements engaged articulate spokespeople in New York City from Al Sharpton to the lawyers at the NYCLU, as well as a handful of media outlets like Pacifica radio's affiliate WBAI and newspapers like the *Village Voice*. In addition to defending the security of Arab and Muslim Americans, these groups criticized the use of widespread detentions on immigration pretexts, the registration of particular nationalities and the closing of court rooms to public scrutiny.

Increased Surveillance

The USA Patriot Act, quickly passed into law on October 26, 2001, created many avenues for increased policing. The Attorney General and the Secretary of State may now unilaterally designate domestic groups involved in virtually any violent activity as terrorist organizations without objective criteria applied equally to all groups. Non-citizens can be detained or deported for providing assistance to such groups. The FBI already had authority to spy on foreign groups without probable cause of crime under the Foreign Intelligence Surveillance Act (FISA) of 1978. The Patriot extends surveillance authority making it easier to spy domestically on Internet use, conduct secret searches, and force a business to turn over a person's educational, medical, financial, mental health or travel records. It also allows for the broad sharing of information in criminal cases with intelligence agencies, including the CIA, the NSA, the INS and the Secret Service, without judicial review or significant safeguards regarding the future use of such information.

The Patriot Act is only the most recent of a series of progressively more expansive laws. In the United States, Congresses approved and Presidents signed numerous pieces of legislation: the Omnibus Diplomatic Security and Antiterrorism Act of 1986, the Antiterrorism Acts of 1987, 1990 and 1992, and the Omnibus Counterterrorism Act of 1995 (see Patton 1997). By the anniversary of the Oklahoma bombing, the Antiterrorist and Effective Death Penalty (AEDP) Act of 1996 was approved by Congress. The AEDP Act allows exceptions to the Posse Comitatus Act of 1878 so that the Attorney General may ask for assistance from the military in domestic situations where chemical or biological weapons have been used (Martin 1996: 224). It lowers the standard for law enforcement officers to obtain a multipoint wiretap (Martin 1996: 227). Several amendments infringe upon the due process of those accused of crimes by allowing conviction based on secret evidence and curtailing the appeals process. It also outlaws material support to foreign terrorist organizations and requires financial institutions that become aware of any funds connected to foreign terrorist

organizations to seize the assets and report them to the Secretary of the Treasury (Patton 1997: 132). This is problematic for those who have donated to organizations that are charitable or religious yet also involved in political activities objectionable to the Secretary of State. Even when the Supreme Court repeatedly held that the First Amendment protects money contributions to political groups, this right can be ignored by the designation of a group as terrorist (Patton 1997: 151). In universities "foreign students and scholars have been harassed, research projects have been stalled, and librarians have been forced to compromise their professional ethics . . . some academics now find their jobs unmanageable, their futures uncertain, or their civil liberties trampled" (Chronicle of Higher Education 2003: A12).

Federal efforts set precedents for local enforcement to expand the scope of their police investigations. In January 2003, Deputy Commissioner Cohen challenged and succeeded in removing the old spying rules, called the 1985 Handschu Guidelines, that limited and monitored police investigations of constitutionally protected activity like street protests, community meetings and political essayists, where there is no indication of crime. Abandoning the Handschu Guidelines, police obtained the power to infiltrate and monitor groups, keep dossiers and freely disseminate information (see Lee 2003).

The new power was apparently exercised on public dissenters against the war in Iraq. As millions of people around the world prepared to demonstrate against the impending war in February 2003, New York City officials only permitted a stationary demonstration, not a march, then blocked participants from reaching it, attacked a handful with pepper spray and horses, and arrested hundreds of others (Solomon 2003). Charged only with minor offenses, arrested demonstrators were interrogated about their political affiliations and prior demonstration activity on a Criminal Intelligence form entitled "Demonstration Debriefing Form" (NYCLU 2003b). By November 2003 major newspapers were reporting on FBI investigations of anti-war demonstrators in cooperation with local law enforcement agencies (see Lichtblau 2003), even likening the operations to J. Edgar Hoover's COINTELPRO campaign against the Black Panthers (Hentoff 2003).

The expansion of racially and religiously selective immigration enforcement at the federal level, followed by the perceived repression of popular dissent by the NYPD, called "arresting protest" by the NYCLU (Dunn et. al. 2003), has made the power paradigm a plausible explanation for the increase in policing. From the civil liberties perspective and power paradigm, national security is again being invoked post 9/11 to justify government repression of social movements against war and tyranny and for global justice.

The Psycho-Cultural Paradigm

Unlike the rational-Enlightenment and power paradigms, the psycho-cultural paradigm says that violence, by state or nonstate actors, may be contrary to a clear, instrumental purpose. It may be neither in the public interest, nor in the interest of perpetrators. The psycho-cultural paradigm points out that those carrying out the antiterrorist mission have also been affected by the personal trauma suffered on 9/11 and the cultural mythology that frames events and decisions to respond. People may engage in self endangering or destructive activity for emotional reasons tied to previous trauma or their sense of identity in a social world.

Post Traumatic Stress and Aggression

Three weeks after the attack, officers began returning to the course I teach to NYPD officers on racism and policing. They were fatigued and expressed disbelief and confusion. Many officers, if not most New Yorkers, were experiencing what Freud called the uncanny (Gampel 2000). A white male officer described his day as starting with taking his kid to school, then being thanked by strangers who previously would have avoided him, and then digging for buried bodies on the "pile" down at Ground Zero. Going back and forth between these scenes, he said, "just can't be a healthy thing." One black female officer related the fear and anger brought on by her experiences, and how she and her colleagues had "gone numb in order to get on with everyday stuff." She thought it was good that she was exhausted from work, because otherwise she probably would not sleep.

We also discussed reactive aggression and how repressed fear and anger can burst to the surface, often out of proportion to the immediate trigger. Some gave personal examples and others described ways they had tried to let out fear and anger a little bit at a time and get a handle on their feelings. Some hesitant to seek counseling in the Department said returning to our class was the one time they were able to stop moving and try to talk about what they were experiencing.

In the weeks that followed, officers began to lament how many uniformed personnel died doing their job, going up the stairs while others were running down. They described a strong identification with and compassion for the victims, fear for themselves and their families, and even remorse, a recurring feeling of guilt, something akin to the survivor's guilt observed by Bruno Bettelheim (1980). This remorse was sometimes expressed as a sense of responsibility. The deaths, it was commonly said, should not be in vain; they should not have died for nothing. Such phrases express and frame feelings, but their vagueness inspires different people to different actions. Many went to dig on the pile. Some said there was a new urgency for increased vigilance in their policing, while a few others, especially one who referred to his army experience during the invasion of Panama, expressed criticism of state violence and his desire for a reform of US militarism.

Cultural Mythology

For some, the most accessible models to interpret what happened and what to do about it were drawn from Hollywood movies. The reason for and solution to terrorism could be imagined by those who saw any number of films in the terrorist genre. A particularly relevant example was the 1998 movie *The Siege* from 20th Century Fox. The movie depicts terrorist attacks in New York City, the Federal Government imposing martial law in Brooklyn, thousands of Arab-Americans arbitrarily detained and brutalized, and thousands of non-Arab Brooklynites coming out to protest the detention of their neighbors. In the end, the hero, an FBI officer played by Denzel Washington, discovers the terrorist leader, who is a Palestinian professor teaching in Brooklyn. There is also a sexual relationship between the male Palestinian terrorist villain and the unsuspecting American CIA agent heroine. They use each other for information, but ultimately he reveals his identity and attempts to kill her. This sexual subplot, typical of Hollywood films, weaves stereotypes of oppressive Arab gender politics with international politics, and implies that the Arab-Muslim terrorist is not just a violent political renegade, but also a sexual beast.

The Oriental man as sexual despot and irrational enemy has been a recurring image of European and American fiction and is something most "terrorist" movies include. This genre of movies, including high profile films like *True Lies, Executive Decision,* and *Delta Force,* all feature a scene of a crazy-eyed and furious Arab man, unlike American heroes who always keep their cool and rarely show emotion. In each of these movies there is at least one scene in which the terrorist beats or grabs a (usually white) woman. There have been substantial studies of the scope, pattern, and variety of such unfavorable portrayals of Arabs in the American media (Ghareeb 1983; Shaheen2001). Edward Said's classic *Orientalism* (1978) gives many examples from generations of French and English literature.

While hijacked airplanes and suicide bombings are fictional dramatizations of real events, the terrorist is usually the only image of Arabs or Muslims that American audiences see. For anyone ignorant to the diversity of Muslims and Arabs, the unsavory types portrayed could easily have been understood as generalized characteristics of many of those in the group. When such images remain unchallenged, the attribution of guilt is made according to vague racial-religious categories. So despite statements by President George Bush and both houses of Congress rejecting racial or religious profiling, there were many reported cases of racial discrimination: at least 80 passengers were removed from airlines after boarding because of perceived ethnicity; there were over 800 reported cases of employment discrimination; and many cases of discrimination in housing and provisions of other services (Ibish 2003).

Guilt by vague association is one problem intensified by images in Hollywood films, but there is another. Not only are the antagonists reduced to flat cliches, but the heroes, too, are no more complicated than GI Joe action figures. Like 20th century Westerns, these films end in a final shootout in which heavily armed Americans save the day. Such resolutions do not communicate the message that although this terrorist was stopped, there is an ongoing political crisis that must be resolved in other ways. The combination of a racialized enemy and total military victory provides powerful imagery lending emotional support only to violent solutions.

Stereotyping and Profiling

In the context of post-trauma stress and cultural myths of villains and heroes, law enforcement personnel can face significant emotional challenges expressed as zealotry. For example, a lawsuit filed in federal district court has challenged ethnic and religious bias in an unnecessary, unjustified, illegal, and degrading search of a 22-year-old United States citizen of Pakistani descent wearing a head covering November 2001 at O'Hare International Airport. After passing through the metal detector without setting it off, a member of the Illinois National Guard told a private security employee that the woman should be strip searched even after a hand-held metal detector search and a pat down of her body found nothing incriminating (ACLU 2002b).

Initiatives like putting the National Guard at airports or Operation Atlas, which put officers at bridges and tunnels, or Operation Hercules, which are roving armored vehicles and battle-ready police, may do little to stop terrorists, but they perform security for a public audience. Based on familiar Hollywood scripts, they may work against terror by projecting to the public that they are being protected. Seeing uniformed officers or armed soldiers might calm some people's fear of flying or entering the Holland Tunnel between Manhattan and New Jersey, but in the context of cultural myths of villains and heroes their stops are also likely to be based on perceived racial-religious cues.

One officer explained that before 9/11, he did not look at Arabs or Muslims as suspicious, but now he does. Even when confronted with the idea that it is prejudice, he said he had to pay attention to his suspicions: "A cop's got to go with his gut, sometimes." Before 9/11, the debate was if there was or was not systematic racial profiling by police of black people. Everyone agreed that it was wrong, but they did not agree that it occurred. After 9/11, the debate became should there be or not be profiling of Arabs and Muslims.

Several students and workers have said they were stopped, but few want to go on record. An exception was a 20-year-old CUNY student who was taking pictures of storefronts on Main Street in Flushing Queens in New York City to document changing neighborhoods for an urban sociology course in February 2003. Three officers became suspicious, began a field interrogation and learned he was a Pakistani named Yasser Hussain (Geron 2003). He was taken into custody in the 109th precinct where the Criminal Intelligence Section of the NYPD questioned and released him about five hours later. Before 9/11 the NYPD formally issued policy statements prohibiting officers from field investigations based only on a person's ethnic or racial identity and that such identity can only be gathered as pedigree information. Race alone cannot justify a stop, but race in addition to a second factor is acceptable. So Hussain's nationality in combination with his suspicious picture taking made the two necessary factors. Other suspicious behaviors mentioned by police were carrying boxes or packages, being overdressed in warm weather, or just standing around.

Like young black men, immigrants might not feel they are in a position to refuse a field interrogation or a consent search. Patrol officers overwhelmingly understand that they are expected to be courteous, professional, and respectful in their engagement with the public, but like the AfricanAmerican community, frequent stops and searches are likely to be experienced as harassment. Understanding its dangers, Commissioner Kelly has warned against racial profiling saying that "profiling generally, irrespective of whether or not it's the moral thing to do or the right thing to do, . . . can really dissipate your resources. It takes away

a lot of energy . . . Profiling, in many ways, is a result of lack of information. So we need more information about activities, about people coming into this country" (Interview on CNBC, December 13, 2002). Profiling may not only be immoral and a waste of resources, it may also be counterproductive. As Kelly indicates, information is key and this requires cooperation with the community, especially to provide intelligence. If the community feels the police are hostile to them, they are less likely to cooperate, their bilingual children are less likely to join the Department, and those who do are likely to endure criticism.

The psycho-cultural paradigm examines the emotional and shared meanings of specific activities or behaviors of police. From this perspective, the consequences of trauma like reactive aggression and remorse, and the mythologies of Hollywood become salient in policing. Behavior stemming from these motivations may or may not coincide with the instrumental logics described by the security-civil liberties debate.

Discussion

The historic increases in policing activities should be examined through a combination of logics including the rational-Enlightenment, the power, and the psycho-cultural paradigms. Whether consultants to security professionals or as political activists in the civil liberties movement, anthropology may provide important insights into the cultural dynamics at work in a given time and place. Anthropologists can explain how fears of ethnic or racial difference create legitimizing discourses for a variety of practices that undermine security and liberty.

For those concerned primarily with security, anthropologists can summarize and translate community perspectives, such as the civil liberties narrative and unconscious psycho-cultural obstacles to law enforcement professionals. For example, recognizing the importance of police-community relations, police managers have been correct to respond to today's profiling problems with racial sensitivity training. Observations here, however, suggest that the problems are deep and management must monitor stops of Muslims and Arabs more carefully, perhaps by including a South Asian or Middle Eastern option on the UF-250 form that officers fill out when they stop, question, search and release a civilian. The UF-250 requires officers to check a box recording the race of the individual: black, white, Hispanic, Asian and other. The racial description is recorded primarily for investigative purposes, but it can also serve to track profiling and patterns of racial disparity. Furthermore, given the fear of cooperation with the Federal government, the old INS, and new DHS in particular, some form of a confidentiality policy could make immigrants feel safer coming forward to cooperate with police.

For those concerned with civil liberties, an anthropology of policing documents the processes that transfer government resources toward more social control through policing and incarceration. Cultural analysis lays bare how a fearful public passively endorses such measures because terrorist images allow ordinary people to detach themselves from the pain of their scapegoats by defining them as less than human. Descriptions of these prejudices presumably unmask the "false consciousness" that sees policing as either rational or for a greater good. Ethnographers writing for the defense of civil liberties may also describe the suffering of those targeted by state security forces in order to heighten sympathy for them and inhibit actions against them.

For either audience, this article explains that policing activities emerge from rational-Enlightenment and power motives, as well as from complicated psycho-cultural dispositions. Discrete acts may be better explained by reference to one of these schools of thought, but to reduce the larger process to a single driving force is usually narrow-minded. Instead, this ethnography of the process indicates a plurality of causes. The goal here has not been to decide which paradigm trumps the others as much as it has been to show how multiple paradigms are simultaneously relevant.

References

Adcock, Thomas; 2003 Pro Bono, Public Interest Projects. New York Law Journal 229:16.

American Civil Liberties Union; 2002a ACLU Files First Post-Sept. 11 Challenge To Closed Immigration Hearings on Behalf of MI Congressman and Journalists. URL:http://www.aclu.org/ImmigrantsRights/ImmigrantsRights.cfm?ID=10198&c=95 (January 29, 2002).

American Civil Liberties Union; 2002b ACLU of Illinois Challenges Ethnic and Religious Bias in Strip Search of Muslim Woman at O'Hare International Airport. URL:http://www.aclu-il.org/news/press/000062.shtml (January 16, 2002).

American Civil Liberties Union; 2003 ACLU Seeks Disclosure of 'Secret Law' on Local Police Enforcement of Federal Immigration Laws. URL:http://www.aclu.org/SafeandFree/SafeandFree.cfm?ID=12358&c=206 (April 14, 2003).

Bettelheim, Bruno; 1980 Surviving and Other Essays. New York: Vintage Books.

Bornstein, Avram; 2001 Border Enforcement in Daily Life: Palestinian Day Laborers and Entrepreneurs Crossing the Green Line Human Organization 60: 298–307.

Bornstein, Avram; 2002 Crossing the Green Line between the West Bank and Israel. Philadelphia: University of Pennsylvania Press.

Bratton, William, with Peter Knobler; 1998 Turnaround. New York: Random House.

Casimir, Leslie; 2003a Muslims: INS Policy is Biased Call It Racial Profiling. Daily News (New York, NY), February 17:12.

Casimir, Leslie; 2003b Arab Cabbie Signed In, Feds May Toss Him Out. Daily News (New York, NY), June 13:10.

Chronicle of Higher Education; 2003 Closing the Gates. Chronicle of Higher Education 49: A12.

Dunn, Christopher, Arthur Eisenburg, Donna Lieberman, Alan Silver and Alex Vitale; 2003 Arresting Protest. New York: New York Civil Liberties Union.

El-Ghobashy, Tamer; 2004 Mock Calamity Helps Nine Agencies Prepare for the Worst, Terror Rescuers Snap To, 1,000 join exercise at Shea. Daily News (New York, NY) March 15:4.

Gampel, Yolanda; 2000 Reflections of the Prevalence of the Uncanny in Social Violence. In Cultures Under Siege: Collective Violence and Trauma. Antonius Robben and Marcelo Suarez-Orozco, eds. Pp. 48–69. New York: Cambridge University Press.

Gardiner, Sean; 2001 WTC Cleanup Costs Hit $500M. Newsday (New York, NY), December 15:A19.

Gardiner, Sean, and Rocco Parascandola; 2002 9/11 One Year Later, Shifting Role for NYC Police, Department Leaders' Main Focus has Shifted to Terrorism. Newsday (New York, NY), September 8:W14.

Geron, Tomio; 2003 Police Detain Honors Student. Clarion (New York, NY), March:5.

Ghareeb, Edmund, ed.; 1983 Split Vision: the Portrayal of Arabs in the American Media. Washington, DC: American-Arab Affairs Council.

Hall, Mimi; 2003 Homeland Security Steps Tightest since 9/11. USA Today (Washington, D.C.), March 19:1A.

Hamill, Denis; 2001 A Hate Unit Cop Polices Own Feelings. Daily News (New York, NY), October 24:20.

Hentoff, Nat; 2003 J. Edgar Hoover Back at the "New" FBI. Village Voice (New York, NY) December 16:30.

Horowitz, Craig; 2003 The NYPD's War on Terror. New York 36/3:34–40.

Human Rights Watch; 2002 "We are not the enemy": Hate Crimes Against Arabs, Muslims, and those Perceived to be Arabs or Muslims after September 11. Washington, DC: Human Rights Watch.

Ibish, Hussein, ed.; 2003 Report on Hate Crimes and Discrimination Against Arab Americans: The Post-September 11 Backlash. Washington, DC: Arab-American Anti-Discrimination Committee Research Institute.

Kappeler, Victor, Richard Sluder, and Geoffrey Alpert; 1994 Forces of Deviance: Understanding the Dark Side of Policing. Prospect Heights, IL: Waveland Press.

Kraska, Peter, ed.; 2001 Militarizing the American Criminal Justice System. Boston: Northeastern University Press.

Lee, Chisun; 2003 The Force Multipliers, NYPD to bring Nationwide Spying Effort Home. Village Voice (New York, NY), February 26:25–28.

Lichtblau, Eric; 2003 FBI Scrutinizes Antiwar Rallies. New York Times (New York, NY), November 23:1,1.

Martin, Thomas; 1996 The Comprehensive Terrorism Prevention Act of 1995. Seton Hall Legislative Journal 20:201–247.

Mastrofski, Stephen, Michael Reisig and John McCluskey; 2002 Police Disrespect Toward the Public: an Encounter-Based Analysis. Criminology 40:519–551.

New York Civil Liberties Union; 2003a NYCLU Hails Inspector General Report Detailing Misconduct In Federal Treatment Of Immigrants Following World Trade Center Attack. URL: http://www.nyclu.org/justiceoig_911 report_060203.html (June 2, 2003).

New York Civil Liberties Union; 2003b In Response to Demand From NYCLU, Police Department to Halt Interrogating Protesters About Political Activity. URL:http://www.nyclu.org/demo_intel_041003.html (April 10, 2003).

New York Law Journal; 2001 NYPD to Interview Middle Eastern Men. New York Law Journal December 6:2.

Parenti, Christian; 1999 Lockdown America. New York: Vintage Press.

Patton, William; 1997 Preventing Terrorist Fundraising in the United States. George Washington Journal of International Law and Economics 30:127–160.

Ridge, Tom; 2003 Secretary Ridge Holds Press Briefing on Operation Liberty Shield. URL:http://www.whitehouse.gov/news/releases/2003/03/20030318-6.html (March 18).

Ruiz, Albor; 2003 Hate Crimes Target Arabs and Muslims. Daily News (New York, NY), April 16:8.

Said, Edward; 1978 Orientalism. New York: Basic Books.

Shaheen, Jack; 2001 Reel Bad Arabs. New York: Olive Branch Press.

Silverman, Eli; 1999 NYPD Battles Crime. New York: New York University Press.

Skolnick, Jerome, and James Fyfe; 1993 Above the Law: Police and the Excessive Use of Force. New York: Free Press.

Solomon, Alisa; 2003 Busted for Peace: When Cops Play Soldier, Protesters become the Enemy. Village Voice (New York, NY), February 26:20–23.

Swarns, Rachel; 2003 Thousands of Arabs and Muslims Could Be Deported, Officials Say. The New York Times (New York, NY), June 7:A1.

Upadhyay, Akhilesh; 2003 U.S.-Rights: 'Keep a Low Profile', U.S. Arabs Advised. Inter Press Service. URL:http://www.ipsnews.net/interna.asp?idnews=17346 (April 5).

Weiss, Murray; 2002 NYPD's Foreign Legion: Antiterror Cops Head for Posts Overseas. New York Post (New York, NY), November 12:2.

Weisburd, David, Stephen Mastrofski. Ann Marie McNally, Rosann Greenspan, and James Willis; 2003 Reforming to Preserve: COMPSTAT and Strategic Problem Solving in American Policing. Criminology and Public Policy 2:421–456.

AVRAM BORNSTEIN is an Associate Professor of Anthropology at the John Jay College of Criminal Justice, CUNY. In addition to studying police in New York City, Bornstein has done research in Israel-Palestine since the late 1980s. He has authored a number of articles and reviews on violence and work, as well as the book Crossing the Green Line between the West Bank and Israel (2002, University of Pennsylvania).

From *Human Organization*, Vol. 64, no. 1, Spring 2005, pp. 52–61. Copyright © 2005 by Society for Applied Anthropology. Reprinted by permission.

Community Policing and Terrorism

MATTHEW C. SCHEIDER AND ROBERT CHAPMAN

A great deal of the responsibility for preparing for and responding to terrorist events rests with local police departments. Community policing presents an overarching philosophical orientation that agencies can use to better deal with the threat of terrorist events and the fear that they may create. The community policing philosophy can be roughly divided into three interrelated elements: organizational change, problem solving, and external partnerships. Each element applies to the issues of terrorism prevention and response, as well as to fear.

Since 11 September, the federal government has greatly increased terrorism prevention and response efforts. However, a large degree of responsibility for dealing with these threats and for alleviating citizen fear rests at the local level. To some degree, the majority of local police departments in the United States have worked to reduce the fear of future terrorist attacks and to prevent and plan for attacks. Law enforcement officials are strategically rethinking public security procedures and practices to maximize the potential of their resources.

The philosophy of community policing is important for police in preparing for possible terrorist acts and in responding to the fear they may create. Community policing involves broadening the nature and number of police functions compared to traditional policing models. It emphasizes organizational change, active problem solving, and external partnerships to address issues that concern both the police and citizens. In recent years, the philosophy of community policing appears to have been adopted to differing degrees by a large number of law enforcement entities in the United States. For example, a 2001 U.S. Department of Justice report indicates that from 1997 to 1999, departments employing personnel designated as community police rose from 34% to 64%.[1] In addition, the absolute number of community policing officers rose from 21,000 to 113,000. However, traumatic events can cause organizations to revert to more traditional modes of operation. The events of 11 September may have been no exception for U.S. law enforcement. Some police departments may have been quick to dismiss community policing efforts and programs for seemingly more immediate and pressing security concerns. However, the community policing philosophy is well positioned to play a central role in local law enforcement responses to terrorism.

Community policing shifts the focus of police by placing equal emphasis on crime control, order maintenance, and service provision.[2,3] In addition, it asks police to work with citizens and with other government agencies in efforts to increase overall quality of life. Thus, the model moves away from police-dominated crime control through reactive responses to calls for service. Community policing models move toward active problem solving centered on the underlying conditions that give rise to crime and disorder and on fostering partnerships between the police and the community.[4,5,6]

There is no one commonly recognized definition of community policing. Here we offer one possible definition that we will then apply to preventing and responding to terrorist events. Community policing can be defined as a philosophy that, through the delivery of police services, focuses on crime and social disorder; the philosophy includes aspects of traditional law enforcement as well as prevention, problem-solving tactics, and partnerships. As a fundamental shift from traditional, reactive policing, community policing stresses the prevention of crime. Community policing requires police and citizens to join as partners in identifying and effectively addressing the underlying conditions that give rise to crime and disorder. Community policing can be roughly divided into three interrelated elements: organizational change, problem solving, and external partnerships.

The Community Policing Philosophy

Organizational Change

Ideally, community policing should be adopted organization-wide and be reflected through department participation at all levels as well as through the organization's mission, goals, objectives, performance evaluations, hiring and promotion practices, training, and all other systems that define organizational culture and activities. One of the most important specific aspects of organizational change relevant to community policing is a flattened organizational structure. Community policing departments are often less hierarchical, supporting management's dispersion of decision-making authority to the lowest organizational level and holding those individuals accountable for the outcomes. A second important element of organizational change is fixed geographic responsibility. Officers or deputies are assigned to fixed geographic areas for extended periods, based on social and cultural considerations and on the assumption that this fosters better communication with residents;

increases the police officers' ability to understand, prevent, and respond to community problems; and enhances accountability to the citizens in that area.

Problem Solving

Community policing departments also actively address the underlying conditions that give rise to or facilitate crime or disorder in an effort to prevent future problems by identifying and analyzing problems and by developing tailored strategies that may include traditional and nontraditional responses that focus on deterring offenders, protecting likely victims, and making locations less conducive to crime and disorder. Departments should use a wide array of relevant traditional and nontraditional data sources to better understand and evaluate the nature of problems and work in conjunction with the community and other organizations to develop effective long-term solutions. Problem solving often manifests itself in the "scanning, analysis, response and assessment" problem-solving model.[7,8] Departments first identify relevant or perceived crime problems (scanning), determine the nature and underlying conditions that give rise to those problems (analysis), craft and implement interventions that are linked to that analysis (response), and evaluate its effectiveness (assessment). The process is understood as continually involving feedback among the components. For instance, through in-depth analysis, agencies may come to define problems differently, effectively returning to the scanning phase. Likewise, an assessment may determine that a response was ineffective and that the problem requires additional analysis.

External Partnerships

Under a community policing philosophy, departments partner with other government, social service, and community agencies in attempts to identify and address persistent problems in the community. They form external partnerships in recognition of other agencies' unique strengths, tools, and expertise that can be leveraged when addressing community problems. The police are only one of a host of local government agencies responsible for responding to community problems. Under community policing, coordination with other government agencies in developing comprehensive and effective solutions is essential. In addition, the police are encouraged to develop working partnerships with civic and community groups to accurately survey community needs and priorities and to use the public as a resource in problem solving and in developing and implementing interventions.

Community Policing and Terrorism Prevention and Response

Organizational Change

A flat organizational structure may ensure more effective terrorist prevention and response. It has been demonstrated that local law enforcement officers are likely to come into contact with those who may be directly or indirectly involved in terrorist activities and most certainly will be among the first responders to any future terrorist attack. Empowering officers at lower levels with decision-making authority and familiarizing them with making (and taking responsibility for) important decisions could be of value in any crisis.

In a terrorist event, there may be little time for decisions to move up the chain of command. Officers who are accustomed to making decisions and retaining authority may be better prepared to respond quickly and decisively to any event. In addition, in terms of prevention, developing a flat organizational structure can help lower-level officers feel free to pursue leads or suspected terrorist activity. In addition, having fixed geographic responsibility may assist officers in identifying possible terrorist threats. Officers who work in a community or neighborhood for an extended time can develop specific intelligence concerning resident and community activities. This street-level knowledge is a vital part of counter-intelligence efforts.

Problem Solving

Problem-solving models are well suited to preventing and responding to terrorist activity. Departments can use many existing data sources ahead of time to develop detailed risk management and crisis plans. Identifying potential terrorist targets in local jurisdictions is an important first step. Police can determine what in their jurisdictions (dams, electric grids, chemical warehouses, large-scale public gatherings) are potential terrorist targets. Community policing encourages agencies to conduct complex analyses of the possible threats and of their relative likelihood of occurring. Finally, agencies in conjunction with other government, social, and community entities can develop detailed crisis prevention and response plans. Finally, the community policing model encourages continual refinement of these plans to suit changing conditions and threat levels.

External Partnerships

The threat of terrorism provides a unique opportunity to create partnerships with citizens, other government organizations, and other law enforcement agencies. Prior apathy toward these partnerships that may have existed is often reduced by the presence of terrorist targets and threats. Recent terrorist events and associated concerns may have created a sense of uneasiness and urgency in many communities. The specter of additional terrorist activity has created an opportunity to galvanize local police to work with their communities, other law enforcement agencies, and local, state, and federal entities.

The community policing model encourages the development of such ongoing and effective partnerships, which can be invaluable in preventing terrorist activity because of increased opportunities for intelligence gathering and sharing. They can also be central to developing coordinated responses to any actual terrorist events.

Community policing encourages agencies to establish and expand upon existing partnerships with a goal of developing model crisis plans and processes to deal with the aftermath of terrorist incidents. These plans and processes would consider the needs and concerns of all community stakeholders. Law enforcement and local government can come together with community partners to develop a plan on how to prepare for such a crisis, what to do in the event of such a crisis, and how to cope with its aftermath.

Community Policing and Fear of Terrorism

By definition, the primary goal of terrorism is to create fear and an atmosphere of uncertainty. This fear can greatly affect the quality of life of many individuals, extending far beyond those who are directly affected by a terrorist event. In the United States the police have increasingly been asked to address the fear of crime generally. The expansion of their role to include quality of life and partnerships with citizens, as emphasized by the community policing philosophy, has increasingly brought fear of crime under the purview of police professionals. As A. Steven Dietz stated in "Evaluating Community Policing," "Reduction of fear of crime has been associated with community policing programs since their inception."[9] It is clear that reducing fear of crime has become an essential element and an often explicitly articulated goal of community policing.[10] Thus, community policing finds itself well positioned to deal with issues of fear that can arise as a direct result of terrorist activity. In addition, dealing directly with citizen fear of crime is important, as unchecked fear of terrorism (or feelings of revenge) can manifest itself in hate crimes and illegal bigotry targeted particularly at people who are Muslim and of Middle Eastern descent. These are important social problems that law enforcement should be prepared to respond to and prevent.

Organizational Change

Adoption of the community policing philosophy partly involves reengineering department processes and resources away from randomness and reactivity and toward information- and service-driven community-based approaches. Police officers are often assigned to specific geographic areas to foster communication with residents and are accountable to those residents and their superiors for the safety and well-being of that area. Other aspects of the agency are realigned to support the most fundamental focus of all activities, the beat.

As a result of this emphasis, police officers should be more attuned to rising levels of community concern and fear and, by virtue of the relationships they have established within the community, be in a position to respond effectively to those needs and concerns. Community policing has been found to engender trust and increased satisfaction among residents for the police,[11] which

in periods of heightened unrest can be parlayed into dealing more effectively with community fear that can be based on both rational and irrational concerns.

Problem Solving

Community policing encourages a deeper understanding of the fear that may result from terrorist events. The first step is to determine whether fear is a problem in the community and to determine the extent of the problem. Police can conduct citizen interviews, surveys, and face-to-face interactions to determine levels of citizen fear. Then they can analyze the underlying conditions that give rise to or encourage fear. Perhaps it is a result of a specific terrorist-related fear such as living near what is perceived to be a potential terrorist target, or the fear may involve fear for loved ones who reside in high-threat areas. Finally, perhaps the fear is a more general fear of terrorism. In any event, law enforcement should work to understand the extent and nature of fear in their community if they want to develop effective responses.

Law enforcement should then work in partnership with other community groups to develop responses aimed at decreasing levels of fear if they are negatively affecting quality of life and are determined to be highly exaggerated. Community policing efforts to deal with citizen fear of crime have included foot and vehicle patrols in high-crime neighborhoods, as well as community meetings, citizen patrols, neighborhood cleanup programs, opening neighborhood substations, and citizen awareness campaigns.[12] Clearly, citizen fear of terrorist events is somewhat different than fear of crime generally. However, some of the same techniques may also be useful for reducing this type of fear. For example, citizen awareness campaigns can inform citizens about what the local police and city government are doing to prevent and prepare for possible terrorist events. Crisis response plans can be discussed in addition to general prevention activities. Citizens can be informed about what they themselves can do—such as preparing emergency survival kits for their own homes—to prepare for possible terrorist events and can be informed of evacuation routes to use in the event of a large-scale disaster. Finally, law enforcement agencies should assess the effectiveness of any fear-reduction efforts and modify their responses accordingly.

External Partnerships

The emphasis on building strong community partnerships encouraged by a community policing philosophy may also help reduce citizen fear of terrorist events. These partnerships may be able to directly reduce fear by increasing citizen feelings of efficacy, increasing the bond among neighbors themselves, and involving citizens in prevention and preparedness activities. Encouraging citizen involvement in neighborhood watch, youth education, and cleanup programs can increase social cohesion among citizens and has been found to result in decreased fear of crime.[13] It is likely that these increasing feelings of efficacy in response to terrorist events may have similar effects. Citizens can be involved to differing degrees in prevention and preparedness discussions.

Conclusion

Immediately following 11 September 2001, local law enforcement agencies in the United States responded to disasters, lost officers, were placed on various levels of alert, provided a visible security presence at public events, partnered with federal intelligence agencies, and investigated hate crimes at greatly increased rates and with a new urgency. Community policing offers law enforcement agencies an overarching orientation from which to conduct this myriad of tasks. Since its inception, the success of community policing has been based on the relationships built between law enforcement and community members. These relationships, often expressed as collaborative partnerships, have served functions as diverse as the communities that maintain them: solving traffic problems, shutting down drug houses, keeping children safe in school and after school, referring offenders to drug courts, and cleaning up abandoned properties. Addressing these quality-of-life issues has helped give citizens a voice in the public safety of their community and an active way to address crime and their fear of crime. For the past 20 years, community policing has encouraged community members to partner with law enforcement to identify potential threats and create a climate of safety. The community policing philosophy is well positioned to take a major role in preventing and responding to terrorism and in efforts to reduce citizen fear. Instead of de-emphasizing community policing efforts, police departments should realize that community policing may be more important than ever in dealing with terrorism in their communities.

Bibliography

Trevor Bennett, "Confidence in the Police as a Mediating Factor in the Fear of Crime," *International Review of Victimology,* vol. 3, 1994, pp. 179–194.

Lee P. Brown and Mary Ann Wycoff, "Policing Houston: Reducing Fear and Improving Service," *Crime and Delinquency*, vol. 33, no. 1, 1987, pp. 71–89.

Gary W. Cordner, "Community Policing: Elements and Effects," in Roger G. Dunham and Geoffrey P. Alpert (eds.), *Critical Issues in Policing* (Prospect Heights, IL: Waveland Press, 1997), pp. 451–468.

A. Steven Dietz, "Evaluating Community Policing: Quality Police Service and Fear of Crime," *Policing: An International Journal of Police Strategies and Management*, vol. 20, no. 1, 1997, pp. 83–100.

Herman Goldstein, *Problem-Oriented Policing* (New York: McGraw-Hill, 1990).

Matthew J. Hickman and Brian A. Reaves, "Community Policing in Local Police Departments, 1997 and 1999," Bureau of Justice

Statistics Special Report (Washington, DC: Office of Justice Programs, U.S. Department of Justice, 2001).

Michael S. Scott, *Problem-Oriented Policing: Reflections on the First 20 Years* (Washington, DC: U.S. Department of Justice, Office of Community-Oriented Policing Services, 2000).

Quint Thurman, Jihong Zhao, and Andrew Giacomazzi, *Community Policing in a Community Era* (Los Angeles: Roxbury Publishing, 2000).

Robert Trojanowicz and Bonnie Bucqueroux, *Community Policing: A Contemporary Perspective* (Cincinnati, OH: Anderson Publishing, 1990).

James Q. Wilson, *Varieties of Police Behavior* (Cambridge, MA: Harvard University Press, 1968).

James Q. Wilson and George L. Kelling, "Broken Windows: The Police and Neighborhood Safety," *Atlantic Monthly*, volume 249, no. 3, March 1982, pp. 29–38.

References

1. Matthew J. Hickman and Brian A. Reaves, "Community Policing in Local Police Departments, 1997 and 1999," Bureau of Justice Statistics Special Report (Washington, DC: Office of Justice Programs, U.S. Department of Justice, 2001).
2. Robert Trojanowicz and Bonnie Bucqueroux, *Community Policing: A Contemporary Perspective* (Cincinnati, OH: Anderson Publishing, 1990).
3. James Q. Wilson, *Varieties of Police Behavior* (Cambridge, MA: Harvard University Press, 1968).
4. Herman Goldstein, *Problem-Oriented Policing* (New York: McGraw-Hill, 1990).
5. Michael S. Scott, *Problem-Oriented Policing: Reflections on the First 20 Years* (Washington, DC: U.S. Department of Justice, Office of Community-Oriented Policing Services, 2000).
6. James Q. Wilson and George L. Kelling, "Broken Windows: The Police and Neighborhood Safety," *Atlantic Monthly*, volume 249, no. 3, March 1982, pp. 29–38.
7. Herman Goldstein.
8. Michael S. Scott.
9. A. Steven Dietz, "Evaluating Community Policing: Quality Police Service and Fear of Crime," *Policing: An International Journal of Police Strategies and Management*, vol. 20, no. 1, 1997, pp. 83–100.
10. Quint Thurman, Jihong Zhao, and Andrew Giacomazzi, *Community Policing in a Community Era* (Los Angeles: Roxbury Publishing, 2000).
11. Trevor Bennett, "Confidence in the Police as a Mediating Factor in the Fear of Crime," *International Review of Victimology*, vol. 3, 1994, pp. 179–194.
12. Lee P. Brown and Mary Ann Wycoff, "Policing Houston: Reducing Fear and Improving Service," *Crime and Delinquency*, vol. 33, no. 1, 1987, pp. 71–89.
13. Gary W. Cordner, "Community Policing: Elements and Effects," in Roger G. Dunham and Geoffrey P. Alpert (eds.), *Critical Issues in Policing* (Prospect Heights, IL: Waveland Press, 1997), pp. 451–468.

Editor's Note: Points of view or opinions contained in this document are those of the authors and do not necessarily represent the official positions or policies of the U.S. Department of Justice or the Office of Community Oriented Policing Services.

ROBERT CHAPMAN is a senior social science analyst with the U.S. Department of Justice, Office of Community Oriented Policing Services, where he is responsible for conducting and managing policy analysis, program development, and evaluation activities. He is enrolled in the graduate program at the Johns Hopkins University School of Government. He previously served as the Deputy Director for Legislative Affairs for the Police Executive Research Forum, a membership organization of police executives from the largest city, county, and state law enforcement agencies.

MATTHEW C. SCHEIDER is a senior social science analyst with the U.S. Department of Justice, Office of Community Oriented Policing Services, in Washington, DC. He is involved in developing, managing, and evaluating federal government programs designed to enhance the community policing capabilities of local law enforcement agencies. He holds a Ph.D. in sociology from Washington State University.

From *Journal of Homeland Security,* April 2003. Copyright © 2003 by Journal of Homeland Security. www.homelandsecurity.org

D.C. Deploys Wireless Net for First Responders

Wireless Integrated Network created Web-based interoperability for first responders.

Carolyn Duffy Marsan

Public-safety officials are focused on getting broadband wireless communications into the hands of first responders. But once police, fire and emergency response officers have this capability, what can they do with it?

That's where an innovative, Web-based application developed for Washington, D.C., is filling the gap.

The Capital Wireless Integrated Network (CapWIN) is a partnership involving Maryland, Virginia and the District of Columbia. Its goal is to create an interoperable data- and information-sharing network for all the first responders in the region.

CapWIN has 1,700 users from 43 government agencies, including the Maryland State Police, the Virginia State Police, the District of Columbia Police Department and the U.S. Park Service.

"We're the first of its kind in the country where multiple agencies across multiple jurisdictions can communicate in a single application to provide data, images and conferencing capability," says Bill Henry, director of field operations for CapWIN.

The University of Maryland began developing CapWIN before Sept. 11, but Congress didn't allocate funds until after the Pentagon was attacked.

CapWIN was started in 1998 after an incident involving a suicide jumper on the Woodrow Wilson Bridge over the Potomac River. Parts of the bridge are in Maryland, Virginia and Washington, D.C. Police from all of the neighboring jurisdictions were at the scene, but they couldn't talk to each other, because they used different types of radios.

"The communications infrastructure was such that they had to send runners back and forth to carry messages to the different participants," says Bill Henry, director of field operations for CapWIN. "The complaints they had that day about interoperability led to CapWIN."

The Department of Transportation funded a pilot project for CapWIN, which was developed from 1999 to 2001. In late 2001, Congress allocated $20 million to roll out a full-fledged system across the region.

Now in its second version, CapWIN offers secure instant messaging and group chat. Users create a chat room for each incident, and the software provides a record of what is happening for managing the response. The software also supports the sharing of images, including maps and photos for users that have enough bandwidth.

CapWIN runs on laptops, but an abridged version is available for handheld devices. The application is carrier agnostic, so that individual users can access it regardless of their wireless service provider. CapWIN is free to government agencies.

"The CapWIN strength is that it provides connectivity to first responders in the field, and it provides information from the field to the command center," Henry says. "In a major catastrophic event, CapWIN would be used as one of the main field communications links and a secondary channel if the commercial wireless or radio systems were down."

The Maryland State Police began using CapWIN in 2004 as part of a three-year, $7.5 million initiative to automate its squad cars. The agency has purchased 1,000 laptops, which are being installing in patrol vehicles along with CapWIN, upgraded radios, cameras and radar systems.

CapWIN comes in handy for calling the roll at the beginning of shifts, and it's a backup for radios when connectivity goes down, says Capt. Terry Custer, commander of the IT division of the Maryland State Police.

"We have some problems with connectivity in western Maryland. We hit some dead spots, which were giving our troops concerns. With CapWIN, we're finding that when our troopers can't contact the barracks with police radios, they can instead use CapWIN," Custer says.

Troopers also run record checks on license plates with CapWIN. Maryland troopers have run more than 80,000 record checks, including drivers' licenses, warrants and vehicle registrations this year using CapWIN. "We have several troopers that run more than 100 record checks per month," Custer says. "The normal response is 10 seconds. So before we approach a car, we know if there's an outstanding warrant for the owner."

What Maryland State Police like best is that they can use CapWIN to communicate with police, fire, emergency and transportation officials statewide.

For example, Maryland State Police in July used CapWIN to help apprehend the driver in a carjacking incident in Cumberland, Md. "The Cumberland City Police started the pursuit. They put it on CapWIN, and our troopers helped make the apprehension," Custer says.

CapWIN complements other communications systems used by first responders in the Washington, D.C., area. For example, police and fire departments in the region have standardized on 800 MHz radios to ensure interoperability. Sometimes radio communication has proven less reliable than the data CapWIN provides.

For example, last March a barge struck the Severn River Bridge near Annapolis, Md. The initial radio reports led law enforcement to believe the accident had happened at the Chesapeake Bay Bridge. However, CapWIN verified that the accident had happened somewhere else.

"At first, law enforcement and transportation officials that were working that issue were not anywhere near where they needed to be. Somebody looked at the CapWIN incident-management system and realized it was the Severn River Bridge," says Roddy Moscoso, communications manager for CapWIN. Incidents like these "help buttress the argument for a significant role for data in emergency response." In the future, CapWIN expects to transmit more photos, images and streaming video. Since July, the Virginia State Police has been using it to send out criminal database photos in response to law-enforcement queries.

"In Maryland, we had an incident where a large World War II ordnance was found by a construction crew," Moscoso says. "The incident was in close proximity to a school. A CapWIN user in the field logged into a mapping application and put in push pins on a map and attached that map to the incident report that he created in the field. With this image, everyone could instantly identify where the ordnance was located."

Among the users of CapWIN's image and data transmission is the U.S. Park Police, which has 23 mobile computers that are equipped with CapWIN. Officials use these systems for law enforcement queries and managing special events, such as the dedication of the World War II Memorial and the annual Fourth of July celebration.

"The Park Police will create an event and broadcast it out to all the participating agencies," says Lt. David Mulholland, commander for information technology and communications for the U.S. Park Police.

"We use CapWIN to communicate not only with law enforcement, fire or emergency services but also with the transportation people. We need to bring them in when we're doing the countdown to the fireworks and we have to evacuate the Mall due to bad weather. We're working toward bringing in nontraditional users like public utilities and the Red Cross," Mulholland says.

The Front Line in Training for Disasters

Community colleges prepare 85% of 'first responders' but say they are shortchanged in competition for federal dollars

BEN GOSE

Owens Community College trains hundreds of firefighters and police officers on its Toledo, Ohio, campus each year. If terrorists ever take aim at the city, odds are good that Owens graduates will be among the first on the scene. So when officials of the college realized that no facility existed near Toledo to simulate such disaster scenarios, they made plans to construct a 110-acre, $25-million training complex.

That was 18 months ago. Today the scheduled completion of the facility has been pushed back from 2005 to the spring of 2006, and the college hasn't raised nearly enough money to cover the price tag. The Ohio Board of Regents has given $2-million to the effort, and several local businesses have contributed materials and props, including rail cars and a full-scale gas station. But the U.S. Department of Homeland Security, and its state office in Ohio, which might seem to be the most obvious sources of support for such a facility, have contributed nothing.

Owens officials aren't happy about the lack of federal money—and they have plenty of company on community-college campuses throughout the country. Those colleges provide initial or continuing education to 85 percent of the nation's "first responders"—police officers, firefighters, and emergency technicians—says the American Association of Community Colleges. A survey by the association in 2004 found that 65 percent of the 344 responding community colleges had retooled their curricula in response to new training needs related to homeland security.

Miami Dade College, for example, has in the past 18 months provided eight hours of entry-level training on the effects of weapons of mass destruction and on the use of personal protective equipment to 8,700 people, including not only first responders but also employees of schools, hospitals, and public-works facilities.

But so far, the dollars flowing to community colleges to support such training are a trickle compared with those spent by the Department of Homeland Security on university research and equipment for fire and police stations. The University of Minnesota, the University of Southern California, and Texas A&M University lead research efforts that have each received $12-million or more in homeland-security funds.

That leaves many community-college officials feeling that their role in preparing for disasters, whether man-made or natural, has gone unappreciated by both the federal government and the state administrators who dole out the majority of homeland-security funds. The colleges say they need additional money to modify their curricula, establish training sites, and train more first responders if the country is to effectively prepare for the kinds of threats that were hardly envisioned before September 11, 2001, as well as for natural catastrophes like Hurricane Katrina.

"We have the expertise," says Paul Unger, Owens's provost. "We want to save the country money by not reinventing the wheel of the training infrastructure."

The problem in community colleges' quest for homeland-security money is a familiar one: They have faced not so much outright discrimination as benign neglect.

Most of the federal homeland-security funds potentially available to community colleges flow through a state office, which then passes along 80 percent of such funds to local or regional decision makers within the state.

The federal government sets certain restrictions on how the money can be spent: It cannot be used for building projects, for example, which explains why Owens Community College has received no funds from Ohio Homeland Security, the state administrator. But in categories like equipment, planning, training, and exercises that simulate disaster scenarios, states and municipalities are free to allocate the money as they see fit. Fire and police chiefs arguably have the greatest say over how the funds are spent at the local level, and they have overwhelmingly funneled the money into equipment—spending more than eight times as much on gear, vehicles, and other hardware as on training and exercises.

"The localities have always wanted to buy equipment, and this has been their chance to do it," says George R. Boggs, president of the American Association of Community Colleges, who has heard a number of college presidents grumble about the challenges of obtaining homeland-security funds. "But one would think that the people buying the equipment would need some training and upgrading of their skills."

Pam Whitelock is president of Prepare America, a coalition of 250 community colleges that is pushing for more federal support for homeland-security training. She says the ubiquitous requests for new equipment—coupled with no federal and very few state requirements about how much homeland-security training is required for first responders—have put community colleges in a difficult position.

"Are we going to argue over the need for an emergency-response vehicle or equipment for a firefighter?" Ms. Whitelock, who recently retired as dean of lifelong learning at Gulf Coast Community College, in Panama City, Fla., asks rhetorically. "So, in most cases, training has gone by the wayside or been handled in a hit-or-miss way."

Aside from state spending, the other potential source of money for community colleges is the department's Competitive Training Grants Program, which supports projects that help the country prevent, respond to, and recover from incidents of terrorism. The program, which has been in existence for two years, distributes $30-million annually, but community colleges have received only three of the 29 awards. Four-year institutions have won 15. The remaining awards were won by institutes, associations, and states.

"We need to move the pendulum more toward the training and particularly the exercising, and away from the equipment. What you don't practice, you're not going to do well."

The training-grants program is small compared to the $2.3-billion in homeland-security spending at the state level, where equipment expenditures reign. And community-college advocates aren't the only ones who are concerned about the relatively modest sums being spent on training and exercises compared with outlays for equipment. Kenneth L. Morckel, director of the Ohio Department of Public Safety, which includes the state's homeland-security division, says he has spoken directly with Michael Chertoff, U.S. secretary of homeland security, about the need for more training.

"We need to move the pendulum more toward the training and particularly the exercising, and away from the equipment," Mr. Morckel says.

Even though federal regulations prevent him from providing money for it, he believes that the Owens training facility would be "a great resource" for first responders in Ohio. He points to the harm caused by the interagency confusion following Hurricane Katrina as an example of why exercises are so important. "What you don't practice," he says, "you're not going to do well."

Marc Short, a spokesman for the Department of Homeland Security, says its officials share the concern that too much of the money that has gone out to the states has been used to purchase

equipment. The requirement that the money be spent within two years may have influenced decisions, he says, since it is easier to buy equipment than to assemble a training program.

Some community-college officials say that the process for distributing training funds is broken, and that the federal government needs to assert greater control.

"I believe we'll see a long-term shift toward the training and the exercises with the continued allocation of those dollars," Mr. Short says.

Beginning in 2006, the department will allow every state to name one or more training partners that would deliver courses that have been approved by the Office for Domestic Preparedness, the arm of the department responsible for preparing the country for acts of terrorism. To date the office has relied most heavily on just a few such partners to provide training, including three universities—Louisiana State, Texas A&M, and the New Mexico Institute of Mining and Technology.

While those institutions and others will continue to provide highly specialized training, more-general training could fall to community colleges in a number of states.

"I think this is a move by ODP to turn some of the authority over to the states and to the community colleges who are the experts in training," says Bryan Renfro, director of the Institute of Corporate and Public Safety at Northwest Arkansas Community College, in Bentonville.

Northwest Arkansas is one of the three community colleges that have won direct awards through the Department of Homeland Security's Competitive Training Grants Program. The college, which received $1-million a year ago, is working closely with three corporations based in or near Bentonville—Wal-Mart, J.B. Hunt, and Tyson Foods—to develop a series of courses that will integrate corporate executives into the community emergency-planning process.

The department, which had indicated an interest in supporting corporate-sector training, encourages partnerships in its grant competitions. "The folks in Washington are really looking for collaborative efforts," Mr. Renfro says. "We had three key corporate partners that could work to bridge that training gap."

Kirkwood Community College, in Cedar Rapids, Iowa, received a $3.1-million award in 2004 from the competitive-grants program to develop a "train the trainer" program in agricultural terrorism. Since the early 1990s, when Kirkwood first received a federal grant to support hazardous-materials training, the college has built a network of 125 community colleges and other partners in 35 states that send educators and technicians to receive instruction from Kirkwood. Those people then return home to train others in their own communities.

The major fear with "agroterrorism" is that an animal disease, such as foot-and-mouth disease, could be introduced in the United States, wreaking economic havoc. Kirkwood's training will show first responders how to control an outbreak.

"When they gave us that grant, the point they made time and time again was that this was a no-brainer," says Doug Feil, Kirkwood's director of environmental-health-and-safety programs. "We have an established network to get the training out, and by having the network, the department didn't have to build a new one."

Only one community college, Waukesha County Technical College, was among the 15 winners in the latest round of competitive-training grants, which were announced in September. The college received $750,000 to develop courses on general aviation and airport security for first responders and airport personnel.

The number of community colleges that have successfully obtained large homeland-security grants through other avenues is tiny. One such institution is St. Petersburg College, a community college that also offers some four-year degrees. The Florida college established its National Terrorism Preparedness Institute in 1998—three years before the September 11 terrorist attacks—and for the past four years has received more than $2-million per year as a training partner with the Office for Domestic Preparedness. Among other things, the funds support monthly broadcasts, transmitted from the college via satellite, of round-table discussions with experts on various aspects of homeland security.

William H. Janes, the institute's director, says he doesn't necessarily agree with the notion that community colleges are being snubbed. "I don't know what a fair amount for community colleges is—I try to avoid those sorts of discussions," he says. "The advantage I have is that by being in existence since 1998, we have the relationships and the credibility."

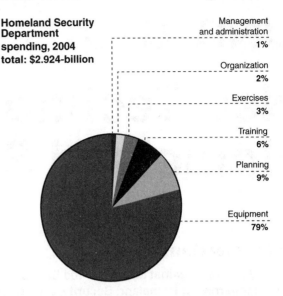

Homeland Security Department spending, 2004 total: $2.924-billion

- Management and administration **1%**
- Organization **2%**
- Exercises **3%**
- Training **6%**
- Planning **9%**
- Equipment **79%**

Figure 1 Overequipped and Undertrained? Community-college officials argue that training for "first responders" is being neglected by the state and local officials who make decisions about how to use money from the U.S. Department of Homeland Security. In 2004 a total of $2.3-billion from the department was used to purchase equipment—more than eight times the amount spent on training and exercises (simulating disaster scenarios).

Note: The total of $2.9-billion includes the following federal grant programs, funds from which are distributed through state administrators: State Homeland Security Program, Law Enforcement Terrorism Prevention Program, Citizen Crops Program, Urban Areas Security Initiative, and Transit Security Program. "Organization" includes payments for overtime and additional staff when first responders are attending training or when a homeland-security threat changes.

Source: Department of Homeland Security

The American Association of Community Colleges and the Transportation Security Administration, a division of the Department of Homeland Security, struck a deal last year in which five colleges around the United States provide self-defense training to airline pilots and flight attendants. But the numbers involved in the program so far have been modest. Miami Dade, for example, holds about one class per month, for 10 to 25 students, and has received about $100,000 in federal funds for its work.

The bigger dollars for training flow through the state administrators. Florida's Department of Education has paid Miami Dade $800,000 in federal homeland-security funds to provide entry-level training to 8,700 first responders and others.

Ronald Grimming, director of the college's School of Justice and Homeland Security, says the overall level of federal support is not sufficient. "Quite frankly, we do a lot of other homeland-security training that we've received no funding for," he says. "We essentially end up having to do this on our own."

Some community-college officials suggest that the process for distributing training funds is broken, and that the federal government needs to assert greater control. The Public Safety Institute at Tarrant County College, in Fort Worth, operates a $20-million, 23-acre training site that includes five buildings

with computer-controlled fires, a swift-water rescue area, and an emergency-driving course. Ted P. Phillips, the institute's division chair, says the college has created its homeland-security training largely on the fly, as public agencies and private companies have come to the college asking for help with instruction and the use of its facility.

"It would make more sense to me if community colleges were in the direct-funding loop from the federal government," Mr. Phillips says. "If they funded us directly, we could offer and deliver the courses that we are doing anyway, but we could better plan, schedule, and staff those courses."

Some training officials at community colleges argue that the current structure is only now beginning to work. The Kentucky Community and Technical College System, which comprises 16 colleges on 65 campuses, recently was hired to coordinate all official training exercises for the state's homeland-security office. That work, coupled with some community outreach, will bring in $940,000 per year.

"The time is close where the research has been done and it's time to start getting boots on the ground," says Bob Hammonds, the system's director of homeland-security initiatives. "I'm very optimistic about the future of training for homeland security at community colleges."

UNIT 6

New Technologies in Homeland Security

Unit Selections

Key Points to Consider

- Have technologies developed in the wake of 9/11 made the United States safer?

- Should anti-missile technology be a priority for the Department of Homeland Security?

- What could the Department of Homeland Security do to improve port security?

Student Web Site

www.mhcls.com/online

Internet References

Further information regarding these Web sites may be found in this book's preface or online.

Government Technology
   http://www.govtech.net/
National Institute of Standards and Technology
   http://www.nist.gov/public_affairs/factsheet/homeland.htm

New technologies have had a tremendous impact on U.S. security. Surveillance cameras, metal detectors, and explosive detection equipment have become commonplace at U.S. airports. Yet, despite the existence of these precautionary measures, the September 11th hijackers managed to board and take over four U.S. aircraft. While some choose to blame the Intelligence Community for the security failures of 9/11, there has been little or no discussion of the failure of technology. Billions of dollars spent on new security measures and millions spent on new explosive detection equipment, installed at major U.S. airports on the recommendations of the Gore Commission after the crash of TWA Flight 800, did not prevent the attacks of 9/11. As we become increasingly dependent on technology in day-to-day security, we must recognize the limits of technology in homeland security. Technological solutions are expensive. They offer limited solutions to specific problems. Once in place, they are vulnerable to countermeasures.

One of the major drawbacks of technology solutions to security issues is cost. Since the first attack on the World Trade Center in 1993, counterterrorism funding has increased significantly. U.S. government spending on counterterrorism has risen from less than $1 billion in 1995 to well over $50 billion in 2005. As the federal budget deficits increase and counterterrorism spending reaches its limits, increased attention must be paid to the nature of investments in technology and the associated tradeoffs.

Technological solutions often focus on very narrow problems. Metal detectors may detect firearms, but are not likely to detect plastic explosives. Databases that maintain information on potential terrorists are only useful if they capture all possible suspects and if they can be easily accessed by those who need them. Passenger profiling software does not identify terrorists who don't fit a specific profile. Systems designed to protect aircraft against heat-seeking missiles do not protect against other types of shoulder-fired weapons or prevent attacks against targets on the ground. The selection of one technology over another thus automatically determines the limitations of the security system.

Once a new technology is in use, it becomes susceptible to countermeasures. Terrorists have proven themselves extremely adept at circumventing existing security. Billions spent on technology for airport security were circumvented by 99 cent boxcutters. Systems that monitor the international transfer of funds have been rendered ineffective by traditional barter and exchange systems. Technology designed to intercept and monitor cell-phone calls has led to the development and use of alternate means of communication. Profiling of terrorists has led to the increased recruitment of individuals who don't meet the profile.

While technology alone cannot solve the complex problems posed by homeland security, the use of technology can significantly improve and enhance existing security. With this caveat, the articles in this unit examine the potential role of new technologies in homeland security.

Guarding Against Missiles

Fred Bayles

Police and, in some instances, the National Guard are patrolling the perimeters and flight approaches of airports in Los Angeles, Chicago, Orlando and other major cities in an effort to stop terrorists from shooting down passenger jets with shoulder-fired missiles.

In San Francisco, New York and Washington, Coast Guard boats keep watch near waterfront runways. Boston Harbor clam diggers use cell phones to report suspicious activity near Logan International.

The increased surveillance is the first step in federal efforts to protect airliners that take off and land an average of 170,000 times a day.

Federal officials won't talk about pending strategies to prevent terrorists from launching heat-seeking missiles at passenger planes. But an unreleased FAA study lists the use of airborne patrols, ground checkpoints, observation posts and high-intensity lights in areas adjacent to airports.

Although there has never been an attack in the USA and federal officials discount the immediacy of the threat, some members of Congress have proposed putting anti-missile systems on airliners within the next year.

One sponsor, Sen. Charles Schumer, D-N.Y., says that with thousands of the missiles on the black market and previous attacks on jets overseas, the risk to the flying public and the airline industry is too great to not take action.

"The damage a terrorist attack could do would be devastating," Schumer says. "Do you think anyone would fly for three to six months after an attack?"

Homeland Security Secretary Tom Ridge also sees the possible use of anti-missile systems on airliners in the future, but only after more study.

"I think the first public dollars we ought to expend should be to take a look at the technology itself to see if adaptation can be made," he told a gathering of reporters recently.

Security experts agree there is no fast or easy fix. They say airport surveillance is limited against a weapon that can be launched from a pickup, boat or rooftop. Many shoulder-launched missiles can hit a jet 4 miles away at altitudes of more than 10,000 feet. According to the FAA report, that would give terrorists a 150-square-mile area around an airport in which to hide and fire at aircraft that are taking off or circling to land.

Congress' hopes for a quick technological solution may be optimistic, too, they say. Adding a complex system of countermeasures to jets could take years to do safely.

"There is no silver bullet," says James Loy, head of the Transportation Security Agency (TSA), which is responsible for air travel safety.

Some federal officials also caution that the threat of shoulder-launched missiles may be overstated. So far, they have a poor record against passenger jets; only one has been downed in six attacks.

"These weapons pose a threat, but there is no specific credible evidence that they are in the hands of terrorists in the United States or that they plan to use them to shoot down airliners," says Brian Roehrkasse, a spokesman for the Department of Homeland Security.

The missiles, called Man Portable Air Defense Systems, or MANPADS, weigh about 35 pounds and can be fired with little training. Honing in on the heat from aircraft engines, the missiles travel at more than 600 mph, three times the takeoff or landing speed of an airliner.

The U.S. version, the Stinger, contributed to the defeat of the Soviet army in the 1980s in Afghanistan, where rebels used them to shoot down assault helicopters and jet fighters.

About 700,000 MANPADS have been produced worldwide since the 1970s. The most common is the 30-year-old Russian SA-7 Strela. The British, French and Chinese also produce them. Intelligence agencies say Al-Qaeda and 26 known terrorist groups have dozens of the weapons.

MANPADS have been used in 35 attacks against civilian airplanes in Africa, Asia, Afghanistan and Central America; 24 were shot down, killing more than 500 people. All but one of the planes shot down were propeller planes. The only jet, a Congo Airlines Boeing 727, was shot down by rebels in 1998.

In May, Al-Qaeda terrorists fired an SA-7 at a U.S. military jet taking off in Saudi Arabia. In November, terrorists launched two SA-7s at an Israeli charter jet leaving Mombasa, Kenya. Both attempts failed.

The day after the Mombasa attack, the White House formed a group to study the threat. In December, the TSA surveyed about 80 major airports to identify vulnerabilities. Two months ago, after London's Heathrow Airport was nearly shut down by

Increasing Runway Security

Steps to improve security on airport grounds include:

- Area checkpoints.
- Perimeter and area observation posts.
- More ground patrols.
- Random ground patrols.
- High-intensity portable lighting directed outward in areas of woods, open waterways or uninhabited areas.
- Airborne patrols, observations using night-vision and heat-vision equipment if available.
- Special surveillance areas beyond the fence line in sectors parallel to the active runways.

Source: *Unpublished 1996 FAA document*

concerns of a possible missile attack, the TSA and FBI visited 22 of the largest airports to develop security plans.

Officials decline to identify the airports or talk about specific tactics. But an FAA study, initiated in 1996, points to possible countermeasures. They include:

- **Denying terrorists access to areas around the airport.** While the report considered this the most practical solution, it noted efforts would require manpower from federal, state and local agencies. It is also far from certain. Capt. Steve Luckey, chairman of the Air Line Pilots Association's security committee, says neighborhoods around urban airports such as Los Angeles International and San Diego offer too many hiding places.

"I don't know how you can defend an airport surrounded by miles of rooftops," he says.

- **Changing flight operations.** Pilots could take off in faster, steeper climbs and descend in spiraling turns over the airport to reduce time spent at lower altitudes. Such changes would be difficult.

"It isn't something that can easily be accomplished given the fixed navigational aids used by the airplanes," says Ian Redhead of Airports Council International, an airport trade association.

- **Installing countermeasures on airliners.** Congress is considering a $30 million appropriation to test a system of lasers and other devices to throw heat-seeking missiles off target. Military aircraft already use flares and lasers to divert missiles. Air Force One and El Al airliners are believed to use similar devices.

"The technology already exists," says Schumer, who favors a bill that would require the system to be installed in 5,000 airliners at an estimated cost of $8 billion.

But aviation safety experts say the use of flares and other incendiary devices creates safety issues in the air and on the ground. They also worry about putting new technology into the already complex systems of a jetliner.

"It would take five to 10 years to do the engineering work to add these systems to a fleet of different aircraft," says Kevin Darcy, a former accident investigator for Boeing.

Modernizing Homeland Security

High-tech data links and inter-agency coordination could stop terrorists from slipping through our fingers again.

JOHN D. COHEN AND JOHN A. HURSON

Last year's terrorist attacks uncovered a deadly lack of integration among America's domestic defenses. Several of the future hijackers were briefly involved with police or other government agencies, which entered their names into government data systems. At least two of the men were sought by the FBI; the names of others were in other intelligence databases. But because the data systems were not linked, the dots were never connected, and the men went on their way. The chance to prevent terrorism was lost.

We know that the nation's law enforcement and emergency response systems do not function cohesively because they are largely tied to geographical jurisdictions or exclusive functions.

Although we'll never know whether better data sharing would have thwarted the horrible attacks, we do know that terrorists often use traditional crime, such as drug trafficking to support their objectives.

We also know that the nation's law enforcement and emergency response systems do not function cohesively because they are largely tied to geographical jurisdictions or exclusive functions. When police and fire departments from Virginia, Maryland, and Washington, D.C. responded to the Pentagon attack, they were unable to radio one another because, like most public safety entities, each department had its own radio frequencies.

To prevent and respond to terrorism, we must change our approach to security.

First, we must redefine our concept of national security to include the pivotal role of states and localities. In the event of new terrorist attacks, some of the first people on the scene will be police officers, followed by local firefighters and healthcare providers. Federal help will be hours and maybe even days away. One way or another, responsibility for homeland defense rests with state and local governments.

Second, our approach to domestic defense must be made national and seamless. In addition to coordinating federal agencies, the Office of Homeland Security must set clear national priorities to guide action for states and localities. And to help state and local governments build a seamless domestic defense, Congress must provide block grants with accountability provisions.

"We must build on existing state and local partnerships and information sharing, resisting the temptation to create stand-alone agencies mobilized only in a crisis."

Third, we must make domestic defense a top priority in the everyday work of government, not just in emergencies. We must build on existing state and local partnerships and information sharing, resisting the temptation to create stand-alone agencies mobilized only in a crisis. Information and communication technology and operational strategies used for emergencies should also support efforts to provide delivery of services by government agencies each day. With this infrastructure, state and local officials will not only have the foundation for efforts to prevent and respond to crises—everyday government will work better, too.

We should begin institutionalizing this new approach by immediately taking several steps. The first involves connecting the dots with the data. To link the information from various arms of the criminal justice system about the people who commit crime and the places where crime occurs, we must launch "integrated justice" information systems.

Just as search engines on the Web allow instantaneous access to vast sources of information, we must create a system in which secure facilities (such as airports) can access resources like the terrorist "watch list" in the National Crime Information Center at the FBI. Public safety information and communication systems should also be interlinked with those of other critical government systems that support transportation, social services, and public utilities. Efforts to "connect the dots with data" in 38 states and the District of Columbia must be accelerated and made universal.

A SMART START: Upgraded anti-terrorist technology, like the U.S. Army's new SmarTruck, can help first responders, like patrolman Robert Berry (inset), of Byram, Connecticut.

In addition, we must integrate emergency response communications systems. This would enable first responders from different agencies and jurisdictions to talk to each other. Efforts to address such deficiencies have been energized following the events of Sept. 11. For example, Maryland launched a project to patch disparate radio systems into an integrated network that offers a model for others.

At the same time, we need to bolster defenses against biological and chemical terrorist attacks. To identify and respond to both naturally occurring disease outbreak and biological and chemical weapon attacks, we must establish an information network linking laboratories, first responders, health care providers, governmental agencies, and other facilities.

Now that terrorism is a clearer threat, it's all the more critical that states be prepared to recognize an outbreak of disease, circulate information to health-care providers, coordinate local response with federal and military systems, and allocate scarce medical resources such as antibiotics and vaccines.

> **State and local leaders should take heart that the best way to prevent and prepare for terrorism is already available in the techniques and technologies now strengthening communities and protecting our neighborhoods.**

A good first step is the Lightweight Epidemiology Advanced Detection & Emergency Response System deployed by hospitals and state medical offices in New York and Phoenix during the World Series. Building on this Web-based system, medical personnel will have the ability to track outbreaks as they are reported by hospitals, map geographic regions where outbreaks are occurring, and determine response capabilities of various medical facilities.

Finally, it is important to connect everyone with 211 and 311. To provide information and services to everyone, we must establish statewide toll-free numbers for non-emergency information and referral services for health care and social services. At the time of the terrorist attacks and the anthrax scare, people called a non-emergency number for information and referral to health and social services when one was available. When a non-emergency number wasn't available, they called 911. But relying on 911 systems is potentially catastrophic, because the system could become inundated with non-emergency calls that clog out emergency calls. We need to expand the use of 211 and 311 as non-emergency information numbers. Connecticut's statewide 211 telephone system for information and referral is a model to follow.

These innovations would be key first steps toward fully integrating America's domestic defenses. State and local leaders should take heart that the best way to prevent and prepare for terrorism is already available in the techniques and technologies now strengthening communities and protecting our neighborhoods. Building on those methods will not only improve homeland security, it will also improve health care, policing, and other government services.

JOHN D. COHEN is president of PSComm LLC and directs the Progressive Policy Institute's Community Crime Fighting Project. JOHN A. HURSON is a member of the Maryland House of Delegates, where he serves as chairman of the Environmental Matters Committee.

Hesitation at Homeland Security

A high-tech missile defense for passenger jets now exists, but plans to install it don't

LORRAINE WOELLERT

It's a horrifying scenario: A lone terrorist hiding near a U.S. airport targets a passenger jet with a shoulder-fired missile. Beyond any immediate carnage, the inevitable ripple of fear could paralyze the travel industry and cripple the economy.

The Bush Administration ranks portable missiles—some of which are thought to be in the hands of al Qaeda and other fanatic groups—as a leading terrorist menace. In September, 2005, the State Dept. warned of "a serious potential threat to passenger air travel [and] the commercial aviation industry."

But at the Homeland Security Dept., the alarm is more tempered. The agency is winding down a three-year study of how to adapt military antimissile technology to civilian planes. Contractors doing the research say results so far are promising. But as Homeland Security phases out its antimissile research budget—to $4.8 million for 2007, down from $109 million this year—the agency shows little interest in buying the gear. "Until we know whether this approach is a good approach or not, I think that that is something we just are not prepared to promise money for," Homeland Security Secretary Michael Chertoff told the House Homeland Security Committee last month.

Another reason for Chertoff's hesitation: The roughly 30 shoulder-fired missile attacks on civilian aircraft in the past three decades were all in overseas hot spots. "We do take it seriously, but we base [Homeland Security's position] on the risk assessment of, 'Could it happen here?'" says Brian Doyle, a department spokesman.

Such ambivalence worries skeptics of every stripe. Alane Kochems, a national security analyst at the conservative Heritage Foundation, says that without Administration leadership, Congress isn't likely to take the initiative and fund defense systems for American planes. Homeland Security "doesn't have clear policy guidelines, and they're not putting a lot of money out there because they don't quite know what they want," she says.

Representative Steve J. Israel (D-N.Y.), asserts that intelligence experts "all agree that this is one of the most glaring vulnerabilities to our homeland security, and the White House and DHS insist on wishful thinking that it's not." Shoulder-fired

missiles typically weigh less than 40 pounds and can be hidden in a golf bag. They can fire up to 23,000 feet, and tens of thousands are unaccounted for around the world. Israel has introduced a bill to force Homeland Security to set a schedule for buying missile-defense devices, but the legislation has little momentum.

It was at Congress' behest in 2004 that the agency began testing military technology on commercial jets. Sensors attached to a plane's hull detect an incoming heat-seeking missile and

Surprise Attacks

Shoulder-fired missile assaults on civilian planes have become a threat:

Nov. 22, 2003
A DHL Airbus A300 cargo jet transporting mail in Iraq landed safely after being hit, but the plane was a total loss.

Nov. 28, 2002
Two missiles missed an Israeli jet with 271 passengers and crew during takeoff from Mombasa, Kenya.

Dec. 26, 1998
UNITA rebels brought down a U.N. Lockheed C-130, the first of two in the span of a week. Fourteen were killed.

Oct. 10, 1998
A Congo Airlines Boeing 727 was downed over the Congo by Tutsi rebels, killing all of the 41 people on board.

Apr. 6, 1994
A small jet carrying the presidents of Rwanda and Burundi was shot down, killing all aboard and sparking regional conflict.

trigger lasers or flares, an alternate heat source that throws the missile off course.

In two studies for Homeland Security, contractors Northrop Grumman Corp. and BAE Systems Inc. are testing the system on working cargo planes—so far with no significant glitches, the companies say. Homeland Security will release early results this spring. "This is an operationally effective system. We've done a lot of work in making it commercially viable," says Stephen duMont, BAE's director of commercial aircraft programs. If the government mandated the technology, BAE and Northrop would expect to profit by selling it.

Homeland Security's Chertoff has warned that the steep cost of defending against missiles would have to be shared by taxpayers and the airline industry. That has made the financially weak industry an opponent of the technology, although air carriers have kept a low profile on the sensitive issue. At an estimated $1 million a plane, it would cost $7 billion to equip the U.S. passenger fleet's 6,800 aircraft. Added maintenance and fuel costs (because of the weight and drag of the gear) could tack on $27 billion or more over 20 years, according to Santa Monica (Calif.) researcher RAND Corp.

"We think the better choice is to continue to work to get those missiles out of the hands of the bad guys and secure airport perimeters," says David A. Castelveter, vice-president of the Air Transport Assn., a trade group. El Al Israel Airlines made a different choice. In December it said it would become the first carrier to install the technology. Five of its planes have been outfitted with the devices.

Thanks, Dubai!

The scrutiny of the ports deal has fast-tracked an idea to make ports more secure. It may also end up saving billions in global trade

TOMAS KELLNER

What good could come out of the politicized debate on who runs shipping terminals? Some new technology to stop terrorists.

U.S. seaports handle 9 million containers per year. Only 5% of these boxes are inspected by the Coast Guard or U.S. Customs officials, a gaping hole in security that remains unaffected by port stewardship. (Of the 3.6 million containers coming in overland, 10% are inspected.) As meager as this level of protection is, considerable sums are being spent on it—$1.5 billion last year by the Coast Guard, plus significant, and mostly uncounted, sums by shippers. To make things worse, the number of incoming containers will double by 2020.

Stephen E. Flynn, a retired Coast Guard commander and expert on port security at the Council on Foreign Relations, wrote in the *Far Eastern Economic Review* that "U.S. government container security policy resembles a house of cards."

High-tech responses to this sorry state of affairs are coming from a variety of companies, including General Electric, IBM and shipper A.P. Moeller-Maersk. They are testing a system in which they rig cargo containers with nimble electronic brains and link them to a constellation of orbiting satellites. Customers and homeland security officials would be able to monitor where cargo goes second by second, from the minute it leaves a factory in China until it reaches a store in Wichita.

GE has linked up with Globalstar and Orbcomm, two formerly bankrupt satellite communications firms now on the mend, to build a rugged plastic box about the size of two cigarette packs that mounts with four screws between the ribs of a shipping container. The box contains a satellite modem, a lithium-ion battery that lasts seven years, a processor that stores data and communications circuitry connecting the box with disposable wireless sensor tags distributed throughout the container.

The tags monitor everything from the door lock, humidity and temperature to radiation and gases like carbon dioxide. It's sensitive enough to spot human breath—and even the ethylene exuded by ripening bananas—anywhere inside the container within 30 seconds. Sensors also measure the container's g-forces, altered when a container accelerates, a telltale indicator of dropped cargo.

The tags then zap the data via low-powered radio to the main box, which beams the intelligence to one of Globalstar's 43 satellites orbiting 875 miles above the Earth. The data takes less than five minutes to zip from a ship to GE's control center.

Thomas Konditi, head of GE's asset intelligence unit, says that the system, which costs as much as $1,000 per container, allows clients to micromanage their supply chains, reduce theft and inventories, and buy cheaper insurance. GE's Equipment Services unit leases out more than 1 million containers to retailers such as Wal-Mart. "This is a billion-dollar business when you start managing all that data," says Konditi.

He's not exaggerating. The U.S. brought in $1.9 trillion of manufactured goods last year, about 60% by sea, says Chip C. White of the Logistics Institute at Georgia Tech. The loss to theft, anywhere between the dock of the factory that loaded the container and the dock of the U.S. warehouse that receives it, is probably in the neighborhood of 0.3%. There are other costs to the way containers are handled now. Bottlenecks at ports, which are sure to increase if the Coast Guard gets tougher with its inspections, are hugely expensive. A medium-size container ship waiting at anchor costs its owner $50,000 a day in lost rent. In 2004 the backlog at the Los Angeles ports got so bad that there were 94 ships held up for as long as a week. GE has tested the device on 500 container and says its system could eventually shave 4% to 8% off ocean-shipping costs by cutting down on theft and port jams.

IBM has teamed up with another once-bankrupt satellite operator, Iridium, to test a similar solution with the Danish shipping giant A.P. Moller-Maersk Group last year, monitoring containers between China, Europe and the U.S. The system eliminates kinks in the sensors, holes in satellite connections and false alarms (as much as 6% of reported incidents). The partners have just launched a pilot program tracking 1,000 containers filled with real cargo.

Later this year IBM will use the system for monitoring its own traffic of high-end business printers between Yokohama, Japan and Rochester, Minn. via the Port of Los Angeles. (About 11 containers a month take the 30-day trip.) IBM estimates it could cut logistics costs by 5% with container-tracking gear.

Satellite operators see a potential bonanza in logistics data. Iridium and Globalstar, which flamed out in the late 1990s trying to sell voice services, are now showing nice operating profits. In 2005 Iridium earned an estimated $48 million (before interest, taxes and amortization), 25% of it from data services, on $190 million in revenue. Globalstar earned $25 million last year on $120 million in revenue, 23% from data. "This is data heroin," Jay Monroe, Globalstar chief executive, says about container radios. "The more data people get used to, the more they want."

The satellite tracking systems have some hurdles to overcome. Shippers may balk at adding a $1,000 piece of equipment to a container that costs only $2,000. The radio systems still need to be certified by U.S. Customs. The system is useless if the false alarm rate stays high. Robert C. Bonner, a recently retired Customs commissioner, favors the expansion of alternative solutions such as advance electronic shipping manifests and container inspection at ports of departure to speed screening at U.S. ports.

Whatever the best technology for stopping bombs, we'd surely be better off trying some of it rather than worrying about who hires the longshoremen.

UNIT 7

Vulnerabilities and Threats

Unit Selections

Key Points to Consider

- How can the threat posed by the theft of highly enriched uranium be reduced?

- How can the threat posed by bioterrorism be lessened?

- How can the United States limit the threat posed by rail transport of hazardous materials?

- How can security at U.S. ports be improved?

Student Web Site

www.mhcls.com/online

Internet References

Further information regarding these Web sites may be found in this book's preface or online.

National Homeland Security Knowledge Base
   http://www.twotigersonline.com/resources.html

National Terror Alert Response Center
   http://www.nationalterroralert.com/

U.S. Customs and Border Protection
   http://www.cbp.gov/xp/cgov/border_security/antiterror_initiatives/border_security_overview.xml

The purpose of this unit is to give the reader a sense of existing threats. The attacks on the World Trade Center and the Pentagon spawned wild speculation and apocalyptic predictions concerning the future of U.S. security. The tragedies and the subsequent anthrax attacks fueled fears and have led to exaggerations of terrorist capabilities. While the existing threats cannot and should not be ignored, the U.S. government and the media often project unrealistic images of terrorists, endowing them with capabilities far beyond their actual reach. These articles, rather than to further perpetuate myths and fears, seek to provide insights into what some believe the future of terrorist threats may look like. Since terrorism is to be a top priority for homeland security, difficult choices must be made. As policymakers attempt to find ways to reassure a concerned public, choices between spending for security today and preparing for the threats of the future are becoming increasingly difficult.

Terrorism will undoubtedly remain a major policy issue for the United States well into the 21st century. Opinions as to what future perpetrators will look like and what methods they will pursue vary. While some argue that the traditional methods of terrorism—such as bombing, kidnapping, and hostage-taking—will continue to dominate the new millennium, others warn that

weapons of mass destruction or weapons of mass disruption, such as biological and chemical weapons, or even nuclear or radiological weapons, will be the weapons of choice for terrorists in the future.

The articles in this unit highlight some of the potential vulnerabilities and threats. "Thwarting Nuclear Terrorism" argues that terrorist organizations have ample opportunities to steal or buy enough highly enriched uranium to build a primitive atomic bomb. It asserts that governments need to redouble their efforts to limit the availability of highly enriched uranium. The second article in this unit warns that our over-reliance on historical precedent in regards to bioterrorism may be dangerous. It claims that the U.S. needs to develop flexible defenses capable of adjusting to the continuing changes of natural sciences. In the third article, Amy Barrett focuses on the vulnerability of trains carrying dangerous chemicals throughout the United States. She suggests that they should be, when possible, re-routed or disguised to reduce the threat of terrorist attacks. Finally, Stephen Flynn claims that efforts to secure domestic ports and monitor foreign points of origin have not been successful. He highlights three important weaknesses of the maritime security apparatus and offers policy recommendations designed to address them.

Thwarting Nuclear Terrorism

Many civilian research reactors contain highly enriched uranium that terrorists could use to build nuclear bombs

ALEXANDER GLASER AND FRANK N. VON HIPPEL

The atomic bomb that incinerated the Japanese city of Hiroshima at the close of World War II contained about 60 kilograms of chain-reacting uranium. When the American "Little Boy" device detonated over the doomed port, one part of the bomb's charge—a subcritical mass—was fired into the other by a relatively simple gun-like mechanism, causing the uranium 235 in the combined mass to go supercritical and explode with the force of 15 kilotons of TNT. The weapon that devastated Nagasaki a few days later used plutonium rather than uranium in its explosive charge and required much more complex technology to set it off.

Despite the production of more than 100,000 nuclear weapons by a few nations and some close calls during the succeeding 60 years, no similar nuclear destruction has occurred so far. Today, however, an additional fearful threat has arisen: that a subnational terrorist organization such as al Qaeda might acquire highly enriched uranium (HEU), build a crude gun-type detonating device and use the resulting nuclear weapon against a city. HEU is uranium in which uranium 235, the isotope capable of sustaining a nuclear chain reaction, has been concentrated to levels of 20 percent or more by weight.

The engineering required to build a gun-type atomic bomb is so basic that the physicists who designed "Little Boy" did not perform a nuclear test of the design before deployment—they had no doubt that if the "gun" fired, the weapon would explode. Experts agree, therefore, that a well-funded terrorist group could produce a workable gun-type mechanism. Indeed, some have raised credible concerns that suicidal malefactors could penetrate an HEU storage facility, construct a so-called improvised nuclear device and detonate it before security guards could respond.

Although the production of HEU is beyond the means of nonstate actors, its procurement through theft or black market purchase is not: the globe is awash in around 1,800 tons of the material created during the cold war mostly by the U.S. and the Soviet Union. HEU today can be found at both civilian and military sites. We will, however, focus on that at civilian facilities

Blueprint for a Bomb

If terrorists obtained 60 kilograms of highly enriched uranium, they could make a nuclear explosive similar to the "Little Boy" atomic bomb that leveled Hiroshima in Japan at the end of World War II. Builders would shape a subcritical mass of the uranium into a "bullet" and place it just in front of a quantity of propellant at the far end of a closed cylinder. The remainder of the uranium [also a subcritical mass] would go at the other end of the "gun" barrel. Detonation of the propellant would send the bullet down the barrel, slamming it into the second uranium mass. The combined masses would then go supercritical and set off an explosive nuclear chain reaction.

in, or intended for use as, fuel for research nuclear reactors. We fret especially about civilian HEU because it is less securely guarded than military stores. (Uranium fuel for generating electricity at nuclear power plants is typically only slightly enriched to 3 to 5 percent uranium 235 by weight.)

More than 50 tons of HEU are in civilian use, dispersed around the globe to support about 140 reactors employed to conduct scientific or industrial research or to produce radioactive isotopes for medical purposes. These sites are often located in urban areas and are minimally protected by security systems and guards. Especially worrisome is Russia's HEU-fueled reactor fleet, which constitutes about one third of the world's total and has associated with it more than half of all the civilian HEU that exists.

Improving security is essential. But in the long run, the most effective solution to the danger posed by nuclear terrorism is to eliminate wherever possible the use of HEU and remove accumulated stocks. The recovered HEU then should be diluted with uranium 238, the much more common uranium isotope that cannot Sustain a chain reaction, to produce what specialists call low-enriched uranium (LEU)—material

Overview/Security Civilian Uranium 235

- Terrorists who acquired less than 100 kilograms of highly enriched uranium [HEU] could build and detonate a rudimentary but effective atomic bomb relatively easily. HEU is also attractive for states that seek to develop nuclear weapons secretly, without having to test them.
- Unfortunately, large quantities of HEU are stored in nuclear research facilities worldwide—especially in Russia, often under minimal security.
- The U.S. and its allies have established programs to bolster security measures, convert reactors to use low-enriched uranium [which is useless for weapons] and retrieve HEU from research-reactor sites around the world. Dangerous gaps remain, however.
- High-level governmental attention plus a comparatively small additional monetary investment could go a long way toward solving the problem for good.

containing less than 20 percent uranium 235—which is not usable in weapons.

That the world has HEU at so many civilian sites stems mainly from the competitive efforts of the U.S. and the Soviet Union during the "Atoms for Peace" period of the 1950s and 1960s. As the two cold war superpowers constructed hundreds of research reactors for themselves, they simultaneously supplied such facilities to about 50 other nations to gain political favor and to establish their respective reactor technologies abroad. Later, in response to demands for longer-lived nuclear fuel, export restrictions were relaxed, which resulted in most research reactors being fueled with the bomb-grade HEU that the rivals were producing in huge quantities for nuclear weapons. This very highly concentrated material is approximately 90 percent uranium 235. As of the end of 2005, some 10 metric tons of exported bomb-grade HEU still resided in countries that do not possess nuclear weapons—enough to make 150 to 200 gun-type explosive devices.

Convert Reactors

The U.S. government first began taking steps in the 1970s to prevent diversion to nuclear weapons of the research-reactor fuel it had exported during the previous two decades. Notably, in 1978 the Department of Energy launched the Reduced Enrichment for Research and Test Reactors (RERTR) program to convert American-designed reactors so that they could run on LEU-based fuel. By the end of 2005, the effort had retrofitted 41 units. Together these converted facilities had received shipments of approximately 250 kilograms of fresh bomb-grade HEU from the U.S. each year.

The replacement of the HEU fuel used in 42 additional reactors is now under way or planned. Unfortunately, it will not be possible to convert to LEU fuel about 10 high-powered research reactors until new LEU fuel types with the necessary performance can be developed. These high-powered reactors, which today burn about 400 kilograms of HEU fuel every year, typically feature compact cores designed to maximize the flow of neutrons for neutron-scattering experiments or materials tests requiring high irradiation levels. Current LEU-based fuel does not perform adequately within compact reactor cores that were originally designed for HEU.

To minimize the impact of the conversion on the high-power reactor designs, researchers in the RERTR program need to make LEU fuel with the same geometry and fuel life as the HEU fuel it is to replace. The job is a major engineering challenge, however. Because about four uranium 238 atoms accompany every uranium 235 atom in the LEU, fuel-element designers need to increase the amount of uranium in the LEU-based fuel elements by about five times without increasing their dimensions. After years of work, the small program to develop LEU fuel appears to be close to mastering fabrication techniques for a promising new generation of high-density fuels.

Retrieve Weaponizable Fuel

In the 1990s the U.S. began to cooperate with Russia on securing and eliminating HEU stocks. This effort was spurred by thefts of fresh, unburned HEU fuel in Russia and other countries of the former Soviet Union. The robberies were usually reported by the authorities only after the material was recovered. No one outside Russia—and perhaps no one inside—knows how much may have been stolen.

To limit the amount of civilian HEU in Russia accessible for unauthorized removal, the U.S. established in 1999 a Material Consolidation and Conversion Program to acquire and blend down initially about 17 tons of surplus Russian civilian HEU. By the end of 2005 about seven tons had been diluted to 20 percent uranium 235 levels.

Another effort focuses on "spent" HEU reactor fuel. Even though about half the uranium 235 has been consumed by the nuclear fission chain reaction inside reactor cores by the time the used fuel is removed, uranium 235 still makes up about 80 percent of the remaining uranium, the same concentration as the atomic charge in the Hiroshima bomb.

For several years after spent fuel is extracted from a reactor, it is "self-protecting" from theft—that is, it is so radioactive that it would surely kill within a matter of hours anyone who tried to handle it. Nuclear workers manipulate such material only by remote means while protected by heavy shielding. The intensity of the radiation danger lessens with time, however. After about 25 years, it would take about five hours for an unshielded person working a meter from a typical five-kilogram research reactor fuel element to collect a radiation dose that would be lethal to about half of exposed individuals. At this level, say experts advising the International Atomic Energy Agency (IAEA), the fuel can no longer be considered self-protecting.

What Nuclear Terrorists Would Need

To make nuclear weapons, terrorists would first have to buy or steal a supply of highly enriched uranium. In nature, uranium consists mainly of the uranium 238 isotope, which does not sustain a fission chain reaction when it absorbs a neutron, and a very low concentration [about 0.7 percent] of the chain-reacting isotope uranium 235. The two isotopes differ in weight by about 1 percent. Engineers can exploit this fact to separate them and concentrate, or enrich, the uranium 235. Terrorists cannot perform these operations themselves, however, because all known techniques are too difficult, time-consuming and costly.

In a mass of HEU that is just barely critical, on average one of the two to three neutrons released by the fission of a uranium 235 nucleus will go on to cause another nucleus to fission. Most of the rest of the neutrons escape through the surface of the mass, so no explosion results. To make a gun-type bomb feasible, builders need about two critical masses of highly enriched uranium so that one fission would on average cause more than one fission, thus generating an exponentially growing explosive chain reaction such as the one that released the energy of the Hiroshima bomb in a millionth of a second.

Less than one critical mass is sufficient to produce a Nagasaki-type implosion weapon. In that design the mass of plutonium was driven to super-criticality by compressing it with specially shaped external explosive charges. This implosion reduced the spaces between the nuclei through which the neutrons could escape from the mass without causing fissions.

Weapons-grade uranium contains 90 percent or more of chain-reacting, or fissile, uranium 235, but experts have advised the International Atomic Energy Agency that all highly enriched uranium (HEU)—any uranium with a uranium 235 fraction above 20 percent—must be considered "direct-use material"—that is, usable in nuclear weapons. Below 20 percent, the critical mass becomes too large to fit in a reasonably sized device. For example, to produce a critical mass using 93-percent-enriched uranium surrounded by a five-centimeter-thick beryllium neutron reflector requires about 22 kilograms, whereas it takes about 400 kilograms using 20-percent-enriched uranium.

—A.G. and F.N.v.H.

Growing Urgency

To cope with the danger of spent HEU fuel around the world that is becoming less and less self-protecting, in 1996 the U.S. government invited foreign countries that had received American HEU fuel to ship back two common types of spent fuel. Six years later the U.S. joined with Russia and the IAEA in an effort to return flesh and spent HEU fuel to Russia. Progress has thus far been modest, though. Spent fuel that originally contained about one ton of American HEU has been repatriated so far—leaving about 10 tons still overseas. One tenth of a ton of fresh HEU fuel has been sent back to Russia, leaving an estimated two tons of HEU in fresh and spent fuel of Russian origin stored in other countries. The spent research-reactor fuel that has been shipped back to the U.S. is currently being stored at the DOE facilities in South Carolina and Idaho. Russia separates out the HEU in its spent fuel and then blends it down to make fresh low-enriched fuel for nuclear power plants.

After the events of September 11, 2001, some nongovernmental organizations and members of the U.S. Congress intensified their pressure on the DOE to step up its attempts to secure civilian HEU stocks worldwide. Former Los Alamos National Laboratory weapons designer Theodore B. Taylor had warned about the danger of nuclear terrorism as early as the 1970s, but the September 11 tragedy greatly enhanced the credibility of his call for action, and demands for a "global cleanout" of nonmilitary HEU grew. In response, the DOE established a Global Threat Reduction Initiative to expand and accelerate some of the programs described above. Current targets aim to repatriate all uniradiated and spent HEU fuel of Russian origin by the end of 2006 and 2010, respectively, and all spent HEU fuel of U.S. origin by 2019. The plan also envisions that all U.S. civilian research reactors will be converted to LEU fuel by 2014.

Some elements of the HEU clean-out effort thus grew more active, but even a funding increase of more than 25 percent in fiscal year 2005 over the previous year (to about $70 million) left the program diminutive compared with multibillion-dollar programs established to deploy a missile defense system and enhance homeland security capabilities. Perversely, the low cost of the crucial HEU elimination project may partly explain why it has had no high-level advocate in any presidential administration and only a few committed supporters in Congress. Officials such as the secretary of energy and the chairs of key congressional appropriations subcommittees spend most of their time battling over big-budget programs.

In Russia, the situation is even worse. The government there appears relatively unconcerned about the danger that terrorists could acquire nuclear-explosive material. It has yet to commit to converting its research reactors to LEU fuel. Unfortunately, President George W. Bush recently backed off from pressing Russia to act. At a February 2005 summit meeting, he and Russian leader Vladimir Putin agreed to limit U.S.-Russian cooperative HEU clean-out efforts to "third countries." Putin's administration has grown increasingly resistant to programs mandating visits by foreigners to Russian nuclear facilities, particularly if those initiatives do not bring large sums of money into Russia.

The HEU clean-out projects that are still active in Russia are therefore employing a "bottom-up" approach. Their representatives negotiate on a local level directly with Russian nuclear institutes one by one, leaving the institutes to obtain permission from their government. Thankfully, a million-dollar effort that seems inconsequential to the Russian government can still be very welcome to a cash-strapped nuclear institute, so several of these projects are ongoing.

Neglected HEU Sources

Current efforts at HEU fuel conversion and recovery address primarily HEU-powered research reactors that require refueling. They largely ignore critical assemblies and pulsed reactors, two other classes of research reactors with cores that collectively contain huge quantities of the dangerous material.

A critical assembly is a physical mockup of a new reactor core that tests whether a core design will indeed sustain a fission chain reaction, or go critical, as the engineers intended. Because these assemblies are typically limited to generating only about 100 watts of heat, they do not require cooling systems, and engineers can construct them simply by stacking up fuel and other materials.

One of us (von Hippel) first encountered such an assembly in 1994, when, as a White House official, he toured the Kurchatov Institute, an atomic energy research center in Moscow, with American nuclear materials security and accounting experts. There, in an unguarded building, they were shown 70 kilograms of almost pure weapons-grade uranium disks stored in what looked like a high school locker. The uranium 235 was intended for a critical mockup of a space reactor. That visit led to the first U.S.-financed upgrade of the security of a Russian nuclear facility. More recently, the Kurchatov Institute and the DOE have begun discussions on a joint project that would "defuel" many of the institute's HEU-powered critical facilities.

Another such site is a critical facility at Russia's Institute of Physics and Power Engineering (IPPE) in Obninsk. This critical facility may possess the largest HEU inventory of any research-reactor site in the world: 8.7 tons, mostly in tens of thousands of thin aluminum- and stainless-steel-clad disks about two inches in diameter. Operators pile the disks in columns that are interleaved with other disks containing depleted uranium to simulate various average fuel-enrichment levels. Because these items emit only low levels of radiation, technicians can stack them by hand. Ensuring that no one walks out with any disks constitutes a security nightmare. We recently conducted an analysis that appears to have convinced the facility director that the laboratory does not need its weapons-grade uranium. Officials at the DOE are interested in establishing a joint project to dispose of this material.

The other under-appreciated users of HEU fuel—pulsed reactors—typically operate at very high power levels for periods of milliseconds or less. Weapons laboratories generally employ pulsed reactors to evaluate the responses of materials and instruments to intense but short bursts of neutrons, such as those generated by nuclear explosions. These systems pose a similar security problem to critical assemblies because their fuel, too, is only slightly radioactive. A pulsed reactor at the All-Russian Scientific Research Institute of Experimental Physics, Russia's first nuclear weapons design laboratory,

located about 400 kilometers east of Moscow, contains 0.8 ton of HEU—enough for 15 Hiroshima bombs. After hearing a talk by one of us (von Hippel) about the dangers of HEU, researchers at the institute proposed to study the feasibility of converting the reactor to LEU.

Although more than 70 HEU-fueled critical assemblies and pulsed reactors exist worldwide—over half in Russia—only a few are needed for research today. Most were built in the 1960s and 1970s and are now technically obsolete. Much of their mission can be accomplished with desktop-computer simulations that calculate the progress of neutron chain reactions occurring in detailed three-dimensional reactor models. Engineers can usually confirm the validity of these mathematical simulations by checking them against the archived results of past criticality experiments. A few multipurpose HEU-fueled critical facilities may still be required to fill in gaps in previous trials, however. Engineers could convert to low-enriched fuel the few pulsed reactors that may still be needed.

More generally, one IAEA specialist has estimated that more than 85 percent of the world's aging research-reactor fleet could be decommissioned. He observed that the services they provide could be better satisfied by a small number of regional neutron sources using the latest technology. To be attractive to the researchers who use reactors, a decommissioning program could invest simultaneously in strengthening the capabilities of the remaining research-reactor centers. European nations and Japan could join with the U.S. in such an endeavor. In fact, the closings could provide a source of funding for the institutes owning reactors with large inventories of lightly irradiated HEU: these stores would bring in about $20 million per ton of HEU after it was blended down to the safe LEU used to fuel nuclear power plants.

Toward a Solution

The effort to convert HEU-fueled reactors has already dragged on for more than a quarter of a century. That the use of HEU continues has little to do with technical reasons. This failure has resulted largely from a dearth of sufficient high-level governmental support. Resistance on the part of reactor operators fearing relicensing or shutdown has also caused holdups.

Despite current concerns over nuclear terrorism, most segments of the HEU clean-out program are still proceeding much too slowly. Governments need to increase funding to accelerate the conversion of reactors for which substitute LEU fuel is available and to ensure that practical replacement fuel elements are developed with which to convert the remaining ones. Further, the program must be broadened to include all HEU fueled critical assemblies, pulsed reactors and a few other civilian users of HEU fuel, such as Russia's nuclear-powered icebreakers.

If the U.S. and its allies were to take seriously the challenge of preventing nuclear terrorism, civilian HEU could be eliminated from the world in five to eight years. Continued delay in completing this task only extends the window of opportunity for would-be nuclear terrorists.

ALEXANDER GLASER and **FRANK N. VON HIPPEL** are colleagues in the Program on Science and Global Security at Princeton University. Glaser, a member of the research staff, recently received his doctorate in physics from Darmstadt University of Technology in Germany, where he studied the technical barriers to research-reactor conversion. Von Hippel, a theoretical nuclear physicist by training, co-directs the program and is professor of public and international affairs. While assistant director for national security in the White House Office of Science and Technology Policy in 1993 and 1994, von Hippel helped launch American efforts to improve the security of nuclear materials in the former Soviet Union. Both work with the newly established International Panel on Fissile Materials, which is attempting to end the use of highly enriched uranium and plutonium.

Bioterrorism—Preparing to Fight the Next War

Davⁱᴅ A. Relman, M.D.

The United States has become preoccupied with the threat of bioterrorism—the potential for the poisoning of the milk supply with botulinum toxin, the hypothetical dissemination of smallpox by self-infected terrorists, the possibility of a massive release of aerosolized anthrax spores in the subway, even the newly raised specter of misuse of a reconstructed 1918 influenza virus. These concerns have had important consequences for the biomedical research agenda, funding priorities, and the regulatory environment.

In fiscal year 2003, $1.5 billion was allocated for biodefense research to the National Institutes of Health (NIH). These new research dollars, which have been reallocated yearly, now account for roughly one third of the budget of the National Institute of Allergy and Infectious Diseases (NIAID) at the NIH. Although some of these funds are intended for the study of emerging infectious diseases, unprecedented attention is being paid to pathogens that currently cause rare diseases. For example, the number of NIH grants for work on *Francisella tularensis* increased from 4 in 2001 to 71 in 2003, although there are only 100 to 150 cases of tularemia in the United States each year; in October 2005, $60 million was awarded by NIAID for work on new tularemia vaccines.

Government concern about bioterrorism has also led to new federal restrictions on the handling of infectious agents; such rules have hampered both the ability of U.S. researchers to participate in international collaborations and efforts to train foreign scientists in this country. All these changes reflect a radical shift in the political and social climate—a shift highlighted by the incarceration in 2004 in federal prison, on charges of improper handling of *Yersinia pestis,* of Dr. Thomas Butler, chief of infectious diseases at Texas Tech University and an expert on plague.

How well founded is this heightened concern about bioterrorism? If it is justified, how can we best allocate our intellectual, technical, and financial resources, given the imminent dangers from avian influenza and other natural threats? On what principles should we build a biodefense strategy?

Policymakers weighing the likelihood and dangers of bioterrorism tend to seek guidance from a past era of large, state-sponsored bioweapons programs that used industrial-scale processes, emphasized quality control, and based their projections of use on traditional military doctrine. The leaders of those programs that then viewed biologic agents as credible strategic weapons believed that a few particular agents had the most potential for use and saw the technology for preparing and delivering those agents as an essential component of a weapons program.

But we cannot assume that the logic behind biowarfare programs of the past will guide future misuses of the life sciences. Indeed, the lessons of this history can be dangerously misleading. First, the notion that only a certain few agents pose a plausible threat is largely an artifact of weapons programs that predated our current knowledge of molecular biology and that selected agents on the basis of their natural properties and the limited technical expertise then available. Among the agents that remain on today's threat lists, anthrax and smallpox make particularly compelling weapons, but as science and technology advance, the number of worrisome agents is expanding greatly.

Furthermore, large-scale industrial processes are not necessary for the development of potent biologic weapons. Increasingly, the means for propagating biologic agents under controlled conditions are being made accessible to anyone. Even our traditional concept of "weaponization" is misleading: nature provides mechanisms for packaging and preserving many infectious agents that can be manipulated through biologic and genetic engineering—for example, by enhancing the virulence of naturally sporulating organisms. Materials science and nanoscale science—advances in encapsulation technology, for instance—will provide new ways to package such agents. And self-replicating agents that are highly transmissible among humans, such as variola virus and influenza virus, need little or no alteration in order to be disseminated efficiently by terrorists.

Nor should we presume, on the basis of history, that when biologic agents are used deliberately and maliciously, they are capable of causing only relatively limited harm. The large biologic-weapons programs of the late 20th century were never unleashed. And the use of such weapons by smaller groups, such as the Aum Shinrikyo cult, has been relatively unsophisticated—far from representative of what moderately well informed groups might do today. The consequences would have been far more dire, for example, had the anthrax spores circulated in the U.S. mail in 2001 been disseminated by more effective routes. Tomorrow's science and technology will present a new landscape with features that are both worrisome and reassuring: the methods and reagents used for reverse-engineering a novel virus, for instance, can also be used to engineer a vaccine against it.

New insights into biologic systems are emerging rapidly, and new tools for manipulating these systems continue to be developed.[1,2] Information is now disseminated globally, many relevant procedures require far fewer resources than ever before, and much life-science technology has been miniaturized. Today, anyone with a high-school education can use widely available protocols and prepackaged kits to modify the sequence of a gene or replace genes within a microorganism; one can also purchase small, disposable, self-contained bioreactors for propagating viruses and microorganisms. Such advances continue to lower the barriers to biologic-weapons development.[3,4]

So far, nature has been the most effective bioterrorist. In the future, however, the ability of experimenters to create genetic or molecular diversity not found in the natural world—for example, with the use of molecular breeding technologies—and to select for virulence-associated traits may result in new biologic agents with previously unknown potency. Although such agents may not survive long in the natural world and could, from an evolutionary standpoint, be dismissed as poorly adapted competitors, they may prove extremely destructive during their lifespan.

In devising a robust biodefense strategy, a key challenge will be to define the optimal balance between fixed and flexible defenses. The Maginot Line built by the French in the 1930s serves as a symbol of static defenses designed to protect against known threats. Although these elaborate fortifications bought the French some time, the advancing German army maneuvered around them. Similarly, the creation of static defenses can be justified for clear, imminent, and potentially catastrophic biologic threats—including avian influenza virus and prominent drug-resistant bacteria, such as *Staphylococcus aureus,* as well as anthrax and smallpox.

For the vast array of other potential threats, however, we should invest even more in flexible, dynamic defenses, which will rely on integrative science, new insights into biologic systems, and advancing technology. We need methods and technologies that can generate effective diagnostics, therapeutics, and prophylactics against a new or variant infectious agent within days or weeks after its characterization.

Lists of specific agents and the scrutiny of past events can inhibit creative thinking about universal tools and generic approaches for a dynamic world. A robust biodefense plan must be anticipatory, flexible, and rapidly responsive. It should exploit crosscutting technologies and cross-disciplinary scientific insights and use broadly applicable platforms and methods that offer substantial scalability. Examples include the use of "lab-on-a-chip" technology, based on advances in microfluidics, for rapid, sensitive, point-of-care diagnostics; computational approaches for predicting drug—ligand interactions; genomic tools such as microarrays and genomewide screening for protective antigens; and automated robotic systems for rapid, high-throughput drug screening and the scale-up of vaccine production. Efforts to understand microbial virulence should emphasize the study of mechanisms and structures that are shared by a variety of agents.

Given the importance of early intervention, a greater emphasis should be placed on approaches to diagnosing diseases early and specifically. We need such tools now for naturally occurring microbial diseases, if only to reduce the inappropriate use of antibiotics. For example, analyses of host responses to infection in which advanced mass spectroscopy or DNA microarray technology is used to assess patterns of protein abundance or genome-wide patterns of transcript abundance may lead to a new capability for diagnosing presymptomatic disease and predicting clinical outcomes or responses to therapy. The NIH, the Centers for Disease Control and Prevention, the Department of Homeland Security—in response to the federal strategic plan for defense against biologic weapons outlined in Homeland Security Presidential Directive 10—and other agencies have discussed these needs,[5] but investments in these broad approaches have been insufficient.

Such efforts will require strengthening our public health bioterrorism—preparing to fight the next war infrastructure, especially in terms of personnel, communications, and surge capacity. Scientists and clinicians will need to play a bigger role in biodefense planning, including the articulation of needs, policymaking, and the assessment of future threats.

It is often said that military forces are trained to fight the last war, not the next one. The same may be true of public health officials and scientists working to strengthen the public health infrastructure. But given the pace of change in the life sciences, we cannot afford to be constrained by the past, nor can we afford to make incremental, short-term fixes. Recent investments in biodefense offer immense potential benefit, if guided by a creative, future-oriented perspective. Now is the time to begin making serious, sustained investments in the science and technology on which we can build agile defenses against an ever-evolving spectrum of biologic threats.

Notes

1. Segal E, Friedman N, Kaminski N, Regev A, Koller D. From signatures to models: understanding cancer using microarrays. Nat Genet 2005;37:Suppl:S38–S45.

2. Tully T, Bourtchouladze R, Scott R, Tallman J. Targeting the CREB pathway for memory enhancers. Nat Rev Drug Discov 2003;2:267–77.

3. Petro JB, Relman DA. Understanding threats to scientific openness. Science 2003;302:1898.

4. Petro JB, Plasse TR, McNulty JA. Biotechnology: impact on biological warfare and biodefense. Biosecur Bioterror 2003;1:161–8.

5. Hirschberg R, La Montagne J, Fauci AS. Biomedical research—an integral component of national security. N Engl J Med 2004; 350:2119–21.

DR. RELMAN is an associate professor in the Departments of Medicine and of Microbiology and Immunology, Stanford University, Stanford, Calif., chief of infectious diseases at the Veterans Affairs Palo Alto Health Care System, Palo Alto, Calif., and a member of the National Science Advisory Board for Biosecurity.

'These Chemicals Are So Deadly'

Hazardous material transported by rail is vulnerable to attack. Here's what to do

Amy Barrett

The U.S. government's inability to anticipate the September 11 attacks in 2001 amounted to a "failure of imagination," according to the committee that investigated the tragedy. Well, imagine this: Terrorists plant a bomb beneath a rail car carrying deadly chlorine gas. The bomb explodes near the National Mall in Washington on July 4, when 500,000 revelers are gathered for fireworks. Within 30 minutes as many as 100,000 could be dead or seriously injured, according to the U.S. Naval Research Lab.

At the moment, public concerns about key infrastructure are focused on the management of some operations at six U.S. ports, which may pass from a British company to the government of Dubai. But railroads could present just as tempting a target to terrorists, and in the years since September 11, little progress has been made toward protecting them. According to the American Association of Railroads, about 1.7 million carloads of hazardous materials are transported on rail lines every year. The cars are easily identifiable, and the routes are hardly a secret. Even minor mistakes can be catastrophic. A derailment last year involving a chlorine car in Graniteville, S.C., killed nine people and put 75 in the hospital. "These chemicals are so deadly, and they are shipped through our urban areas in large quantities," says Richard A. Falkenrath, former deputy homeland security adviser to the President.

Yet the problems of safeguarding the transport of "hazmats" are not intractable. Here are some steps that would greatly ameliorate the risk:

Permit Limited Rerouting

Last year city council members in Washington pushed through a measure forcing the railroad CSX Corp. to divert shipments of hazardous materials that would otherwise run near the Capitol to less populated areas. CSX and the federal government are now fighting the ordinance in court. Some experts contend that the District of Columbia lacks authority to interfere with interstate commerce. That has not stopped Baltimore, Chicago, and Cleveland from proposing similar measures.

The railroads argue that changing the routes could significantly increase the amount of time hazardous cargo is on the tracks while sending the material out on less suitable and less safe rails. Theodore S. Glickman, a professor at George Washington University, says that in some cases rerouting may be safer, but that railroads resist because they might have to hand off cargo to competitors. The solution, says Glickman, is to engage a neutral body to rule on a case-by-case basis.

Mask the Cargo

Railcars with hazardous materials currently carry placards bearing easily visible identification numbers. Those numbers are a code for the material in the cars and are spelled out in widely published manuals to ensure that emergency responders know exactly what hazards they face. But the codes are equally available to would-be terrorists. The solution: Replace the placards with electronic tags that identify the contents of each car to police and first responders. "Right now it is too easy for the bad guys," says James R. Blaze, planning director with transportation consulting firm Zeta-Tech Associates Inc.

Monitor the Hazmats

Global positioning systems, electronic tagging, and other techniques can provide minute by minute information on the location and condition of each locomotive and car on the rails, says Steven R. Ditmeyer, a professor at the National Defense University. Some of this technology is in place already. But the railroads don't have tracking capability everywhere, and sometimes they can't access temperature or other information captured on sensors installed by companies that lease the cars. These systems need to be put in place so the location of all hazmats can be pinpointed at any time, and data between the railroads and shippers need to be integrated.

Find and Use Chemical Alternatives

The best way to cut down on risk is simply to ship fewer dangerous substances in the first place. Some water-treatment plants have begun substituting substances such as sodium hypochlorite for potentially lethal chlorine. Users of these materials must keep up the pressure on chemical companies to find substitutes while reducing their reliance on the most hazardous substances. In the end the best solution will be to eliminate the target, not just reroute it.

Port Security Is Still a House of Cards

Stephen E. Flynn

As one of the world's busiest ports, it is fitting that Hong Kong played host to the World Trade Organization's December 2005 meeting. After all, seaports serve as the on- and off-ramps for the vast majority of traded goods. Still, the leaders of the 145 delegations that convened in Hong Kong undoubtedly did not have much more than a sightseer's interest in the host city's magnificent and frenetic harbor. For the most part, finance and trade ministers see trade liberalization as involving efforts to negotiate rules that open markets and level the playing field. They take as a given the availability of transportation infrastructures that physically link markets separated by vast distances.

But the days when policy makers could take safe transportation for granted are long past. The Sept. 11, 2001 attacks on New York and subsequent attacks on Madrid and London show that transport systems have become favored targets for terrorist organizations. It is only a matter of time before terrorists breach the superficial security measures in place to protect the ports, ships and the millions of intermodal containers that link global producers to consumers.

Should that breach involve a weapon of mass destruction, the United States and other countries will likely raise the port security alert system to its highest level, while investigators sort out what happened and establish whether or not a follow-on attack is likely. In the interim, the flow of all inbound traffic will be slowed so that the entire intermodal container system will grind to a halt. In economic terms, the costs associated with managing the attack's aftermath will substantially dwarf the actual destruction from the terrorist event itself.

Fortunately, there are pragmatic measures that governments and the private sector can pursue right now that would substantially enhance the integrity and resilience of global trade lanes. Trade security can be improved with modest upfront investments that enhance supply chain visibility and accountability, allowing companies to better manage the choreography of global logistics—and, in the process, improve their financial returns. In short, there is both a public safety imperative and a powerful economic case for advancing trade security.

A Brittle System

Though advocates for more open global markets rarely acknowledge it, when it comes to converting free trade from theory to practice the now-ubiquitous cargo container deserves a great deal of credit. On any given day, millions of containers carrying up to 32 tons of goods each are moving on trucks, trains and ships. These movements have become remarkably affordable, efficient, and reliable, resulting in increasingly complex and economically expedient global supply chains for manufacturers and retailers.

From a commercial standpoint, this has been all for the good. But there is a problem: as enterprises' dependence on the intermodal transportation system rises, they become extremely vulnerable to the consequences of a disruption in the system. To appreciate why that is so requires a brief primer on how that system has evolved.

Arguably, one of the most unheralded revolutions of the 20th century was the widespread adoption of the cargo container to move manufactured and perishable goods around the planet. In the middle of the last century, shipping most goods was labor intensive: items had to be individually moved from a loading dock at a factory to the back of a truck and then offloaded and reloaded onto a ship. Upon arrival in a foreign port, cargo had to be removed by longshoremen from the ship's holds, then moved to dock warehouses where the shipments would be examined by customs inspectors. Then they were loaded onto another transportation conveyance to be delivered to their final destination. This constant packing and repacking was inefficient and costly. It also routinely involved damage and theft. As a practical matter, this clumsy process was a barrier to trade.

The cargo container changed all that. Now goods can be placed in a container at a factory and be moved from one mode of transportation to another without being manually handled by intermediaries along the way. Larger vessels can be built to carry several thousand containers in a single voyage. In short, as global trade liberalization accelerated, the transportation system was able to accommodate the growing number of buyers and sellers.

Arguably, East Asia has been the biggest beneficiary of this transportation revolution. Despite the distance between Asia and the U.S., a container can be shipped from Hong Kong, Shanghai, or Singapore to the West Coast for roughly $4,000. This cost represents a small fraction of the $66,000 average value of goods in each container that is destined for the U.S.

However, multiple port closures in the U.S. and elsewhere would quickly throw this system into chaos. U.S.-bound container ships would be stuck in docks, unable to unload their cargo. Marine terminals would have to close their gates to all incoming containers since they would have no place to store them. Perishable cargo would spoil. Soon, factories would be idle and retailers' shelves bare.

In short, a terrorist event involving the intermodal transportation system could lead to unprecedented disruption of the global trade system, and East Asia has the most to lose.

What Has Been Done?

The possibility that terrorists could compromise the maritime and intermodal transportation system has led several U.S. agencies to pursue initiatives to manage this risk. The U.S. Coast Guard chose to take a primarily multilateral approach by working through the London-based International Maritime Organization to establish new international standards for improving security practices on vessels and within ports, known as the International Ship and Port Facility Code (ISPS). As of July 1, 2004, each member state was obliged to certify that the ships that fly their flag or the facilities under their jurisdiction are code-compliant.

The Coast Guard also requires that ships destined for the U.S. provide a notice of their arrival a minimum of 96 hours in advance and include a description of their cargoes as well as a crew and passenger list. The agency then assesses the potential risk the vessel might pose. If the available intelligence indicates a pre-arrival security check may be warranted, it arranges to intercept the ship at sea or as it enters the harbor in order to conduct an inspection.

The new U.S. Customs and Border Protection Agency (CBP), which was established within the Department of Homeland Security, mandated that ocean carriers must electronically file cargo manifests outlining the contents of U.S.-bound containers 24 hours in advance of their being loaded overseas. These manifests are then analyzed against the intelligence databases at CBP's National Targeting Center to determine if the container may pose a risk.

If so, it will likely be inspected overseas before it is loaded on a U.S.-bound ship under a new protocol called the Container Security Initiative (CSI). As of November 2005, there were 41 CSI port agreements in place where the host country permits U.S. customs inspectors to operate within its jurisdiction and agrees to pre-loading inspections of any targeted containers.

Decisions about which containers will not be subjected to an inspection are informed by an importer's willingness to participate in another post-9/11 initiative, known as the Customs-Trade Partnership Against Terrorism (C-TPAT). C-TPAT importers and transportation companies agree voluntarily to conduct self-assessments of their company operations and supply chains, and then put in place security measures to address any security vulnerabilities they find. At the multilateral level, U.S. customs authorities have worked with the Brussels-based World Customs Organization on establishing a new framework to improve trade security for all countries.

In addition to these Coast Guard and Customs initiatives, the U.S. Department of Energy and Department of Defense have developed their own programs aimed at the potential threat of weapons of mass destruction. They have been focused primarily on developing the means to detect a "dirty bomb" or a nuclear weapon.

The Energy Department has been funding and deploying radiation sensors in many of the world's largest ports as a part of a program called the Megaport Initiative. These sensors are designed to detect radioactive material within containers. The Pentagon has undertaken a counterproliferation initiative that involves obtaining permission from seafaring countries to allow specially trained U.S Navy boarding teams to conduct inspections of a flag vessel on the seas when there is intelligence that points to the possibility that nuclear material or a weapon may be part of the ship's cargo.

Finally, in September 2005, the White House weighed in with its new National Maritime Security Strategy. This purports to "present a comprehensive national effort to promote global economic stability and protect legitimate activities while preventing hostile or illegal acts within the maritime domain."

A House of Cards

Ostensibly, the flurry of U.S. government initiatives since 9/11 suggests substantial progress is being made in securing the global trade and transportation system. Unfortunately, all this activity should not be confused with real capability. For one thing, the approach has been piecemeal, with each agency pursuing its signature program with little regard for other initiatives. There are also vast disparities in the resources that the agencies have been allocated, ranging from an $800 million budget for the Department of Energy's Megaport initiative to no additional funding for the Coast Guard to support its congressionally mandated compliance to the ISPS Code. Even more problematic are some of the questionable assumptions about the nature of the terrorist threat that underpin these programs.

East Asia has the most to lose if a terrorist event disrupts the global trading system.

In an effort to secure funding and public support, agency heads and the White House have oversold the contributions of these new initiatives. Against a backdrop of inflated and unrealistic expectations, the public is likely to be highly skeptical of official assurances in the aftermath of a terrorist attack involving the intermodal transportation system. Scrambling for fresh alternatives to reassure anxious and angry citizens, the White House and Congress are likely to impose Draconian inspection protocols that dramatically raise costs and disrupt crossborder trade flows.

The new risk-management programs advanced by the CBP are especially vulnerable to being discredited, should terrorists succeed at turning a container into a poor man's missile. Before stepping down as commissioner in late November 2005, Robert Bonner repeatedly stated in public and before Congress that his inspectors were "inspecting 100% of the right 5% of containers." That implies the CBP's intelligence and analytical tools can be relied upon to pinpoint dangerous containers.

Former Commissioner Bonner is correct in identifying only a tiny percentage of containers as potential security risks. Unfortunately, CBP's risk-management framework is not up to the task of reliably identifying them, much less screening the low- or medium-risk cargoes that constitute the majority of containerized shipments and pass mostly uninspected into U.S. ports. There is very little counterterrorism intelligence available to support the agency's targeting system.

That leaves customs inspectors to rely primarily on their past experience in identifying criminal or regulatory misconduct to determine if a containerized shipment might potentially be compromised. This does not inspire confidence, given that the U.S. Congress's watchdog, the Government Accountability Office (GAO), and the U.S. Department of Homeland Security's own inspector general have documented glaring weaknesses with current customs targeting practices.

Prior to 9/11, the cornerstone of the risk-assessment framework used by customs inspectors was to identify "known shippers" that had an established track record of engaging in legitimate commercial activity. After 9/11, the agency expanded that model by extracting a commitment from shippers to follow the supply chain security practices outlined in C-TPAT. As long as there is no specific intelligence to tell inspectors otherwise, shipments from C-TPAT-compliant companies are viewed as low-risk.

The problem with this method is that it is designed to fight conventional crime; such an approach is not necessarily effective in combating determined terrorists. An attack involving a weapon of mass destruction differs in three important ways from organized criminal activity.

First, it is likely to be a one-time operation, and most private company security measures are not designed to prevent single-event infractions. Instead, corporate security officers try to detect infractions when they occur, conduct investigations *after* the fact, and adapt precautionary strategies accordingly.

Second, terrorists will likely target a legitimate company with a well-known brand name precisely because they can count on these shipments entering the U.S. with negligible or no inspection. It is no secret which companies are viewed by U.S. customs inspectors as "trusted" shippers; many companies enlisted in C-TPAT have advertised their participation. All a terrorist organization needs to do is find a single weak link within a "trusted" shipper's complex supply chain, such as a poorly paid truck driver taking a container from a remote factory to a port. They can then gain access to the container in one of the half-dozen ways well known to experienced smugglers.

Third, this terrorist threat is unique in terms of the severity of the economic disruption. If a weapon of mass destruction arrives in the U.S., especially if it enters via a trusted shipper, the risk-management system that customs authorities rely on will come under intense scrutiny. In the interim, it will become impossible to treat crossborder shipments by other trusted shippers as low-risk. When every container is assumed to be potentially high-risk, everything must be examined, freezing the worldwide intermodal transportation system. The credibility of the ISPS code as a risk-detection tool is not likely to survive the aftermath of such a maritime terrorist attack, and its collapse could exacerbate a climate of insecurity that could likely exist after a successful attack.

Moreover, the radiation-detection technology currently used in the world's ports by the Coast Guard and Customs and Border Protection Agency is not adequately capable of detecting a nuclear weapon or a lightly shielded dirty bomb. This is because nuclear weapons are extremely well-shielded and give off very little radioactivity. If terrorists obtained a dirty bomb and put it in a box lined with lead, it's unlikely radiation sensors would detect the bomb's low levels of radioactivity.

The flaws in detection technology require the Pentagon's counterproliferation teams to physically board container ships at sea to determine if they are carrying weapons of mass destruction. Even if there were enough trained boarding teams to perform these inspections on a regular basis—and there are not—there is still the practical problem of inspecting the contents of cargo containers at sea. Such inspections are almost impossible because containers are so closely packed on a container ship that they are often simply inaccessible. This factor, when added to the sheer number of containers on each ship—upwards of 3,000—guarantees that in the absence of very detailed intelligence, inspectors will be able to perform only the most superficial of examinations.

In the end, the U.S. government's container-security policy resembles a house of cards. In all likelihood, any terrorist attack on U.S. soil that involved a maritime container would come in contact with most, or even all, of the existing maritime security protocols. Consequently, a successful seaborne attack would implicate the entire security regime, generating tremendous political pressure to abandon it.

The Way Ahead

We can do better. The Association of Southeast Asian Nations should work with the U.S. and the European Union in authorizing third parties to conduct validation audits in accordance with the security protocols outlined in the International Ship and Port Facility Security Code and the World Customs Organization's new framework for security and trade facilitation.

A multilateral auditing organization made up of experienced inspectors should be created to periodically audit the third party auditors. This organization also should be charged with investigating major incidents and recommending appropriate changes to established security protocols.

To minimize the risk that containers will be targeted between the factory and loading port, governments should create incentives for the speedy adoption of technical standards developed by the International Standards Organization for tracking a container and monitoring its integrity. The technology now used by the U.S. Department of Defense for the global movement of military goods can provide a model for such a regime.

Asean and the EU should also endorse a pilot project being sponsored by the Container Terminal Operators Association (CTOA) of Hong Kong, in which every container that arrives passes through a gamma-ray content-scanning machine, as well as a radiation portal to record the levels of radioactivity within the container. Optical character recognition cameras then photograph the number painted on several sides of the container. These scanned images, radiation profiles, and digital photos are then stored in a database where they can be immediately retrieved if necessary.

The marine terminals in Hong Kong have invested in this system because they hope that a 100% scanning regime will deter a terrorist organization from placing a weapon of mass destruction in a container passing through their port facilities. Since each container's contents are scanned, if a terrorist tries to shield radioactive material to defeat the radiation portals, it will be relatively easy to detect the shielding material because of its density.

Another reason for making this investment is to minimize the disruption associated with targeting containers for portside inspection. The system allows the container to receive a remote preliminary inspection without the container leaving the marine terminal.

By maintaining a record of each container's contents, the port is able to provide government authorities with a forensic tool that can aid a follow-up investigation should a container with a weapon of mass destruction still slip through. This tool would allow authorities to quickly isolate the point in the supply chain where the security compromise took place, thereby minimizing the chance for a port-wide shut-down. By scanning every container, the marine terminals in Hong Kong are well-positioned to indemnify the port for security breaches. As a result, a terrorist would be unable to successfully generate enough fear and uncertainty to warrant disrupting the global trade system.

This low-cost inspection system is being carried out without impeding the operations of busy marine terminals. It could be put in place in every major container port in the world at a cost of $1.5 billion, or approximately $15 per container. Once such a system is operating globally, each nation would be in a position to monitor its exports and to check their imports against the images first collected at the loading port.

The total cost of third-party compliance inspections, deploying "smart" containers, and operating a cargo scanning system such as Hong Kong's is likely to reach $50 to $100 per container depending on the number of containers an importer has and the complexity of its supply chain. Even if the final price tag came in at $100 additional cost per container, it would raise the average price of cargo moved by, say, Wal-Mart or Target by only 0.06%. What importers and consumers are getting in return is the reduced risk of a catastrophic terrorist attack and its economic consequences.

In short, such an investment would allow container security to move from the current "trust, but don't verify" system to a more robust "trust but verify" regime. That would bring benefits to everyone but criminals and terrorists.

Mr. Flynn is the Jeane J. Kirkpatrick senior fellow for national security studies at the Council on Foreign Relations and author of America the Vulnerable (HarperCollins, 2005).

UNIT 8

Civil Liberties and Civil Rights

Unit Selections

Key Points to Consider

- Does the detention of prisoners at Guantanamo undermine the war on terrorism?

- Should torture be used as an interrogations tool?

- Should private companies be allowed to amass personal data of American citizens for profit?

Student Web Site
www.mhcls.com/online

Internet References
Further information regarding these Web sites may be found in this book's preface or online.

Homeland Security and Civil Liberties
http://www.strategicstudiesinstitute.army.mil/pubs/display.cfm?PubID=697

Center for Democracy and Technology: Security and Freedom
http://www.cdt.org/security/nsa/briefingbook.php

There is an inherent tension between the need for security and the need to insure the protection of our civil liberties. Terrorism exploits this tension. While terrorists may have different objectives, one of the main purposes of terrorism is to provoke government overreaction. As governments indiscriminately target communities and groups that may pose, or are perceived to pose, a potential threat, the rights of innocent people are violated. Terrorists gain support. Violence escalates.

Democratic governments are in a difficult position. If governments fail to protect their citizens from terrorist attacks, they fail to fulfill one of their fundamental obligations and will inevitably lose the support of the public. If governments, in order to prevent terrorism, violate the civil rights of their citizens and threaten civil liberties, they undermine the very principles upon which they were founded. There is little room to maneuver between the two. There is little room for error.

Critics of the Bush administration and its legislative initiatives after 9/11 claim that the U.S. government is violating civil rights and jeopardizing civil liberties in its war on terrorism. They accuse the Attorney General and the Bush administration of using "McCarthy-like" tactics in the persecution of minorities. They fear that new powers, derived from legislation like the U.S. Patriot Act, will be used against U.S. citizens. They are concerned about the increased access of government agencies to personal information. They argue that the indefinite detention of terrorist suspects without charges, justified by the creation of special categories of prisoner, undermines basic constitutional protections.

Supporters of the administration claim that the U.S. Patriot Act has been instrumental in creating better cooperation and more effective information exchange between the CIA and the FBI. They argue that terrorists hide behind and seek to abuse the inherent protections offered by democratic societies in order to destroy them. They believe that in order to weed out those who would abuse our system, they need greater access to public records and personal information. They claim that in order to protect our national security and prevent the occurrence of another 9/11, they must have greater flexibility in the treatment and interrogation of terrorist suspects. They see the creation of special categories of prisoners and the use of prison camps outside of the United States as vital. They see the extraction of valuable information from terrorist suspects without legal constraints as vital to American interests. They believe that our right to be free from terror is more important than a terrorist suspect's right to legal representation and due process. They think that the use of special military courts is essential, as it will allow for the use of classified information by the prosecution while being able to limit the access of the accused.

The articles in this unit reflect the tenor of the ongoing civil rights debate in homeland security. While most are openly critical of the administration's excesses and warn of increased government intrusion into our private lives, few offer viable alternatives to existing policies.

Island Mentality

Why the Bush administration defends Guantanamo

SPENCER ACKERMAN

The detainee, by all appearances, is resigned to his fate. Throughout his hearing, he remains stoic, not once even shifting in his chair, let alone jostling the restraints that bind his wrists and ankles. His tan jumpsuit indicates his compliance with the camp guards. (The infamous orange jumpsuits are reserved for "problem" detainees.) When the panel of American military officers asks if he wants to submit additional statements on his behalf, he declines. Despite a statistical glimmer of hope—of over 160 detainees who've gone through this process, four have been designated for release—he seems to know what's in store for him: another year in Guantánamo Bay.

Maybe that's the right outcome. According to a briefing I was given, the detainee earned a grisly nickname—suitable for a comic-book villain—fighting with Taliban affiliates in his native Afghanistan. (In order to learn that, I had to sign a contract preventing me from reporting what that nickname is.) Yet the counts against him fall decidedly short of meriting the "worst of the worst" designation that Donald Rumsfeld once gave Guantánamo's inmate population. The military, citing information from "many agencies," says that he is suspected of "involvement in rocket attacks" on U.S. forces in Afghanistan, as well as the manufacture of false visas; he was in charge of investigation and interrogations for the Taliban's Eighth Division in a section of the eastern Paktia province; and he has been affiliated with the Osama bin Laden-connected jihadist organization run by warlord Gulbuddin Hekmatyar. A bad guy he may be. Khalid Shaikh Mohammed he isn't.

"I admit it," he says through a civilian interpreter. "I worked for the Taliban, but for a construction project. I wasn't the boss or foreman, just a simple worker." For the first time, the detainee starts to get agitated. He doesn't think the officer advising him has clearly instructed the three-officer panel about seemingly exculpatory information. After several minutes of questioning from the panel—did he know anyone who attacked U.S. forces? (No.) Did he receive weapons training at a refugee camp in Pakistan? (No.)—he begins to plead. "You didn't tell me what kind of scars I have. If you think they're war injuries, no," he says, in an apparent attempt to convince the panel that he was not wounded while trying to kill Americans. An officer assures him, "We understand the injuries you have are not from war." By the time the unclassified portion of the hearing closes, the detainee is silent and still, once again acquiescent to another year of probable detention—either at Guantánamo or, under a deal announced last week to send detainees to prisons in their own countries, in Afghanistan.

The outcome of the hearing was probably not in question—in large part because it was not a legal proceeding. The officer advising the detainee is not a lawyer. His job is not to challenge the government's case for continued detention, but rather to help the detainee "understand" the proceedings. The hearing doesn't ascertain the detainee's guilt or innocence, but rather the threat he poses to the United States, as well as what intelligence value he possesses. (That consideration is undertaken in a classified hearing.) What I saw, however, made it difficult to escape the conclusion that the detainee's guilt is largely taken for granted. Justice, conventionally understood, is not a priority at Guantánamo. But that doesn't seem to bother the officers in charge—after all, they say, the process, known as an Administrative Review Board, has been created on the fly. "Quite frankly," shrugs Captain Eric Kaniut, a Pentagon official involved with the review process, "it's unprecedented."

That's a common sentiment among Kaniut's colleagues. "We freely admit we're learning this as we go along," Paul W. Butler, a Rumsfeld adviser and an architect of Guantánamo detentions, told *The Washington Post* last year. Indeed, that rationale is used to justify the perpetuation of numerous contradictory stances. For example, the Bush administration has contended simultaneously that Guantánamo Bay is foreign soil (in order to deprive its inmates of access to U.S. courts) and that it "is included within the definition of the special maritime and territorial jurisdiction of the United States" (in order to circumvent the federal Torture Statute, which governs overseas conduct). And, as described in a recent Pentagon report on interrogations at Guantánamo Bay, "degrading and abusive treatment" did not, as General Bantz Craddock of Southern Command put it in congressional testimony last month, "violat[e] U.S. law or policy"—despite relentless assurances from the White House that policy dictates that enemy combatants at Guantánamo be treated humanely.

Little wonder, then, that American liberals have joined the outcry against Guantánamo previously reserved largely for foreigners. *New York Times* columnist Thomas L. Friedman has implored the administration to "just shut it down." But

Friedman's call for shuttering Guantánamo was based on neither the "deeply immoral" abuse at the prison nor the policies that drove it—but instead on "how corrosive Guantánamo has become for America's standing abroad," undermining U.S. efforts to win Muslim hearts and minds. Likewise, Senator Joseph Biden, one of the leading Democratic foreign policy voices, told ABC's George Stephanopoulos in June, "[T]his has become the greatest propaganda tool that exists for the recruiting of terrorists around the world. I think more Americans are in jeopardy as a consequence of the perception that exists worldwide with [Guantánamo's] existence than if there were no Gitmo."

But Guantánamo is more than just an image problem; it is a moral, legal, and strategic one as well. Indefinite detention and the embrace of torture as policy are betrayals of fundamental American principles. Sometimes in war, moral tradeoffs are necessary, but that's not the case at Gitmo, which yields intelligence of little value and where suspect interrogation techniques threaten the legal prosecution of terrorist suspects—an increasing problem as the war on terrorism morphs into more of a law-enforcement struggle. Simply shutting down the facility would do nothing to address these issues. After all, Guantánamo may be the flagship of the post-September 11 enemy-combatant detention apparatus, but the system extends to Bagram Air Base in Afghanistan, the Indian Ocean island of Diego Garcia, and other far-flung corners of the globe that the administration doesn't disclose. The only way to "solve" Guantánamo is to introduce human rights protections and due process for its inmates—and, more importantly, to abandon the principle that underlies the Bush administration's entire post-September 11 U.S. detention system: that the only way to win the war on terrorism is to grant nearly limitless authority to the president.

The interrogation chamber in Camp Five, Guantánamo's recently constructed high-tech prison facility—Camp Six is due next year—is as austere as it is intimidating. Inside a triangular cinderblock room with its frosted-glass window blocked off by a translucent sheet of paper is a small, gray table with two folding chairs on one side. Across the table, as the room converges to its point, is a third chair, which is handcuffed to a metal bar in a dug-out section of the floor. The detainee sits there. On the wall, behind where the interrogators sit, is a red button marked DURESS to alert guards of an emergency.

How much "duress" a detainee endures in the interrogation room is a matter of both confusion and controversy. FBI interrogators who visited Guantánamo in 2003 and 2004 informed their superiors that, "on a couple of occasions," they found detainees "chained hand and foot in a fetal position to the floor"—that is, secured to the small bar I saw—"with no chair, food or water. Most times they had urinated or defecated on themselves, and had been left there for 18–24 hours or more." The air conditioning was set to make interrogation rooms so cold that the detainee was violently shaking or so "unbearably hot" that the detainee, who endured the temperature for hours, was practically unconscious and had "apparently been literally pulling his own hair out throughout the night." Detainees had been blasted with "extremely loud" songs by Lil' Kim and Eminem, as well as a Meow Mix cat food commercial, for extended periods. In June, *Time* magazine published excerpts from the interrogation log of the suspected would-be twentieth September 11 hijacker, Mohammed Al Qatani, which states, among other things, that Qatani's questioners injected him with massive amounts of fluids and forced him to urinate on himself.

In response to the public disclosure of the FBI accounts—not the accounts themselves—the Pentagon assigned Generals Randall Schmidt and John Furlow to investigate Guantánamo interrogations. Their report, released last month, is euphemistic and disingenuous. Schmidt and Furlow maintain that they found "no evidence of torture or inhumane treatment," while simultaneously confirming many of the FBI descriptions. Their most startling conclusion is that nearly every incident they investigated was "authorized" by Pentagon guidelines—guidelines Donald Rumsfeld approved between October 2002 and April 2003. Sometimes, to reach this conclusion, Schmidt and Furlow shoehorn in new definitions to the Army's field manual on interrogations, which complies with the Geneva Conventions. For instance, Schmidt and Furlow consider sexual coercion by female interrogators—including the smearing of fake menstrual blood on a detainee, who subsequently "threw himself on the floor and started banging his head"—to fall within the boundaries of the manual's "Futility" technique. (One veteran of an Army intelligence unit fighting the war on terrorism told me sexual manipulation is decidedly not "Futility.") Qatani, Schmidt and Furlow found, was the subject of a "Special Interrogation Plan." That meant he endured, among other things, high-blast air conditioning that slowed his heartbeat until he required medical attention; was interrogated for 18 to 20 hours daily for 48 days out of a 54-day stretch; was straddled by a female interrogator; and was led on a leash and forced "to perform a series of dog tricks." As their report states: "[E]very technique employed against [Qatani] was legally permissible under the existing guidance."

That is exactly what military lawyers, known as judge advocates general (JAGs), feared would happen when the Bush administration relaxed interrogation guidelines for the Guantánamo facility. When they learned, in 2003, what Rumsfeld was considering for detainees, they worried about high-level authorization of war crimes. "Approving exceptional interrogation techniques may be seen as giving official approval and legal sanction to the application of interrogation techniques that U.S. Armed Forces have heretofore been trained are unlawful," Deputy Air Force JAG Jack L. Rives warned that February, according to a memo declassified two weeks ago. The Navy JAG, Rear Admiral Michael F. Lohr, bluntly called the techniques "inconsistent with our most fundamental values."

But the problem of Guantánamo is not simply a problem of values—it's also a problem of the camp's actual utility in fighting terrorism. The biggest evasion in Schmidt and Furlow's report—and the most significant for the administration's prosecution of the war on terrorism—is their face-value acceptance of the claim that Qatani's "degrading and abusive" interrogation "ultimately provided extremely valuable intelligence." They do not elaborate. Indeed, no Pentagon investigation has challenged this central contention of the administration: that Guantánamo detainees provide invaluable intelligence about Al Qaeda—intelligence that requires, in many cases, the brutal techniques approved by Rumsfeld—despite how dubious it is.

Guantánamo Bay officials didn't grant my repeated requests for interviews with either the Joint Task Force commander, Brigadier General Jay Hood, or his deputy for intelligence operations, Steve Rodriguez, a civilian Pentagon official. Nor was I permitted to speak with any Guantánamo interrogator. As a result, it's difficult to ascertain exactly what intelligence value Guantánamo inmates possess. But there are several reasons not to believe the Pentagon's claims. For one, despite the intimations of some on the right—namely Senator Jeff Sessions of Alabama—professional American interrogators don't consider abuse a useful tool for extracting trustworthy information. It's difficult to take seriously the idea that a detainee exposed to suffocating heat nearly to the point of unconsciousness or smeared with what he believed was menstrual blood produced information of any merit. Not surprisingly, FBI interrogators don't take it seriously. One Bureau official caustically e-mailed his superior in December 2003, "These tactics have produced no intelligence of a threat neutralization nature to date." In fact, an unconventional-war expert at the Naval Postgraduate School told the *Post* that the "best actionable intelligence in the whole war" came not from Guantánamo interrogations but from captured e-mails sent by Khalid Shaikh Mohammed.

Then there's the fact that there may not be very much useful intelligence among the camp's inmates to obtain. Despite the mantra that Guantánamo houses "the worst of the worst," Qatani, the thwarted hijacker, is the highest-ranking Al Qaeda detainee acknowledged to be at Camp Delta. Senior Al Qaeda captives—such as Khalid Shaikh Mohammed, the mastermind of September 11, or terrorist-recruiting chief Abu Zubaydah—are held at undisclosed locations across the U.S. detention apparatus. What's left are largely what one former White House counterterrorism official dubs "the ash-and-trash jihadi picked up in Afghanistan," as opposed to the "honest-to-God, cardcarrying members of Al Qaeda—operatives who are worth a shit." Many detainees picked up in Afghanistan in the first year after September 11, 2001, and taken to Guantánamo were initially captured by Northern Alliance fighters looking to settle scores and collect rewards. Indeed, Rodriguez told *The New Yorker*'s Jane Mayer that only about one-quarter of Guantánamo's approximately 520 detainees possess any intelligence value for him.

What those 130 or so inmates have to offer, however, is still questionable. Most of Guantánamo's population has been in the camp for its entire three-and-a-half-year existence, and, according to Kaniut, only about ten detainees have arrived in the past year. "Obviously," says a recently retired senior intelligence official with counterterrorism experience, "the longer he's there, the less he has to tell you in terms of fresh actionable stuff. After a certain time, it becomes historic research data." That's not to say *that* information can't be useful. As the former

White House official explains, the detainees might still be able to reveal "how do people interact, how do they communicate, what ethnic group will work with another ethnic group, where are the fault lines within the organization . . . pieces of the jihadi and Sunni extremism jigsaw puzzle."

But, as the former official cautions, even those pieces lose their worth after awhile. And that's because the jigsaw puzzle is changing. Simply put, Al Qaeda in 2005—as both a terrorist network and a broader jihadist movement—looks very little like Al Qaeda in 2002. Most Guantánamo detainees were captured on the Afghan battlefield. Yet Al Qaeda's center of gravity is increasingly moving out of Afghanistan and Central Asia: In a series of classified reports this year, the CIA has warned that the next wave of the global jihadist movement lies with new recruits who travel to Iraq to gain on-the-job training killing U.S. forces and Iraqi civilians before returning to their homes in the Middle East, North Africa, and, increasingly, Europe—to say nothing of those who, as is likely with some of the culprits of last month's thwarted London attacks, taught themselves terrorism in the relative isolation of the British midlands. And Pentagon officials have testified to Congress that jihadists captured in Iraq *can't* be sent to Guantánamo Bay, because Iraqis must be treated in compliance with the Geneva Conventions. Guantánamo's population, in other words, can tell us next to nothing about this "Class of '05" problem—the future of Al Qaeda.

Al Qaeda's increasing European profile suggests that Guantánamo is providing little useful intelligence. But Guantánamo and the rest of the U.S. detention apparatus are also actually undermining prosecution of the war on terrorism, because Europe won't accept evidence procured via torture or duress. In January, for example, British officials arrested Moazzam Begg, Feroz Abbasi, Martin Mubanga, and Richard Belmar—British nationals who had been recently released after being detained for three years at Guantánamo—immediately after they stepped off a plane at Heathrow Airport. As London's then-police chief, Sir John Stevens, explained, information American officials had shared with their British counterparts indicated that the men were truly dangerous. "There was no other course of action—we would not have been doing our duty—if we had not arrested them and questioned them," Stevens said. There was only one problem: No information from Guantánamo Bay was admissible in British court, because it had been obtained under dubious legal circumstances. Despite the palpable worries British authorities had about them, all four walked out of a police station the next day, free men.

The issue is not one of European weakness in fighting terrorism, as conservatives often suggest: Investigating judges like Spain's Baltasar Garzón and France's Jean-Louis Bruguière have been relentless in hunting down Al Qaeda affiliates in their countries. Rather, European counterterrorist officials, politicians, and publics simply will not accept the Bush administration's legal contentions about abusive interrogation and indefinite detention, and they won't change their judicial systems to accommodate Washington. And, since Al Qaeda's evolution means that it is European officials who will increasingly have to combat the jihadists, this transatlantic disconnect runs the risk of allowing probable terrorists like the London four to go free.

In some cases, as with the recent trials in Spain of Al Qaeda suspects, the United States has resisted turning over information that could assist European prosecutions for fear of revealing sources and methods. In others, even when the United States has cooperated, the detention apparatus it has set up has undermined the usability of its evidence. Consider the case of Mounir Motassadeq. Motassadeq, who signed Mohammed Atta's will and had power of attorney over hijacker Marwan Al Shehhi's bank account, was convicted in Germany in 2003 of 3,000 counts of accessory to murder for his complicity in the September 11 plot. But an appeals court overturned his conviction in 2004, and the case is now snarled, in large part because of seemingly endless challenges over the admissibility of evidence obtained under probable duress and torture.

In short, Guantánamo opens the door for terrorists to go free amid the legal crossfire over the admissibility of the information they provide—a growing problem as the law enforcement side of the war on terrorism becomes increasingly important. Yet the Bush administration shows no sign of jettisoning abusive interrogation or indefinite detention in recognition. And that's because the administration has elevated these policies to the level of principle.

Guantánamo officials eagerly told me about a conversation they had with another journalist who recently visited Camp Delta, Al Jazeera correspondent Mohammed Yamlahi Alami. Alami was prepared to entertain the premise that there are indeed terrorists at Guantánamo, something the officials considered a p.r. coup. But Alami then said the detainees need to "have their day in court"—which would be a tremendous departure from current policy, under which only four out of 520 detainees at Guantánamo are facing charges before the administration's legally controversial military commissions and under which the administration reserves the right to detain the rest in perpetuity. "Bottom line," Alami told an on-base publication, "is try these guys, show me the evidence, and hang them if they deserve to die. If not, let them go." It's hard to argue with that. But the administration does. Furiously.

For nearly four years, the White House has claimed the ability to hold enemy combatants indefinitely, without any guaranteed trial. It has argued both that the Guantánamo detentions are justifiable given that the fight against terrorism is a war, and that the war on terrorism is "a different kind of war" that requires, as Bush said in 2002, "new thinking in the law of war." Unfortunately, that "new thinking" has been a euphemism for the replacement of law with policy: policy that, among other things, made application of the Geneva Conventions contingent on "military necessity"; allowed for abusive interrogation; and claimed the right to hold enemy combatants in perpetuity. And, even more unfortunately, the White House has held to those policies even as it has become clear that, as in the case of Guantánamo, they are woefully counterproductive.

The Bush administration has adopted this radical approach because it is defending the idea that the Constitution empowers the president to conduct war exclusively on his terms. A series of memos written by the Justice Department's Office of Legal Counsel in 2002 effectively maintained that any law restricting the president's commander-in-chief authority is presumptively unconstitutional. (When GOP Senator Lindsey Graham recently quoted to Pentagon lawyer Daniel Dell'Orto the inconvenient section of Article I, Section 8, granting Congress the authority to "make rules concerning captures on land and water," he farcically replied, "I'd have to take a look at that particular constitutional provision.") Last month, when some GOP senators tried to bar "cruel, inhuman, or degrading treatment" of detainees in an amendment to the 2006 defense bill, the White House sent them a letter threatening to veto any attempt to "restrict the President's authority to protect Americans effectively from terrorist attack and bring terrorists to justice," and Vice President Dick Cheney warned senators against usurping executive power. For good measure, the White House instructed the Senate leadership to pull the entire half-trillion-dollar bill from the floor, lest the offending language within it pass.

It would not be difficult to solve the indefinite-detention problem: Pass a law allowing for a circumscribed period in which officials interrogate the detainee and accumulate evidence before bringing charges against him. This is how it works in countries like Great Britain and Israel, both mature democracies that have fought terrorist threats militarily and legally for decades. But the administration has strongly resisted any move to introduce legal protections to Guantánamo Bay. When the Supreme Court ruled last year that Guantánamo inmates could bring habeas corpus challenges to their detentions in federal court—settling the question of whether detainees had recourse to the U.S. legal system—the Justice Department adopted the bewildering position that, once detainees file their claims, they possess no further procedural or substantive legal rights at all, an absurdity to which the administration is sticking.

That's not all. Before a Senate panel last month, Dell'Orto argued that Congress shouldn't create a statutory definition of the term "enemy combatant," since the administration needs "flexibility in the terminology in order to . . . address the changing circumstances of the type of conflicts in which we are engaged and will be engaged." The very next week, before an appellate court panel, Solicitor General Paul Clement, arguing for the continued detention without charge of American citizen and suspected Al Qaeda terrorist José Padilla, explained what the administration has in mind for its "flexible" definition. Federal appellate Judge J. Michael Luttig, a Bush appointee, noted that, since Padilla was arrested not on an Afghan battlefield but at a Chicago airport, the administration's discretion to detain an American citizen ought to be fettered, "unless you're prepared to boldly say the United States is a battlefield in the war on terror." Clement immediately replied, "I can say that, and I can say it boldly." In essence, the administration is claiming authority to detain anyone, captured anywhere, based not on any criteria enacted by law but rather at the discretion of policy, and to hold that individual indefinitely.

That position—that the war on terrorism requires executive latitude at odds with hundreds of years of law—has animated every single step of the administration's approach to the war. It's why Bush has kept NATO allies at arm's length while simultaneously trumpeting their absolute necessity to the defeat of Al Qaeda. It's why he didn't just oppose the creation of an independent 9/11 Commission to investigate the history of counterterrorism policy, he also argued it would be an unacceptable burden on his prosecution of the war. And it's why he's blasted any move by the courts to exercise oversight of the war as a dangerous judicial overreach: When a district court judge last year challenged the constitutionality of the administration's military commissions for the trial of enemy combatants, the Justice Department "vigorously disagree[d]," as a spokesman put it, and contested the ruling until the commissions were reinstated on appeal last month. For the administration, its expansion of executive power is synonymous with victory in the war—regardless of the real-world costs to the war effort.

The appeal of jettisoning established law in favor of broad executive prerogative during wartime, and especially during asymmetric or unconventional wars, is nothing new. "There is a very strong temptation in dealing both with terrorism and with guerrilla actions for government forces to act outside the law, the excuses being that the processes of law are too cumbersome, that the normal safeguards in the law for the individual are not designed for an insurgency, and that a terrorist deserves to be treated as an outlaw anyway," Sir Robert G. K. Thompson, the architect of the successful British counterinsurgency in Malaya and adviser to the U.S. command in Vietnam, warned in the mid-'60s. "Not only is this morally wrong, but, over a period, it will create more practical difficulties for a government than it solves."

Indeed, the real danger—to the war on terrorism, American values, and the rule of law—is unchecked executive authority. There would be nothing wrong with keeping detainees at Camp Delta and elsewhere if they were provided legal protection and their interrogations were restricted to the Geneva Conventions-compliant Army Field Manual on interrogations. Nor would there be any harm to national security. Senator Graham, a former Air Force JAG, stated two weeks ago that, when he recently visited Guantánamo, he asked "all the interrogators there: Is there anything lacking in the Army Field Manual that would inhibit your ability to get good intelligence? And they said no. I asked: Could you live with the Army Field Manual as your guide and do your job? They said yes." Whether the Bush administration can live within those rules is another matter.

SPENCER ACKERMAN is an associate editor at TNR.

The Truth about Torture

**One side deploys pieties. The other side, euphemisms.
It's time to be honest about doing terrible things.**

CHARLES KRAUTHAMMER

During the last few weeks in Washington the pieties about torture have lain so thick in the air that it has been impossible to have a reasoned discussion. The McCain amendment that would ban "cruel, inhuman, or degrading" treatment of any prisoner by any agent of the United States sailed through the Senate by a vote of 90–9. The Washington establishment remains stunned that nine such retrograde, morally inert persons—let alone senators—could be found in this noble capital.

Now, John McCain has great moral authority on this issue, having heroically borne torture at the hands of the North Vietnamese. McCain has made fine arguments in defense of his position. And McCain is acting out of the deep and honorable conviction that what he is proposing is not only right but is in the best interest of the United States. His position deserves respect. But that does not mean, as seems to be the assumption in Washington today, that a critical analysis of his "no torture, ever" policy is beyond the pale.

Let's begin with a few analytic distinctions. For the purpose of torture and prisoner maltreatment, there are three kinds of war prisoners:

First, there is the ordinary soldier caught on the field of battle. There is no question that he is entitled to humane treatment. Indeed, we have no right to disturb a hair on his head. His detention has but a single purpose: to keep him *hors de combat*. The proof of that proposition is that if there were a better way to keep him off the battlefield that did not require his detention, we would let him go. Indeed, during one year of the Civil War, the two sides did try an alternative. They mutually "paroled" captured enemy soldiers, i.e., released them to return home on the pledge that they would not take up arms again. (The experiment failed for a foreseeable reason: cheating. Grant found that some paroled Confederates had reenlisted.)

Because the only purpose of detention in these circumstances is to prevent the prisoner from becoming a combatant again, he is entitled to all the protections and dignity of an ordinary domestic prisoner—indeed, more privileges, because, unlike the domestic prisoner, he has committed no crime. He merely had the misfortune to enlist on the other side of a legitimate war. He is therefore entitled to many of the privileges enjoyed by an ordinary citizen—the right to send correspondence, to engage in athletic activity and intellectual pursuits, to receive allowances from relatives—except, of course, for the freedom to leave the prison.

Second, there is the captured terrorist. A terrorist is by profession, indeed by definition, an unlawful combatant: He lives outside the laws of war because he does not wear a uniform, he hides among civilians, and he deliberately targets innocents. He is entitled to no protections whatsoever. People seem to think that the postwar Geneva Conventions were written only to protect detainees. In fact, their deeper purpose was to provide a deterrent to the kind of barbaric treatment of civilians that had become so horribly apparent during the first half of the 20th century, and in particular, during the Second World War. The idea was to deter the abuse of civilians by promising combatants who treated noncombatants well that they themselves would be treated according to a code of dignity if captured—and, crucially, that they would be denied the protections of that code if they broke the laws of war and abused civilians themselves.

Breaking the laws of war and abusing civilians are what, to understate the matter vastly, terrorists do for a living. They are entitled, therefore, to nothing. Anyone who blows up a car bomb in a market deserves to spend the rest of his life roasting on a spit over an open fire. But we don't do that because we do not descend to the level of our enemy. We don't do that because, unlike him, we are civilized. Even though terrorists are entitled to no humane treatment, we give it to them because it is in our nature as a moral and humane people. And when on rare occasions we fail to do that, as has occurred in several of the fronts of the war on terror, we are duly disgraced.

The norm, however, is how the majority of prisoners at Guantanamo have been treated. We give them three meals a day, superior medical care, and provision to pray five times a day. Our scrupulousness extends even to providing them with their own Korans, which is the only reason alleged abuses of the Koran at Guantanamo ever became an issue. That we should have provided those who kill innocents in the name of Islam with precisely the document that inspires their barbarism is a sign of the absurd lengths to which we often go in extending undeserved humanity to terrorist prisoners.

Third, there is the terrorist with information. Here the issue of torture gets complicated and the easy pieties don't so easily apply. Let's take the textbook case. Ethics 101: A terrorist has planted a nuclear bomb in New York City. It will go off in one hour. A million people will die. You capture the terrorist. He knows where it is. He's not talking.

Question: If you have the slightest belief that hanging this man by his thumbs will get you the information to save a million people, are you permitted to do it?

Now, on most issues regarding torture, I confess tentativeness and uncertainty. But on this issue, there can be no uncertainty: Not only is it permissible to hang this miscreant by his thumbs. It is a moral duty.

Yes, you say, but that's an extreme and very hypothetical case. Well, not as hypothetical as you think. Sure, the (nuclear) scale is hypothetical, but in the age of the car- and suicide-bomber, terrorists are often captured who have just set a car bomb to go off or sent a suicide bomber out to a coffee shop, and you only have minutes to find out where the attack is to take place. This "hypothetical" is common enough that the Israelis have a term for precisely that situation: the ticking time bomb problem.

And even if the example I gave were entirely hypothetical, the conclusion—yes, in this case even torture is permissible—is telling because it establishes the principle: Torture is not always impermissible. However rare the cases, there are circumstances in which, by any rational moral calculus, torture not only would be permissible but would be required (to acquire life-saving information). And once you've established the principle, to paraphrase George Bernard Shaw, all that's left to haggle about is the price. In the case of torture, that means that the argument is not *whether* torture is ever permissible, but *when*—i.e., under what obviously stringent circumstances: how big, how imminent, how preventable the ticking time bomb.

That is why the McCain amendment, which by mandating "torture never" refuses even to recognize the legitimacy of any moral calculus, cannot be right. There must be exceptions. The real argument should be over what constitutes a legitimate exception.

Let's take an example that is far from hypothetical. You capture Khalid Sheikh Mohammed in Pakistan. He not only has already killed innocents, he is deeply involved in the planning for the present and future killing of innocents. He not only was the architect of the 9/11 attack that killed nearly three thousand people in one day, most of them dying a terrible, agonizing, indeed tortured death. But as the top al Qaeda planner and logistical expert he also knows a lot about terror attacks to come. He knows plans, identities, contacts, materials, cell locations, safe houses, cased targets, etc. What do you do with him?

We have recently learned that since 9/11 the United States has maintained a series of "black sites" around the world, secret detention centers where presumably high-level terrorists like Khalid Sheikh Mohammed have been imprisoned. The world is scandalized. Black sites? Secret detention? Jimmy Carter calls this "a profound and radical change in the . . . moral values of our country." The Council of Europe demands an investigation, calling the claims "extremely worrying." Its human rights commissioner declares "such practices" to constitute "a serious human rights violation, and further proof of the crisis of values" that has engulfed the war on terror. The gnashing of teeth and rending of garments has been considerable.

I myself have not gnashed a single tooth. My garments remain entirely unrent. Indeed, I feel reassured. It would be a gross dereliction of duty for any government *not* to keep Khalid Sheikh Mohammed isolated, disoriented, alone, despairing, cold and sleepless, in some godforsaken hidden location in order to find out what he knew about plans for future mass murder. What are we supposed to do? Give him a nice cell in a warm Manhattan prison, complete with Miranda rights, a mellifluent lawyer, and his own website? Are not those the kinds of courtesies we extended to the 1993 World Trade Center bombers, then congratulated ourselves on how we "brought to justice" those responsible for an attack that barely failed to kill tens of thousands of Americans, only to discover a decade later that we had accomplished nothing—indeed, that some of the disclosures at the trial had helped Osama bin Laden avoid U.S. surveillance?

Have we learned nothing from 9/11? Are we prepared to go back with complete amnesia to the domestic-crime model of dealing with terrorists, which allowed us to sleepwalk through the nineties while al Qaeda incubated and grew and metastasized unmolested until on 9/11 it finished what the first World Trade Center bombers had begun?

Let's assume (and hope) that Khalid Sheikh Mohammed has been kept in one of these black sites, say, a cell somewhere in Romania, held entirely incommunicado and subjected to the kind of "coercive interrogation" that I described above. McCain has been going around praising the Israelis as the model of how to deal with terrorism and prevent terrorist attacks. He does so because in 1999 the Israeli Supreme Court outlawed all torture in the course of interrogation. But in reality, the Israeli case is far more complicated. And the complications reflect precisely the dilemmas regarding all coercive interrogation, the weighing of the lesser of two evils: the undeniable inhumanity of torture versus the abdication of the duty to protect the victims of a potentially preventable mass murder.

In a summary of Israel's policies, Glenn Frankel of the *Washington Post* noted that the 1999 Supreme Court ruling struck down secret guidelines established 12 years earlier that allowed interrogators to use the kind of physical and psychological pressure I described in imagining how KSM might be treated in America's "black sites."

"But after the second Palestinian uprising broke out a year later, and especially after a devastating series of suicide bombings of passenger buses, cafes and other civilian targets," writes

Frankel, citing human rights lawyers and detainees, "Israel's internal security service, known as the Shin Bet or the Shabak, returned to physical coercion as a standard practice." Not only do the techniques used "command widespread support from the Israeli public," but "Israeli prime ministers and justice ministers with a variety of political views," including the most conciliatory and liberal, have defended these techniques "as a last resort in preventing terrorist attacks."

Which makes McCain's position on torture incoherent. If this kind of coercive interrogation were imposed on any inmate in the American prison system, it would immediately be declared cruel and unusual, and outlawed. How can he oppose these practices, which the Israelis use, and yet hold up Israel as a model for dealing with terrorists? Or does he countenance this kind of interrogation in extreme circumstances—in which case, what is left of his categorical opposition to inhuman treatment of any kind?

But let us push further into even more unpleasant territory, the territory that lies beyond mere coercive interrogation and beyond McCain's self-contradictions. How far are we willing to go?

This "going beyond" need not be cinematic and ghoulish. (Jay Leno once suggested "duct tape" for Khalid Sheikh Mohammed.) Consider, for example, injection with sodium pentathol. (Colloquially known as "truth serum," it is nothing of the sort. It is a barbiturate whose purpose is to sedate. Its effects are much like that of alcohol: disinhibiting the higher brain centers to make someone more likely to disclose information or thoughts that might otherwise be guarded.) Forcible sedation is a clear violation of bodily integrity. In a civilian context it would be considered assault. It is certainly impermissible under any prohibition of cruel, inhuman, or degrading treatment.

Let's posit that during the interrogation of Khalid Sheikh Mohammed, perhaps early on, we got intelligence about an imminent al Qaeda attack. And we had a very good reason to believe he knew about it. And if we knew what he knew, we could stop it. If we thought we could glean a critical piece of information by use of sodium pentathol, would we be permitted to do so?

Less hypothetically, there is waterboarding, a terrifying and deeply shocking torture technique in which the prisoner has his face exposed to water in a way that gives the feeling of drowning. According to CIA sources cited by ABC News, Khalid Sheikh Mohammed "was able to last between 2 and 2 1/2 minutes before begging to confess." Should we regret having done that? Should we abolish by law that practice, so that it could never be used on the next Khalid Sheikh Mohammed having thus gotten his confession?

And what if he possessed information with less imminent implications? Say we had information about a cell that he had helped found or direct, and that cell was planning some major attack and we needed information about the identity and location of its members. A rational moral calculus might not permit measures as extreme as the nuke-in-Manhattan scenario, but would surely permit measures beyond mere psychological pressure.

Such a determination would not be made with an untroubled conscience. It would be troubled because there is no denying the monstrous evil that is any form of torture. And there is no denying how corrupting it can be to the individuals and society that practice it. But elected leaders, responsible above all for the protection of their citizens, have the obligation to tolerate their own sleepless nights by doing what is necessary—and only what is necessary, nothing more—to get information that could prevent mass murder.

Given the gravity of the decision, if we indeed cross the Rubicon—as we must—we need rules. The problem with the McCain amendment is that once you have gone public with a blanket ban on all forms of coercion, it is going to be very difficult to publicly carve out exceptions. The Bush administration is to be faulted for having attempted such a codification with the kind of secrecy, lack of coherence, and lack of strict enforcement that led us to the McCain reaction.

What to do at this late date? Begin, as McCain does, by banning all forms of coercion or inhuman treatment by anyone serving in the military—an absolute ban on torture by all military personnel everywhere. We do not want a private somewhere making these fine distinctions about ticking and slow-fuse time bombs. We don't even want colonels or generals making them. It would be best for the morale, discipline, and honor of the Armed Forces for the United States to maintain an absolute prohibition, both to simplify their task in making decisions and to offer them whatever reciprocal treatment they might receive from those who capture them—although I have no illusion that any anti-torture provision will soften the heart of a single jihadist holding a knife to the throat of a captured American soldier. We would impose this restriction on ourselves for our own reasons of military discipline and military honor.

Outside the military, however, I would propose, contra McCain, a ban against all forms of torture, coercive interrogation, and inhuman treatment, except in two contingencies: (1) the ticking time bomb and (2) the slower-fuse high-level terrorist (such as KSM). Each contingency would have its own set of rules. In the case of the ticking time bomb, the rules would be relatively simple: Nothing rationally related to getting accurate information would be ruled out. The case of the high-value suspect with slow-fuse information is more complicated. The principle would be that the level of inhumanity of the measures used (moral honesty is essential here—we would be using measures that are by definition inhumane) would be proportional to the need and value of the information. Interrogators would be constrained to use the least inhumane treatment necessary relative to the magnitude and imminence of the evil being prevented and the importance of the knowledge being obtained.

These exceptions to the no-torture rule would not be granted to just any nonmilitary interrogators, or anyone with CIA credentials. They would be reserved for highly specialized agents who are experts and experienced in interrogation, and who are known not to abuse it for the satisfaction of a kind of sick sado-masochism Lynndie England and her cohorts indulged in at Abu Ghraib. Nor would they be acting on their own. They would be required to obtain written permission for such interrogations from the highest political authorities in the country (cabinet level) or from a quasi-judicial body modeled on the Foreign Intelligence Surveillance Court (which permits what would ordinarily be illegal searches and seizures in the war on terror). Or, if the bomb was truly ticking and there was no time, the interrogators would be allowed to act on their own, but would require post facto authorization within, say, 24 hours of their interrogation, so that they knew that whatever they did would be subject to review by others and be justified only under the most stringent terms.

One of the purposes of these justifications would be to establish that whatever extreme measures are used are for reasons of nothing but information. Historically, the torture of prisoners has been done for a variety of reasons apart from information, most prominently reasons of justice or revenge. We do not do that. We should not do that. Ever. Khalid Sheikh Mohammed, murderer of 2,973 innocents, is surely deserving of the most extreme suffering day and night for the rest of his life. But it is neither our role nor our right to be the agents of that suffering. Vengeance is mine, sayeth the Lord. His, not ours. Torture is a terrible and monstrous thing, as degrading and morally corrupting to those who practice it as any conceivable human activity including its moral twin, capital punishment.

If Khalid Sheikh Mohammed knew nothing, or if we had reached the point where his knowledge had been exhausted, I'd be perfectly prepared to throw him into a nice, comfortable Manhattan cell and give him a trial to determine what would be fit and just punishment. But as long as he had useful information, things would be different.

Very different. And it simply will not do to take refuge in the claim that all of the above discussion is superfluous because torture never works anyway. Would that this were true. Unfortunately, on its face, this is nonsense. Is one to believe that in the entire history of human warfare, no combatant has ever received useful information by the use of pressure, torture, or any other kind of inhuman treatment? It may indeed be true that torture is not a reliable tool. But that is very different from saying that it is *never* useful.

The monstrous thing about torture is that sometimes it does work. In 1994, 19-year-old Israeli corporal Nachshon Waxman was kidnapped by Palestinian terrorists. The Israelis captured the driver of the car used in the kidnapping and tortured him in order to find where Waxman was being held. Yitzhak Rabin, prime minister and peacemaker, admitted that they tortured him in a way that went even beyond the '87 guidelines for "coercive interrogation" later struck down by the Israeli Supreme Court as too harsh. The driver talked. His information was accurate. The Israelis found Waxman. "If we'd been so careful to follow the ['87] Landau Commission [which *allowed* coercive interrogation]," explained Rabin, "we would never have found out where Waxman was being held."

In the Waxman case, I would have done precisely what Rabin did. (The fact that Waxman's Palestinian captors killed him during the Israeli rescue raid makes the case doubly tragic, but changes nothing of the moral calculus.) Faced with a similar choice, an American president would have a similar obligation. To do otherwise—to give up the chance to find your soldier lest you sully yourself by authorizing torture of the person who possesses potentially lifesaving information—is a deeply immoral betrayal of a soldier and countryman. Not as cosmically immoral as permitting a city of one's countrymen to perish, as in the Ethics 101 case. But it remains, nonetheless, a case of moral abdication—of a kind rather parallel to that of the principled pacifist. There is much to admire in those who refuse on principle ever to take up arms under any conditions. But that does not make pure pacifism, like no-torture absolutism, any less a form of moral foolishness, tinged with moral vanity. Not reprehensible, only deeply reproachable and supremely impracticable. People who hold such beliefs are deserving of a certain respect. But they are not to be put in positions of authority. One should be grateful for the saintly among us. And one should be vigilant that they not get to make the decisions upon which the lives of others depend.

Which brings us to the greatest irony of all in the torture debate. I have just made what will be characterized as the pro-torture case contra McCain by proposing two major exceptions carved out of any no-torture rule: the ticking time bomb and the slow-fuse high-value terrorist. McCain supposedly is being hailed for defending all that is good and right and just in America by standing foursquare against any inhuman treatment. Or is he?

According to *Newsweek*, in the ticking time bomb case McCain says that the president should disobey the very law that McCain seeks to pass—under the justification that "you do what you have to do. But you take responsibility for it." But if torturing the ticking time bomb suspect is "what you have to do," then why has McCain been going around arguing that such things must never be done?

As for exception number two, the high-level terrorist with slow-fuse information, Stuart Taylor, the superb legal correspondent for *National Journal*, argues that with appropriate legal interpretation, the "cruel, inhuman, or degrading" standard, "though vague, is said by experts to codify . . . the commonsense principle that the toughness of interrogation techniques should be calibrated to the importance and urgency of the information likely to be obtained." That would permit "some very aggressive techniques . . . on that small percentage of detainees who seem especially likely to have potentially life-saving information." Or as Evan Thomas and Michael Hirsh put it in the *Newsweek* report on McCain and torture, the McCain standard would "presumably allow for a sliding scale" of torture or torture-lite or other coercive techniques, thus permitting "for a very small percentage—those High Value Targets like Khalid Sheikh Mohammed—some pretty rough treatment."

But if that is the case, then McCain embraces the same exceptions I do, but prefers to pretend he does not. If that is the case, then his much-touted and endlessly repeated absolutism on inhumane treatment is merely for show. If that is the case, then the moral preening and the phony arguments can stop now, and we can all agree that in this real world of astonishingly murderous enemies, in two very circumscribed circumstances, we must all be prepared to torture. Having established that, we can then begin to work together to codify rules of interrogation for the two very unpleasant but very real cases in which we are morally permitted—indeed morally compelled—to do terrible things.

CHARLES KRAUTHAMMER is a contributing editor to *The Weekly Standard*.

"The Land of the Controlled and the Home of the Secure"

Civil Liberties and Homeland Security

Valerie L. Demmer

In response to the terrorist attacks of September 11, 2001, the Bush administration reacted swiftly and boldly, implementing programs it claimed would strengthen the security of the United States. President George W. Bush, Secretary of Defense Donald Rumsfeld, and Attorney General John Ashcroft have all adopted a firm and unyielding stance in executing their focused reply to the menace of global terrorism. An unfortunate byproduct of these aggressive moves, however, is the erosion of civil liberties. The administration has gone beyond the legitimate needs of national security and is infringing on constitutional freedoms in the name of patriotism and security.

The Patriot Act (Provide Appropriate Tools Required to Intercept and Obstruct Terrorism Act) was signed into law by Bush on October 26, 2001, after being rushed through Congress without giving members time to properly read or interpret its provisions. According to Representative Ron Paul of Texas (one of only three Republicans in the House to vote against the bill), "The bill wasn't printed before the vote—at least I couldn't get it . . . . It was a very complicated bill. Maybe a handful of staffers actually read it, but the bill definitely was not available to members before the vote."

In an interview given to *Insight,* Paul further said, "The insult is to call this a 'patriot bill' and suggest I'm not patriotic because I insisted upon finding out what is in it and voting no. I thought it was undermining the Constitution, so I didn't vote for it—and therefore I'm somehow not a patriot. That's insulting."

Ostensibly an anti-terrorist bill, the Patriot Act makes changes to over fifteen different statutes. Of particular concern, the legislation permits the government to arbitrarily detain or deport suspects; to eavesdrop on Internet communications, monitor financial transactions, and obtain individuals' electronic records; and to clandestinely survey records of religious and political organizations, whose privacy rights have usually been upheld in the courts. Critics of the act contend that these McCarthy-like tactics strip citizens of their fundamental rights while not being effective in—and often not having anything to do with—stopping terrorism.

The act even allows increased surveillance of church finances and bookstore records. For example, instead of being able to ask a court to quash a subpoena for customer information, booksellers may be required to turn records over immediately. The act allows surveillance through all types of electronic communications and affects telecommunications companies, Internet providers, cable companies—indeed anyone using this technology. Jim Dempsey, deputy director of the Center for Democracy and Technology, worries that investigators "will collect more information on innocent people and be distracted from the task of actually identifying those who may be planning future attacks."

Russ Feingold (Democrat–Wisconsin), the only dissenting voice in the Senate, addressed his colleagues in the Senate before the bill's passage, pointing out that the framers of the U.S. Constitution, even though they'd just been through a war with Britain, "wrote a Constitution of limited powers and an explicit Bill of Rights to protect liberty in times of war, as well as in times of peace." Feingold added:

> Of course there is no doubt that, if we lived in a police state, it would be easier to catch terrorists. If we lived in a country that allowed the police to search your home at any time for any reason; if we lived in a country that allowed the government to open your mail, eavesdrop on your phone conversations, or intercept your email communications; if we lived in a county that allowed the government to hold people in jail indefinitely based on what they write or think, or based on mere suspicion that they are up to no good, then the government would no doubt discover and arrest more terrorists.

> But that probably would not be a country in which we would want to live. And that would not be a country for which we could, in good conscience, ask our young people to fight and die. In short, that would not be America.

> Preserving our freedom is one of the main reasons that we are now engaged in this new war on terrorism. We will lose that war without firing a shot if we sacrifice the liberties of the American people.

And sacrificing liberties is just what the Bush administration would do. It announced last fall that 5,000 men between the ages of eighteen and thirty-three were being rounded up by the FBI for questioning. The young men have been in the country for two years and are from "suspect" countries. The list was provided by Ashcroft, who emphasized that "the objective is to collect any information that the individuals on this list may have regarding terrorist elements in this country and abroad. These individuals were selected for interviews because they fit the criteria of persons who might have knowledge of foreign-based terrorists." This action was denounced by the Center for Constitutional Rights in a press release which stated: "Questioning individuals without any evidence of wrongdoing amounts to the very definitions of racial profiling. . . . Since September 11, we have already seen thousands of people who have been harassed by local authorities over immigration matters totally unrelated to the attacks."

In another disturbing development, Ashcroft approved a rule that permits eavesdropping by the Justice Department on the confidential conversations of inmates and uncharged detainees with their lawyers—communication that is supposed to be inviolate. Robert Hirshon, president of the American Bar Association stated: "Prior judicial approval and the establishment of probable cause. . . are required if the government's surveillance is to be consistent with the Constitution and is to avoid abrogating the rights of innocent people." Ashcroft's rule, however, was pushed through as an emergency measure without a waiting period. Senator Patrick J. Leahy (Democrat–Vermont), in a letter to Congress said, "I am deeply troubled at what appears to be an executive effort to exercise new powers without judicial scrutiny or statutory authorization."

Indeed, unilateral executive action is becoming a trend of this administration. For instance, on November 13, Bush issued a military order directing Rumsfeld to be responsible for military tribunals to try noncitizens charged with terrorism. Secret trials without benefit of a jury or the requirement of a unanimous verdict, as well as nondisclosure of evidence for "national security reasons," would be authorized by the use of these tribunals. Representative John Conyers (Democrat–Michigan, and the ranking member of the House Judiciary Committee) called Bush's order "a civil liberties calamity in this country" that puts the "executive branch in the unattainable role of legislator, prosecutor, judge and jury." At a press conference, Conyers, other Democratic legislators, and Representative Bob Barr (Republican–Georgia) described the military tribunals as an abuse of executive power jeopardizing the nation's civil liberties. Immediate hearings were called for by Barr. Representative Dennis Kucinich (Democrat–Ohio) said, "We should never be so fearful as to think somehow we can gain a great measure of security by being willing to set aside the Bill of Rights or any other hallowed legal principle that forms the bedrock of our society."

On December 6, Ashcroft appeared before the Senate Judiciary Committee for a lengthy hearing on Bush's order to use military tribunals, the Justice Department's monitoring of phone conversations between suspects and their lawyers, and the questioning of thousands of people of Middle Eastern heritage. Ashcroft was defiant, denied these actions undermine civil liberties, and charged that accusations promoting fear of lost freedom aid terrorists. The next day, the American Humanist Association commented, "Our nation is built on diversity, not

unanimity, and is not bolstered by governmental attempts to suppress dissent. We appeal to Congress and the president to halt Ashcroft's assault on America's civil liberties."

With this wave of patriotism has come a zeal that affects all areas of our lives and threatens the very ideals the United States stands for.

Unfortunately, the current crackdown on civil liberties is nothing new, and the Bush administration is using earlier infringements on freedoms to justify its new policies. In World War I there was press censorship. During World War II, Japanese-Americans and other foreign-born citizens were interned. The Cold War era had its McCarthyism with black-listing of suspected communist sympathizers. During the Vietnam War, anti-war protest groups were infiltrated, harassed, and spied on. The Gulf War saw media coverage controlled through "pool reporting." As Feingold put it: "Wartime has sometimes brought us the greatest tests of our Bill of Rights."

In the first days and weeks immediately following the September 11 tragedies, a wave of nationalism swept across the United States the likes of which hadn't been seen since World War II. But with this wave of patriotism came a zeal threatening the very ideals the United States stands for.

In particular, the right to freedom of expression has been compromised. In one incident, the cartoon *Boondocks* was pulled from some newspapers in New York because it was deemed either "un-American" or too political. Rick Stromoski, cartoonist of *Soup to Nutz* and spokesperson for the National Cartoonists Society said, "I find that a little scary, that just because someone can take another point of view they're seen as unpatriotic or sympathetic to the terrorists. . . . Papers are afraid of offending their communities and losing even more readers."

The same could be said about television programs. Bill Maher's *Politically Incorrect* was dropped by fifteen stations after remarks he made after September 11 were deemed inappropriate—and most likely his contract won't be renewed in 2002.

Airport security has understandably been a prime concern since the terrorist attacks. But in the name of "national security" some passengers' civil liberties have been violated. Green Party USA coordinator Nancy Oden was stopped by government agents while trying to board an American Airlines flight in Bangor, Maine, in October. She wasn't arrested for anything—merely prevented from flying. Oden had been scheduled to speak at the Greens' national committee meeting in Chicago to work on details of a campaign against biochemical warfare and the party's peace agenda. According to Oden, "An official told me that my name had been flagged in the computer. . . . I was targeted because the Green Party USA opposes the bombing of innocent civilians in Afghanistan." Chicago Green activist Lionel Trepanier commented, "The attack on the right of association of an opposition political party is chilling. The harassment of peace activists is reprehensible."

On November 1 Circuit Court Judge James Stucky upheld the three-day suspension handed down by Sissonville High School officials against Charleston, West Virginia, student Katie Sierra for promoting an "Anarchy Club" and wearing anti-war T-shirts in school. In October, high-school student Aaron Pettit of Fairview Park, Ohio, was suspended for ten days for displaying anti-war posters on his locker—one depicting an eagle with a tear drop and others with bombers drawn on them with messages like "May God have mercy, because we will not." Pettit sued the school in federal court and was reinstated. Even teachers have been suspended for merely voicing their views about the military action and policies now enacted.

Websites have also been shut down. Hypervine, an Internet service provider, forced Cosmic Entertainment to pull three radio show sites on the Internet, among them *Al Lewis Live,* because they allegedly contained pro-terrorist materials. The sites were reportedly forced from the Net when Hypervine received calls from someone identifying himself as a federal agent and threatening seizure of Hypervine's assets if the sites weren't shut down. Al Lewis, who played Grandpa in the 1960s television show *The Munsters,* said, "I lived through the McCarthy period. It will get worse."

Apparently intimidated by developments immediately following the terrorist attacks, the Sierra Club and the Natural Resources Defense Council began *voluntarily* removing ad material that criticized Bush's environmental policies. The Sierra Club went so far as to remove material critical of Bush *prior* to September 11.

An October 4 article by Brook Shelby Biggs, contributing editor of MotherJones.com aptly sums up the clamp down on civil liberties:

> Far more surprising than government attempts to stifle criticism is the seeming willingness of the media, politicians, and activist groups—particularly those on the left—to censor themselves. Some may be backing off to avoid the kind of public crucifixion endured by *Politically Incorrect*'s Bill Maher. Others, however, apparently truly believe that frank and vibrant discourse is damaging to the country's moral fiber.

The trauma of the terrorist attacks has caused many people to seek solace in religion—and religionists are taking advantage of it. The phrase "God Bless America" is everywhere these days. Besides the endless renditions of the song at sporting and other public events, there is a movement afoot in Congress to have the song declared a national hymn and to have the slogan "God Bless America" displayed in schools and public buildings. Moreover, a minister of the United Church of Christ has observed that the message implied by "God Bless America" is: "to be genuinely patriotic you must be conventionally religious."

Stefan Presser, legal director of the Pennsylvania American Civil Liberties Union, referring to a lawsuit that challenges the constitutionality of displaying the Ten Commandments in a public courthouse in West Chester, Pennsylvania, eloquently summarized this issue by saying, "Even if 99 out of 100 people are in favor of keeping the plaque, the point of the Bill of Rights is that the majority does not rule when it comes to religious issues. Each person, in their own privacy, gets to make religious decisions." In our zeal to protect the country from the terrorist threat let us not forget the menace posed by religious excess.

Some of these encroachments on our civil liberties—those with sunset provisions—will expire automatically unless renewed by Congress. Others will be challenged in the courts as violations of the Constitution. Still others seem destined to become permanent encroachments—what Bush and his cronies believe are "necessary accommodations" to a changing world.

We would do well to remember the words of Supreme Court Justice Oliver Wendell Holmes Jr., who said many years ago, "The life of the law has not been logic: it has been experience. The felt necessities of the time. . . have had a good deal more to do than the syllogism in determining the rules by which men should be governed."

The question we must now ask ourselves is: how do we *feel* about the necessities of our time? You can be sure our laws are following close behind. If you don't agree with the laws curtailing your rights and the actions of your officials, this is the time to tell your legislators and your neighbors how you feel. It's the patriotic thing to do.

VALERIE L. DEMMER holds a degree in management from the University of Phoenix. She is an editorial consultant at the Humanist and lives in Middleport, New York.

From *The Humanist,* January/February 2002. Copyright © 2002 by Valerie L. Demmer. Reprinted by permission of the author.

Homeland Security and the Lessons of Waco

MARY ZEISS STANGE

I t did not have to happen. We know this now. The 51-day siege at Mount Carmel, the Branch Davidian complex near Waco, Tex., cost 84 lives: four federal agents of the Bureau of Alcohol, Tobacco and Firearms and six Branch Davidians who died in the initial assault on February 28, 1993; and 74 Davidians who perished in the April 19th conflagration that bought the standoff to its disastrous close.

Why did it happen the way it did? Why did it happen at all? Those questions take on a special urgency now, 18 years later, given the current war against Iraq and the more amorphous homeland "war on terror." The USA Patriot Act, and its sequel-in-progress, the Domestic Security Enhancement Act, give federal agents unprecedented power to violate the religious and other rights of individuals and groups. Unchecked, an administration that feels as firmly as the current one does that God is on its side can be counted on to use those weapons against "dangerously divergent" groups—today, more likely to be Islamic than Christian. The more the political universe arranges itself into oppositions between "patriotic" Americans and "evildoers," the more nervous Americans become, to the point of willingly abrogating the rights of "divergent" individuals and groups. Thus the events in Waco demand revisiting.

As far as most Americans knew in 1993, the Branch Davidians were a sinister "doomsday cult" founded by an unsavory character named David Koresh. In fact, however, the Davidian sect had been in existence in the Waco area since the 1920s, an offshoot of Seventh-Day Adventism. Indeed, the apocalyptic worldview that united the Mount Carmel community, Koresh's role there, and the content of his preaching are all incomprehensible without some understanding of Adventist millennialism.

Yet federal agents steadfastly spurned such understanding. FBI negotiators, some purportedly so clueless as to think that the seven seals Koresh referred to were aquatic mammals, dismissed his scriptural interpretation as "Bible babble." Religious-studies scholars tried in vain to convince them that in Koresh they were dealing with a religious leader, not a madman surrounded by weak-willed lunatics. But the FBI preferred its fiction of cultic crazies, which the national news media obligingly reinforced.

Koresh was hardly blameless. Although allegations of child abuse now appear to have been baseless, he probably would have been found guilty of statutory rape under Texas law. Yet that charge was never brought; had it been, it would have been a matter for local rather than federal authorities.

The feds were there because of the Davidians' guns. Since most evidence was destroyed either in the fire or shortly thereafter by FBI bulldozers, it will never be clear whether the Davidians had, as the Bureau of Alcohol, Tobacco and Firearms had claimed, illegally converted semiautomatic to fully automatic firearms. But even if true, as one Texan quipped at the time, "down here in the 50-Caliber Belt" that crime was as serious as "spitting on the sidewalk."

Even when the FBI unwittingly stepped into the role that Davidian apocalypticism assigned it, Koresh and company were at best an unwilling Army of the Lord. One survivor, Livingstone Fagan, explained afterward that "it was not inevitable that events had to end the way they did. The final outcome was contingent on our adversaries' response to our efforts to communicate our position of faith . . . . All our efforts were ignored. Evidently the government wanted its deception, both for itself and its people."

T he question, as pertinent now as then, is: Why the deception? Why did the FBI prefer the advice of anticult "experts" over the more reliable information available from religious-studies scholars? Why did it persist in creating its cult fiction? Why the government wanted to exterminate members of an offbeat religious group that had never indicated the slightest intention of doing harm remains a largely unanswered question. What made Koresh and his followers such targets of government hostility?

It may be that what makes religious groups like the Branch Davidians especially threatening from a more "mainstream" point of view is their sheer devotion to a life-altering, and explicitly countercultural, message. Most Americans balk at that much commitment, and will tolerate only certain familiar forms of religious (or quasi-religious) zeal—the anti-abortion movement, animal rights, environmental activism. Beyond that, we as a people cannot, in T. S. Eliot's words, "bear very much reality."

Two days after the Mount Carmel conflagration, in an op-ed piece for the *Los Angeles Times,* I made essentially this case, arguing that applying the "crazy" label to the Branch Davidians effectively allowed the government, and the media-consuming public, not to see the Branch Davidians as a religious group at all. Another religious-studies scholar, in no less a venue than the *Journal of the American Academy of Religion,* insisted that I was undermining "the reputation of our profession" by lending the Branch Davidians the merest hint of credibility. He argued that spurious figures like Koresh did not deserve to be understood, lest the attempt lend their viewpoints some degree of plausibility.

Today, a kindred argument against religious understanding has reasserted itself with special ferocity.

I've experienced this firsthand. Within days after 9/11, I wrote an op-ed essay for *USA Today* in which I argued, countering those who claimed there was "nothing religious" about the terrorists' point of view, that religion can sometimes drive people to do terrible things. (This was after Muhammad Atta's "last night" letter had come to light, clearly illustrating that for Atta, his was a religious act.) While I received some positive responses, I also received some truly vicious hate mail, including a disturbingly suspicious package that I turned over unopened to our postal inspector. My institution received angry letters from alumni, threatening to withhold contributions.

What was especially interesting about the hostile responses is that they continued 10-year-old themes: That I should not suggest that we try to understand how Muslim radicals construct their worldview. That to grant Al Qaeda's position even a whiff of comprehensibility is to commit a mortal sin against not only religion, but democracy. That, whatever coherence the study of religion might discern in radical or divergent points of view, those findings are better left unspoken.

One of the most alarming aspects of the 51-day assault on Mount Carmel is that it passed without significant protest. It was as if, as one commentator remarked, the American people were watching a miniseries. Today, the readier analogy might be to reality television, a depressingly accurate assessment of what mainstream journalism has become.

The stars of *Waco: the Miniseries* were Koresh, in the role of mad prophet, squared off against heroic FBI agents, there to avenge the deaths of their fallen comrades. Janet Reno also starred, in her debut as attorney general. The 130 Mount Carmel residents were simply extras. The government kept it that way: Videotapes made by the Davidians—which demonstrate that as a group they were educated, articulate, and anything but brainwashed—were withheld from the news media and the public by the FBI. The media failed to obtain their release. In any case, it was easier, and more ratings-friendly, to promote the image of the "wacko from Waco" and his anonymous, zombified flock.

The Branch Davidians' civil rights were violated in a number of ways the USA Patriot Act has actually rendered legal.

Of course, in situations of war and law enforcement, the authorities can exert considerable control over information. But that does not excuse the extent to which the news media served as government spokespersons at Waco. The FBI, praised for their nonaggression, subjected the Branch Davidians to harassment akin to torture. Federal agents were lauded for their "restraint" in withholding fire when an unarmed Davidian left the complex. When the final assault came on April 19, agents used armored vehicles to block exists, lobbed incapacitating, cyanide-producing gas and incendiary tear gas into the tinder-dry complex in high-wind conditions, and detained rescue workers and firefighters a mile from the scene. The news media called the result mass suicide. And the American public eagerly believed.

Rarely has there been a more blatant case of victim blaming. But in the popular imagination, the Branch Davidians barely qualified as victims. To the extent that they existed at all, they were not merely faceless, they were unworthy of public sympathy. They were child abusers. They practiced polygamy. They owned all those weapons. They were zealots, probably crazy. They brought it on themselves, and they deserved whatever they got. So even if they were to some extent victims, they weren't innocent ones. Twenty-one children died, some argued, because they had bad mothers.

The discourse, like the death count, belongs to the winning side. As the FBI's tanks were battering down the walls, a voice on the loudspeaker kept intoning: "This is not an assault. This is not an assault." If victims are by definition guilty, then the aggressor must perforce be righteous. Which is what we are seeing today in Iraq: The way to achieve peace is through war, which is defined as a "humanitarian" action. Closer to home, the war on terror demands the suppression of rights, in the name of freedom.

Waco is thus eerily relevant. Ultimately, the federal authorities employed the same arguments for their "pre-emptive" strike against Mount Carmel as the Bush administration has for war against Iraq. The federal authorities prohibited news-media access to the Davidians in much the same way, and for essentially the same reasons, that journalists today are kept from learning the precise number, let alone the names, of detainees at Guantánamo Bay and elsewhere. Then as now, the mainstream media colluded in the process of demonizing the "other." The Branch Davidians' civil rights were violated in a number of ways the USA Patriot Act has actually rendered legal, although their former illegality neither stopped the federal agents nor led to any sanctions against them.

It is easier, and alarmingly more acceptable, to violate the rights of a broader spectrum of individuals and groups today than ever before. Recently, Supreme Court Justice Antonin Scalia underscored that point when he commented that the Constitution "just sets minimums" and that, especially during wartime, the government has considerable room to scale back people's rights.

David Thibodeau, one of a handful of Davidian survivors, has lamented that in the aftermath of Waco he came to see himself "as an outcast from an America that had always been mine." The steps being taken in the name of homeland security and the war on terror may leave untold numbers of Americans in a similar position, for religious or other reasons of conscience.

The current assaults on civil and human rights in the United States demonstrate that too few Americans read the message in the flames that flared on that windswept plain 10 years ago.

MARY ZEISS STANGE is an associate professor of women's studies and religion at Skidmore College and, most recently, the co-author of Gun Women: Firearms and Feminism in Contemporary America (New York University Press, 2000).

Terrorism and civil liberties

Heading in the Wrong Direction

The Bush administration is making a dangerous hash of its terrorism laws

In 1962 the apartheid regime in South Africa, no respecter of civil liberties, picked up a suspected terrorist leader who had just returned from training in bomb-making and guerrilla warfare in Ethiopia. It marked the start of 27 years in jail, but Nelson Mandela was given access to lawyers and his prosecutors had to follow rules of due process. Last year, the world's foremost democracy, the United States, detained one of its own citizens, José Padilla, at Chicago airport as a witness to a grand-jury probe and then categorised the so-called dirty bomber as an "enemy combatant"—which, according to the government, gives it the right to hold him indefinitely, with no access to a lawyer and minimal judicial review.

Though Mr Padilla is unlikely to become a Mandela, his treatment is but one cause for concern about the Bush administration's approach to civil liberties. Of course, September 11th prompted America to reconsider the balance between liberty and security, and to favour the latter; America's freedoms seemed to have helped 19 hijackers to live and train in the country for up to two years. And given the relative lack of a legal structure to deal with terrorism, the American government has often had to think on its feet. Yet even allowing for all this, George Bush is heading in the wrong direction.

The Importance of Due Process

If you accept, as most do, that the war on terrorism justifies wider powers of surveillance and detention, then two principles still need to be applied. First, the government's new powers should, where possible, be enacted in clearly-worded terrorism laws, passed by Congress. Second, wider powers should be balanced by wider review. Spies, now less constrained, should be more answerable for their actions; suspects, deprived of their lawyers for longer periods, should eventually have more opportunity to present their case to a judge and, where possible, a jury; and the whole process should be subject to political and judicial review.

Precisely the opposite has happened. Far from establishing new checks and balances, the government has moved repeatedly to quash those that exist. It whistled one new terrorism law, the USA Patriot Act, through Congress soon after September 11th; now a draconian new "Patriot II" may be pushed through during a war with Iraq. But the government has also claimed new powers by executive fiat, citing precedent from tangentially related cases. Mr Padilla's strange status is justified by an obscure second world war ruling, putting him in a legal limbo similar to that of the "enemy combatants" in Guantanamo Bay. In practice, the government's main legal defence has been delay: it could take ages for the challenges to its behaviour to reach the Supreme Court.

The irony is that, particularly when it comes to surveillance, there is a good case for stronger powers. Despite fiddling with the FBI, America lacks a proper domestic intelligence-gathering service equivalent to Britain's MI5. Similarly, many of the ideas that so exercise American civil libertarians—such as the notion of government agents snooping on places of worship—seem reasonable precautions. But Mr Bush could make his case much more easily if he could also show that the use of these new snooping powers was itself being watched, and questioned, by judges and politicians.

The most disturbing aspect of America's approach comes once terrorist suspects have been arrested. Again, proper terrorism laws should allow a government to treat such people differently from normal criminals, as they are potentially more dangerous than humdrum law-breakers. But the differences should be of degree. By all means hold a terrorist suspect longer before he has access to a lawyer or before specific charges need to be made; but let the lawyer appear in due course. As for claims to be able to hold people indefinitely, powers like these smack of third-world dictatorship.

This week, John Ashcroft, Mr Bush's attorney-general, boasted that the government's tougher methods are yielding results. Recent arrests strengthen his argument. But would his immediate anti-terrorism battles have been so much less effective if he had paid more attention to the basic rules of due process? The public-relations cost has been frightful—particularly among groups such as immigrants and Muslims, whose help is most needed in battling terrorism.

Achieving a balance between security and liberty was never going to be easy. "For a vast and free nation, there is no such thing as perfect security," Mr Bush reflected last week. But America has jumped too far in one direction. A reassessment is called for, if it wants to avoid rude comparisons with South Africa four decades since.

Mining Personal Data

One company keeps tabs on the public in the name of post-9/11 security

Robert O'Harrow Jr.

It began in 1997 as a company that sold credit data to the insurance industry. But over the next seven years, as it acquired dozens of other companies, Alpharetta, Ga.-based ChoicePoint Inc. became an all-purpose commercial source of personal information about Americans, with billions of details about their homes, cars, relatives, criminal records and other aspects of their lives.

As its dossier grew, so did the number of ChoicePoint's government and corporate clients, jumping from 1,000 to more than 50,000 today. Company stock once worth about $500 million ballooned to $4.1 billion.

Now the little-known information industry giant is transforming itself into a private intelligence service for national security and law enforcement tasks. It is snapping up a host of companies, some of them in the Washington area, that produce sophisticated computer tools for analyzing and sharing records in ChoicePoint's immense storehouses. In financial papers, the company itself says it provides "actionable intelligence."

"We do act as an intelligence agency, gathering data, applying analytics," said company vice president James A. Zimbardi.

ChoicePoint and other private companies increasingly occupy a special place in homeland security and crime-fighting efforts, in part because they can compile information and use it in ways government officials sometimes cannot because of privacy and information laws.

ChoicePoint renewed and expanded a contract with the Justice Department in the fall of 2001. Since then, the company and one of its leading competitors, LexisNexis Group, have also signed contracts with the Central Intelligence Agency to provide public records online, according to newly released documents.

Attorney General John D. Ashcroft and other government authorities have said these new tools are essential to national security. But activists for civil liberties and privacy, and some lawmakers, say current laws are inadequate to ensure that businesses and government agencies do not abuse the growing power to examine the activities of criminals and the innocent alike.

These critics said it will soon be hard for individuals looking for work or access to sensitive facilities to ever shake off a criminal past or small transgression, such as a bounced check or minor arrest.

Chris Hoofnagle, associate director of the Electronic Privacy Information Center, a nonprofit group in the District, said ChoicePoint is helping to create a " 'Scarlet Letter' society."

The information industry has traditionally fought regulations, arguing that it can police itself. But hoping to avoid a regulatory backlash that could curtail his company's access to information, ChoicePoint chief executive Derek V. Smith said he'll be reaching out to Capitol Hill in the coming months to promote the industry's benefits—and express his willingness to work with lawmakers to develop new regulations.

"We have a new responsibility to society, and we want to make sure that's legitimized," Smith said. "We'd like everybody to play by the same rules and standards that society believes are correct."

An entire industry has mushroomed during the past decade because of extraordinary increases in computing power, the expansion of telecommunications networks and the ability of companies like ChoicePoint to gather and make sense of public records, criminal histories and other electronic details that people now routinely leave behind.

Some of these companies—including the three major credit bureaus—have become multi-pronged giants that regularly refresh information about more than 200 million adults and then sell that data to police, corporate marketers, homeland security officials and one another.

In doing so, they wield increasing power over the multitude of decisions that affect daily life—influencing who gets hired, who is granted credit or who can get on an airplane.

ChoicePoint is not alone in eyeing the government for new business. LexisNexis and others also work closely with national security and intelligence officials. To compete in the homeland security market, LexisNexis paid $775 million last year for Seisint Inc., a rival company with a supercomputer and a counter-terrorism system dubbed Matrix.

ChoicePoint, though, has distinguished itself through 58 acquisitions in recent years. Those purchases have recently been companies that have close ties to the government or have products that will sate the demand for more refined details about people and their activities.

One ChoicePoint acquisition last year, Alexandria-based Templar Corp., was initially conceived by the departments of Defense and Justice to improve information sharing. Templar's system helps draw information together instantly from multiple databases. A District firm called iMapData Inc., also acquired by ChoicePoint last year, creates electronic maps of "business, economic, demographic, geographic and political" information. Its customers include intelligence and homeland security agencies.

For a time in 2003 and last year, ChoicePoint even offered a background-check-in-a-box sold on the shelves of Sam's Club.

ChoicePoint, Templar and iMapData help operate a fledgling law enforcement network in the Hampton Roads region of Virginia called the Comprehensive Regional Information Management and Exchange System, or CRIMES. A similar system operates in south Florida. ChoicePoint officials hope the system will be a model for a national information-sharing network mandated last fall when Congress approved intelligence reform legislation.

In marketing materials distributed to government officials, ChoicePoint says the system offers investigators "the ability to access all relevant information with a single query."

Earlier this month, ChoicePoint also completed the acquisition of i2 Ltd., a British technology firm with a subsidiary in Springfield, i2 Inc., that creates computer software to help investigators and intelligence analysts in the United States and scores of others countries finds links among people, their associates and their activities.

In 2001, the FBI announced a $2 million deal to buy i2 software over three years. Company officials said their software was used by the military to help find Saddam Hussein in Iraq.

In an interview, i2 Inc. President John J. Reis said analysts increasingly use the software to head off crimes or attacks, not just investigate them after the fact. "We are principally a company whose focus is all about converting large volumes of information into actionable intelligence," he said.

Police, lawyers, private investigators, reporters and many others have been using commercial information services for years, as the availability of personal information skyrocketed during the 1990s. But those commercial services did not play such an important role in the secretive, high-technology realm once dominated solely by the National Security Agency and other members of the government intelligence community.

The government still maintains some of the world's most sophisticated eavesdropping and spy gear. But officials often depend on commercial systems for public records, identity verification and automated analysis, such as finding anomalous personal information that might suggest a person has hidden ties to risky groups. Growing numbers of commercial systems offer "scoring" services that rate individuals for various kinds of risks.

To expand its presence in the intelligence community, Choice-Point hired a team of prominent former government officials as homeland security advisors in late 2003. They included William P. Crowell Jr., the former deputy director of the National Security Agency; Dale Watson, a former FBI executive assistant director of counter-terrorism and counterintelligence, and Viet D. Dinh, a former assistant attorney general and primary author of the USA Patriot Act.

Current and former government officials praise the new services as important to efforts to investigate criminal and terrorist activity and to track down people who pose a threat. But some of those same officials, including Pasquale D'Amuro, an assistant director at the FBI and head of its New York office, also expressed qualms about whether ChoicePoint and other information services operate with enough supervision.

"There are all kinds of oversight and restrictions to the federal government, to Big Brother, going out there and collecting this type of information," he said. "Yet there are no restrictions in the private sector to individuals collecting information across this country, which potentially could be a problem for the citizens of this country."

Hoofnagle, the privacy activist, recently filed a complaint with the Federal Trade Commission claiming that ChoicePoint has worked hard to avoid triggering oversight under existing laws, including the Fair Credit Reporting Act. If ChoicePoint's reports about people are not legally considered consumer reports under the act, Hoofnagle said in the letter, then the law should be expanded to include them.

Hoofnagle's letter, co-authored with George Washington University law professor Daniel J. Solove, described the Fair Credit Reporting Act as a "landmark law that ensures that compilations of personal information used for many different purposes are accurate, correctable, fairly collected."

In a response, ChoicePoint said the thrust of Hoofnagle's letter was baseless. The Fair Credit Reporting Act was "not meant to be omnibus privacy legislation," the company's letter said. "Information used for investigative, law enforcement or governmental purpose is not regulated in the same manner as the information used to make decisions related to credit, insurance, or employment."

ChoicePoint started as a spin-off from Equifax Inc., the credit bureau and information service. It was considered an underperforming division, with its main source of revenue coming from the insurance industry. ChoicePoint examined credit records and other personal information to help top insurers assess customers and vet insurance applications for signs of fraud.

Smith and other ChoicePoint executives wanted much more. Intent on becoming a national data and analysis clearinghouse, the company went on a buying spree. ChoicePoint bought one company that screens new employees for signs of illicit drug use. It purchased another that specializes in the use of DNA to identify people, living or dead. In 2002, it bought VitalChek Network Inc., a Nashville company that provides the technology and networks to process and sell birth, death, marriage and divorce records in every state.

It collected data in other ways, too. Through an employee screening system called Esteem, the company compiles reports from dozens of retailers such as Target, Home Depot and others about employees who have admitted to, or been convicted of, shoplifting.

For a time in 2003 and last year, ChoicePoint even offered a background-check-in-a-box sold on the shelves of Sam's Club. The $39.77 package included a "How To Hire Quality Employees" handbook, a CD containing an online background screening package and one complimentary drug test.

By 2003, ChoicePoint could claim to have the leading background screening and testing business in the nation, analyzing job applicants, soccer coaches, day-care workers and Boy Scout volunteers. About 5 million criminal records searches that year turned up almost 400,000 applicants or others who had recent criminal records.

Since its inception, Smith said, his company has focused primarily on making the country a safer place, especially in the wake of the Sept. 11, 2001, terrorist attacks.

Smith said he recognizes that there have to be limits on what his company can do, if only to maintain the trust of the many millions of people whose information fuels his business.

"Whatever the country decides to do, I'm willing to accept, as long as it's done in an enlightened way," Smith said. "The stakes have escalated since 2001."

Some reporting for this story was done for ROBERT O'HARROW's book, "No Place to Hide," published by Free Press, copyright 2005. O'Harrow also received financial assistance from the Center for Investigative Reporting.

UNIT 9

Intelligence and Homeland Security

Unit Selections

Key Points to Consider

- How can the Central Intelligence Agency be reformed?

- Are the intelligence agencies or policy makers responsible for intelligence failures?

- Does the appointment of a Director of National Intelligence undermine the role of the CIA?

- What additional reforms are needed to improve U.S. Intelligence?

Student Web Site
www.mhcls.com/online

Internet Reference
Further information regarding these Web sites may be found in this book's preface or online.

Office of the Director of National Intelligence
  http://www.dni.gov/

The U.S. Intelligence Community has received much of the blame for the failure to prevent the attacks on 9/11. Critics argue that the Intelligence Community failed in its primary task: to protect the United States from foreign threats. After numerous inquiries and commissions reports into the intelligence failures of 9/11, in December of 2004, the President signed into law the Intelligence Reform and Terrorism Prevention Act. The center piece of the legislation was the appointment of a new Director of National Intelligence (DNI) to oversee the Intelligence community, a function previously carried out by the Director of the Central Intelligence Agency. While hailed as "the most sweeping intelligence reform since the national security act of 1947," little has changed. While the agency directors talk openly about increased cooperation, the turf wars continue. Behind the scenes, intelligence officials appear more concerned with protecting their own fiefdoms and budgets from the potential encroachment of other agencies than pursuing the reforms needed to address future threats.

The U.S. Intelligence Community was established by the National Security Act of 1947 to cope with the rapidly growing Soviet threat. For more than 40 years, most of its resources were targeted at the Soviet Union. Organizational structures and collection systems were developed specifically to gather intelligence from state actors. The dominant role of the military agencies in the community reflects cold war priorities. After the fall of the Soviet Empire in 1990, despite significant debate and calls for reform, no significant structural reforms were made.

In the mid 1990's, in response to changing priorities and emerging threats, the Intelligence Community began to shift its focus increasingly to international terrorism and non-state actors. Rather than designing new systems to deal with these threats, the intelligence community attempted to use existing systems to spy on non-state actors. Little effort was made to reform its huge bureaucracies, eliminate the duplication of effort, address the lack of interoperability, and improve inter-agency communications. Rather than rethinking its approach to intelligence collection and analysis, state centric models of threat assessment continued to prevail. The fundamental flaw of this approach was reflected in the belief that the best way to protect the homeland and prevent terrorism was to attack or invade a country.

The articles in this unit examine the role of the Intelligence Community in homeland security. The first focuses on persistent problems within the Central Intelligence Agency. The second article explains the difficulty of collecting and interpreting accurate intelligence. It asserts that intelligence officials and policy makers are equally to blame for intelligence failures. The next article examines the impact of the appointment of a Director of National Intelligence. It suggests that the appointment of the DNI may enable the Director of Central Intelligence to focus on much needed reforms in the Central Intelligence Agency. The last article in this unit highlights the continuing need for intelligence reforms, particularly in the areas of human intelligence, military intelligence, and organizational leadership.

U.S. Intelligence: A Losing Proposition

Why it is inadequate and how to fix it.

ANGELO M. CODEVILLA

Conventional wisdom used to be that U.S. intelligence was the lifeblood of the war on terror. By 2004 no one contested that intelligence, especially the CIA, was at the heart of policies that had failed to stem terrorism and had turned military victory in Iraq into embarrassment. The high level commissions that examined current failures began to suspect that these reflected long-standing, basic faults. They only scratched the surface. In fact, U.S. intelligence in all its functions—collection, quality control (otherwise known as counterintelligence), analysis, and covert action—is hindering America's war.

The public, accustomed in recent years to stories of botched anti-Saddam coups, had learned that CIA covert action works only in the movies. But in the summer of 2004 newspaper readers were shocked by the CIA's admission to Senate investigators that it had precisely zero agents in Iraq in the years prior to the invasion, because getting and keeping agents in such places is tough. Was it not the CIA's job to have agents in tough places?

The attentive public also remembered that the president had struck specific bunkers at the start of the Iraq war because the CIA's most valued sources assured us Saddam was staying there. But U.S. troops inspecting the wreckage had found neither Saddam nor bunkers. Wasn't the CIA supposed to know enough not to help play America for a sucker? The commissions seemed most impressed that the CIA had translated scarce and bad information into misleading analyses without dissent. Groupthink, they called it. Voters and taxpayers wonder how an institution in which so many had placed so much trust could suddenly have been found to be such a loser.

To those close to the intelligence business, however, such things are an old story. There never was a golden age of the CIA. Its performance against terrorism is not so different from what it was during the Cold War.

Not least of the CIA's problems, then as now, has been its preference for influencing U.S. policy over striving for clarity about the outside world. It has done so by substituting its many judgments for the few hard facts it has. Phrases like "we believe . . ." and "we have no conclusive evidence that . . ." (longhand for yes and no) conveyed its prejudices to policymakers and favored media alike, feeding strife in American politics. Because the CIA vouched for the existence of Weapons of Mass Destruction in Iraq, the Bush team chose "disarmament" as the official justification for invading that country. The Democrats campaign against the Bush team for believing the CIA on WMDs (as they themselves believed it), but also for disbelieving its judgment that Iraqi intelligence was not connected with 9/11—because the Democrats themselves want to disbelieve. Such quarrels becloud the essential question: Who are the people whose death will free us from terror?

Now all agree that the CIA fouled up, and all are foursquare for reform. But the main proposals embraced by Democrats and Republicans with equal mindlessness, consist of rearranging bureaucratic wiring diagrams. It is anyone's guess how such "reform" would increase knowledge of the outside world, instill the self-criticism necessary for quality control, produce intellectual rigor out of wanton analytical sloppiness, or turn U.S. covert action from bloody *opera buffa* to a serious instrument of policy. Just as important, no one seems to have asked whether any intelligence system imaginable could bring success to the current policy of trying to discover individual terrorists before they strike.

To consider what it would take to turn U.S. intelligence into an asset in the war on terror, we must first look at its basic problems.

Collection

U.S. intelligence has never had more than a few sources of human reporting of which it could be certain, and the capabilities of U.S. technical collection devices, both imaging and electronic, are too well known.

Money has never been the problem with the CIA's espionage. Its clandestine service has some 2,500 "case officers" abroad. But this "clandestine" service is clandestine in name only. Ninety-eight percent of its officers are spooks only to the point of claiming they report to some part of the U.S. government other than the CIA. The 2 percent *super* spooks hide their connection to the U.S. government but make no attempt to hide the fact that they are Americans. Rather than prowling the back alleys pretending to be Ruritanian arms dealers, or using identities of convenience to worm information out of unwitting sources, CIA officers are limited to the kinds of contacts that U.S. embassy personnel have. Because personnel standards at the CIA are lower than for the Foreign Service, the quality of CIA reporting seldom has equaled that of the State Department.

In Iraq they live and work behind a screen of American soldiers. Everywhere they deal either through translators or with English-speaking foreigners. They know languages even less than diplomats, or the substance of any subject matter that would lead to natural contact with sources. As for work that requires the use of weapons, CIA policy has always been to hire contractors. In sum, the CIA's concept of its case officers as gentleman spies is the wrong concept, resulting in a service full of the wrong people.

Satellites travel paths and cover areas at times that are predictable years in advance. They neither see beneath roofs nor into the hearts of men.

Their relationship with spies typically consists of managing relations with foreigners who seek them out—so-called walk-ins. The chief problem here is figuring out whether self-proposed agents are really working for a hostile intelligence service. That problem is most serious when foreign intelligence services themselves are providing information. This is especially so regarding terrorism, since Arab governments—whose agendas run counter to America's—supply a substantial portion of the CIA's information on it. The smelliest information comes from "interrogations" conducted by ignoramus officers, of prisoners who may or may not know anything but who are constrained to say *something*.

Collection by various kinds of cameras and electronic intercepts suffers from problems not entirely dissimilar. The CIA wallpapered its lobby with a drawing of downtown Moscow copied from satellite photos, showing every building. Its implication, added to the well-advertised fact that the best resolution of satellite photography could theoretically read license plates, gives the impression of omniscience. The equally well-advertised fact that U.S. antennas on satellites, on land, sea, and air, intercept billions of communications strengthens that impression. Theoretically, these antennas can also tell when a truck's engine is on, among other things. Yet cameras and antennas are much less useful than they seem, especially with regard to terrorism.

Satellites travel paths and cover areas at times that are predictable years in advance. They neither see beneath roofs nor into the hearts of men. Hiding from high altitude photography is child's play, as is spoofing it. The U.S. and Britain misrepresented D-Day preparations to confuse German aircraft, the Soviets prevented U.S. satellites from seeing any thing of its fourth generation missiles except holes in the ground that may or not have been filled, and during the Gulf War Saddam Hussein managed to hide from satellites and aircraft every last one of the mobile Scud launchers that hit Israel and U.S. troops.

When the U.S. government has struck terrorism on the basis of satellite reconnaissance, its bombs and missiles have destroyed empty mud huts. "Pounding sand" is what the Pentagon calls it. When the Pentagon used satellites to pick targets for its "shock and awe" campaign against Iraq in 2003, it ended up destroying empty buildings.

Electronic intercepts are even more problematic. Theoretically, if the enemy does not know that his electronic messages are intercepted, we can read them. And if the enemy does know, he must choose between having them intercepted and not sending them. In fact, just as in the case of satellites, the enemy can use his knowledge to give us the impressions he wishes, while sending messages either non-electronically or through means he knows are safe. The Soviets long ago developed unbreakable codes. Most governments and serious criminals nowadays have them. Mere individuals as well as governments use multiple cell phone numbers or calling cards from public phones for real communications, while our enemies call between phones they know are monitored to watch in glee as we scramble with security measures.

Quality Control

If the flow of intelligence on terrorism were subjected to the discipline of counterintelligence and the CIA were to reject all that was not secure, its analysts would have to come to terms with poverty. This would force policymakers to take responsibility for doing what they can on the basis of what they know. But in this field as in others, scarcity presses the CIA to take what garbage comes its way and call it good.

It has always been so. From the 1950s to the 1970s the CIA treated James Angleton's small, independent counterintelligence office as a pest, and spread accusations that Angleton's concerns for the integrity of sources amounted to aspersions on the loyalty of CIA case officers, or reflected his own paranoia. In fact the CIA resented the obstacles that Angleton placed in the way of self-congratulation—and self-promotion—for passing on insecure information. And so in 1975 the CIA got rid of Angleton and independent quality control. Since then each geographic division has judged its own integrity—which is more corrupting than having Arthur Andersen audit Enron.

During the Cold War, scarcity of hard information combined with political prejudice to produce Groupthink at the CIA.

As it turned out, Angleton was more correct than he feared. Every last CIA agent in or on Cuba was working for Castro's intelligence. All but three in or on East Germany were working for the Stasi. This and much more was due to mere incompetence. The Soviet KGB's total control of the human intelligence that reached the U.S. government resulted from the treason of Aldrich Ames and Robert Hanssen, in charge of quality control respectively for the CIA's and the FBI's anti-Soviet espionage.

None of these discoveries led to any serious efforts at quality control.

Nor did the discovery that Geoffrey Prime had told the Soviets U.S. satellites were intercepting their communications affect the way in which those satellites were funded, nor how their information factored into the rest of our intelligence. Finally, neither the revelation that, because of one John Walker, the Soviets were privy to all U.S. naval communications, nor the fact that U.S. intelligence had overlooked countless indications that this was so, make those in charge of U.S. intelligence any more skeptical about what they were seeing and hearing.

The CIA's uncritical acceptance of "low hanging fruit" regarding terrorism is part of the same phenomenon. Paranoia would not have been necessary to ask why, if the Arab intelligence services that told us that al Qaeda was responsible for terrorism knew so much about it, they were powerless to prevent it from operating in their police states. After the 1998 U.S. cruise missile attack on an innocent Sudanese pharmaceutical factory that Arab intelligence had designated and U.S. technical sources had confirmed as an al Qaeda chemical warfare facility, common sense would have counseled skepticism about those sources. No way. In 1993 the CIA decided that Arab regimes were innocent, that "loose networks" of renegades and Islamic extremists were responsible for terrorism, and that to confirm the validity of a source one need only confirm the truth of some of its details.

Since then, the CIA has held to its paradigm of terrorism with acts of denial and definition that shock common sense. Foremost is its squaring of the facts with the dogma that no Arab regime, especially that of Iraq, was responsible for the 1993 or (and) the 2001 attack on the World Trade Center.

Here is a thumbnail sketch. One of the 1993 bombing's masterminds is a secular person who entered the U.S. on an Iraqi passport as Ramzi Yousef (the name under which he was convicted and sent to federal prison). He left the U.S. for Baghdad as Abdul Basit Karim, on a Pakistani passport obtained on the basis of Kuwaiti documents that had been doctored during Iraq's 1990 occupation of Kuwait. The real Kasim, who disappeared during that occupation, was physically different from Yousef. Only Iraqi intelligence could have merged the two identities.

The man who the CIA says is Yousef's superior and uncle, and who it calls the mastermind of the 2001 attack, who also took part in the 1993 one, and joined Yousef in the 1995 Philippines plot to bomb U.S. airliners over the Pacific, is a secularist Baluch who goes by the name Shaik Khalid Mohammed. A third secularist by the name of Ali, otherwise known as Ammar al Baluchi, provided funds for all three attacks. Only Mohammed had anything to do with al Qaeda, and that only after 1996, long after his own network had performed operations like that of 9/11. Where did the money and motivation for that network come? Could it be that this network thinly disguised as a family worked for Iraqi intelligence, which had long recruited Baluchs for a variety of tasks?

The CIA, however, absolved Iraq of responsibility for any of the attacks by this fictitious Baluchi family, while pinning all of them on Islamic extremism and just the 2001 attack on Osama bin Laden's al Qaeda. Go figure. Worse, it refuses to question the sources or the line of reasoning that led to this conclusion.

Analysis and Groupthink

During the Cold War, scarcity of hard information combined with political prejudice to produce Groupthink at the CIA. In the 1960s and 1970s CIA analysts distorted reality concerning Soviet missiles even more radically than they did regarding Iraq in 1993–2003. Just as in Iraq, the CIA's human collectors did not know what characteristics the other side intended to endow its weapons. And our technical devices were able to discern only indirect indications of what these might be. Nevertheless, to maintain their prejudices, CIA analysts had to ignore the plainest facts—just as in Iraq.

> **There is no reason, then, to be surprised at CIA analysis' judgment that Iraq was virtually uninvolved with terrorism and full of Weapons of Mass Destruction.**

In the mid-1960s the Soviet Union began a massive buildup of its missile force, and of warheads with the combination of power and accuracy for disarming "first strikes." But the CIA's dogma had it that the Soviets would not try to match the number of U.S. missiles or seek that capacity. When the Soviets' numbers did, CIA analysts judged that they would not exceed them. When their missiles exceeded ours in number, the CIA judged that the Soviets would not endow them with accuracy. When they did that, the CIA judged that this would not matter because the Soviets just had to know that it would be unreasonable to use the force they had built. This line of reasoning developed over a decade, and involved countless redefinitions of what technical evidence was and was not acceptable. Each redefinition prejudiced conclusions in favor of the CIA's dogma. Only in 1977, when an independent commission was given access to all data available to the CIA, did this intellectual house of cards fall.

Similarly, CIA dogma held that the Soviet Union was not spending a greater proportion of its GDP on military matters than was the U.S.—in those days, some 5 to 6 percent. To support this prejudice, the CIA built an elaborate econometric model, complete with its own valuation of the ruble. It turned out of course that the Soviets had been spending on the order of 40 percent of GDP on their military. A glance at the *Statistical Abstract of the United States* for the 1980s, compiled with CIA data, shows even more egregious prejudice. According to the CIA, you see, the per capita GDP of East Germany and West Germany were roughly equal. This was news to all but the CIA analysts who made up the econometric models.

There is no reason, then, to be surprised at CIA analysts' judgment that Iraq was virtually uninvolved with terrorism and full of Weapons of Mass Destruction. To reach the first part of that judgment, they only had to term "inconclusive" the existence of the training camp for foreign terrorists at Salman Pak, the financing of terrorism in Israel (which the CIA does not admit is really terrorism), the reported meeting of 9/11 captain Mohamed Atta with Iraqi case officer al Ani (al Ani's denial of the meeting beats Czech intelligence's affirmation of it, you see), the overlap of personnel between the first and second attack on the World Trade Center, Ramzi Yousef's possession of identity documents doctored by Iraqi intelligence, and much more. To affirm Iraq's possession of WMDs, CIA analysts only had to go with the flow of legalistic argument: The U.N. had required Iraq to submit to inspections. Iraq had not done so. It had to be hiding WMDs. Easy. Besides, focusing on WMDs averted America's attention from the role that Arab regimes play in terrorism. The CIA wanted to make sure of that.

Action

Not only has the CIA's covert action, full of half-measures and bloody betrayals, produced countless dead Kurds, Hmong, and other would-be allies, it has also crippled America's capacity to deal with terrorism. That is because much of the CIA's interference in the affairs of the world has consisted of promoting precisely the regimes and ideas that are the matrices of terrorism.

> **Not only has the CIA's covert action, full of half-measures and bloody betrayals, produced countless dead Kurds, Hmong, and other would-be allies, it has also crippled America's capacity to deal with terrorism.**

From its earliest days, the CIA built a dysfunctional relationship with the "third world." CIA Director Allen Dulles financed political revolution aries such as Egypt's Gamal Abdel Nasser, as well as intellectuals such as Frantz Fanon, author of *The Wretched of the Earth*, the ur text of anti-Westernism. Though the CIA did not invent the Ba'ath Party, no one who knows the region would suggest that such a party would have come to power without the CIA. To Iraq, the CIA sent a young thug named Saddam Hussein. The CIA's assumption was that these movements would take its advice, and at least that the CIA would retain the loyalty of enough of their members never to lack for excellent sources of information about them.

Wrong on all counts. Third World movements turned against America. Meanwhile the CIA's large emotional and organizational investment in these movements led it to be their advocate within the U.S. government. To ordinary Americans a Yassir Arafat is a disgusting thug. But to the CIA he is always full of hopeful signals. Sunni, Ba'athist domination of Iraq might be patently disastrous to any number of people, but to the CIA Saddamism, first with, later without Saddam, has been the way to go. The CIA's political prejudices color whatever realities U.S. intelligence comes across.

Reform

No one has attempted to show how the main proposals for "reform" proposed by the 9/11 Commission and endorsed by

both 2004 presidential candidates would remedy any fault of U.S. intelligence whatever. Creating the post of Director of National Intelligence with budgetary and programmatic authority (Kerry) or supervision (Bush) over all intelligence agencies, as well as a national counter terrorism center to direct all aspects of intelligence about as well as action against terrorism, side-steps all substantive questions about what intelligence is to be sought, how its integrity is to be guarded, how controversies over its interpretation ought to be resolved, and what action ought to be taken. Much less could anyone show how either of these organizational changes would safeguard America.

The proposal for a Director of National Intelligence has been around since the 1970s. Its implementation would have few if any effects beyond somewhat complicating an already complex bureaucracy. But a national counterterrorism center that could order any agency to collect in certain ways, come to certain conclusions about who is a terrorist, and act on those conclusions without the adult supervision of, say, the Secretary of Defense or State, would likely spawn any number of embarrassing activities. All to naught. Since incentives for terrorism continue to increase, opportunities for attack are irreducible, and fundamental intelligence faults remain unaddressed, events will surely discredit such irrelevant "reforms."

Putting resources into boxes with the proper label does not produce good outcomes. These depend on people knowing the right things to be done, and actually getting them done. Alas, intelligence officials whose work has been their own secret for two generations have defined excellence simply as whatever they happen to turn out.

There is no substitute for firing massive numbers of people who have performed badly or are just useless, and replacing them with persons picked for their capacity to do the job expected of them. But there is the rub. Someone at the top must define the job. Intelligence is an instrument of conflict. In any given conflict, intelligence is good insofar as it contributes to victory. Whoever is responsible for any operation must—as part of the exercise of his responsibility—define what information is needed for that operation's success.

For that reason, the idea behind the creation of the Central Intelligence Agency, namely to separate responsibility for knowing the world from responsibility for defense and foreign affairs, was a bad idea. Intelligence reform should proceed from the premise that intelligence is naturally the handmaiden of strategy.

> **There is no substitute for firing massive numbers of people who have performed badly or are just useless, and replacing them with persons picked for their capacity to do the job expected of them.**

Strategy and Policy

The faults of U.S. intelligence in anti-terrorism come as much from the outside as from the inside. In 1993 the Clinton administration decided that individuals, not regimes, were responsible for terrorism and demanded that U.S. intelligence comb through thousands of persons about whom we know nothing, while discounting the fact that terrorist activities breed in authoritarian regimes as expressions of those regimes. The Bush team has not reversed that judgment. And so, as wealthy Saudis spread the Wahabi movement through oil billions and Syrian dictators and Palestinian warlords rail on TV with impunity against America and all its works, U.S. intelligence interrogators are "going after" the small fry. No problem can be dealt with well if it is defined badly. No intelligence can save unintelligent policy or make up for lack of a strategy for victory.

Intelligence can light a path to victory if we make war on the basis of what we know for sure. Policymakers for whom the pursuit of victory is contingent on intelligence beyond their reach are making intelligence a scapegoat for their own incompetence.

Angelo M. Codevilla, a professor of international relations at Boston University, a fellow of the Claremont Institute, and a senior editor of TASMI, was a Foreign Service officer and served on the staff of the U.S. Senate Intelligence Committee between 1977 and 1985. He was the principal author of the 1980 presidential transition report on intelligence.

In Defence of the Intelligence Services

The committees of inquiry into American and British intelligence failures may have left the West less secure, argues Efraim Halevy, an ex-chief of Mossad.

EFRAIM HALEVY

When commissions of inquiry investigate intelligence failures of extraordinary magnitude, their conclusions inevitably have an overwhelming influence on the conduct of intelligence chiefs and their political masters for generations to come. Whatever the practical steps taken by the powers-that-be to implement this or that recommendation of the Senate Intelligence Committee, the September 11th commission, and the British committee headed by Lord Butler, the language and rhetoric of these documents are destined to have an enormous impact on the manner in which world leaders, both in intelligence and in politics, will perform in times of crisis and war. Several assumptions and concepts, implicit or explicit in the reports, warrant close study.

There is an inherent understanding in the findings that the shortage of information on the threats—from Islamic terrorism and from Iraq's weapons of mass destruction (WMD)—was at the root of the intelligence breakdown on these two fronts. It seems only logical that the more you know, the safer you are and the greater the chance that you will get things right.

Yet Israel's most costly and fateful failure was its mistaken estimate of Egyptian and Syrian intentions, on the eve of the Yom Kippur war in 1973, when the two armies unexpectedly attacked Israel in a bid to regain the territories lost in the 1967 war. At the time, Israel had it all: superior intelligence coverage, excellent human resources with good access, high-level and discreet dialogue with more than one Arab or Muslim leader, and an intelligence-evaluation arm that had provided an early warning several months before the war, thus preventing it from breaking out at that time. But despite all of the above, we got it all wrong. The abundance of information led us to intelligence "hubris": we trusted our superior analytical prowess rather than ominous indicators on the ground.

Naturally, one should not conclude from this that the less you know, the better your judgment. On the other hand, one should understand that, although knowledge is strength, knowledge by itself is no guarantee of safety.

A second assumption relates to structures and the flow of information. There is the belief that the more the system is streamlined, the greater the possibility that the final product will be accurate and properly exploited. That better organisation is

always desirable cannot be disputed; nor that a better flow of information can save lives. However, this in itself will never produce the ultimate panacea, and should not be a central focus of action.

A third element in the reports focuses on the danger of "group thought" and the tendency to blur reservations and caveats as the intelligence product makes its way to the top. Intelligence is not a science, certainly not a natural science. It is an art or a craft, and as such it cannot be governed by the basic tenets of logic.

Intelligence officers must be gifted with imagination and creativity, enabling them to peer behind the curtain of apparent reality. On this last count, the September 11th commission got it right. The commission spoke of a lack of imagination on the part of the evaluators. In the absence of hard intelligence, it is incumbent on the intelligence chief to try to imagine the unimaginable. But in the unique circumstances of September 11th, this was no easy matter. I will come back to this point later.

The Buck Stops with the Chief

There has to be a clear understanding among the clients of the product that, in the final analysis, any institutional evaluation is a "group-think" effort. Officers can sit around a table and hotly debate an issue but, at the end of the day, someone has to be assigned to draw up a draft that is designed to reflect the mainstream consensus. If there is consensus, is this "group think"? If there is no agreement whatsoever, what benefit can a political master derive from receiving a paper with five or six conflicting opinions on a given issue?

After all, these are not academic exercises but action-orientated briefs. When there is no agreement, the time comes for an intelligence chief to step in and determine what the official estimate shall be. He could and should indicate if there are major reservations, and what these might be, but the ultimate responsibility lies with the chief. He must state his view and he, and he alone, must bear official responsibility for the estimate. Nobody else shoulders real and accountable responsibility, either for the estimate, or for the ultimate mistake, if it emerges that there has been one.

There is a fourth inherent assumption in the reports: that if it is necessary to collect information, it can always somehow be done. In other words, where there is a will there is a way. For a considerable period of time, it has been known and clear that there have been grave deficiencies in the collection of information both on Islamic terrorism and on the proliferation of weapons of mass destruction.

However, to do the intelligence services justice, it is fair to mention the enormous difficulty that must have been encountered in trying to spot, recruit and run sources in Iraq throughout the years when a virtual siege was laid around the country by the world at large. Similarly, the task of penetrating international Islamic networks was, and is, a daunting challenge.

Israel's Singular Advantages

On this latter point, it is appropriate to recall that Israel has scored singular successes in its fight against "local" terrorism. Yet one should not forget that we were present in the "territories," the main breeding grounds of terrorism, for over 20 years, that we are still in control of large chunks of land and parts of the Palestinian population, that we enter areas controlled by the Palestinian Authority whenever we consider it necessary for the security of Israel, and that our close proximity to the territories has enabled us to make spectacular and novel use of a variety of our intelligence capabilities.

And yet, even so, the Israeli score on terror has become a debatable one. There are those who will say that the decision by Ariel Sharon, Israel's prime minister, to disengage unilaterally from the Gaza strip and an initial few settlements in the northern West Bank is in itself a triumph for the al-Aqsa *intifada*, which has claimed more than 1,000 Israeli lives since it began in September 2000.

The fifth assumption in the reports is that the failure in the collection of information, assuming that there was such a failure, was matched by a complementary debacle on the assessment side. I wish to take issue with these findings, on both subjects: terrorism and the WMD.

Three times within close to a quarter of a century, Saddam Hussein has attempted to develop capabilities in the field of WMD, with emphasis on the nuclear area. In the early 1980s, Israel destroyed his French-supplied nuclear reactor. In the early 1990s, the first Gulf war, launched after Iraq invaded Kuwait, revealed extensive Iraqi activity in all three WMD fields (nuclear, chemical and biological); the UN destroyed some of these capabilities after the war, and tried to monitor others before it withdrew from Iraq in 1998 and was not allowed back. And in the years leading up to the American-British invasion of Iraq in 2003, there was evidence that Saddam was trying to renew his nuclear and ballistic missile programmes, and to restore his original capabilities. Nobody outside Iraq knew how far he had succeeded.

In assessing the situation, an intelligence chief would have to give due weight not only to the current available information, but also to past performance. He would have to take into account indications of intention, and also the nature and known character of the adversary. And he would have to assess the significance of Saddam's adamant obstruction of UN efforts to renew its monitoring activities on the ground.

Obviously, he would have to take into account all the caveats and reservations of all the officers involved. But in the end he would have to form an overall picture, a credible view of his own, for which, as stated previously, he would have to bear full formal responsibility.

On the terrorist scene, it became obvious when two American embassies, in Nairobi and Dar es Salaam, were simultaneously attacked in 1998, that al-Qaeda had entered a new phase in its war against the United States. This threat was clearly recognised by the American intelligence community. Serious collection efforts were initiated. However, I believe that if the Central Intelligence Agency had come up with proposals to adopt measures like those that were hastily implemented after September 11th 2001, the American public would not have been capable of approving them.

Even if the powers-that-be at the time had been as imaginative as possible, and if, for instance, the director of the CIA had publicly imagined the horror of a simultaneous attack on the White House, Congress, the Pentagon and the New York twin towers, I seriously doubt that the president would have found support for what was sanctioned after that fateful day.

Tenet Got It Right

I have reason to believe that George Tenet, the director of the CIA who resigned in June and left in July, got it right on both key issues. He correctly assessed the terrorist threat, and his basic approach to the Iraqi conundrum was similarly accurate. The fact that WMD have not yet been found in Iraq is no proof that there was nothing there; those who can conceal complete squadrons of aircraft in the sand could easily act similarly when it comes to WMD.

There is a sixth element in the reports which deserves mention and elaboration. There is always a unique relationship between intelligence chiefs and their political masters. The political master has to rely on his intelligence chief for threat assessment, and for the cautious and professional conduct of the service. There must be an unusual degree of trust between them, and it has to be mutual. This cannot be achieved and preserved on a purely formal and official basis.

I believe, therefore, that it was not only permissible but mandatory that, at a given moment, George Bush should turn to George Tenet and say to him something like this: "Listen George, let us stop for a moment and turn off all the audio and other recording devices. Let us talk a little maybe alone, just the two of us. I know that information is scant and incomplete but I cannot afford to wait around endlessly, years after the UN has left the scene in Baghdad. Tell me on the basis of what you know and what you feel, your gut-feeling and intuition: is Saddam into WMD for real?"

I do not know if such a conversation took place. I have certainly not spoken of it to Mr Tenet. But if it did not take place, that would have been a grave fault. Moreover, if such a conversation can henceforth never take place, then grievous damage has been rendered by the commissions that investigated intelligence shortcomings. The security of the United States and the world at large is that much worse off.

This leads me to another aspect of the reports that I believe to be of paramount importance: the treatment of individuals. For exchanges like the above to take place, there has to be a suitable climate, both political and cultural, that permeates the domestic and international scene. Mr Tenet was in office for seven years and his many successes cannot be publicly revealed. But there is one achievement of which one can speak: the rare knack he had of pulling together a genuine international effort in this third world war against Islamic terror and the proliferation of WMD.

American leadership in these sensitive areas cannot be taken for granted. Mr Tenet inspired the confidence of his subordinates and peers in all four corners of the earth, and this was a vital ingredient in the war effort. It still is. The manner of Mr Tenet's departure, and his public castigation at the hands of the inquiry commissions, will make it extremely difficult for any successor to lead the world in the clandestine war which is such a key theatre in the current international conflict.

Butler's Way Was Better

There may be many individuals in far-flung places who played a part in some of Mr Tenet's real achievements who will in future think twice before committing themselves. I believe that on this count, Lord Butler and his colleagues performed a singular service in treating individuals in the British intelligence community as they did: neither Richard Dearlove, the former head of Britain's Secret Intelligence Service (M16), nor John Scarlett, the current one, was held responsible. The committee understood its responsibility for the future, and gave this precedence over settling accounts of the past.

One of the principal dangers of inquiries like the present ones is that they focus on the failures at hand, making the necessary recommendations to ensure that such failures never happen again. They do not deal with future challenges, currently unknown. But it is surely these new and unknown threats that will bring about future intelligence setbacks. In these professional areas the reports are deafeningly silent.

Moreover, to the best of my knowledge, nobody came up with any new ideas as to how to collect information from countries like Iraq, or from targets like al-Qaeda. If the collection efforts did not produce the desired results, how should they be carried out in the future? Ideas like these would have given the Senate report an aura of genuine professionalism, which it now sadly lacks.

I cannot avoid the comparison between these reports and that of the Agranat Commision in Israel which investigated the failure of Israel's intelligence services to predict the Arab attack in 1973. The Israeli commission recommended the appointment of a special adviser on intelligence who would go through all the intelligence estimates, and would advise the prime minister on

them. It was not clear if the adviser would monitor the reports, and decide which should go on to the prime minister's desk, or if he would add evaluations of his own. Only two people filled this slot for relatively short periods, and both left office in frustration.

Now there is a recommendation to appoint an intelligence "tsar" in the United States. In my humble opinion no greater mistake could be made so far as the intelligence community is concerned. If the new tsar is to assume command responsibility for the intelligence community, then he will be de facto director of the CIA and the other intelligence agencies in the country. He, and he alone, will be responsible for the content and standard of the evaluation. The professional director of the CIA will be responsible to the tsar, and the president of the United States will be functioning through a "proxy" on matters of war and peace. In intelligence, there can be no sharing in responsibility; it is, and will always remain, indivisible.

There are no "legal" rules and regulations in the dense field of intelligence, espionage and collection. It is not by chance that the international statute book has neither a chapter nor a verse on espionage, although this has been a vital tool of war from time immemorial. We are in the throes of a world war which is distinct and different from all the wars the world has hitherto experienced. There are no lines of combat; the enemy is often elusive and escapes identification.

Support the Men in the Trenches

The rules of war are incumbent on the defendant but not on he or she who attacks. International law, the Geneva conventions and the other well-known humanitarian provisions do not apply to the aggressor in this current confrontation. In circumstances like these, the future probably has in store crisis situations the like of which we have never experienced before. Rather than seeking long-term overhauling and restructuring of the system, and the creation of new high-level slots, surely this is a moment in history when the body politic should swing behind those who are already in the trenches and give them encouragement and support in this fateful battle that has been thrust upon us.

Those who have experienced times of acute crisis know that lines often get blurred and formal functions and positions do not reflect the real influence of various players on the scene. You will find political masters absorbing copious quantities of raw intelligence and forming their own estimates and evaluations of the situation. You will also find intelligence chiefs not only passing on information and assessments, but also advocating specific courses of action. This is simple human nature and no rule or regulation can change it.

This is especially so when the intelligence chief not only has his army of assessment officers but also has units and forces and assets directly involved in the conflict. At such a time, the attempt to apportion blame and responsibility between the political and executive levels of government becomes artificial and obsolete. They are in it together for better or worse.

In an ideal world, each player performs his part. In reality, personalities often shine way beyond their limited bailiwick.

This happens more often than not when others melt into the woodwork under the intense pressures of war. An intelligence chief can never wither in the heat. Let us hope, for the sake of us all, that the inquiry commissions will not create a climate wherein the George Tenets and Richard Dearloves and John Scarletts of this planet will not be able to function. After everything has already been said, let us never forget that there are not all that many of them around.

EFRAIM HALEVY was head of Mossad, Israel's intelligence service, from 1998 to 2002. Since 2003 he has been head of the Centre for Strategic and Policy Studies at the Hebrew University of Jerusalem

America's intelligence reforms

Can Spies Be Made Better?

In the wake of recent shocks, intelligence-gathering is being reformed on both sides of the Atlantic. The task is daunting. We begin in America.

"We tend to meet any new situation in life by reorganising," Petronius Arbiter, a 1st-century Roman satirist, is supposed to have remarked. "And what a wonderful method it can be for creating the illusion of progress while producing confusion, inefficiency and demoralisation." Wonderful, indeed, for John Negroponte, America's ambassador to Iraq, who will leave Baghdad this month to become America's first director of national intelligence (DNI). Mr Negroponte may come to question which job is the more harrowing. On one side, murder and mayhem; on the other, mayhem and mystery.

The creation of the DNI was a well publicised reform, approved by both Republicans and Democrats, which was intended to improve the performance of America's intelligence agencies in the wake of the terrorist attacks of September 11th 2001. But precisely what power it will confer on Mr Negroponte is, as yet, unknown. So too is what power he will subtract from others within the 15 arcane agencies he will direct. The Central Intelligence Agency (CIA), the best known, accounts for only about a tenth of the intelligence budget; the biggest of all, the National Security Agency (NSA), with 30,000 employees, resides in the Department of Defence (DOD) under the pugnacious Donald Rumsfeld. As Mr Negroponte turns his thoughts away from bombs and gunfire inside the green zone, he may hear a rattle of daggers being drawn in Washington, Arlington and Langley.

America's secret world is inefficient and demoralised, and has been for some time. The CIA in particular is an unreformed, substantially unaccountable bureaucracy, which has almost never sacked anyone, which appears deluded by its own mythology and which, despite some notable successes, is burdened by a miserable run of failures. The entrance-hall at Langley is decorated with a black star for every CIA officer killed fighting the cold war. A more telling record, according to several former spooks, is that the agency in those years did not recruit a single mid-level or high-level Soviet agent. Every significant CIA informant was a volunteer. And the agency was comprehensively infiltrated. At one point, every CIA case-officer working on Cuba was a double agent. All but three CIA officers working on East Germany allegedly worked for the

Stasi. As for those brave volunteer agents, Aldrich Ames, a greedy drunkard in the CIA directorate of operations who was bought by the Russians, put paid to many—as did another mole, Robert Hanssen, in the FBI.

When it comes to recruitment and filing intelligence from the field, quantity has often mattered most. In cold-war Africa, American spooks allegedly paid for the same information obtained for nothing by American diplomats over lunch. One recent case-officer, Lindsay Moran, says she was aware that an agent she was running in the Balkans was peddling worthless information, but she was repeatedly refused permission to end the contact. "It gets depressing," she said. "You start to wonder whether we can do anything good at all."

More recent events have brought shame on the intelligence agencies as a whole. They failed to predict both the Soviet invasion of Afghanistan in 1979 and the Soviet Union's break-up a decade later. In 1998, America's spies were taken by surprise when India tested a nuclear bomb; they then advised Bill Clinton to flatten one of Sudan's few medicine factories, wrongly believing that it made nerve gas. The next year, on the agencies' mistaken advice, an American warplane bombed China's embassy in Belgrade.

The two main prompts to reform, however, have been the September 11th attacks, in which some 3,000 Americans died, and the spooks' hallucinations about Iraq's weapons programmes, which were used to justify a war and bloody peace that have cost tens of thousands of lives. The fallout from Iraq—especially a report by the Senate Intelligence Committee last year, which accused the agencies of "a lack of information-sharing, poor management, and inadequate intelligence collection"—forced George Tenet, the CIA's second-longest-serving boss, to resign in June.

Porter Goss's Burdens

Under Mr Tenet's successor, Porter Goss, a former Republican congressman and spy, a dozen senior spooks have been sacked and two dozen have quit in fury. Mr Goss's aides—most of whom have had no previous experience of intelligence work—are said to be thuggish managers. Mr Goss is meanwhile finding his job tough. On March 2nd, he said he was "a little amazed at the workload," which was "too much for this mortal". Merely preparing the president's daily intelligence briefing takes him five hours.

It was partly to ease this burden that the DNI was created, in a package of reforms passed in December. These were broadly in line with recommendations made by the bipartisan 9/11 Commission, whose vivid report into the attacks was a deserved, if unlikely, bestseller last year. (The recommendations were not informed by the foul-up on Iraq; a presidential commission into the pre-war Iraq intelligence is due to report later this month.)

The DNI will be charged with co-ordinating all the secret agencies, a job which the CIA's chief—as the director of central intelligence—has performed only in theory hitherto. The DNI will thus be held accountable for the performance of each agency. Alongside a new multi-agency National Counterterrorism Centre (NCTC)—which will have wider powers than its existing equivalent, and may be the prototype for more specialist centres, focused on China and proliferation issues—the DNI represents the biggest organisational change to America's spy world since 1947.

The 9/11 Commission's report told mostly the story of the months and moments leading up to the attacks, with many details of the agencies' bungling. The CIA noticed that two known terrorists had obtained American visas, but failed to inform the Federal Bureau of Investigation (FBI), which is responsible for domestic counter-terrorism. Notoriously, certain FBI bosses failed to pick up on a report that a group of Arab men was learning to fly planes, but not to land them. Overall, the commissioners diagnosed a grave reluctance to share information within and among the agencies. Most seriously, they found that the FBI's two main departments, responsible for intelligence and criminal investigations, barely communicated. In part, they were deterred by laws safeguarding Americans from government meddling, though the reach of these laws was often exaggerated.

More generally, the commission observed a "failure of imagination" in the agencies' response to the warning signs they did observe. A CIA report filed in 1998 had warned that al-Qaeda might carry out suicide attacks with hijacked planes; but the report's authors later said they could barely remember having included the detail. The problems were only partly organisational. Indeed, the commission noted that, when tipped off that al-Qaeda was planning a range of horrific attacks to mark the end of the last millennium, the agencies performed well; a number of bomb attacks on embassies in the Middle East were averted.

The commission proposed that a DNI, crudely analogous to the head of the armed forces, the chairman of the joint chiefs of staff, should be hired to oversee all the agencies and correct what had gone wrong. To lend weight to his admonishments, the DNI was to be given charge of the agencies' combined $40 billion budget, though most of that is controlled by the Pentagon. The DNI would be just what the agencies had not been: vigilant, imaginative and single-minded.

Devilment in the Details

Nobody really disputes the idea that America's intelligence system, which was designed in 1947, was out of date, disorganised and had no recognisable chief. Its 15 squabbling baronies, which were set up to deal with conventional enemies, display precious little cohesion (with the Pentagon particularly protective of the agencies it controls). It was thus not surprising that the 9/11 commissioners fastened on the idea of appointing an overall chief to bring the muddle together. The question is whether this new job, without any other structural reform, can actually improve the system.

By the time the commission delivered its recommendations, some of the more useful ones were almost three years out of date. The commission's period under investigation ended on September 11th 2001; the commission's report was delivered 34 months later. In the intervening time, the war on terror was launched and changes were made. First, under the Patriot Act, many of the inter-agency firewalls protecting Americans' civil liberties were broken down. FBI and other agents were obliged to share intelligence on terrorists within and among the agencies. The director of the FBI, Robert Mueller, was required to attend the president's daily intelligence briefing, given by the director of central intelligence (DCI).

Huge resources were shifted to counter-terrorism. In January 2003, a multi-agency counter-terrorism think-tank, the Terrorist Threat Integration Centre, was formed inside the CIA's headquarters. The centre produces a daily briefing on terrorist threats and counter-terrorism operations, which the president hears after the DCI's.

When the 9/11 Commission added its own recommendations to the pile, they were accepted rapidly. John Kerry, the Democratic presidential candidate, endorsed the report almost before he could have read it. Bereaved relatives of the hijackers' victims rallied behind its recommendations. Reluctantly, and to Mr Rumsfeld's great annoyance, Mr Bush endorsed it too.

To general surprise, Mr Bush after his reelection made good on that endorsement, signing into law the Intelligence Reform and Terrorism Prevention Act. It was modelled on the commission's recommendations, with a few modifications insisted on by pals of Mr Rumsfeld. For example, in keeping with the commission's demands, the act authorises the DNI to "design and deliver" a unified intelligence budget. But it also says that the authority of the cabinet secretaries should be upheld.

This has created confusion over who will, in fact, control the purse-strings. To extricate the defence intelligence budgets from the wider defence budget could take several years and a staff of several hundred experts. It might not even be desirable. America's generals almost always get first dibs on the intelligence assets, such as spy satellites, that they share with civilian agencies, and in wartime they always do. The law similarly gives the DNI control over the agencies' personnel, but here too there is devilment in the detail: in practice, the DNI can veto the appointment of some second-tier officials, but he will not be able to sack agency chiefs.

To shore up the DNI's putative powers, Mr Bush has suggested that Mr Negroponte, not Mr Goss, will deliver his morning intelligence briefing. In theory, this should allow Mr Goss to concentrate on managing the CIA. In practice, the briefing is likely still to be prepared by the CIA and Mr Goss will still be required to attend the meetings, with Mr Negroponte appearing as an over-qualified court herald. Alternatively, he too could spend half his working day drafting the briefing. He will exert even less control over what goes into the counter-terrorism briefing that follows it, because although the DNI will be in overall charge of the NCTC, the agency chiefs retain control of their operations. Yet Mr Negroponte is to be held accountable for their mistakes.

These uncertainties have fuelled a noisy and ill-tempered debate about the reforms in a country whose spies have traditionally excited fierce passions, and where national security is a national obsession. Left-wingers loathe the CIA, in particular, for its cold-war habit of plotting to murder left-wing leaders, including Patrice Lumumba of Congo and Fidel Castro of Cuba. On the right, the CIA is often considered a nest of liberals, bureaucratic and broken beyond repair, whose salvageable assets should be handed over to the Pentagon. Some hawks justify the policy of preemption on the ground that the agencies cannot be trusted to give warning of imminent threats. And, of course, moderate opponents of all the above tend to take the opposite view.

A Cornucopia of Incompetence

Such passions lie behind the unerring certainty with which America's politicians and pundits speak of a world that remains, after all, secret. For many right-wingers, the DNI office will prove disastrous, adding an unwanted layer of bureaucracy to an already constipated system. At worst, it will go the way of the Office of Homeland Security, which was created after the September 11th attacks with a mandate to co-ordinate agencies such as customs and the coast guard, but which has since proved toothless and wasteful. Others note the few factors in Mr Negroponte's favour. His chosen deputy, Lieut-General Michael Hayden, is a well-respected former head of the NSA. Above all, Mr Negroponte will have daily access to a president who holds him in high regard.

The truth is, no one knows how the reforms will proceed. Mr Negroponte may gain a modicum of control over the agencies. At best, he may ensure that the information channels opened within and between the agencies after the hijack attacks stay open. Yet, on his own at least, he will not be able to fix the agencies' most grievous problems, highlighted by their performance on Iraq.

Last year's Senate report into the Iraq debacle found America's spies—and especially the CIA—negligent and incompetent at every stage of the intelligence-collection and analysis process. The CIA had not a single agent in Iraq after the UN's weapons inspectors were expelled in 1998. They had no fresh intelligence to claim, as they did, that Iraq had chemical and biological weapons. Their claim that Iraq was "reconstituting its nuclear programme" was based on the country's import of some aluminium tubes that could have been used for other purposes, and was fiercely contested by most experts across the agencies. They did not, at least, suggest that Iraq was in cahoots with al-Qaeda, although members of the government, notably Dick Cheney, the vice-president, did so often.

The key to the agencies' misapprehensions, the committee found, was a predilection to "group-think." In other words, they failed to re-examine received truths—for example, the historical fact that Iraq had prohibited weapons. This was made manifest in numerous ways. The CIA's analysis was seldom double-checked; detection of dual-purpose materials, that might possibly be used in weapon programmes, was routinely taken as proof that such programmes existed; and ambiguous scraps of intelligence were compiled to reach an unambiguous conclusion, a process known as "layering." These problems, said the report, stemmed "from a broken corporate culture and poor management, and will not be solved by additional funding and personnel."

The spies' friends (and Mr Bush's enemies) rebut this. On chemical and biological weapons, they say, the agencies were not all that wrong—the report acknowledged that Iraq had retained the technology to rebuild its stockpiles—and, moreover, no other western intelligence service thought differently. On Iraq's nuclear programme, they say, the government was to blame: under intense pressure to provide the case for a war that Mr Bush had already decided to fight, doubters were muffled and caveats were cut.

Another defence is that intelligence, whether human or, far more commonly, electronic, rarely yields the smoking-gun proofs that policymakers may wish for. It is an accumulation of indicators, contradictory and unreliable, which intelligence analysts turn into an estimation of a hidden reality—or, even more precariously, use to predict the future. Intelligence is inherently faulty. True: but why then did Mr Tenet—in a phrase quoted by Bob Woodward, which Mr Tenet has not disputed—describe the case for Iraq having banned weapons as "a slam-dunk"?

Mr Negroponte's Uses

Despite all the recommendations, the rot may be hard to stop. After a decade of cuts—the CIA's budget was chopped by 23% under Bill Clinton—the agencies are indeed getting more money and more spies. This year, the CIA will graduate its biggest-ever class of case-officers. With only around 1,200 stationed overseas, more case-officers are needed, but only if they are properly equipped for the latest challenges. Around half of all the CIA's case-officers are in Baghdad. But with only a handful of them fluent in Arabic, they are mostly confined to the green zone, condemned to interview Iraqi interpreters and watch endless episodes of "Sex and the City" on DVD.

Further organisational reform would not eliminate the problem. America's spies do not necessarily need shifting;

a good few need sacking. Mr Negroponte is in too lofty and exposed a seat to manage such a programme. But if he can shoulder some of the DCI's more onerous duties, including the president's briefing and the intelligence budget, he might free a dynamic cia director to wield the axe for him. There is no time to waste. In a precarious world, the full range of American intelligence and intelligence-gathering on, for example, China's military build-up and Iran's nuclear ambitions needs urgent re-evaluating. But that dynamic director may not be Mr Goss, who sounds awfully tired.

We Have Not Correctly Framed the Debate on Intelligence Reform

Saxby Chambliss

Over the last decade, our intelligence community has failed us. It wasn't able to penetrate the al Qaeda terrorist organization, and we paid a high price for that failure. The terrorist attacks on 11 September 2001 were the first significant foreign attacks on the US mainland since the War of 1812. In the weeks and months leading up to 9/11, we failed to interpret, analyze, and share information gathered. Subsequently the intelligence community failed the President by presenting an inaccurate analysis of the quantities and capabilities of Saddam Hussein's weapons of mass destruction (WMD). While there should be no doubt whatsoever that Saddam's intentions were to reconstitute his WMD programs and become a supplier of these weapons to the radical Islamist terrorists who are bent on the destruction of democratic and secular Western societies, the fact remains that the CIA did not have a single agent inside Iraq to verify the true state of these programs before coalition forces, led by the United States, attacked Iraq in 2003.

Today, the intelligence community is struggling to stay ahead of a host of threats to our security—the insurgency in Iraq that is taking American lives daily, the continuing war on terrorism, and the nuclear threat posed by Iran and North Korea, to name but a few. And there is an intelligence breakdown every time an improvised explosive device is detonated in Iraq killing American soldiers and marines.

We have had huge, glaring intelligence failures, and the Administration and the Congress are working assiduously to improve our intelligence community as quickly as possible to better protect our people and our allies. On 17 December 2004, President Bush signed into law the most sweeping intelligence reform legislation since the National Security Act of 1947.

The centerpiece of this intelligence legislation—articulated by the 9/11 Commission in its report,[1] embraced by the President, and endorsed by the Congress—is the creation of a new position to lead our intelligence community, the Director of National Intelligence (DNI). The DNI will not head any single agency, as was the case when the 1947 National Security Act created the Central Intelligence Agency and dual-hatted the Director as the chief intelligence officer of the United States as well as running the CIA. Another positive aspect of the legislation is the creation of the National Counterterrorism Center (NCTC),

which will conduct strategic operational planning for joint counterintelligence operations.

Our country is in the midst of a national debate on intelligence reform. In any endeavor of this type, the end result is largely dependent upon how the debate is framed, and we have not done a good or complete job of framing the debate on this issue of vital importance to the American people. Creating the DNI is an extremely important decision, and it forms the very foundation that is necessary to continue building intelligence capabilities. However, it is the beginning of a long process, not the end.

Human Intelligence

Last year's debate on intelligence reform should have centered on espionage, which we call human intelligence, or HUMINT, or spying. As we reframe the intelligence debate this year, we need to make sure HUMINT gets the right emphasis.

Americans like technology and we are good at it. Our ability to monitor certain activities via satellites, signals intelligence, or other technical means, while not perfect, is pretty good. Our weak point is HUMINT, which has atrophied to the point that it must be rebuilt. Human intelligence, relative to the other intelligence disciplines, can tell us what the enemy is thinking. The strength of good HUMINT is that it can answer this key question: What are the enemy's intentions about when, where, and how to strike?

In July 2002, as the Chairman of the Subcommittee on Terrorism and Homeland Security in the House of Representatives, it was my responsibility, along with Ranking Member, Representative Jane Harman, to submit the first detailed report to Congress on intelligence deficiencies that existed prior to 11 September 2001. We identified several systemic problems in the CIA, and we also noted that there were significant problems in sharing intelligence within the intelligence community, especially between the CIA and the FBI.

"The intelligence community is struggling to stay ahead of a host of threats to our security."

We pointed out that the CIA had lost its focus on HUMINT missions and needed to put more collectors on the streets, rely less on other foreign intelligence agencies, and find ways to penetrate terrorist cells. I am particularly pleased that immediately following the release of our report, the CIA rescinded the so called "Deutch guidelines" that were implemented in 1995. Those guidelines prohibited the expenditure of tax money being paid to individuals providing us intelligence if they had a criminal record or any kind of disparaging record in their past.

Having met personally with CIA agents in countries with known terrorist activities, I heard firsthand how these guidelines, while relaxed after 9/11, were still a major hindrance for our agents to collect and gather intelligence. Terrorist networks like al Qaeda are comprised of the meanest, nastiest killers in the world, and it simply was not smart for us to limit the operatives our intelligence agents could recruit to infiltrate terrorist groups. For us, this was a small but important victory with respect to improving human intelligence.

HUMINT is a dirty business, a dangerous profession, and we must be prepared to accept the risks associated with spying on those who seek to harm us, whether they be a small terrorist cell, a larger international terrorist organization, or a rogue nation-state. North Korea, for example, is developing the means to deliver nuclear weapons to close and important allies, like Japan, or to our own state of Hawaii and our Pacific Coast—we cannot afford to let down our guard or relax our intelligence awareness.

The "risk-avoidance" culture that had infected the CIA and prevented us from getting into the inner circles of al Qaeda or the regime in Iraq before the 2003 war must be changed, and new CIA Director Porter Goss is working hard to do just that. However, it will take time and a team dedicated to a new way of thinking.

All of our intelligence capabilities need improvement, but it is important to stress that HUMINT is where we need to put our priority of effort. Not all intelligence collection disciplines are of equal importance for every threat we face. And it is clear that human intelligence offers us the best chance to protect ourselves and successfully win the war on terrorism.

That brings us to this vital question: How does the new intelligence reform legislation measure up relative to human intelligence? During the national debate on intelligence reform last year, there was general acknowledgment that HUMINT needed to be improved; however, it was not afforded the primacy in the legislation that I believe it deserved. In fact, HUMINT is not mentioned even once in the 26-page summary of the Intelligence Reform and Terrorism Prevention Act of 2004 prepared by the Congressional Research Service. The reason al Qaeda was able to attack us was because we didn't have spies to infiltrate their organization. It had nothing to do with intelligence budget execution or the reprogramming of funds.

The intelligence community is undoubtedly entering a period of turmoil caused by the intelligence reform legislation. During the coming implementation of that legislation,

the Congress must make certain the primacy of HUMINT is emphasized and the morale of our intelligence officers, especially those serving in dangerous undercover positions, is protected. In this regard, it is my hope that the Senate Select Committee on Intelligence will introduce a subcommittee structure and that one of the subcommittees will be devoted to human intelligence.

Engaging the Full Spectrum

Contemporary definitions of national and tactical intelligence are now archaic and do not reflect the sophistication of 21st-century collection, analysis, and distribution methods of intelligence. Nor does the "end-user" of intelligence have the same meaning in today's environment. The real shortcoming of the framework being used in our debate on intelligence reform is that it is too narrowly focused on what is referred to as the "national level." Too many so-called "intelligence experts" want the Director of National Intelligence to have control of national intelligence assets and are content to leave the military with the tactical intelligence assets.

This type of thinking is fallacious and dangerous. Intelligence reform is a lot more complicated than creating a DNI and giving him or her stronger control over "national" intelligence systems.

Real intelligence reform must look beyond the definitions of "national" and "tactical." It must address the intelligence needs of the President in the White House, but it must also address the needs of the US Army private in Baghdad or the US Marine lance corporal in Fallujah. We cannot send American military forces into battle without the full spectrum of support from the entire intelligence community.

If we do not succeed in stabilizing the security situation in Iraq, which can be achieved only with accurate and timely intelligence to the troops on the ground, the United States and its coalition partners will suffer an enormous strategic setback in the war on terrorism and in promoting a lasting peace in the greater Middle East. Islamist terrorists will become more emboldened to strike us again here at home if they perceive us as weak and incapable of providing security in Iraq.

"Our weak point is HUMINT, which has atrophied to the point that it must be rebuilt."

Finding out who an insurgent is in a town in Iraq may fit someone's definition of tactical intelligence, but the nature of our mission in Iraq makes almost everything we do there of vital importance at the national level. People who perpetuate the distinction between "national" and "tactical" intelligence during our debate on intelligence reform simply do not understand the sophistication of our intelligence and communication systems.

The series of Unmanned Aerial Vehicles (UAVs) now in use and under development is a case in point. Early UAV versions probably fit the definition of "tactical intelligence systems" because of their limited range and capabilities, but not anymore. The Predator B, for example, is a long endurance, high-altitude, unmanned aircraft system for surveillance, reconnaissance, and targeting missions. It also can be used as a weapons platform carrying air-to-air and air-to-ground missiles. In fact, an earlier version of the Predator tracked a vehicle in Yemen in 2002 carrying terrorists and destroyed it with a Hellfire missile.

These advanced UAVs collect their surveillance imagery from synthetic aperture radar, video cameras, and a forward-looking infra-red (FLIR) system, which can be distributed in real time to the front-line soldier, to the operational commander, and simultaneously to national intelligence agencies in near-real time via military satellite communication links. If a UAV like the Predator B is giving intelligence to a soldier in Iraq and to an analyst at the CIA at virtually the same time, then how can one define it as purely a "tactical" or a "national" system? The answer is, one can't, and we need to get beyond this kind of limiting terminology and thinking.

As a current member of the Senate Select Committee on Intelligence, I was involved with the report released on 7 July 2004 by Senators Pat Roberts and Jay Rockefeller dealing with the intelligence community's prewar assessments on Iraq.[2] This 511-page report is another that's highly critical of our intelligence analysis and collection capabilities. Like the House report mentioned earlier, it also singles out human intelligence as the weakest link in our intelligence chain.

It is important to note that in the Senate's review of the intelligence relating to Iraq's WMD programs, it became abundantly clear that our intelligence problems were not the result of the quality of our personnel. In fact, the Senate Select Committee on Intelligence was singularly impressed with the dedication and professionalism of the hard-working men and women in our intelligence community. What we need to do is give these people a new national intelligence structure that will be worthy of their efforts.

It is abundantly clear that we don't have enough spies on the ground, and that we need to make this an issue of the highest priority. Yet somehow during the debates in Congress and among the political pundits in the media on intelligence reform, the focus shifted from fixing our HUMINT capabilities and further improving information-sharing within and among all relevant agencies of the government to discussing why there is such a large percentage of the total US intelligence budget in the Defense Department.

Improving—Not Degrading—Military Intelligence

As some see it, the military's share of the overall intelligence budget, estimated at about 80 percent, is too large, and if a portion of this were transferred to the DNI our intelligence capabilities would somehow improve. The apportionment of the intelligence budget is a legitimate issue to discuss, but we should not allow it to divert our focus away from the pressing problems that need fixing, such as human intelligence and information-sharing.

HUMINT is a relatively inexpensive intelligence discipline compared to the high-technology systems and platforms used by the military. When we put a military intelligence satellite into orbit, the intelligence budget needs to pay for its research and development, its production, the launch vehicle, ground stations, support personnel, and communication links. And the military collects intelligence from a great variety of platforms. In addition to satellites, the military services use ships, submarines, aircraft, UAVs, ground vehicles, and small sensors used by individual soldiers on the ground. In order to move the resulting vast amounts of intelligence worldwide, securely and in near-real time, the military has built information networks that are the best in the world and continually improves them with new technologies. Consequently, it is not at all surprising that the military's share of the intelligence budget is so large.

Last October, Lieutenant General Keith Alexander, Chief of Intelligence for the Army, discussed the fusion of intelligence and communication networks. He noted that "the [communications] network must provide tactical teams with timely intelligence in minutes, not hours or days, which the Army calls 'actionable' intelligence. That's what we have to get to. Additionally, such a network must eventually connect from a soldier on patrol through national-level agencies to truly leverage intelligence capabilities." He also, correctly in my opinion, elevated the importance of HUMINT when he said, "Today's threat is people embedded in the population, bent on changing governments to the way they believe those governments should be—a global insurgency. Thus, the intelligence emphasis has changed from one focused on signals and imagery intelligence to human intelligence and counterintelligence."[3]

> **"Human intelligence offers us the best chance to protect ourselves and successfully win the war on terrorism."**

Another element that needs to be added to our national debate on intelligence reform is how the Director of National Intelligence will interact with the military and vice-versa. The DNI will inherit an intelligence community made up of 15 separate members, eight of which are in the Department of Defense. Collectively, these eight members are huge, comprising tens of thousands of uniformed military and civilian personnel, and multibillion-dollar budgets. How someone outside the military, like the DNI, could adequately and efficiently manage these vast intelligence capabilities by dealing with eight separate Department of Defense members is beyond me. This is a major issue, and it must be addressed; otherwise the DNI may have an unrealistically large span of control.

That is why I, in conjunction with my Democrat colleague from Nebraska, Senator Ben Nelson, plan to reintroduce legislation in the 109th Congress to create a unified combatant command for military intelligence, to be called INTCOM. This command would, for the first time, bring the majority of the intelligence capabilities in the Department of Defense under a single commander.

INTCOM would be the single point of contact for the DNI in dealing with military intelligence. The INTCOM Commander would have the dual responsibility of being the one source for informing the DNI of military intelligence requirements requiring support from the entire intelligence community, and being the one source for assigning military intelligence capabilities to assist in fulfilling the DNI's broader intelligence responsibilities.

One of the US Army's nine Principles of War is Unity of Command. When this principle is properly used, there is a common focus on reduction of duplication and wasted efforts, vastly improved coordination, and—above all—accountability. The military already applies this principle very successfully to several functional areas, and has created unified combatant commands for transportation, joint forces, and special operations. The latter one, by the way, was established by legislation over the objections of the then-Secretary of Defense and Chairman of the Joint Chiefs of Staff. There is no objection today, however, to our Special Operations Command, or to any other unified command. The fact is, whenever the military has created either a functional or a geographic unified command, we have seen a better resulting focus on the mission, better support from the military services, and improved capabilities. A unified command for intelligence will have the same benefits.

One of the major responsibilities of the DNI will be to better integrate the current 15 members of the US intelligence community. The DNI's task will be far easier to accomplish if there is an INTCOM Commander to coordinate the disparate eight Department of Defense members into one, thus reducing the total number of intelligence community members from 15 to eight.

Sharing Data

Another issue not yet addressed in our national debate on intelligence reform is the outdated intelligence cycle model that ends with a final intelligence product that very much reflects the bias of whatever organization "produced" the intelligence. Lest anyone have any doubts about the dangers associated with this type of intelligence cycle, reading the report prepared by the Senate Select Committee on Intelligence dealing with WMD in Iraq will dispel them.

What the DNI will need to do is change the entire intelligence information management structure. The notion of "data ownership" must be eliminated if we are ever to have real "all-source" analysis. The minute one element of the intelligence community withholds some information from the rest of the community, then "all-source" loses its meaning.

Intelligence is not an end in itself, but it is an essential ingredient to formulating good policy and protecting our nation's interests. The key is to harness all the information we have and put it into a form that is manageable and useful. Integral to this process is the ability to share the information with those who need it and to continually update it.

Consider a commercial travel website such as Expedia.com or Travelocity. com. When you want to travel on a certain date, you access the database, and the program gives you all possible flights, connections, times, prices, and will also help you make your hotel and rental-car reservations. In short, every bit of information about traveling to your destination is at your fingertips for you to make your decision. We need the equivalent of an Expedia.com or Travelocity.com for intelligence. Our analysts and policymakers should be able to access common databases where information is constantly being posted as it comes in so they can get the most complete and current picture possible.

The Road Ahead

The process of intelligence reform is just beginning, and there is a lot of important work ahead to make sure we get it right. We have made an important decision in creating a Director of National Intelligence who is not beholden to the CIA, the Department of Defense, or any other agency. It is a good step, but it is just the first step in a long process of intelligence reform.

If the new intelligence reform legislation does not allow us to "connect the dots" and provide more "dots to connect" to prevent further attacks on the United States and US interests, then we have failed in our effort to reform the intelligence community.

No one knows at this point if the new legislation will work or not. But it has a better chance to succeed it we keep focused on these points:

- Recognize the problems with HUMINT and take the necessary steps to fix it, including accepting the risks associated with it, so we can actually infiltrate organizations bent on our destruction.

- Improve the quality of congressional oversight of the intelligence community by instituting a subcommittee structure in the Senate Select Committee on Intelligence.

- Organize military intelligence by bringing unity of command to the enormous defense intelligence community to better help the DNI succeed in bringing unity of effort to the broader intelligence community.

- Devise ways to improve information-sharing, and the management of enormous amounts of intelligence. In this regard, we could take some lessons from our commercial databases.

In the final analysis, we need to frame our debate on intelligence reform so it includes getting the right information, at the right time, to the right person, from the US President to the newest US Army private in harm's way.

Notes

1. *The 9/11 Commission Report*, Final Report of the National Commission on Terrorist Attacks Upon the United States by the 9/11 Commission (Washington: GPO, 22 July 2004).

2. US Senate, Select Committee on Intelligence, *Report on the U.S. Intelligence Community's Prewar Intelligence Assessments on Iraq* (Washington: GPO, 7 July 2004), http://intelligence.senate.gov/iraqreport2.pdf.

3. Remarks by Lieutenant General Keith Alexander, G-2 of the Army, at the DefenseWriters Group breakfast, 14 October 2004.

United States Senator SAXBY CHAMBLISS, a Republican representing Georgia, serves on the Senate Intelligence and the Senate Armed Services Committees. In the Congress, Senator Chambliss has been a strong voice on issues regarding national security, intelligence, and homeland security matters.

From *Parameters,* Spring 2005, pp. 5–13. Published in 2005 by U.S. Army War College. Reprinted by permission of Senator Saxby Chambliss.

UNIT 10

The Future of Homeland Security

Unit Selections

Key Points to Consider

- What are Secretary Chertoff's major goals? Are these goals practical and feasible?

- Is the United States losing the war on terrorism?

- How can the Department of Homeland Security be restructured to make it more agile?

- What role should the U.S. military have in domestic security? Explain.

Student Web Site

www.mhcls.com/online

Internet Reference

Further information regarding these Web sites may be found in this book's preface or online.

Securing Our Homeland: U.S. Department of Homeland Security Strategic Plan
   http://www.dhs.gov/interweb/assetlibrary/DHS_StratPlan_FINAL_spread.pdf

It seems early to speculate about the potential future of homelandsecurity. Yet, as the DHS matures, questions about the long-term goals of the department continue to surface. The DHS faces monumental challenges. It must not only protect the United States from future attacks but also respond effectively to both natural and man-made disasters. So far, despite its best efforts, the DHS has failed to inspire public trust and confidence. How well it will be able to accomplish its mission in the future remains to be seen.

The long-term success of U.S. homeland security policy depends on three main factors: the relative effectiveness of the Department of Homeland Security, future developments in international terrorism, and continued public support of homeland security policies.

The future of homeland security policy depends on the ability of the DHS to continue to mature and complete the ongoing merge into an effective organization. In this multi-year process, Michael Chertoff, like his predecessor Tom Ridge, must continue to reform, restructure, and integrate twenty-two different agencies into a cohesive unit capable of protecting the homeland. Organizational cultures, past interagency rivalries, and turf wars with other government agencies must be overcome in order for the DHS to be effective.

The success of U.S. homeland security policy also depends on future developments in international terrorism. International terrorism continues to evolve. While the United States has focused almost exclusively on al-Qaeda and Islamic fundamentalist inspired terrorism around the world, significant changes have taken place in Latin America. New leaders are increasingly challenging U.S. hegemony in the Western hemisphere, as popular discontent with U.S. policies is on the rise. The proliferation of nuclear technologies has given rise to increased concerns about the use of Weapons of Mass Destruction (WMD) by international terrorists. For the DHS, changes in international terrorism pose a two-fold problem. If terrorists choose to limit their activities and focus on attacks against U.S. resources abroad, political and economic support for domestic security may eventually wane. If terrorists manage to repeatedly attack targets in the United States, the competence and utility of the new department will soon be questioned.

Lastly, and most importantly, the success of homeland security is dependent on public support. After the attacks on 9/11, there was a tremendous amount of support for homeland security policy. While some have voiced concerns about actions taken by the Bush Administration, most accepted the fact that the primary motive for these action was to protect the American people. Most Americans trusted the U.S. government to act in their best interest. U.S. policies overseas and scandals at home have increasingly eroded this trust. Increased domestic surveillance, indefinite detentions, and accusations of torture and abuse of prisoners continue to undermine public support for the administration and its homeland security policy. In the long run, homeland security will only be successful if it has the support and trust of the American people.

The articles in this unit examine the prospects for the future of homeland security. They highlight the continuing need for a long-term strategic vision for homeland security.

Department of Homeland Security: Charting a Path Forward

MICHAEL CHERTOFF

I want to thank Heritage first of all for hosting me. I also want to thank Heritage for allowing us to shamelessly steal their ideas and some of their personnel in the course of setting up the Department of Homeland Security. Heritage, as you know, has produced a number of very thoughtful reports about the challenges at Homeland Security.

We've adopted a lot of the recommendations. One of the notable ones was the creation of a policy office. I'm pleased to say we've pirated a top person from Heritage to come and help us get that up and running. I think the recommendations have been very thoughtful. And so this is, I think, a very appropriate place for me to discuss the way forward.

It has been a little bit over a year since my coming on board as Secretary, and it certainly has been a very eventful year of facing challenges—from the bombings in London in July of last year, to Hurricane Katrina, to many of the budget challenges we have, and including other hazards that may come up in the next year, such as the avian flu.

I think we have had an opportunity now to look back over a year and learn some very interesting and important lessons about how Homeland Security can work and should work. Before I get into the substance, though, I want to pay special tribute to Attorney General Ed Meese. I actually served under him at a very low position; I'm sure he didn't know who I was. I was an Assistant U.S. Attorney at the time.

But he provided tremendous leadership to the Justice Department, and he continues to do so to the country as a whole, in terms of bringing very thoughtful suggestions about how we order ourselves in some of the most fundamental ways that government operates; where the proper allocation of responsibility is among the various levels of government; what it means to be part of the rule of law; and of course, his very important work in terms of making sure that our courts are functioning as envisioned by the Framers.

This Friday, I'm going to Asia to meet with my counterparts in Japan and China, Hong Kong and Singapore. This is, therefore, a good opportunity for me to talk about three areas which I think will be the critical points of triangulation in terms of our next year of opportunity and challenge at the Department of Homeland Security. One of these is preparedness. This past year, we set up for the first time a director of preparedness with the sole function of creating accountability for the execution of true preparedness for all hazards in the United States.

The second is addressing the issue of illegal migration. Illegal migration is a problem that has been with us for over 20 years. We have addressed it in fits and starts. Clearly, the American public in 2006 has reached the point of demanding serious solutions. And when I say serious solutions, I don't mean cosmetic solutions or feel-good solutions, but I mean solutions that have a real prospect of providing a durable resolution of the challenge of illegal migration—the challenge that it brings to the rule of law, the challenge in terms of our national security concern, but also the challenge it poses to our desire to reconcile our ideals about border protection with the realities of the economic demand that is bringing literally hundreds of thousands of migrants into this country every single year.

And the third piece I want to talk about briefly is protecting our critical infrastructure. We've had a lot of discussion in the last several weeks about protecting the ports. My job, however, is not to go from protecting the ports to protecting the railroads to protecting this and protecting that, following along as the media focuses in fits and starts on the particular news of the day. My job is to always make sure that our approach to protecting critical infrastructure is comprehensive, that it looks at all of the threat, not merely the one that happens to be capturing public attention at any given moment, and to make sure that it's balanced, to make sure that we do not take steps in the name of protecting ourselves that are so destructive to our way of life and to the foundations of what our society is about that we in effect burn down the village in order to save it.

The essence of Homeland Security is recognizing the tradeoffs and managing the risks. And that means, as I've said before, not pretending that we can guarantee every single person against every bad thing happening at every moment in every place. We can't do that. And if we could do it, it would be at such a horrendous cost, that I think it would transform this country. So I think we need to continue to drive through an intelligent and properly risk-managed approach to critical infrastructure.

Preparing for Disasters

Now, let me turn to each of these topics in turn. We look at the issue of preparedness against the background of one of the most catastrophic natural disasters in American history, which was Hurricane Katrina. Actually, there were three hurricanes in a row: There was Katrina; there was Rita, which came very closely thereafter; and then there was Wilma, which was actually the most powerful of the storms. Taken singularly and certainly taken together, these storms posed a challenge to our preparedness and our response unlike we've ever had in our history.

Look at Katrina, which devastated 90,000 square miles—that's roughly the size of Great Britain. Well over a million people had to move out of the area. More people migrated after Katrina than in any other previous mass migration in American history, except for the Dust Bowl, which took place over a period of decades and not over a period of days. When you consider all of those things, you realize that the lessons learned from Katrina are both salient but also a little bit extraordinary, and we have to be careful when we apply those lessons not to confuse the truly super-catastrophe with the ordinary disaster, which is more or less with us on a year-in and year-out basis.

But we can make some generalizations. The essence of preparedness is planning and integration of execution. If you don't have a proper plan, improvisation is not going to give you the answer that you need when you're in the middle of the storm. And from the same standpoint, if you don't integrate all of your organs of power and all of your authorities and all of your capabilities, if you stovepipe them, you are going to have very much less than the totality of effort which I think the public rightfully expects when we do have a catastrophe.

So we have to look forward and ask ourselves what are the kinds of planning and what are the kinds of integrated capabilities we need to have going forward to be truly prepared. And we do that against the looming date of June 1, which is the onset of hurricane season for this year. It doesn't mean the first hurricane will come on June 1, but it does mean that some time after June 1 we will get a hurricane; we'll get a number of hurricanes. I can't tell you whether they will be stronger than last year's or more frequent than last year's, but I can tell you we will be more prepared than we were last year.

How are we going to do that? Well, first we have to remember the primacy of the role of state and local government in disaster preparedness and response, not just a matter of our federal system under the Constitution, but as a matter of common sense. Ultimately, preparedness and response has to begin in the first instance with your state and local responders. They understand the landscape; they understand the people; they understand the particular challenges when a hazard comes in a particular location. Any effort to try to build a plan or to execute a plan that is not built around state and local capabilities is doomed to failure.

As a consequence of the recognition of this core fact, the President directed last fall—very soon after Katrina, when he spoke in Jackson Square in New Orleans—that we begin an immediate evaluation with our state and local partners of the state of their evacuation and emergency plans. We completed stage one of that on February 10, meeting our deadline. It showed, frankly, a mixed bag. Using the red, yellow, green type of evaluation structure which we often see, there were some greens; there were some yellows; there were also some reds. He told us we had a significant amount of work to do. We are now, as we speak, in the process of working with our state and local partners on getting that work done.

The first place we're looking to do this is in the Gulf. We recognize the Gulf faces an unusual challenge this year because we have only partly rebuilt communities. And so we're going to probably need to pay more attention to what the requirements are and what the capabilities are in the Gulf than in any other place in the country. In the next two weeks, I'm going to direct George Foresman, our Undersecretary for Preparedness, and David Paulison, our Acting Director of FEMA, to personally go down to the Gulf and to continue the process of planning we have already undertaken by meeting with political leaders and making sure we are very clear that we must be on a path to being completely prepared for hurricane season by June 1.

We must understand what the plans are; we must understand what the state and local requirements are; we must have a clear, blunt assessment of what their capabilities are. When we get that, we will be prepared to look at what additional capabilities we need to bring to the table. We're going to undertake this planning, not only using the resources of DHS, but the resources of all of the other departments of the federal government including the Department of Defense. But of course, we have to get our own house in order, as well.

So even as we are working with the state and local authorities on their plans and preparedness, we have to begin the process of re-tooling FEMA for the 21st century. What does that mean? Well, it means first of all, we ought to have the ability to manage and track our supplies—food, water, other necessary items—using the same kind of visibility that UPS uses when you send a pair of sneakers to your kid at college and they track the sneakers from the time they get picked up to the time they get delivered. We have to be able to do that for the necessary commodities that come into play anytime there is a disaster. So we are going to be contracting this year in anticipation of June 1 for total asset visibility on all of the guards and commodities that we're going to be calling upon in the case of a disaster.

We also have to re-tool our way of dealing with such things as what I call claims management, people who are victims who need to become registered, who need to know what is available to them under the law by way of emergency care and emergency compensation. Last year we were overwhelmed by the sheer, massive numbers of people, literally hundreds of thousands of people seeking aid. This year we have to put into effect and we will put into effect contracts that give us a surge capability to deal with hundreds of thousands of telephone calls for people who are displaced if we should have another mass catastrophe.

Third, we have to address some of the issues that arise with our current contracting on debris removal. You know, there was a story in the paper today about people complaining that the cost of debris removal when the federal government executes it is very much greater than when local businesses do it. The fact of the matter is, this past year we actually changed our rules to encourage communities to hire local construction firms to do debris removal—to actually create an incentive to move them away from the Army Corps of Engineers and into local contractors.

We want to continue to build on that. The Army Corps will be available to do debris removal when communities feel they need to get someone to come in quickly and do the job entirely on its own. But where local communities want to have debris removal done with local firms, which makes economic sense and which is cheaper, we have constructed a system that will allow them to do it with as much financial incentive as if they used the Army Corps.

Finally, communications: We're going to be putting enhanced communications capabilities into the hands of our responders in the field and state responders in the field to deal with those circumstances where the basic operability of communications collapses.

Before I leave the area of preparedness, though, I have to turn to that group of people who have the single most important responsibility when it comes to preparedness, and that is individual American citizens. It's been doctrine and been understood by firefighters and other emergency responders for decades that you cannot count on help coming in the first 24 or even 48 hours of a catastrophe. People who prepare themselves by having food and water and necessary medicine, radios, and plans so that families know, for example, if they're separated to go to a particular place in order to meet; people who are prepared with that kind of planning do much better if they have to wait 24 or 48 hours than people who don't do that planning.

The fact of the matter is we all face risks, but we all as individual citizens have it in our power to deal with those risks because we can prepare ourselves. There are a lot of tools available; there are tools on the Web; there are Web sites that DHS has, that HHS and other government agencies have that will tell people what they need to know to do the preparation. But the real power and determination can only be supplied by the individual citizen and by individual families.

And I would say that taking the steps to prepare yourself as an American citizen is not only a way of empowering yourself but it is discharging a civic responsibility, because those who are able-bodied and fail to prepare distract the responders from helping those who are not able to help themselves and therefore are simply unable to prepare. So I think we all owe it to each other to do the kind of preparation that allows responders to focus on those most in need.

Securing America's Borders

Let me turn to the border. As I said before, the border challenge has been with us for decades. But certainly in the wake of 9/11 there is a new urgency from a national security standpoint to dealing with the border. Some people say we can't surmount the challenge; they say it is inevitable we will lose, and therefore they disparage our efforts to try. I do not believe that. I remember—and I think General Meese will remember—that before the 1980s people believed traditional organized crime would be with us forever, and we would never be able to make inroads against the leadership of the Mafia. But I can tell you that in the 1980s, with some very good planning and the application of smart resources, we actually began the process of dismantling organized crime, getting them out of labor unions, getting them out of legitimate businesses, While the job isn't done, traditional organized crime is only a shadow of what it once was.

So I am convinced that with the proper planning and application of resources in an intelligent fashion we can do the same thing to get control of our border. What does that mean? First, it means an integrated, sensible, systems-based approach to how we deal with illegal migration as it comes across the border. It does require additional personnel. The President's budget this year adds 1,500 border patrol agents on top of the 1,500 we put in last year, which will get us up to almost 14,000 border patrol agents on the border. It certainly means more roads and more fences and vehicle barriers in critical, strategic locations, and we are on track to providing that. But it also means hi-tech, using some of the tools that we can bring to the challenge that the criminal organizations don't have. We've got unmanned aerial vehicles that we are now using to get better visibility about who's coming across remote parts of the border. We have the capability to use satellite imagery to help us locate threats across the border.

As we are in the process of integrating all of these hi-tech capabilities through a process we call SBI Net, which is underway this year. We are going to build ourselves what I call a virtual fence. This is not a fence of barbed wire and bricks and mortar, which I will tell you simply doesn't work, because people just go over the fence, but rather a smart fence, a fence that makes use of physical tools, but also tools about information sharing and information management that let us identify people coming across the border and let us plan the interception and apprehension in a way that serves our purposes and maximizes our resources, thereby giving our border patrol the best leverage they can have in order to make sure they are apprehending the most people.

But there's another part of this. When we catch people, what do we do with them? Up until this past year, non-Mexicans who couldn't simply be sent back across the border to Mexico were released because we didn't have enough beds to detain them, and when we detained them it took too long to send them back home. Now common sense is going to tell you this is a completely unacceptable way to do business. For one thing it sends a perverse incentive out. It basically says to non-Mexicans, "Get across the border; get caught, and you'll be released." So, not surprisingly, we saw non-Mexicans coming up through Mexico and crossing the border into the United States.

We're committed to changing that now. We are now moving this year from catch-and-release to catch-and-return at the border. That means every person that we get at the border who is here illegally will be detained until they are removed. To do that, we are, first of all, cutting the removal time, making it quicker by using modern technology and also, frankly, by negotiating vigorously with our overseas partners to make sure they take their migrants back. Second, we're bringing more beds into play so that we have more capability to detain people while we are arranging to remove them.

I will tell you that we have essentially succeeded in ending catch-and-release for all but three groups of people who are coming across the border. The first group is families. Up until now, we have not had the ability to detain families that have come across as a group because we don't have the capability to keep them together in a detention facility. Again, to show the perverse incentive involved, we've actually got anecdotal information that some smuggling groups now essentially pay for children to come across the border with people being smuggled so they can create fictitious family groups because they understand that they'll be released if they are families, as opposed to individuals.

So we're going to address that by opening up, in early May, a family-focused detention facility, so that we will now be able to detain families that come across illegally. This is, by the way, not only a smart way to defeat this incentive for bringing children in as, I guess you call them window dressing for smugglers, but it actually is humanitarian, because we want to discourage people from bringing children on what is a very dangerous journey across the border into the United States.

The second thing we're going to do is to work with the countries that are still a little bit slow to take their migrants back. I expect to begin conversations with the leaders of a couple of those countries in the next few weeks. I'm hopeful that they will understand the importance to them and the importance to us of making sure that when their citizens cross into our country illegally, they have to work with us to get them back home as quickly as possible. So that's the second challenge that we have and the way we're going to meet that challenge.

The third is, frankly, the most complicated. There is one group of illegal migrants that come in across the border that we are not permitted to remove in an expedited fashion; that is people from El Salvador. And the reason for that is because there is an almost 20-year-old court order, dating back to the time that El Salvador was in a civil war, that essentially makes it impossible to apply expedited removal to illegal migrants from that country. Now that court order was issued at a time that we had INS, we had a civil war in El Salvador, and we had a group of people who were running INS. Those people have gone, INS no longer exists as an organization, and there's no longer a civil war in El Salvador. All we have left from that period is the weight of a court order that is almost 20 years old.

We are seeking to go back to the courts and get that order lifted and to use other legal tools to allow us to finally bring expedited removal to this last group. I can tell you that if we are permitted to use expedited removal with this last group of migrants, we will not only have catch-and-remove by the end of this fiscal year, which is what I promised almost a year ago, we'll actually do it this summer. But we need to have help in getting over these final obstacles.

Finally, I can't leave the border without talking about interior enforcement. The fact of the matter is that the strong demand that pulls people across the border is an illegal demand; it's a demand for illegal workers. To deal with that demand, we have to use two approaches. We have to come up with a method that allows people to satisfy that demand for workers in a regularized, legal channel that is not an amnesty. I think that the solution there is a temporary worker program, as the President has outlined.

But the second piece is that we have to sanction those who are unwilling to follow the law, and that means sanctioning not only the migrants themselves but sanctioning the people who employ the migrants. Right now, we find ourselves hamstrung in this regard as well. For example, currently the Social Security Administration compiles information about Social Security numbers that do not match names or Social Security numbers that consist of simply a string of zeros, which is pretty obviously not a legitimate Social Security number. But we still do not have the ability to access that information in a way that would allow us to identify people who are working illegally and that would allow us to help employers make that kind of identification.

There's currently an effort in Congress to correct that, to give us the ability to send requests to the Social Security Administration to identify for us numbers in Social Security that are being used fraudulently for illegal purposes, including illegal work. If we can get that legislative fix, that will give us another tool that we need in order to make sure we can get the job that the American people want done actually accomplished, and that is to get control of our borders, to get control of this illegal work force, and to satisfy legitimate work in a legitimate fashion.

Safeguarding Critical Infrastructure

Finally, let me turn to critical infrastructure. A lot of attention has been paid to ports in the last few weeks, as I've said, and I'd be the first person to tell you we have more work to do. But I also need to tell you that a

lot of work has been done. It is not fair to suggest that the ports are in the same condition they were from the standpoint of vulnerability four years ago; quite the contrary. I will tell you that if you consider the President's fiscal year 2007 proposed budget, if that passes, we will have spent almost $10 billion on port security, including billions of dollars on the Coast Guard and hundreds of millions of dollars on Customs and Border Protection, which have the responsibility for maintaining security in our American ports.

We will, by the end of the year, be putting two-thirds of containers through radiation portal monitors either overseas or in this country, and next year we will get close to 100 percent. We are rolling out additional new next-generation radiation detection technology that is more precise and easier to use starting within the next couple of months. Our Container Security Initiative that gives us the ability to inspect high-risk cargo overseas will by the end of the year cover over 80 percent of the container cargo that comes into this country. The fact of the matter is, we screen 100 percent of containers that come into this country to see whether they are a risk. And containers that pose a high risk are inspected either through X-ray machines or actually by physically breaking bulk. So while we have more we can do, we have done quite a bit.

What is the way forward here? I think it involves even better information about the constituents of the supply chain, going back from the time of manufacture all the way through the transporting process before the cargo gets to the container. The more information we have, the better the targeting, and the better the targeting, the more precise our ability to inspect. It also involves exploiting new technology. For example, I know there's a pilot program in Hong Kong now that looks to do some form of scanning of containers before they even get loaded. I look forward to visiting the Port of Hong Kong on my trip to Asia; I want to see it for myself. If there are some valuable techniques we can adapt, we'll adapt those techniques because, again, we want to raise the level of security, but we want to do it in an intelligent way.

Finally, we need to finish the job of getting our transportation worker identification credential into play here in U.S. ports. This is an initiative which languished for too long. We're committed to getting this underway in the next few months, and that will be the final piece of security that we need to make sure that we are covering the entirety of the supply chain from the point of loading to the point of unloading here in the United States.

But I want to leave you with this thought: Sometimes I hear people say, "Well, you don't come close to physically inspecting 100 percent of the cargo that comes into this country." And the answer to that is: That's right; we don't. Because if we were to do so, we would destroy the maritime shipping industry in the United States; it would simply be too slow. We have got to be smarter about security; it doesn't mean we have to be more heavy handed about security. And of course, the people who would lose, in addition to the consumers, would be all those dock workers and people who work in the maritime industry who would find themselves thrown out of work.

That comes back to the fundamental principle of risk management. We don't eliminate risks; we manage risks; we prioritize risks, and then we focus on the risks that are the most significant and use smart methods to minimize and get rid of the risks, as opposed to clumsy and heavy handed methods. Cargo coming through the ports, however, is not the only area of vulnerability. Rail security, which was in the headlines last July, has faded from the headlines, but it hasn't faded from our agenda. We learned a lot of valuable lessons after the London attacks working with our colleagues in Britain.

The President's budget adds $200 million in fiscal year 2007 for transportation infrastructure protection grants that can be used for rail security. We are now piloting what we call "Viper Teams," which are specialized teams of trained TSA employees with dogs that we can send out when there is an elevated risk in a transit system to do more effective searching for explosives and other kinds of threats. We've got additional funding for rail inspectors, and we are looking at additional kinds of screening technology that would give us a better capability of screening for explosives when people come into areas like rail terminals or rail stations.

One of the things in particular I think we're interested in pursuing is video surveillance, which proved itself in Britain, not so much as a preventer of terrorism, but as a wonderful forensic tool that allowed the British to identify people who had carried out an attack and thereby created a head start on finding their confederates and their coconspirators.

Air cargo security: Obviously, we screen everybody's baggage when they get in an airplane, but we have to look at the cargo as well. And that means we are starting to apply to the air-cargo supply chain what I've described we're doing with respect to the maritime cargo supply chain—a risk-managed, threat-based approach that elevates the security against the significant risks without destroying the air-cargo system itself. There are a lot of techniques we're using: threat assessments, random screening, and enhanced capabilities for explosive detection. TSA has established an air-cargo working group to get feedback from stakeholder. The goal here, as with maritime cargo, is to screen 100 percent of air cargo and inspect 100 percent of the high-risk cargo.

This summer TSA will deploy an automated known-shipper management program, and we've got additional money in the budget this coming fiscal year to allow us to progress forward on this very important air-cargo security initiative.

Finally, let me turn to chemical security. Again, this is a subject which waxes and wanes in the news cycle but remains for us ever-present as a very, very significant challenge. The fact of the matter is chemical plants and in fact, transportation of chemicals remains a vulnerability because, as we know, terrorists tend to want to exploit our own technology and our own capability against us by making our infrastructure into a weapon to be used against our own people. Clearly, certain categories of chemicals do raise a risk of being exploited by terrorists who want to cause havoc either by creating explosions or by having toxic inhalation affecting significant parts of the population.

The chemical industry itself, of course, has done a lot to increase security, but that may not be enough. In particular, I'm concerned about the problem of free riders. Individual chemical companies or plants that do not want to invest in security because they count on the fact that the industry in general has a good level of investment and they figure they will hide among the weeds and essentially freeload on the security work done by others.

That's not acceptable to the public, and it's not acceptable to those chemical companies which are good corporate citizens. Progress on this has stalled for too long. We do need legislation and congressional action and leadership on this point. I know there's a bill in Congress; we look forward to working to working with Chairman Collins and Senator Lieberman on their bill and having some back-and-forth dialogue with them. I think we look forward to working with anybody else who's got a bill.

Tomorrow, I will set forth publicly the basic principles that we believe any congressional bill should contain. The goal here again is to raise the overall level of security but not to strangle the business or burn down the village in order to save it. It is to have flexibility, appropriate risk management, smart use of technology and not heavy handed strangulation or overregulation.

Risk Management the Right Way

I've covered a lot of ground because we have a lot of ground to cover. My basic message is this: Whether something's in the news cycle or out of the news cycle, we are paying attention to these threats 24/7. This department—and in fact the federal government as a whole—and our state and local partners, have done a lot to elevate the general baseline of security in this country. It doesn't mean that the job is over or that we've done it perfectly, but it does mean that we need to recognize that a lot has been done.

At the same time, we need to have a very clear sense of the overall strategy going forward. We are in this business to protect the country for a long period of time; this threat will not go away in a year or five years or 10 years. We have to build an architecture for managing risk that addresses the serious risks, deals with them effectively but does so in a way that doesn't compromise our fundamental values, whether those values are civil liberties or our economic system which provides the engine for prosperity in our country.

This department is committed to risk management in the right way. We will listen to suggestions; we will continue to learn and adapt; we will continue to make progress; and I look forward to working with this institution and others in building a stronger, safer, and prosperous America.

The Honorable **MICHAEL CHERTOFF** is the U.S. Secretary of Homeland Security.

From *Heritage Lectures*, No. 933, March 20, 2006, pp. 1–8. Copyright © 2006 by Heritage Foundation. Reprinted by permission.

The Terrorism Index

Is the United States winning the war on terror? Not according to more than 100 of America's top foreign-policy hands. They see a national security apparatus in disrepair and a government that is failing to protect the public from the next attack.

Following the terrorist attacks of Sept. 11, 2001, Americans understandably rallied around the flag. Having just suffered the deadliest attack ever on U.S. soil, huge percentages believed another attack was imminent. But Americans also had enormous faith that the Global War on Terror would help keep them safe. Just one month after 9/11, for instance, 94 percent of Americans told an ABC News/*Washington Post* poll that they approved of how the fight against terrorism was being handled. The United States then quickly went to war in Afghanistan, closing down a terrorist sanctuary and capturing or killing a number of high-level al Qaeda operatives in the process.

Since 2001, terrorists have found their targets on almost every continent, with bombings in Bali, London, Madrid, and elsewhere. Five years on, however, America has yet to experience another attack. But Americans appear less convinced that their country is winning the war on terror. In the face of persisting threats, including a growing number of terrorist attacks around the world, numerous reports show that Americans are losing faith in their government's ability to wage the war successfully and to protect them from the terrorists' next volley. Barely half of Americans today approve of the way in which the war on terror is being handled, and more than one third believe the United States is less safe today than it was before 9/11.

These pessimistic public perceptions could easily be attributed to the high cost, in both treasure and lives, of counterterrorism efforts. After all, Americans are constantly being told by their elected leaders that their pessimism is wrong, that the war is being won. But they're also told that another attack is inevitable. Which is it? To find out, FOREIGN POLICY and the Center for American Progress teamed up to survey more than 100 of America's top foreign-policy experts—Republicans and Democrats alike. The FOREIGN POLICY/Center for American Progress Terrorism Index is the first comprehensive effort to mine the highest echelons of America's foreign-policy establishment for their assessment of how the United States is fighting the Global War on Terror. Our aim was to draw some definitive conclusions about the war's priorities, policies, and progress from the very people who have run America's national security

Thinking about the present situation, would you say that the world is becoming safer or more dangerous for the United States and the American people?

Much or somewhat safer   **10%**
Much or somewhat more dangerous**86%**

In your view, what is the single greatest threat to U.S. national security?

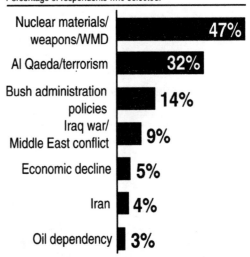

Percentage of respondents who selected:

Nuclear materials/weapons/WMD	**47%**
Al Qaeda/terrorism	**32%**
Bush administration policies	**14%**
Iraq war/Middle East conflict	**9%**
Economic decline	**5%**
Iran	**4%**
Oil dependency	**3%**

President Bush has stated that the United States is winning the war on terror. How do you feel about that statement?

Political Affiliation	Percentage of respondents who selected:	
	Agree	**Disagree**
Total	13	84
Conservative	23	71
Moderate	8	90
Liberal	9	89

With Friends Like These

Wars have a way of making unlikely bedfellows, and the Global War on Terror is apparently no different.

Asked to name the country that has produced the largest number of global terrorists, the index's foreign-policy experts pointed to Saudi Arabia, Egypt, and Pakistan—three of America's marquee allies in the Muslim world. Nearly two thirds (62 percent) identified Saudi Arabia as the leading culprit. Thirteen percent pointed to Egypt, and 11 percent said Pakistan produces the most terrorists. "The jihadist movement," says index participant and Sarah Lawrence College Professor Fawaz Gerges, "was born in Egypt in the late 1960s. After September 11, however, Saudi Arabia has emerged as the leading theater of jihadist-Salafist thought and action."

Although these three states may be widely believed to be incubating terrorists, the cooperation they have offered the United States in fighting terrorism presents a more mixed picture. Approximately two thirds of the experts say that U.S. cooperation with Egypt and Pakistan has been effective. The experts are more divided as to whether Saudi Arabia is doing what it can to counter the terrorist threat.

These perceptions cut to the heart of some of the dilemmas facing the United States. Egypt, for instance, has received more than $50 billion in U.S. military and economic assistance since 1979, yet it resisted recent U.S. efforts to promote political reform. America designated Pakistan a major non-NATO ally in 2004, despite allegations that it has not done enough to capture bin Laden. Saudi Arabia has helped crack down on financial support flowing to terrorist groups, but Saudi leaders have been slow to move against radical elements within their own population. Is the United States doing a poor job of choosing its friends? Maybe. Then again, it may just be keeping its friends close, and its enemies closer.

Which single country has produced the largest number of global terrorists?

Percentage of respondents who selected:	
Saudi Arabia	**62**
Egypt	13
Pakistan	11
Palestine	1
Yemen	1
Iraq	1
Lebanon	1
Afghanistan	1
Iran	1

The Popular Front

Foreign-policy experts may know the issues, but they can sometimes be guilty of groupthink, and the public has a mind of its own. Here's a look at where the index's experts and the American public agree—and part ways.

America is winning the war on terror.

	Agree	Disagree
Experts	13%	84%
Public	56%	41%

How likely is a major terrorist attack in America this year?

	Likely	Unlikely
Experts	35%	62%
Public	66%	33%

Has the war in Iraq had a positive or negative impact on the war on terror?

	Positive	Negative	No Impact
Experts	10%	87%	3%
Public	38%	44%	8%

The United States should close down the detention facility at Guantánamo Bay.

	Agree	Disagree
Experts	66%	27%
Public	36%	58%

Becoming less dependent on foreign sources of energy will strengthen national security.

	Agree	Disagree
Experts	82%	11%
Public	90%	8%

Sources: CNN/*USA Today*/Gallup Poll, Jan. 20–22, 2006; Harris Poll, Feb. 7–14, 2006; Pew Research Center for the People and the Press, March 16, 2006; CNN/*USA Today*/Gallup Poll, June 16–19, 2005; Public Agenda Confidence In U.S. Foreign Policy Index, January 2006

The Next Attack

Americans are consistently told that the next terrorist attack on U.S. soil is a question of when, not if. The index's results overwhelmingly agree that the next attack is just a matter of time.

Eighty-four percent of the experts said they believe a terrorist attack on the scale of Sept. 11, 2001, is likely or certain to happen in the next five years. More than a quarter said a 9/11-scale attack is certain to occur in America within the next decade. Asked about the likelihood of a smaller strike akin to the July 2005 London bombings, 91 percent agreed that such an attack is likely or certain by 2016; more than half said that such an attack could happen this year.

But how will the terrorists strike? Roughly two thirds of the experts said that some part of America's infrastructure—a port, train station, or major landmark—will be targeted. That is no surprise, given that terrorists have repeatedly struck these locales in the past. But it may be more alarming that almost the same percentage predict that the next attack will come in the form of a suicide bombing. These results, says index participant Bruce Hoffman, a terrorism expert at the Rand Corp., "reflect a recognition of how easy terrorism has become." Such attacks, he says, "are cheap, unpredictable, and difficult to prevent. All that is required is the will to kill and the will to die, neither of which seems in short supply today."

Americans have never feared a suicide bombing the way the people of Amman or Jerusalem have. But there may be reason to think that will soon change. A recent study by Rand found that 81 percent of all suicide attacks in the past 30 or so years have occurred since Sept. 11, 2001, and the primary motivation for each of these attacks was a military intervention or occupation such as the ongoing operations in Iraq. The odds that America can continue to elude the world's most popular form of terrorism may be fading fast.

What is the likelihood of a terrorist attack on the scale of 9/11 occurring again in the United States in the following time frames?

Percentage of respondents who selected:	No chance or unlikely	Likely or certain
By the end of 2006	**65**	35
By the end of 2011	21	**79**
By the end of 2016	16	**84**

Now consider an attack on the scale of those that took place in London and Madrid . . .

Percentage of respondents who selected:	No chance or unlikely	Likely or certain
By the end of 2006	43	57
By the end of 2011	16	84
By the end of 2016	9	91

Regardless of what you think about the timing of an attack, what two methods are most likely to be used in America by global terrorists?

Percentage of respondents who selected:	
Suicide bombing attack	**67**
Attack on major infrastructure	66
Attack using radiological weapon	20
Cyberattack	12
Attack on chemical or nuclear plants	11
Chemical weapon attack	10
Biological weapon attack	9
Nuclear weapon attack	6

apparatus over the past half century. Participants include people who have served as secretary of state, national security advisor, retired top commanders from the U.S. military, seasoned members of the intelligence community, and distinguished academics and journalists. Nearly 80 percent of the index participants have worked in the U.S. government—of these more than half were in the executive branch, one third in the military, and 17 percent in the intelligence community.

Despite today's highly politicized national security environment, the index results show striking consensus across political party lines. A bipartisan majority (84 percent) of the index's experts say the United States is not winning the war on terror. Eighty-six percent of the index's experts see a world today that is growing more dangerous for Americans. Overall, they agree that the U.S. government is falling short in its homeland security efforts. More than 8 in 10 expect an

attack on the scale of 9/11 within a decade. These dark conclusions appear to stem from the experts' belief that the U.S. national security apparatus is in serious disrepair. "Foreign-policy experts have never been in so much agreement about an administration's performance abroad," says Leslie Gelb, president emeritus of the Council on Foreign Relations and an index participant. "The reason is that it's clear to nearly all that Bush and his team have had a totally unrealistic view of what they can accomplish with military force and threats of force."

Respondents sharply criticized U.S. efforts in a number of key areas of national security, including public diplomacy, intelligence, and homeland security. Nearly all of the departments and agencies responsible for fighting the war on terror received poor marks. The experts also said that recent reforms of the national security apparatus have done little to make Americans

Energy's Highest Price

If you could make something a higher priority in fighting the war on terror, what would it be? A little more than one third of the index's experts said killing or capturing terrorist leaders such as Osama bin Laden. About the same number favored promoting democracy in the Muslim world. More than two thirds said stopping the proliferation of nuclear weapons to rogue states. But devising a more aggressive energy policy?

It may surprise, but the index's experts said that ending America's dependence on foreign oil may be the U.S. government's single most pressing priority in winning the war on terror. Eighty-two percent of the experts said that policymakers should make ending America's dependence on foreign oil a higher priority. And nearly two thirds said that current U.S. energy policies are actually making matters worse, not better. "We borrow a billion dollars every working day to import oil, an increasing share of it coming from the Middle East," says index participant and former CIA director James Woolsey. "[F]or example in Saudi Arabia, billions are transferred to the Wahhabis and like-minded groups who then indoctrinate young people to hate Shiites, Sufis, Jews, Christians, and democracy, and to oppress women horribly."

If U.S. policymakers don't take this vulnerability seriously, terrorists do. Ayman al-Zawahiri, al Qaeda's No. 2, has labeled the global energy infrastructure a key strategic target for terrorists. In February, Saudi Arabia's government foiled an al Qaeda plot to attack the Abqaiq oil facility, the country's largest. Some 30,000 security forces are now guarding the country's oil fields. Global oil markets are so tight that even the threat of a supply disruption can cause a spike in price. These tight markets are partially responsible for the higher prices Americans will pay at the pump this summer. But the index suggests that there may be a greater price for our energy policy: losing the war on terror.

Please rate the impact of these actions or policies on protecting the American people from global terrorist networks.

Percentage of respondents who selected:	Positive impact	Negative impact
War in Iraq	10	87
Guantanamo	16	81
Energy policy	3	**64**
Iran policy	12	60
Public diplomacy	5	58
North Korea policy	1	49
War in Afghanistan	93	4

Please indicate whether each of the actions listed below should be given a higher or lower priority in the war on terror.

Percentage of respondents who selected:	Higher priority	Lower priority
Reduce foreign oil use	**82**	11
Improve intelligence	76	1
Stop loose nukes	68	12
Strengthen the U.N.	68	12
Strengthen DHS	65	9
Kill terrorist leaders	37	16
Increase military	30	36

safer. Asked about recent efforts to reform America's intelligence community, for instance, more than half of the index's experts said that creating the Office of the Director of National Intelligence has had no positive impact in the war against terror. "Intelligence reform so far has been largely limited to structural reorganization that in most cases produced new levels of bureaucracy in an already overly bureaucratic system," says index participant Bill Gertz, a journalist who has covered the intelligence community for more than 20 years.

The index's experts were similarly critical of most of the policy initiatives put forward by the U.S. Congress and President George W. Bush since September 11. Eighty-one percent, for instance, believe the detention of suspected terrorists at Guantánamo Bay, Cuba, negatively affects the war on terror. The index's experts also disapprove of how America is handling its relations with European allies, how it is confronting threatening regimes in North Korea and Iran, how it is controlling the spread of weapons of mass destruction, and its dealings with failing states, to name just a few. "We are losing the war on terror because we are treating the symptoms and not the cause," says index participant Anne-Marie Slaughter, dean of Princeton University's Woodrow Wilson School of Public and International Affairs. "[O]ur insistence that Islamic fundamentalist ideology has replaced communist ideology as the chief enemy of our time . . . feeds al Qaeda's vision of the world."

These conclusions about the United States' performance in the war thus far are all the more troubling considering that, although Americans appear to be growing tired of the war on terror, the index's experts appear to believe that the battle has just begun. Accordingly, a majority agrees that the war requires more emphasis on a victory of ideas, not just guns. That is hardly surprising, considering that nearly 80 percent believe a widespread rejection of radical ideologies in the Islamic world is a critical element to victory. To win the battle of ideas, the experts say, America must place a much higher emphasis on its nonmilitary tools. More than two thirds say that U.S. policymakers must strengthen the

Grading the Government

A room full of foreign-policy experts can be a tough crowd. So it's hardly surprising that the index experts were highly critical of how the various branches of the U.S. government are fighting the war on terror. Only the National Security Agency received an above-average score of 5.2, on a 0 to 10 scale, where 0 represents the worst possible job of guarding the United States. Every other agency received below-average marks.

Experts gave the Department of Homeland Security (DHS) the worst grade. Its average score was just 2.9. In fact, 36 percent of the experts indicated that the newly created DHS has had a negative impact on America's national security, and nearly 1 in 5 thought the department's funding should be slashed. The U.S. State Department received relatively high marks. Surprisingly, this opinion was not limited to the liberal internationalist wing of foreign-policy elites. Even conservative experts, who have sometimes taken a dimmer view of the State Department's diplomatic efforts, believed that the department's budget is a good investment and that it should be moderately or substantially increased. Overall, 87 percent of the index's experts believe that Foggy Bottom requires more funding, including 72 percent of conservatives.

The index's experts also have a strong opinion of how that money should be spent. Nearly 80 percent agree that a widespread rejection of extremist ideologies around the globe is critical to "winning" the war on terror. Yet the experts simultaneously rated America's public diplomacy efforts the lowest of any policy initiative, with a median score of just 1.8. Clearly, few believe that the United States is doing its best to win friends and influence people.

Rate each agency's effectiveness at protecting the American people on a scale of 0 to 10.

	Mean score
Dept. of Homeland Security	2.9
Dept. of Defense	4.4
Dept. of State	**4.8**
Dir. of National Intelligence	3.9

Indicate whether agencies should receive an increase or decrease in funding.

Percentage of respondents selecting:	Decrease	Increase
Dept. of Homeland Security	19	43
Dept. of Defense	52	15
Dept. of State	7	**87**
Dir. of National Intelligence	13	39

United Nations and other multilateral institutions. At the same time, the experts indicate that the U.S. government must think more creatively about threats. Asked what presents the single greatest danger to U.S. national security, nearly half said loose nukes and other weapons of mass destruction, while just one third said al Qaeda and terrorism, and a mere 4 percent said Iran. Five years after the attacks of September 11, it's a reminder that the greatest challenges may still lie ahead

Building an Agile Homeland Security Establishment

The best way to secure America's homeland is to enlist the help of its citizens and local governments.

VINCE KASTEN, RALPH WELBORN

A glance at the landscape of American society three years after the terrorist attacks of September 11 reveals a bevy of new structures: a federal Homeland Security Department, parallel agencies in nearly every state, and new or enhanced intelligence bureaus in most large police departments. A visitor from abroad meets employees of the new federal Bureau of Customs and Border Protection on his way into the country, and has his luggage checked by Transportation Security Administration screeners on the way out. Every day, the new Terrorism Threat Integration Center helps prepare the president's Homeland Security Briefing. Local police departments have sent many of their best detectives to expanded FBI-run Joint Terrorism Task Forces. Private businesses, likewise, have spent millions on disaster planning, bought crisis-incident-management software, and reactivated long-dormant office building shelters. Fences are stronger, power plants better protected, and computer networks more secure. More than a thousand localities have created Citizen Corps Councils to coordinate first aid, evacuation, and disaster assistance following a terrorist attack or natural disaster.

America has taken two approaches in our response to the terrorism threat: target-hardening and bureaucratic restructuring. Neither of these approaches address a key reality of the terrorist threat: a foe who can change tactics, targets, and ideology quickly and unpredictably. Responding to an enemy as agile as today's international terrorist groups requires homeland security practices with the same agility.

Agile Foe

Target-hardening lacks the agility and responsiveness necessary to protect against many terrorist attacks. It involves making individuals, institutions, and computer systems safer by reinforcing known weak points against probable threats, but it does little to protect against a foe who can create new threats against different targets. In the years before September 11, 2001, for example, airport baggage screening became more stringent, and airline personal began questioning passengers in greater detail. The

U.S. Department of Transportation (DOT) even built a passenger screening system that successfully identified several of the September 11 hijackers as potential threats. Muhammad Atta and his gang, however, evaded these target-hardening methods by splitting up the known threats and hijacking planes by using items DOT had not banned. Despite previous chemical weapons attacks and a multimillion-dollar investment in improved mail screening, likewise, a crafty terrorist still smuggled Ricin into Congress in February of 2004.

Bureaucratic restructuring within the government—ranging from the creation of local police intelligence bureaus to the $35 billion U.S. Department of Homeland Security—are premised on the hope that new lines of command and missions will focus and energize agencies to confront terrorist threats. And, no doubt, they will. The nature of the terrorist threat, however, limits the intrinsic value of such restructuring. After all, any organization can only handle a finite range of tasks. As James Q. Wilson describes in his book *Bureaucracy* (1989), the best-run government agencies focus on "behaviors, which, if successfully performed by key organizational members, would enable the organization to mange its critical environmental problem." Wilson calls these behaviors "critical tasks." Wilson distinguishes between such task-specific actions and "goals," which prove hopelessly vague upon even cursory analysis. As Wilson shows, providing good government service is often inconsistent with flexibility. For example, under J. Edgar Hoover's leadership, the FBI focused nearly all of its resources on the critical task of capturing every person who robbed a bank or worked as an intelligence agent for a hostile government. This focus, however, steered the FBI away from recognizing emerging threats such as organized crime and, critically, terrorists working for non-state entities.

Task focus, a major purpose of bureaucratic restructuring can indeed reduce the ability of an organization to sense new challenges and respond to them rapidly, effectively, and efficiently—to be *agile*. Agility, as an organizational capability, requires recognition that an organization cannot be constructed to handle every conceivable threat. Rather, it must continually look beyond its current threat perimeter for novel dangers, and learn to respond rapidly and effectively. This will require increased cooperation with other organizations, and for many organizations, particularly in government, it will require a wholesale re-evaluation of the way they operate.

Such a re-evaluation is vital today because nearly all terrorist threats will require a multi-agency reaction—the response at Ground Zero in New York City, for example, involved more than four hundred government agencies and at least three hundred private contractors. To make themselves agile and able to collaborate effectively, the multitude of federal, state, and local organizations that comprise the homeland security establishment must understand how they interacts with one another, with the private sector, and with other government entities. The establishment must also understand how it relies on the conventional information and secure intelligence that forms the basis of its operation; the processes it uses to manage that information; and, finally, the technology that enables those processes. Given the ever-changing nature of the threat environment, each organization must recognize its dependency on the expertise and competencies of other organizations, and must create the structures and capabilities to facilitate effective collaboration.

The bureaucratic structures needed to confront terrorism already exist. Now these bureaucracies must look within, to create the conditions—the culture, organizational structures, internal governance, business processes, and technology—for agility. They must also look outside themselves for the agile partnerships and collaborative forms—both long-lasting strategic partnerships and short-lived, threat-specific relationships—to allow for rapid responses to external challenges. These relationships may involve government agencies working with one another, governments partnering with private entities, and private citizens working as volunteers.

Government agencies committed to an agile homeland security policy should build information frameworks that facilitate rapid, effective, efficient collaboration. This suggests three specific courses of action: collaborative agreements, better communications-systems interoperability, and improved intelligence sharing.

Creating Agility

Responding to and preventing terrorist attacks will require short-term collaboration between agencies that ordinarily have little reason for cooperation. Formal agreements and specifications can provide the ground rules for these collaborations. The Bush administration has recognized the necessity of interagency cooperation, and ongoing grant programs are facilitating formal agreements, where needed, between various government entities at the local, state, and federal levels to delineate lines of responsibility. Some types of cooperative agreements don't even cross state lines: for example, New York City's Police and Fire Departments have a legacy of separation and lack of cooperation, but are slowly working towards a joint-command structure for emergencies.

When it comes to attempting many collaborative tasks, today's public-safety agencies are hampered by *semantic disconnects*—speaking different dialects of the same language and assigning different significance and meanings to events. For example, all emergency-management agencies watch for potential disasters, organize evacuations, and help rebuild, but the specific methods by which they do these things can differ. With appropriate and useful shared semantics—via creation and use of standard language and meaning to define and execute mission, process, and technology—two state emergency-management agencies facing a single terrorist attack can ensure collaboration that prevents separate evacuation plans from sending too many people to the same shelters.

Some of the most useful interagency agreements embrace shared semantics in the form of standards—whether *de facto* or *de jure*—that cover command, control, communication, computing, intelligence, surveillance, and reconnaissance (C4ISR) systems as well as rules that govern procurement, contract administration, and project and program management. Encouraging public-safety agencies to implement information systems that comply with C4ISR standards and other common industry standards (for example, web services which let computer systems exchange data with little human intervention) facilitates agility. Using such standards, two public safety agencies responding to a terrorist attack could grant one another's personnel selective access to their internal e-mail traffic, radio frequencies, and intelligence files while maintaining stewardship of the information, controlling what the other agency could see and for how long.

Intelligence-sharing, seen as an overriding concern for many police agencies, could flow naturally from the improved communications environment that would result from widely shared semantics. So far, however, most analysts see this task as largely distinct from communications interoperability. A 2003 report from a blue-ribbon commission assembled by the New York-based Markel Foundation concluded that a special, secure network for exchanging homeland security-related information topped the list of requirements for homeland security. A joint task force has begun to examine the question, but it may be five years before a national network goes online. Even when it does, making the network effective will require the integration of intelligence databases in all state police agencies and most large cities without forcing the replacement of systems already in place. Many public-safety managers will approach this effort with reluctance: sharing poses security risks, imposes costs, and, given that most localities will never experience a major terrorist attack, offers few rewards. Any attempt to impose an intelligence-sharing network from the top down, in other words, will pose great problems. A bottom-up approach might work better. If each police agency focused on reaching the very achievable goal of creating the conditions for agility within their own organization, then a national network could be a straightforward extension of those achievements—possibly self-organizing as each organization independently realizes, then leverages, the benefits of collaboration with others who share similar concerns. When a public agency prepares to collaborate in the face of rapidly changing conditions, the exchange of necessary information becomes part of its very fabric. It remains only to provide the regulatory environment to define the conditions for such exchange, and the secure channels for the information to flow through.

In its relations with the government, the private sector must also examine potential of short-term partnerships and collaborations. When it comes to sharing information with the government, a desire to protect personal privacy and trade secrets sometimes prevents private entities from collaborating with governments. Disney Corporation, for example, which runs the country's largest and second-largest resorts, keeps certain aspects of its security operations secret from most officers in the Orlando and Anaheim Police Departments and county sheriffs' offices.

The combination of standards-based business processes for handling sensitive information, encryption technology, and a helping hand from local police forces and emergency management agencies offers the potential for better short-term partnerships. Encryption technologies, for example, could allow private entities to give public-safety agencies encoded directories, including floor plans, executives' mobile phone numbers, and locations of particularly valuable property. The information could sit in police or emergency-management-agency computers, with shared business processes defining ways the government can use the information. Information systems based on these shared processes can control access to private information, ensure enforcement of notification and privacy policies, and create transparent, auditable records of any use of the information. Such a system could help in the response to a local threat, and could automatically react to changes in the national threat-advisory level. Governmental homeland-security agencies might also examine how they can serve as consultants to the private sector, by, for example, providing major private institutions advice on evacuation plans and shelter-in-place models. Although hard-pressed police, fire, and emergency-management agencies might consider such security consulting an extravagance, providing it often saves more than it costs: cities such as Simi Valley and Long Beach California maintain low crime levels with police forces far smaller than their eastern counterparts in part because they provide free crime prevention advice to nearly anyone who asks. The same practices can extend to data security. These consulting relationships would allow public-safety agencies to gather an unusual amount of information about private entities while maintaining an arm's-length relationship and ensuring privacy.

Citizen Soldiers

Improved agility can also greatly increase the ability of ordinary citizens to play a valuable role in homeland security. Today, roughly one-thousand local Citizen Corps Councils, sponsored by the U.S. Federal Emergency Management Agency (FEMA) and Corporation for National Service, focus on training all-volunteer Community Emergency Response and Training (CERT) teams (composed largely of senior citizens) in a nationally standardized forty-hour course that covers first aid, CPR, and efforts to mitigate attacks committed with atomic, chemical, and biological weapons. The training program, however, offers little local flexibility: Los Angeles, which runs the country's largest CERT program, includes no training about the specific dangers associated with earthquakes, but it does give information on how to transport accident victims through a forest.

Obviously, this approach lacks agility: Rather than training people to deal with specific disasters, citizen volunteers should work to improve collaboration. A CERT's members could help provide the semantics for collaboration between voluntary organizations and serve as the nexus for disseminating information about national threats. They could also involve experts on possible crises specific to their locations: Los Angeles, for example, should involve local earthquake experts and collaborate with other councils in the western United States on CERT best practices for responding to wildfires.

The inherently unpredictable nature of terrorist attacks makes it difficult to predict exactly what training the volunteers will need: an attack on an isolated oil pipeline, for example, might not require a response from many doctors or police officers but would require an army of volunteer welders. In addition to more flexible CERT training, therefore, efforts to involve ordinary citizens might also require the creation of standby "virtual emergency response teams." Such teams would be able to leverage their existing job skills to help out if a crisis erupted. Hence, these virtual emergency response teams might actually consist of a detailed resume databank, keyed and indexed according to common threat and capability semantics. When a particular need arose, computer systems or emergency managers could telephone or e-mail specific categories of volunteers, allowing localities to instantly access a volunteer pool perfectly suited to face the crisis at hand.

Most agencies and organizations involved in homeland security have begun to understand that they must become more agile in order to fight terrorism. Agility is not easy to achieve, but the conditions for agility—effective and efficient collaboration, enabled by shared semantics and achieved through standards, methods, and tools—are well understood. Organizations still must make it a priority. Focusing on the underlying structure of effective collaborative behavior will enhance existing investments in bureaucratic restructuring and target-hardening while letting public-safety agencies do what we need them to do, sense new threats and respond to them rapidly, effectively, and efficiently.

The exigencies of homeland security are so dynamic that its practitioners must sense and respond relentlessly if they are to keep the nation safe, secure, and assured. At the same time, the homeland security establishment cannot fall victim to fear and erect barriers where none ought to exist, or shudder at the very thought of change. Inflexible strategies, after all, will do little good when fighting a flexible foe. The most effective approach to homeland security involves breaking down walls that separate government agencies while helping private entities and individual citizens prepare themselves to face a nearly limitless range of threats.

VINCE KASTEN is business and technology strategists, focusing particularly on transformation, agility, and collaboration. His recent book, *The Jericho Principle: How Companies Use Strategic Collaboration to Find New Sources of Value* (John Wiley & Sons, 2003), details the transforming power of organizational collaboration.

RALPH WELBORN is business and technology strategists, focusing particularly on transformation, agility, and collaboration. His recent book, *The Jericho Principle: How Companies Use Strategic Collaboration to Find New Sources of Value* (John Wiley & Sons, 2003), details the transforming power of organizational collaboration.

Fighters, Not First Responders

The case against a larger domestic role for the U.S. military

MACKUBIN THOMAS OWENS

The magnitude of the Katrina disaster and the subsequent failure of local, state, and federal agencies to react in a timely manner have led some to call for an expansion of the military's role in domestic affairs. "The question raised by the Katrina fiasco," writes Daniel Henninger of the *Wall Street Journal,* "is whether the threat from madmen and nature is now sufficiently huge in its potential horror and unacceptable loss that we should modify existing jurisdictional authority to give the Pentagon functional first-responder status."

The president has apparently agreed that the issue deserves a look. In a national address last month, President Bush asked Congress to consider a larger role for U.S. armed forces in responding to natural disasters. "It is now clear that a challenge on this scale requires greater federal authority and a broader role for the armed forces—the institution of our government most capable of massive logistical operations on a moment's notice."

In a recent press briefing, he returned to the issue: "Is there a natural disaster—of a certain size—that would then enable the Defense Department to become the lead agency in coordinating and leading the response effort? That's going to be a very important consideration for Congress to think about."

The president is even contemplating using the military to address public health crises, specifically an outbreak of avian flu. In response to a reporter's question, President Bush suggested that an outbreak might trigger the need for a quarantine. "And who is best to be able to effect a quarantine? One option is the use of a military that's able to plan and move." He continued by observing that, as governor of Texas, he didn't like the idea of the president telling him how to command the Texas National Guard. "But Congress needs to take a look at circumstances that may need to vest the capacity of the president to move beyond that debate. And one such catastrophe, or one such challenge, could be an avian flu outbreak."

Some in Congress had already raised the issue. Even before the president's speech, John Warner of Virginia, chairman of the Senate Armed Services Committee, wrote a letter to Defense Secretary Donald Rumsfeld, saying that his committee would be looking into "the entire legal framework governing a president's power to use the regular armed forces to restore public order in . . . a large-scale, protracted emergency." He asked the secretary of defense to take the issue under consideration. In response, Rumsfeld informed Warner that the Pentagon was reviewing pertinent laws, including the 1878 Posse Comitatus Act, to determine whether revisions that would give the military a greater role during major domestic disasters are needed. In response, Admiral Timothy J. Keating, commander of U.S. northern command, the joint command responsible for homeland defense, has proposed that the military create an active-duty force specifically trained and equipped to assist the National Guard in response to major national disasters.

On the one hand, the call for increasing the military's role in domestic affairs is understandable. The military can respond to disaster in ways that local, state, and other federal agencies can't. On the other hand, those who demand a greater domestic role for the military must consider the impact of such a step on healthy civil-military relations in the United States. In addition, they must also take account of the fear, traditionally expressed by officers, that involving the military in domestic tasks will undermine the war-fighting capabilities of their units and cause their "fighting spirit" to decline.

A decade ago, an Air Force staff judge advocate officer painted a disturbing picture of future civil-military relations if the military became involved in domestic affairs. Charles Dunlap described his article, "The Origins of the American Military Coup of 2012," published in the Winter 1992–93 issue of *Parameters,* the professional journal of the U.S. Army, as a "darkly imagined excursion into the future." The article takes the form of a letter from an officer awaiting execution for opposing the military coup that has taken place in the United States. The letter argues that the coup was the result of trends identifiable as early as 1992, including the massive diversion of military forces to civilian uses.

In words eerily similar to those we hear in today's debate, Dunlap's doomed officer opines that in the 1990s Americans became disillusioned with the apparent inability of elected government to solve the nation's dilemmas. "We were looking for someone or something that could produce workable answers. The one institution of government in which the people retained faith was the military." Buoyed by the military's obvious competence in the first Gulf War, the public increasingly turned to it for help. Americans called for an acceleration of trends begun in the 1980s: tasking the military with a variety of new, nontraditional missions, and vastly escalating its commitment to formerly ancillary duties.

> Though not obvious at the time, the cumulative effect of these new responsibilities was to incorporate the military into the political process to an unprecedented degree. These additional assignments also had the perverse effect of diverting focus and resources from the military's central mission of combat training and war-fighting.

What Dunlap describes in this article is the "salami slice" method of overthrowing democratic government: Instead of a *coup d'état* that seizes the government all at once, power is taken one slice at a time. The military is asked to do more and more in the domestic arena and finally concludes that it might as well run the government as a whole. This coup is the result of an accretion of power by the military. But in the end, the result is the same: a military good at maintaining itself in power, but unable to defeat a foreign enemy.

Dunlap's essay was the opening shot of a decades-long debate over the state of American civil-military relations. During the 1990s, a number of events led observers to conclude that all was not well with civil-military relations in America. Some of the most highly publicized events reflected cultural tensions between the military as an institution and liberal civilian society, mostly having to do with women in combat and open homosexuals in the military.

But more serious examples of civil-military tensions included the military's resistance (foot-dragging) to involvement in constabulary missions and the charge that General Colin Powell, then chairman of the Joint Chiefs of Staff, was illegitimately invading civilian turf by publicly advancing opinions on foreign policy. In addition, there were many instances of downright hostility on the part of the military toward President Bill Clinton, whose anti-military stance as a young man during the Vietnam war did not endear him to soldiers. Many interpreted such hostility as just one more indication that the military had become too partisan (Republican) and politicized.

These events generated an often-acrimonious public debate in which a number of highly respected observers concluded that American civil-military relations were in crisis. In the words of Richard Kohn, a distinguished professor of history at the University of North Carolina and one of the country's foremost experts on the nexus between civilians and the uniformed military in the United States, civil-military relations during this period were "extraordinarily poor, in many respects as low as in any period of American peacetime history."

Some observers claimed that the civil-military tensions of the 1990s were a temporary phenomenon, attributable to the perceived antimilitary character of the Clinton administration.

But these tensions did not disappear with the election and reelection of George W. Bush as president. If anything, relations have become more strained as a result of clashes between the uniformed services and Defense Secretary Donald Rumsfeld over efforts to "transform" the U.S. military and the planning and conduct of U.S. military operations in Afghanistan and Iraq. Much of the uniformed services' campaign against Rumsfeld has been conducted by leaks to the press.

All of these tensions will be exacerbated if the statutes and regulations are changed to permit increased military participation in domestic affairs. Even if we don't reach the point described by Dunlap, it is almost a given that the military will be politicized to a dangerous extent. Indeed, the main reason Congress passed the Posse Comitatus Act in 1878 was concern that the Army at the time was being increasingly politicized.

A perusal of recent articles reveals the undeniable fact that most commentators do not understand the Posse Comitatus Act at all. The Posse Comitatus Act does not constitute a bar to the use of the military in domestic affairs. It does, however, insist that such use be authorized only by the highest constitutional authority: Congress and the president.

Contrary to what many Americans believe, the Constitution itself does not prohibit the use of the military in domestic affairs. Indeed, the U.S. military has intervened in domestic affairs some 167 times since the founding of the Republic. In the Anglo-American tradition, the first line of defense in enforcing the law was the *posse comitatus*, literally "the power of the county," understood to be the people at large who constituted the constabulary of the shire. When order was threatened, the "shire-reeve" or sheriff would raise the "hue and cry," and all citizens who heard it were bound to render assistance in apprehending a criminal or maintaining order. Thus, the sheriff in the American West would "raise a posse" to capture a lawbreaker.

If the *posse comitatus* was not able to maintain order, the force of first resort was the militia of the various states, the precursor of today's National Guard. In 1792, Congress passed two laws that permitted implementation of Congress's constitutional power "to provide for calling forth the militia to execute the laws of the union, suppress insurrections, and repel invasions." They were the Militia Act and the "Calling Forth" Act, which gave the president limited authority to employ the militia in the event of domestic emergencies. In 1807, at the behest of President Thomas Jefferson, who was troubled by his inability to use the regular Army as well as the militia to deal with the Burr Conspiracy of 1806–07, Congress also declared the Army to be an enforcer of federal laws, not only as a separate force, but as a part of the *posse comitatus*.

Accordingly, troops were often used in the antebellum period to enforce the fugitive slave laws and suppress domestic violence. The Fugitive Slave Act of 1850 permitted federal marshals to call on the *posse comitatus* to aid in returning a slave to his owner. In 1854, Franklin Pierce's attorney general, Caleb

Cushing, issued an opinion that included the Army in the *posse comitatus*, writing that

> A marshal of the United States, when opposed in the execution of his duty, by unlawful combinations, has authority to summon the entire able-bodied force of his precinct, as a posse comitatus. The authority comprehends not only bystanders and other citizens generally, but any and all organized armed forces, whether militia of the states, or officers, soldiers, sailors, and marines of the United States.

Thus, in April 1851, federal marshals in Boston arrested Thomas Sims, a 17-year-old slave who had escaped from Georgia. He was held in a courthouse guarded by police and soldiers for nine days while his case was argued before a federal commissioner. When the commissioner decided in favor of Sims's owner, 300 armed deputies and soldiers took him from the courthouse before dawn and marched him to the Boston Navy Yard, where another 250 soldiers waited to place him aboard a ship that would carry him back into bondage.

In May 1854, a deputy marshal arrested Anthony Burns, an escaped Virginia slave, also in Boston. While a federal commissioner decided Burns's fate, abolitionists tried to rescue him. President Pierce sent federal troops to Boston to keep the peace, admonishing the district attorney to "incur any expense to insure the execution of the law." Troops were also used to suppress domestic violence between pro- and anti-slavery factions in "Bloody Kansas." Soldiers and Marines participated in the capture of John Brown at Harpers Ferry in 1859.

After the Civil War, the U.S. Army was involved in supporting the Reconstruction governments in the southern states, and it was the Army's role in preventing the intimidation of black voters and Republicans at southern polling places that led to the passage of the Posse Comitatus Act. In the election of 1876, President Ulysses S. Grant deployed Army units as a *posse comitatus* in support of federal marshals working to maintain order at the polls. In that election, Rutherford B. Hayes defeated Samuel Tilden with the disputed electoral votes of South Carolina, Louisiana, and Florida. Southerners claimed that the Army had been misused to "rig" the election.

While the Posse Comitatus Act is usually portrayed as the triumph of the Democratic party in ending Reconstruction, the Army welcomed the legislation. The use of soldiers as a posse removed them from their own chain of command and placed them in the uncomfortable position of taking orders from local authorities who had an interest in the disputes that provoked the unrest in the first place. As a result, many officers came to believe that the involvement of the Army in domestic policing was corrupting the institution.

And this is the crux of the issue. The Posse Comitatus Act (Section 1385, Title 18 U.S.C.) prohibits the use of the military to aid civil authorities, in enforcing the law or suppressing civil disturbances *except in cases and under circumstances expressly authorized by the Constitution or Act of Congress*. As Robert W. Coakley, one of the foremost authorities on the use of the military in domestic affairs, has written:

> All that [the Posse Comitatus Act] really did *was to repeal a doctrine whose only substantial foundation was an opinion by an attorney general* [Caleb Cushing], *and one that had never been tested in the courts. The president's power to use both regulars and militia remained undisturbed by the Posse Comitatus Act. . . .* But the Posse Comitatus Act did mean that *troops could not be used on any lesser authority than that of the president* and he must issue a "cease and desist" proclamation before he did so. Commanders in the field would no longer have any discretion, but must wait for orders from Washington [italics added].

The fact is that the Posse Comitatus Act, in conjunction with the so-called Insurrection Act, provides the president with all the power he needs to employ the military in domestic affairs if he believes it necessary. Although intended as a tool for suppressing rebellion when circumstances "make it impracticable to enforce the laws of the United States in any State or Territory by the ordinary course of judicial proceedings," presidents used this power on five occasions during the 1950s and '60s to counter resistance to desegregation decrees in the South. Reports indicate that President Bush chose not to invoke the Insurrection Act in the case of Katrina because of concerns that such an action would have been viewed as federal bullying of a Southern Democratic governor.

Do we really want to return to the days when "lesser authority" than the president could use the military for domestic purposes? The issue here is not the Posse Comitatus Act but the quality of American civil-military relations and a healthy military establishment.

The U.S. military is currently stretched thin by missions in Iraq and Afghanistan. But the issue goes beyond stress on the force, active and reserve. History teaches that increasing the use of the military for domestic purposes adversely affects its ability to wage war. In a 1991 commentary on the relationship between pre-World War II Canadian military policy and the subsequent battlefield disasters the Canadians suffered at the beginning of the war, the late Harry Summers warned that when militaries lose sight of their purpose, the results can be catastrophic.

The U.S. military is structured to play "away games." It is good at protecting the United States by threatening the sanctuary of adversaries abroad. There are, of course, things the military can and should do to enhance the security of the American homeland, but we should not be blurring further the distinction between military activities and domestic affairs. To paraphrase what Caspar Weinberger said in opposition to the use of the military in the drug war, weakening the statutes that govern the use of the military in domestic affairs in response to Hurricane Katrina makes for terrible national security policy, poor politics, and guaranteed military failure sometime in the future.

The response to Katrina indicates that procedures at all levels of government must be streamlined. But the maintenance of both healthy civil-military relations and a combat-ready force dictates that we not repeal or modify the Posse Comitatus Act or give the president power beyond that of the Insurrection Act. And by no means should we expect the military to go beyond its current mission of supporting civil authorities in the event of domestic emergencies.

MACKUBIN THOMAS OWENS is an associate dean of academics and professor of national security affairs at the Naval War College.

From *The Weekly Standard,* October 24, 2005, pp. 28–31. Copyright © 2005 by Weekly Standard. Reprinted by permission.

Index

Index

Test Your Knowledge Form

We encourage you to photocopy and use this page as a tool to assess how the articles in *Annual Editions* expand on the information in your textbook. By reflecting on the articles you will gain enhanced text information. You can also access this useful form on a product's book support Web site at *http://www.mhcls.com/online/*.

NAME: _____   DATE: _____

TITLE AND NUMBER OF ARTICLE: _____

BRIEFLY STATE THE MAIN IDEA OF THIS ARTICLE:

_____

LIST THREE IMPORTANT FACTS THAT THE AUTHOR USES TO SUPPORT THE MAIN IDEA:

_____

WHAT INFORMATION OR IDEAS DISCUSSED IN THIS ARTICLE ARE ALSO DISCUSSED IN YOUR TEXTBOOK OR OTHER READINGS THAT YOU HAVE DONE? LIST THE TEXTBOOK CHAPTERS AND PAGE NUMBERS:

_____

LIST ANY EXAMPLES OF BIAS OR FAULTY REASONING THAT YOU FOUND IN THE ARTICLE:

_____

LIST ANY NEW TERMS/CONCEPTS THAT WERE DISCUSSED IN THE ARTICLE, AND WRITE A SHORT DEFINITION:

We Want Your Advice

ANNUAL EDITIONS revisions depend on two major opinion sources: one is our Advisory Board, listed in the front of this volume, which works with us in scanning the thousands of articles published in the public press each year; the other is you—the person actually using the book. Please help us and the users of the next edition by completing the prepaid article rating form on this page and returning it to us. Thank you for your help!

ANNUAL EDITIONS: Homeland Security, 2/e

ARTICLE RATING FORM

Here is an opportunity for you to have direct input into the next revision of this volume.
We would like you to rate each of the articles listed below, using the following scale:

1. **Excellent: should definitely be retained**
2. **Above average: should probably be retained**
3. **Below average: should probably be deleted**
4. **Poor: should definitely be deleted**

Your ratings will play a vital part in the next revision.
Please mail this prepaid form to us as soon as possible.
Thanks for your help!

RATING	ARTICLE	RATING	ARTICLE
	1. Homeland Security		22. Hesitation at Homeland Security
	2. How Much Are We Willing to Take?		23. Thanks, Dubai!
	3. Lethal Fantasies		24. Thwarting Nuclear Terrorism
	4. Why We Don't Prepare		25. Bioterrorism—Preparing to Fight the Next War
	5. Are We Ready for the Next 9/11?		26. These Chemicals Are So Deadly
	6. Revisiting Homeland Security		27. Port Security Is Still a House of Cards
	7. Shifting Priorities		28. Island Mentality
	8. Airport Security Screening: Privatize or Federalize?		29. The Truth about Torture
	9. The Doom Boom		30. Civil Liberties and Homeland Security
	10. Immigration and National Security		31. Homeland Security and the Lessons of Waco
	11. Senators Say Scrap FEMA and Start Over		32. Heading in the Wrong Direction
	12. Terrorism's Impact on State Law Enforcement		33. Mining Personal Data
	13. State of Readiness		34. U.S. Intelligence: A Losing Proposition
	14. New York State of Mind		35. In Defence of the Intelligence Services
	15. Blame Amid the Tragedy		36. Can Spies Be Made Better?
	16. Antiterrorist Policing in New York City After 9/11: Comparing Perspectives on a Complex Process		37. We Have Not Correctly Framed the Debate on Intelligence Reform
	17. Community Policing and Terrorism		38. Department of Homeland Security: Charting a Path Forward
	18. D.C. Deploys Wireless Net for First Responders		39. The Terrorism Index
	19. The Front Line in Training for Disasters		40. Building an Agile Homeland Security Establishment
	20. Guarding Against Missiles		41. Fighters, Not First Responders
	21. Modernizing Homeland Security		

HOMELAND SECURITY

ABOUT YOU

Name _____ Date _____

Are you a teacher? ❏ A student? ❏
Your school's name _____

Department _____

Address _____ City _____ State _____ Zip _____

School telephone # _____

YOUR COMMENTS ARE IMPORTANT TO US!

Please fill in the following information:
For which course did you use this book?
_____

Did you use a text with this ANNUAL EDITION? ❏ yes ❏ no
What was the title of the text?
_____

What are your general reactions to the Annual Editions concept?
_____

Have you read any pertinent articles recently that you think should be included in the next edition? Explain.
_____

Are there any articles that you feel should be replaced in the next edition? Why?
_____

Are there any World Wide Web sites that you feel should be included in the next edition? Please annotate.
_____

May we contact you for editorial input? ❏ yes ❏ no
May we quote your comments? ❏ yes ❏ no